Better Cities, Better World

Better Cities, Better World

A Handbook on Local Governments
Self-Assessments

Catherine Farvacque-Vitkovic
and Mihaly Kopanyi

WORLD BANK GROUP

CONTENTS

Boxes

Figures

Maps

Tables

FOREWORD

This book is about cities and towns around the world. It is about helping them unleash their true potentials for the pursuit of:

- Efficient and effective use of public resources
- Sustainable growth and economic prosperity
- Social inclusion
- Greater transparency and accountability in the selection of public investments
- Making the right decisions at the right time with the right resources
- Being "smarter"
- Reducing their environmental footprint through the use of proper regulations and appropriate technologies.

In many ways, the urbanization wave and the unprecedented urban growth of the past 20 years have created a sense of urgency for action and an impetus for change. In 2014, 54 percent of the world's population, or 3.9 billion people, lived in urban areas. That proportion is likely to rise to 68 percent by 2050, while it used to be one-third in the 1950s. More than half of city dwellers live in cities of fewer than 1 million, but there are 28 megacities of more than 10 million. In the 1950s, most of the world's urban residents were in Europe and the Americas. Now, Asia and Africa host the world's largest and fastest-growing cities. Although the planet is becoming increasingly urban, it has become clear that "business as usual" is no longer possible.

In this new configuration, great hopes and expectations are placed on local governments. While central governments are subject to instability and political changes, local governments are seen as more inclined to stay the course; because they are closer to the people, the voice of the people is more clearly heard for a true democratic debate over the choice of neighborhood investments and the choice of citywide policies and programs. In a context of skewed financial resources and of incredibly complex urban challenges—which range from the provision of basic traditional municipal services to issues of social inclusion, economic development, city branding, emergency response, smart technologies, and green investments—cities are searching for more effective and more innovative ways to deal with new and old problems.

Things are indeed changing in some parts of the world. The incredible leap in technology has enabled cities to have access to and appetite for spatially based data and to take into account the importance of location in decision making. New thinking has evolved on the function of city planning. No longer viewed as a reactive function, city planning is perceived to be at the front and center of city management and is no longer seen as the realm of stodgy planners left in a dusty corner of City Hall. City planners have become in many places very vocal voices for change. New planning techniques aim to (1) provide proactive guidance and orientations for future urbanization; (2) take into account new technologies and smart ideas to address environmental concerns; (3) embrace social inclusion challenges; (4) foster and support city "branding"; (5) listen to various interest groups, including citizens; and (6) play a new role of "broker" between public and private interests. However, city planners, for the most part, are still left out of the investment programming process and are still very much disconnected from the financing decisions. The Urban Audit/Self-Assessment (UA/SA) aims to fill this gap and, in many ways, can contribute to furthering the professionalization of municipal staff by promoting a new breed of city planners.

While the decentralization process is progressing, and the missions of local governments are becoming ever more complex, their financial base is not keeping up with the increasing pressure for competitive financing needs. Assessing the financial position of a municipality and its capacity to sustain key capital and recurrent investments, and connecting it to its investment needs and priorities, is more essential than ever. This is where the Municipal Finances Self-Assessment (MFSA) comes in. Collecting "data with a purpose," budgeting and reporting effectively and transparently, projecting future trends, and having a holistic understanding of revenue generation potentials and expenditure needs will help cities better manage their finances. Equally important, these activities will facilitate municipalities' relationships with central government and citizens and their dealings with financial partners (access to credit and to other financing mechanisms through banks or development partners). Again, this calls for a new breed of municipal staff who can actively participate in the future of their city.

This book is at the heart of this debate. It outlines a grid for analysis, a framework for data-based policy dialogue, and a common language that, for the first time, helps connect the dots between investment programming (Urban Audit/Self-Assessment) and financing (Municipal Finances Self-Assessment).

- Chapter 1 provides (1) a genesis of Local Governments Self-Assessments (LGSAs) and of the key urban challenges they aim to address; (2) a definition and explanation of the key underlying objectives and rationales for LGSAs;

and (3) an overview of the process and methodology of the assessments, including answers to some fundamental questions commonly asked on the what, why, and how.

- Chapters 2 and 3 provide a thorough and detailed roadmap for two key functions of the municipality, which are often disconnected from each other and typically carried out on parallel tracks. These are (1) the needs assessment of municipal infrastructure and services and the prioritization of key investments supported by the Urban Audit/Self-Assessment and (2) the management of municipal finances supported by the Municipal Finances Self-Assessment, focusing on the assessment of the financial position of a city and the identification of the key triggers required to strengthen its financial capacity.

- Chapter 4 focuses on how these self-assessments are turned into transformative actions, and how they can impact the way cities conduct their business and deliver on their promises.

The book has a bit of everything for everyone. Central governments will be attracted by the purposefulness and clarity of these tools, their impact on local government capacity and performance building, and the way they improve the implementation of transformative actions for policy change. City leaders and policy makers will find the sections on objectives and content instructive and informative because each urban issue is placed in its context. Municipal staff in charge of day-to-day management will find that the sections on tasks and the detailed step-by-step walk through the process give them the pragmatic know-how they need. Cities' partners—such as bilateral and multilateral agencies, banks and funds, utility companies, and private operators—will find the foundations for more effective collaborative partnerships.

Ede Jorge Ijjasz-Vasquez
Senior Director
Social, Urban, Rural, and
Resilience Global
Practice
World Bank, Washington, DC

Sameh Wahba
Director
Urban and Territorial
Development, Disaster Risk
Management and Resilience
World Bank, Washington, DC

ACKNOWLEDGMENTS

We are thankful for the support and guidance received, over the years, from our colleagues at the World Bank, in particular Ede Jorge Ijjasz-Vasquez (Senior Director, Social, Urban, Rural, and Resilience Global Practice), Sameh Wahba (Director, Urban and Territorial Development, Disaster Risk Management and Resilience), David Sislen (Practice Manager, Europe and Central Asia), Dean Cira (Lead Urban Specialist), and Roland White (Global Lead for City Management, Finance and Governance). We would like to give much appreciation and thanks to our formal reviewers for their valuable advice and constructive comments—especially Sylvie Debomy (Practice Manager, Urban and DRM, Africa Region, World Bank), Lourdes Germán (Director, International and Institute-Wide Initiatives, Lincoln Institute of Land Policy), and Rama Krishnan Venkateswaran (Lead Financial Management Specialist, World Bank). We are also grateful to the many other colleagues who provided, at one time or another, valuable information and showed a general interest in this endeavor, including Christophe Crépin (Practice Manager, Environment and Natural Resources, Asia Region, World Bank), Sandra Kdolsky (Social Development Specialist), Holy-Tiana Rame (Senior Public Finance Specialist, PEFA Secretariat), Harris Selod (Senior Economist, Development Economics, World Bank), and Asha Ayoung (Lead Procurement Specialist), as well as the respective SD Program Leaders who cover the countries mentioned in this book.

This work has greatly benefited from the technical contribution of Anne Sinet (Municipal Finances Consultant, AllNext) and the late Lucien Godin (Urbanist and International Expert and Cofounder of Groupe Huit). They provided long-term intellectual inputs into the conceptualization and design of the tools, as well as technical support to their implementation under several World Bank projects.

What makes the key messages and the overall content of this book powerful is the fact that many cities and towns around the world have taken part in the early design, piloting, or scaling up of these tools. There would be no Local Governments Self-Assessments without local governments.

Although there are too many mayors, city managers, and heads of technical or financial departments to mention here, we would like to acknowledge the important contributions made by the following individuals: Chekhou Diop, Massar Sarr, Modi Ka, Mamadou Ndiaye, Alioune Sarr, Sory Kouyate, Dian Diallo, Abdoulaye Keita, Ljiljana Brdarevic, Marjan Nikolov, Natasa Obradovic, Anto Bajo, Merita Toska, Anila Gjika, Dritan Shutina, Kejt Dhrami, Brankica Lenic, Goran Rakic, and Ibrahim Gjylderen. We are also grateful for the cooperation and support of Kelmend Zajazi (Executive Director, Network of Associations of Local Authorities of South-East Europe) as well as numerous national associations of local governments. We are thankful to Türda Osmen for his professional guidance and contribution to the rating methodology.

Last but not least, we are very grateful to Sabine Palmreuther, former Senior Specialist at the World Bank and former task manager of the Urban Partnership Program, and Tamara Nikolic, Operations Officer and current task manager, World Bank. They provided the steering and the push and shared our passion for a job well done. We would also like to acknowledge and thank the Austrian government, which helped finance parts of this work under the World Bank–Austria Urban Partnership program.

We also appreciate the contributions of World Bank Cartographer Bruno Bonansea and Knowledge Management Analyst Syed Abdul Salam.

Finally, special thanks go to the World Bank Publications Department, especially Jewel McFadden, and Mary Fisk and her team, who skillfully guided the publication process.

This book is dedicated to our friend and colleague, Lucien Godin, who devoted his life to the urban cause and whose legacy continues to inspire many of us. He was at the forefront of much of the current thinking on cities and peri-urban areas, spent his life in the trenches, and was a great believer in tools and toolkits. More than 20 years ago, we started working together on the development of some of these tools and writing books about them. In that time, we notably spent endless hours conceptualizing and designing what eventually became the local government self-assessments. Without him, this book would not be.

ABOUT THE AUTHORS

Catherine Farvacque-Vitkovic has more than 30 years of World Bank experience in many regions of the world. As Lead Urban Development Specialist at the World Bank, she has led the preparation and implementation of a large number of urban development, municipal management, and infrastructure projects in many cities around the world. She is the author or coauthor of several sector studies as well as several books. Among them are the following:

- *Reforming Urban Land Policies and Institutions in Developing Cities/ Politiques foncières des villes en développement* (available in English and French)

- *The Future of African Cities: Challenges and Opportunities for Urban Development/L'Avenir des villes Africaines, enjeux et priorités* (available in English and French)

- *Street Addressing and the Management of Cities* (available in English, French, Portuguese, and Spanish) and companion E-Learning Program

- *Municipal Finances: A Handbook for Local Governments* (available in English, French, Mandarin, and Spanish) and companion E-Learning Program.

She has a keen interest in translating lessons from experience and cutting-edge know-how into practical knowledge products and capacity-building programs for local governments around the world. Her interests, work experience, and extensive field practice have led her to connect the dots between land management, city planning, investment programming, and municipal finances.

Mihaly Kopanyi has more than 25 years of World Bank experience and has worked in cities in 30 countries and on four continents. His key areas of expertise include financial management, municipal finances, own-revenue enhancements, and property taxation. He led the Municipal Finance Thematic Group of the World Bank for over a decade until his retirement. He is a municipal finance adviser to project teams in urban lending projects and capacity-building programs, with special focus on assessing the financial health of local governments and seeking options for improvements.

He has written or edited numerous books and book chapters, and dozens of papers for the World Bank and the London School of Economics. Major volumes he has coauthored for the World Bank include *Municipal Finances: A Handbook for Local Governments* (2014) (English, French, Mandarin, and Spanish); "Municipal Finances E-Learning Program" (2015); *Intergovernmental Finances—A Case of Hungary* (2004); and the MFSA Online Application (a forthcoming companion document prepared by the authors).

ABBREVIATIONS

CAPEX	capital expenditure
CDFs	community development facilities
CIP	capital investments plan
COFOG	classification of functions of governments
CPI	consumer price index
D/E	debt-to-equity ratio
DeMPA	Debt Management Performance Assessment
DSCR	debt service coverage ratio
EIRR	economic internal rate of return
ERR	economic rate of return (synonym of EIRR)
FMA	financial management assessment
FIRR	financial internal rate of return
FOREX	foreign exchange
FX	foreign exchange
GDP	gross domestic product
IFMIS	integrated financial management information systems
IPIE	Inventaire pour la programmation des infrastructures et equipements
IPSAS	International Public Sector Accounting Standards
IPSASB	International Public Sector Accounting Standards Board
IPSI	Inventory for Programming of Services and Infrastructure
GIS	geographic information system
LGSA	Local Governments Self-Assessment
LVC	land value capture
MC	municipal contract
MFSA	Municipal Finances Self-Assessment
NPV	net present value
OECD	Organisation for Economic Co-operation and Development
O&M	operation and maintenance
OPEX	operating expenditures

PEFA	Public Expenditure and Financial Accountability Assessment
PIMA	Public Investment Management Assessment
PIP	Priority Investment Program
PPP	public–private partnership
R&M	repair and maintenance
SASCR	self-assessed shadow credit rating
TIF	tax increment financing
TODS	transit-oriented development schemes
TTIP	tax on transfer of immovable property
UA/SA	Urban Audit/Self-Assessment

CHAPTER 1

Genesis, Objectives and Rationale, Process and Methodology

The Story behind Local Governments Self-Assessments

Genesis

This book is a follow-up and companion document to *Municipal Finances: A Handbook for Local Governments* by the same authors and published by the World Bank. The *Municipal Finances Handbook* set the stage for the fundamentals of sound local government finances and drilled the issues of (1) intergovernmental relations, (2) revenues management, (3) expenditures management, (4) financial management, (5) assets management, and (6) external resources management.

Better Cities, Better World picks up where chapter 8 of the *Municipal Finances Handbook* left off and focuses on Local Governments

Self-Assessments (LGSAs): the Urban Audit/ Self-Assessment (UA/SA) and the Municipal Finances Self-Assessment (MFSA). It (1) outlines a genesis of the key urban problems that LGSAs aim to address; (2) provides an introduction to what these self-assessments are and why they are important; (3) offers some lessons learned from implementation of UA/SAs and MFSAs in different contexts; (4) outlines a clear methodology/road map to carry out the assessments successfully and productively in a self-paced format; and (5) discusses the transformative policy actions generated by the use of these tools. *Better Cities, Better World* has been purposefully designed to help city leaders better manage the process of city investment planning and budgeting, as well as to provide citizens, financial partners, donors, and other interest groups with a clear picture of the investment needs of a particular city and its matching current and projected financial position.

A Context Ripe for Local Governments Self-Assessments

Economists have long argued that reducing the gap between citizens and the level of government responsible for service provision will lead to greater efficiency in the use of resources. Over recent decades, many countries have devolved a growing list of expenditure responsibilities to local governments, often without corresponding decentralization of resources to finance them. As a result, in both highly developed and developing nations, one can find examples of municipal government failures to provide many services to residents and shortfalls in infrastructure and public service investments. In many countries, there is a large difference between the local government expenditure share and the local government revenue share. This difference, often referred to as a *fiscal gap*, provides a very rough measure of the amount of intergovernmental transfers needed to ensure that local governments have sufficient revenues to meet their expenditure responsibilities.

In municipalities where there is coordination between spatial and economic development planning and public finance, thoughtful and strategic investments can be visible and generate positive results for economic performance. However, the biggest expenditure challenge facing governments at all levels is the growing gap in infrastructure financing. Over the next 15 years, an estimated US$93 trillion of infrastructure will need to be built globally, 70 percent of it in cities. This new infrastructure will require annual investments exceeding 5 percent of global gross domestic product (GDP), consuming most of the tax revenues of subnational governments. New revenue sources will need to be found to take on this challenge, and national and state/provincial governments will need to expand intergovernmental transfers to municipal governments, enable local governments to raise new sources of revenues, strengthen local government accountability to residents, and motivate local governments to exploit scale economies by

Box 1.1
The Changing Geography of Urbanites

In 2014, 54 percent of the world's population, or 3.9 billion people, lived in urban areas. That proportion is likely to rise to 66 percent by 2050, while it used to be one-third in the 1950s. More than half of city dwellers live in cities of fewer than 1 million, but there are 28 megacities of more than 10 million. In the 1950s, most of the world's city dwellers were in Europe and the Americas. Now, Asia and Africa host the world's largest and fastest-growing cities. Cities in just three nations—China, India, and Nigeria—are expected to add nearly 1 billion residents in coming decades, with most of the growth occurring in cities of fewer than 1 million. By 2050, nearly 75 percent of urbanites will be in Asia and Africa.

A larger understanding of urban infrastructure systems is necessary to move from data to information to knowledge and, ultimately, to action for urban sustainability and human well-being.

Source: Science 2016.

consolidating planning and expenditures at metropolitan rather than jurisdictional levels.

Genesis of LGSAs: The Story behind Them

Early Generation of Local Governments Assessments: Municipal Audits in Africa

The seed for the LGSAs presented in this book started in the 1990s as part of the World Bank's engagement in Africa, where the World Bank was very actively involved in supporting urban development. Between 1993 and 2003, it financed about 50 urban development projects in the cities of Sub-Saharan Africa, totaling about US$2 billion, or 20 percent of its investments in urban projects globally. The context for assessing municipal capacity was ripe on a continent fast becoming urbanized and faced with rapid decentralization trends. Cities were becoming more densely populated, with rising demand on existing services and infrastructure. Their responsibilities were becoming more complex, with an increasing number of new devolved functions unmatched by skewed financial resources and limited intergovernmental transfers. In addition, cities were not the key development priority of central governments. For example, in Cameroon, government's investments in 18 cities and towns represented less than 1 percent of national budget, and spending was mostly concentrated in the largest cities of Yaounde and Douala. In Senegal, urban areas contributed 60 percent of the country GDP, yet the municipalities collected only 1 percent of the urban GDP, or US$6–8 per capita.

This kind of imbalance in budget allocations, compounded with growing urban poverty and total dysfunction of institutions and service delivery, is precisely what propelled the need to step up our engagement in urban Africa. Grounded in the recognition that (1) reliable data were hard to find, (2) local government capacity was patchy and needed hands-on, project-based accompanying support, (3) a fracture existed in citizens' confidence in their own governments as well as between the various levels of government, and (4) local governments urgently needed support in their core mission to fill the gap in infrastructure and service delivery, the World Bank supported the development and introduction of Municipal Audits in close partnership with local counterparts.

Over the decade of the 1990s and early 2000s, more than 200 local governments (capital cities, cities, and towns) in West Africa alone completed Municipal Audits. These Municipal Audits included a two-track process:

- A Financial and Organizational Audit (the first generation of what we have renamed the MFSA) aimed at shedding light on the financial position of the municipality and identifying key actions for reform.

- An Urban Audit (a simplified version of what is presented in this book) aimed at assessing the level of services and infrastructure, mapping the gaps, and facilitating the programming, financing, and implementation of Priority Investment Programs. In the case of Africa, the Financial and Organizational Audit led to the formulation of a Municipal Reform/Adjustment Program (focused on revenue and expenditure reforms, improvement of financial practices, and adjustment to staffing and skills). We even developed a Catalogue of Capacity Building Measures to help local governments make the right decisions for their specific contexts and grasp up-front what each action required in terms of responsibility and costs. The Urban Audit led to the formulation of a Priority Investment Program and a Priority Maintenance Program, which were the results of a consultative screening process of identification and selection of infrastructure/services projects based on social, economic, financial, and environmental criteria. To support the final selection process, we also developed a Catalogue of Urban Investments that helped local governments' final decisions and provided key information on unit costs, standards, and operational requirements.

These two programs—Municipal Adjustment Programs (finances) and Priority Investment Programs (infrastructure)—were then outlined in a partnership agreement called the municipal contract or the city contract. This contract proved to be an effective way to hold all parties accountable for their part of the bargain (especially when it came to central government's actions) and to propel the concept of a data-based, consultation-based municipal program rather than atomized projects. Some of the major reforms on transfers, tax collection, and decentralization agendas, as well as the building of schools, clinics, roads, solid waste transfer zones, municipal facilities, and infrastructure, can be attributed to these contractual programs. Most of these contracts have led to second, third, and fourth generations

Box 1.2
Senegal: Genesis of Municipal Audits

The Senegal Urban Development and Decentralization Program (UDDP), developed in the 1990s, opened the path to many other similar projects in Africa, where the model was cloned and implemented. The Senegal UDDP introduced for the first time the concept of municipal audits and municipal contracts in Africa. The Municipal Development Agency supported 67 municipalities (including Dakar) in implementing a sustainable priority investment program while providing them with a financing plan commensurate with their financing absorptive capacity and combining soft loans, grants, and savings. The Urban Audit led to the identification and implementation of a Priority Investment Program and a Priority Maintenance Program. The Financial and Organizational Audit led to the identification and implementation of a Municipal Adjustment Program, to be carried out by the local government, and a realistic set of macro reforms to be conducted by the central government. All programs were clearly outlined and specified in an agreement (the municipal contract) between the local government and the central government; the agreement typically included the ministry of finance, the ministry of local governments, and the technical ministry in charge of urban infrastructure.

Although not legally binding, the municipal contract became a respected reference document for all parties involved. Both the emphasis on public consultations as an integral part of the municipal audits and of the formulation of the municipal contracts and the fact that public scrutiny and public media kept a close eye on the implementation progress (the municipal contracts were published in local newspapers) limited potential deviances and unwanted political gains. The first generation of municipal contracts were signed for four- to five-year periods and paved the way for the next generations of municipal contracts up to this day. It was not uncommon to see municipal contracts continue beyond the political mandate of mayors, as the municipal contract was perceived by local beneficiaries as a tool to "get things done" and by donors, such as the World Bank or Agence française de développement, to improve disbursements of painfully slow lending projects as well as to ensure quality of outputs ("getting the right things done"). An Independent Evaluation Group study on municipal decentralization found that the municipal contract approach and its legacy were highly satisfactory.

Source: Farvacque-Vitkovic and Godin 2003.

of municipal contracts and are still ongoing today. Benin, Burkina Faso, Cameroon, Chad, Côte d'Ivoire, Guinea, Madagascar, Mali, Mauritania, Niger, Rwanda, and Senegal are part of this batch of municipal contract countries (see box 1.2). At the same time, East African countries and South Africa simultaneously developed the use of performance grants or performance contracts to support central–local government relationships and monitor the use of public funds. Such grants were implemented in Ethiopia, Ghana, Kenya, South Africa, and Tanzania. In South Africa, the Division of Revenue bill introduces the conditional allocations to municipalities from the national government's share of revenue raised nationally to supplement the funding of functions funded from municipal budgets. The program in Ethiopia provides LGs with a broad investment menu from which they will prioritize and choose investments in consultation with citizens.

A New Generation of Municipal Audits: The Local Governments Self-Assessments and the Implementation Experience in Southeast Europe

Fast-forward to the 2010s, when a new generation of municipal audits was launched in Southeast Europe. Under Austrian financing, the World Bank was asked to design and implement a capacity-building program for municipalities in Southeast Europe. Initial discussions with central and local counterparts and a quick analysis of the situation on the ground showed that key emerging priorities focused on a nexus connecting the dots between land and city planning, municipal finances, and service delivery, intertwined with issues of social inclusion, governance, and transparency. The countries of the region had been badly hit by the 2008 financial crisis, which showed the vulnerability of local finances and the dependency on land-based revenues and transfers.

At the same time, a raging civil war had caused major fractures in the social fabric, as well as a collapse of traditional forms of governance and a rise of informal activities in the absence of rule of law. In this context, the unlikely journey of self-evaluation started, under the Urban Partnership Program designed and monitored by the World Bank, with the introduction in the region of the MFSA and, later on, of the Urban Audit/Self-Assessment.

As of 2019, five years into implementation, the process of municipal LGSAs/audits has been refined. The key achievements can be summarized as follows: 76 municipalities have completed or are completing an MFSA, which was the first self-assessment tool to be introduced in the program and which benefited from an already developed grid of analysis or analytical framework; and 16 municipalities have completed Urban Audits/SA. The smaller number of Urban Audit/Self-Assessments reflects the fact that (1) urban audits were purposefully introduced at a later stage in the program; (2) urban audits' analytical grid required fine-tuning and adjustment to the local context; and (3) unlike MFSAs, which have easily identifiable counterparts within the financial department of the city administration, urban audits require a skill set that spans several city departments. Many municipalities are today into their second- or third-generation audits, which means both that the data for the LGSAs have been updated by local authorities and that some of the key actions identified in their municipal improvement programs are underway (box 1.3).

On the basis of lessons learned from the previous experiences of the first generation of municipal audits in Africa, some adjustments were made in the design/content and implementation/process of the LGSAs in Southeast Europe:

- First, the first generation of municipal audits was designed and carried out in full partnership with local governments, but both the novelty of the tool and the varying

Box 1.3
Improving Local Government Capacity: The Experience of Local Governments Self-Assessments in Southeast Europe — The Case of Belgrade, Serbia

The City of Belgrade has been a partner of the World Bank–Austria Urban Partnership Program (UPP) since the beginning in 2012. Belgrade is the largest city among UPP partners; as a result, the city has greater capacities than most in financial, management, and technical fields. Despite that capacity, testing and implementing a Municipal Finances Self-Assessment (MFSA) appeared to be a very innovative change and a cultural shift for participating city leaders. The most challenging first step was to restructure financial results from regular city reports into MFSA templates, which are compatible with approaches of financial and capital markets as well as rating agencies. Second, municipal staff had to analyze results. Finally, results had to be discussed with various departments and stakeholders in order to identify corrective measures and agree on key financial and development targets.

During this first phase, the city benefited from the punctual assistance of a local consultant and international experts of the World Bank. The results are palpable. In order to prepare market-based financing, in October 2016 the city obtained a B1 investment grade credit rating from Moody's, equivalent to the sovereign rating. This rating was upgraded to B3a in March 2017. The deputy mayor in charge of finance confirmed that—bearing in mind the complexity of financial operations in the City of Belgrade—the MFSA had greatly helped during the credit rating analysis. He stated at one of the seven City to City Dialogues (held in Belgrade on October 25, 2016):

> The City of Belgrade had consolidated all of its financial data for the period of five years in one place, the MFSA, which provides a historical overview of Belgrade's financial situation, including also the City's future prospects and trends based on the analysis of its financial position and long-term projections. This way we were ready for the first meeting held with Moody's credit rating agency and for completing the credit rating questionnaire very quickly for the first time. The information we had to provide to the agency, e.g. macroeconomic indicators, demographic profile, budget, financial debt, liquidity, off-balance sheet items and other liabilities, had already been mostly prepared according to the MFSA methodology recognized by the credit rating agency; these allowed us to complete the entire process expeditiously and efficiently.

Belgrade has updated its MFSA every year by itself and has, subsequently, completed a medium-term capital improvement plan. The analysis in this plan is a logical next step and a derivative of the MFSA program, but it also includes elements of the Urban Audit. In short, the MFSA has helped Belgrade analyze its own financial position from a completely new perspective, namely, that of investors and financial institutions. The City used the MFSA not only to demonstrate its creditworthiness but also to prepare ambitious infra- and superstructure development projects, many of them foreseen as public–private partnership investments.

Belgrade has also produced a short city brochure, standardized under the UPP, which summarizes the city's socioeconomic situation, financial strength, and plans in a very user-friendly format, easy to understand by citizens and other stakeholders, politicians included. In short, the UPP and the LGSA tool have contributed to improve both Belgrade's understanding of its own situation and its communication with financial partners. Publishing results and making information accessible on the city's website have also contributed to greater transparency and accountability.

capacity level of partner municipalities required hands-on assistance from World Bank staff and consultants. In the case of Southeast Europe, the same approach was maintained with the exception of two differences: (1) a purposeful effort to build the capacity of local national consultants to help local governments and (2) a continued effort to put the local governments in the driver's seat and to identify early in the process the key nominative counterparts (hence the change in label to "self-assessment"). These differences represent a purposeful effort to improve the original paradigm with a strong emphasis on capacity building and learning by doing.

- Second, the original/initial templates of both the Urban Audit and the Financial Audit have been refined, with additions on financial projections and credit shadow ratings, land, and environmental concerns.

Better Cities, Better World presents these updated templates and is an additional step in the effort to make the philosophy, methodology, and how-to templates available to the largest number of beneficiaries. As we strive to improve the tools in these uncharted waters, and as more cities engage in this process, lessons from experience show that the next frontier or challenges that remain to be addressed will need to focus on four key areas:

- Consultation and participation
- Formulation and identification of the Action Plans derived from both the Urban Audit/SA and the MFSA
- Implementation of the Action Plans (both the Priority Investments Program and the MFSA Action Plan), including searching for financing opportunities to support implementation
- Institutionalization of self-assessment tools in day-to-day local government practice.

Objectives and Rationale for Local Governments Self-Assessments: Connecting the Dots between Municipal Investments and Finances

Things are changing in parts of the world, but they are not changing equally for all—which may result in a larger gap between the haves and the have-nots. The incredible leap in technology has enabled cities to have access to and an appetite for spatially based data and to take into account the importance of location in decision making. New thinking has evolved on the function of city planning. No longer seen as a reactive function, city planning is perceived to be at the front and center of city management and no longer as the realm of stodgy planners left in the dusty corner of City Hall. City planners have become, in many places, very vocal voices for change. New planning techniques aim to (1) provide proactive guidance and orientations for future urbanization; (2) take into account new technologies and smart ideas to address environmental concerns; (3) embrace social inclusion challenges; (4) foster and support city "branding"; (5) listen to the voices of various interest groups, including citizens; and (6) play a new role of "broker" between public and private interests.

Despite this new awareness of the importance of city planning, city planners, for the most part, are still left out of the investment programming process and are still very much disconnected from financing decisions. The UA/SA aims to fill this gap and, in many ways, can contribute to further the professionalization of municipal staff by promoting a new "breed" of city planners. Although the decentralization process is progressing, and the missions of the local governments are becoming ever more complex, their financial base has not kept up with the increasing pressure for competitive financing needs. Assessing the financial position of a municipality, along with its capacity to sustain key capital and recurrent investments, and connecting that position to the municipality's investment needs and priorities are therefore more essential than ever.

This is where the MFSA comes in. Collecting "data with a purpose," budgeting and reporting effectively and transparently, projecting future trends, and having a holistic understanding of revenue generation potentials and expenditure needs will help cities better manage their finances. Equally important, these functions

---

Box 1.4
Objectives of Local Governments Self-Assessments

Local Governments Self-Assessments (LGSAs) represent a radical departure from traditional city planning and financial management practices and aim to promote the following mutually reinforcing objectives:

- Promote performance measurement.
- Ensure greater accountability, and support the change process in local public administration (accountability).
- Encourage local governments to get the right data/information and to share it with other municipalities as well as inform central government, local associations, and citizens about their current situation and program (visibility in the use of public funds).

- Encourage financial and other relevant municipal departments to work together on capital investment programs anchored in a realistic financial forecast (prioritization).
- Monitor the financial situation and the investment programs and act on a set of key actions (efficiency and transparency).
- Use a common set of concepts and internationally accepted indicators so as to improve communications and negotiations with banking institutions, the private sector, and donors (access to external funding).
- Secure cost-sharing of investment projects.
- Enhance participation of all interest groups in the choice and selection of municipal/city programs and projects.

Box 1.5
Why Conduct Local Governments Self-Assessments?

- The assessments came from the recognition that data are hard to come by and that we seem to reinvent the wheel
- Initially developed by the World Bank as a project preparation tool. Evolved as a tool to help LGs improve their financial management capacity as well as their investments programming capacity
- Help flag key problems and identify key solutions

- Help communicate with a common language: the assessment template provides an analytical framework (the action-oriented dashboard and city management tool) with key ratios, which are essential for benchmarking, acting on key findings, and monitoring
- Connect the dots between finances, city planning, and municipal investments (reframing them as one integrated municipal program rather than a series of projects)

will help cities improve their relationships with central government and citizens, and their dealings with financial partners (access to credit and to other financing mechanisms through banks or development partners). Again, this change calls for a new breed of municipal staff who can actively participate in the future of their city. LGSAs are very much needed to bridge the skills and data gap, build the capacity of local governments, and induce the implementation of transformative actions for change (boxes 1.4 and 1.5).

Local Governments Self-Assessments: Process and Methodology

This section reviews the process and methodology of LGSAs and attempts to address some of the questions commonly asked. First, what is the process involved in carrying out LGSAs (figure 1.1)? What does it take to start the process? Can it be done anywhere—in large cities or smaller cities? Should LGSAs be carried out simultaneously or by themselves? Do LGSAs replace existing channels of reporting or existing planning documents? Where can the information/data of LGSAs be found, and who are the key interlocutors? How do LGSAs fit with other diagnostic tools? How does the consultation process work? How do LGSAs move forward the agenda of green cities, smart cities, compact cities, and sustainable and resilient cities? What about social inclusion? Beyond the nuts and bolts of LGSAs, what are the key transformative outcomes derived from their application?

Figure 1.1   Local Governments Self-Assessment Process

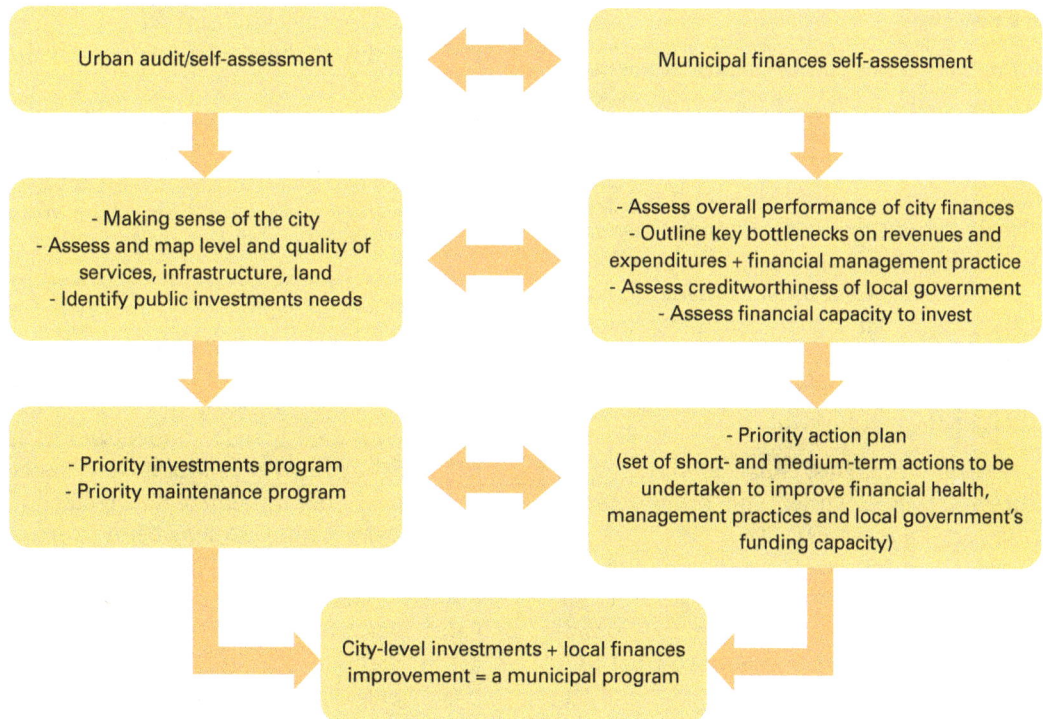

What Does It Take to Start the Process?

Two things are of primary importance: a political will and the right people in the driver's seat. The process must start on the right footing and obtain up-front approval and buy-in from key stakeholders:

- *Town hall*: Mayors and city managers need to be on board at the very beginning of the process. They need to understand why LGSAs are important and what these assessments will do for them: (1) clarify policies and, when needed, policy reforms; (2) provide a road map for action, linking investment decisions to supporting capacity-building measures; (3) ensure transparency and accountability in public spending decisions; and (4) articulate a clear message. Without municipal leaders' political will, the adoption, adaptation, and operationalization of the LGSAs' key findings will be short-lived.

- *Key municipal departments*: Experience shows that identifying the key local counterparts early in the process is essential. Local government staff need to understand that the process of LGSAs does not add to their current data collection and reporting but rather facilitates it while providing a platform for wider use and dissemination of their work. An added bonus is the connection among various departments that might not typically cooperate or work together within the city government.

- *Central ministries*: (finance, local governments, public works, and other relevant sectoral ministries): The ministries are essential partners. First, they want and need to be kept informed, so accurate and timely reporting is of prime importance. Second, they want and need to trust their local partners; LGSAs can help build this trust by providing a data-based platform and a foundation for intergovernmental negotiations. Third, many actions identified in the MFSA Action Plan or the Urban Audit Investment Program require actions by the central government, and the Action Plans will clearly identify the various tiers of responsibilities for unlocking specific issues. It is therefore vital to bring in the key interlocutors early on in the process so that all participants understand their roles and responsibilities.

- *Associations of local governments*: Their role cannot be underestimated because they are the brokers between central and local governments. If they do their job properly, they can be the voice of the local governments and can articulate those governments' position and point of view at the national level. However, many associations around the world are plagued by a number of issues that hinder their capacity to properly fulfill their role. Highest on the list is politics. Second is a general lack of funding, which prevents them from hiring the appropriate staff and addressing the full spectrum of relevant issues. Third is the temptation to get funding from bilateral donors and the result of seeing their work program priorities hijacked by those donors' agenda. They, too, need to understand what LGSAs will do for them. Among many benefits, LGSAs will help (1) articulate a "position" on local issues and provide data-based arguments for their policy dialogue with central governments; (2) support their mission of data collection and curation (an LGSA may be the perfect instrument to develop long-awaited urban observatories, including national aggregated data as well as city-level data); and (3) strengthen their role as providers of training and capacity-building activities.

Can LGSAs Be Done Anywhere?

The current track record shows that LGSAs can be carried out anywhere. Larger cities are more prone to have staff, data, or both more readily available. However, the size of the city and the scale of technical sectoral issues will likely bring a level of complexity to the task. Smaller cities may initially lack adequate staff and available data. The awareness of what is missing both in terms of capacity and data is, in itself, a useful exercise and the prelude for addressing those gaps or shortcomings in the LGSAs' Action Plans. In both cases, the first generation of LGSAs may initially require the involvement of local consultants. These local consultants can be trained in the methodology of LGSAs and provide initial support for data collection and analysis. The idea with using local consultants is not to substitute for municipal staff but rather to work together and "learn by doing." A great deal of capacity-building effort goes into working through LGSAs with a goal to increase the skills of local governments to better record, analyze, present, and act on key findings.

For Municipalities on the Fence: LGSA Version "Light"

LGSAs require some level of capacity and a high level of commitment from all parties involved. The payoff and results emerging from the process are well worth the effort; however, some cities and towns may not be ready for such an engagement. For those local governments that are on the fence—ready but not quite equipped to carry out a full-fledged Urban Audit/Self-Assessment and MFSA—appendix A provides a simplified framework (Version "Light") for a more modest self-assessment that can provide an entry point into a full-fledged LGSA process later. The key objective is to carry out a quick assessment or diagnostic focusing on the urban, financial, and organizational situation of the municipality and helping it to identify a Preliminary Investment Program and a Preliminary MFSA Action Plan. The key goal of this simpler version is to assess the absorptive capacity of the local government and to outline a matching program of investments ready for implementation. The objective is to help the municipality make informed investment decisions while taking steps to improve its urban, organizational, and financial position.

Should LGSAs Be Carried Out Together?

Conducting the Urban Audit/Self-Assessment and the MFSA simultaneously has many obvious benefits. First are the benefits created by the immediate connection and collaboration between various departments (technical and financial) that traditionally do not communicate much among themselves: talking to each other, sharing data, understanding the implications of one department's policy for the other, and understanding the trade-offs of one department's decisions are all much-needed ingredients in creating an integrated municipal/city program. Second are the level of comprehensiveness and the greater understanding of the local situation, challenges, gaps, constraints, and opportunities that arise from a simultaneous use of LGSAs. Combining an assessment of the physical investment needs concurrently with an assessment of the financial position will ensure a fuller understanding of the city's priorities and a better picture of policy implications and required actions. Third, there is something to be said for the power of combining both instruments and achieving both (1) the identification and selection of a municipal investment program and (2) the implementation of key supporting reform and policy actions.

If the local government/city does not wish to engage in a simultaneous Urban Audit/ MFSA process, it can adopt an incremental approach—starting first with the MFSA or the Urban Audit/SA or completing one of the two and delaying the final decision on the way forward. The choice will be based on a number of factors: (1) the political will, as discussed above; (2) the timing and the assessment that LGSAs are the right thing to do; (3) the identification of the right municipal staff; and (4) the identification of local experts/consultants who can help jump-start the process and build the capacity of the relevant departments, if needed. In any case, step 1 of any single LGSA should be the city profile, which gives an overview of (1) spatial and urban governance, (2) demographics and densities, (3) stakeholders and share of functions and responsibilities, (4) urban economy and city branding, and (5) main urban investment challenges.

Do LGSAs Replace Existing Channels of Reporting or Current Planning Practices?

The overarching objective is not to replace existing channels of reporting or current documentation practices. Rather, the objective is to facilitate the actual elaboration of these documents and to improve their speed, accuracy, quality, use, application, relevance, and implementability.

Where Can the Information/Data of LGSAs Be Found, and Who Are the Key Interlocutors?

On the urban investments side, data for the Urban Audit/Self-Assessment can be found in four key locations: (1) the city planning office, (2) the city technical department, (3) utility companies, and (4) sectoral agencies and private operators (land, housing, economic development, and so on). Depending on the level of sophistication of the city or municipality, data will be available in varying formats and accessible on the city's website, portal, interactive maps, geographic information system, and

apps. In other cases, data will be available but not presented in a format that can easily lead to policy decisions. In many cities and towns around the world, data may not be available at all and must be collected, compiled, and analyzed.

- The city's planning office is the number one entry point. As mentioned earlier, most cities have begun to take their planning function more seriously and have come to realize that city planning guidance, in an ever-growing physical environment and ever-shrinking financial context, is crucial. Planning documents have adapted to the local reality and to the need to be both more proactive and more interactive. Long gone is the time when dusty planning offices, supported by an army of technical expatriate assistants, cranked out big master plans whose accuracy would fail along with the pace of urbanization and the disregard for regulations, permits, and the rule of law. City planning documents today are living documents, documents that can adapt and guide investments decisions. They typically include (1) citywide plans, (2) neighborhood-level plans, (3) thematic sector plans, and (4) land development project-based plans at any given time for specific development or redevelopment projects.

- The second key entry point is the technical department of the city government, which takes the brunt of day-to-day maintenance and repairs and is on the frontline and at the receiving end of both the local administration's demands and the citizens' expectations.

- The third key entry point is utility companies. They have their own database and geographic information systems designed to address their specific goal of billing collection and network maintenance.

The city planning office, technical department, department of public works, and the various sectoral agencies typically host map-based data on a vast array of topics: census tract boundaries, city limits, land use plan, zoning plan, address attributes, addressing system (including map and street index), zip code boundaries, street and road network, road traffic data and plan, bicycle plans and pedestrian walkways, educational facilities (primary and secondary schools), health facilities, recreation facilities (libraries, community centers, sports centers, performance centers), parks and open spaces, emergency facilities (fire stations and fire hydrants, police stations, data on emergency response and evacuation), solid waste service boundaries, solid waste service provider data, street sweeping routes, public works easements, commercial facilities, business or enterprise zones, business improvement zones, historic places, subdivision activities, development areas, building permits, inner city development/redevelopment projects, construction inspection areas, tax assessment data, maps of environmentally sensitive areas, and management data on flood-prone areas.

A key challenge is that, in many cities of the world, these various agencies do not communicate their data. As a result, the mass of information collected by various parts of the local government administration, more often than not, does not add up to a coherent, funded, sustainable municipal program. The UA/SA is an opportunity to bring coherence and connectivity in the selection of public investments while integrating the prioritization process with the funding capacity (current and projected) of the city.

Regarding the MFSA, the city finance departments are the key interlocutors for MFSA data collection and the natural "hosts" of most city-level financial information. They generate a dozen or more monthly, quarterly, or annual financial reports in formats prescribed by national public financial management rules and are often defined as specific output tables of integrated financial management information systems (IFMIS), both of which are generally consistent with the MFSA (figure 1.2).

Information sources for the MFSA are typically the following:

- Financial databases are based on information from annual closing financial reports (closing budgets) prepared with varying levels of detail, ranging from very detailed programmatic budget reports to short, single-summary financial statements, or three statements: income, cash flow, and balance sheets, depending on the accounting systems. The finance departments are also supposed to keep tax and debt ledgers but often have no up-to-date, detailed, and reliable tax or debt databases; nor do they have dedicated teams for daily debt or asset/liability management.

- Expenditures and fee revenues are often managed by separate service entities in various forms and of varying quality, and only key summary figures are shared with city finance departments. This absence of coordination hampers the strategic management of revenues and expenditures: integrated financial management systems too often focus on city finance department data and lack tax, fee, labor/salary, goods and services, or asset modules. In such cases, the various service entities or functional units are the only de facto key interlocutors that maintain and record this information—information that is vital to the MFSA process because it lists and analyzes expenditures by function, separates capital and current expenditures, and measures the level and scope of the city's maintenance effort.

The MFSA analysis requires filling up a dozen well-defined and interlinked financial

Figure 1.2 Sources of Municipal Finances Self-Assessment Data

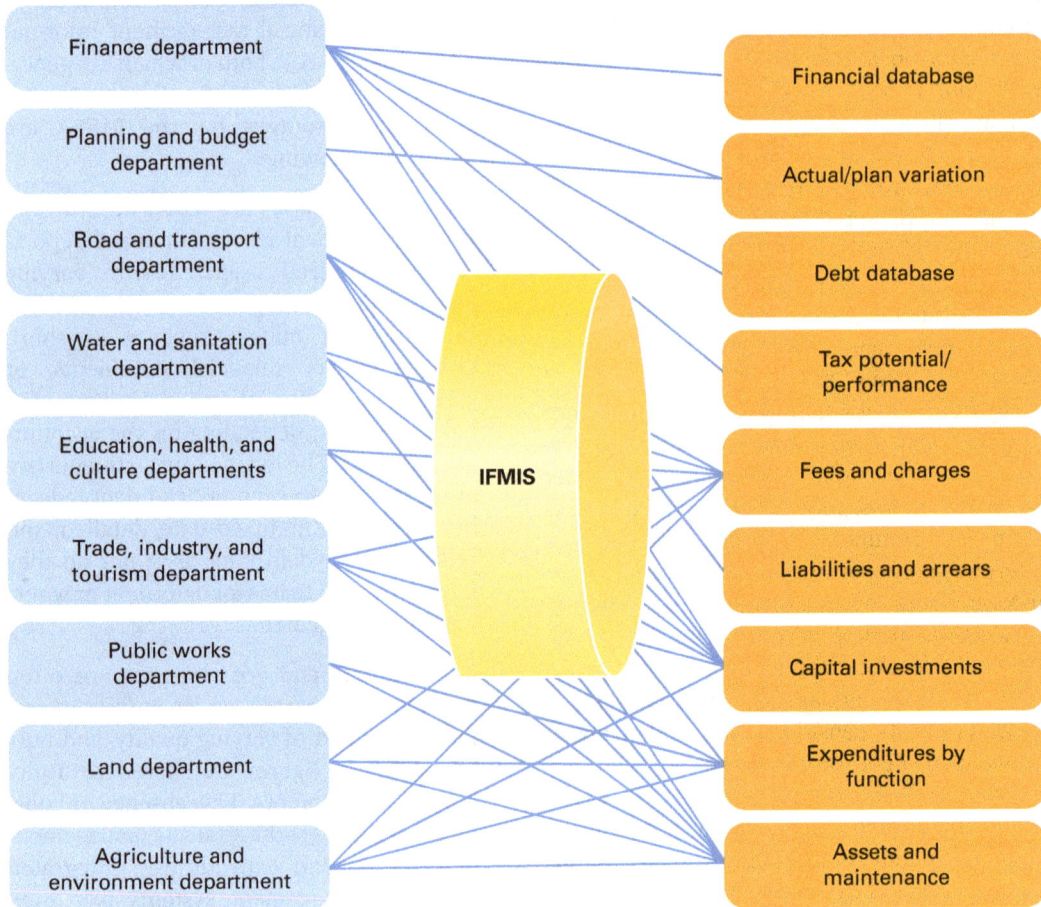

Finance department		Financial database
Planning and budget department	**IFMIS**	Actual/plan variation
Road and transport department		Debt database
Water and sanitation department		Tax potential/performance
Education, health, and culture departments		Fees and charges
Trade, industry, and tourism department		Liabilities and arrears
Public works department		Capital investments
Land department		Expenditures by function
Agriculture and environment department		Assets and maintenance

Note: IFMIS = integrated financial management information system.

or related tables. The task may seem daunting; however, the vast majority of the required information is stored in the vaults of various municipal departments, albeit often disconnected and in different and inconsistent structures. Preparing the MFSA analysis requires locating and slightly restructuring information to fit the MFSA analytical grid.

Having a formatted grid such as the MFSA provides an opportunity to (1) speak with a common language, (2) improve quality and accuracy of planning and budgeting documents, (3) improve forecasting with trend analyses and projections, and (4) open a path away from shortsighted incremental budgeting to a more programmatic harmonization of finances and investment needs. The MFSA represents a quantum leap in data analysis and promotes a new culture of using financial reports for self-assessment of the financial situation and systematic projections of future options. By doing so, the MFSA goes far beyond the common practices in developing countries—that is, preparing financial reports with minimal quality screening (if any) just because they are mandated and using them only to report to upper government bodies. The MFSA moves users beyond simply recording financial data and teaches them how to analyze, understand, and use financial information to draw specific lessons that guide future city-level/municipal actions. In short, the MFSA helps cities move from plain bookkeeping to analysis and action.

If municipalities lack the staffing capacity or the data to complete the full MFSA grid, they may opt for a simpler version (Version "Light"/appendix A) that focuses only on the following key items:

- Fill out the core financial database.

- Complete a historical analysis.

- Complete the municipal finance qualitative assessment (fill out questionnaire and score).

- Draft an action plan.

The better option remains the full-fledged MFSA; however, completing the full MFSA in increments is a possible alternative if needed.

How Do LGSAs Fit with Other Diagnostic Tools?

There are a number of diagnostic tools that aim to focus on some parts of the financial management process. One of them is Public Expenditure and Financial Accountability (PEFA), a methodology for assessing public financial management (PFM) performance and reporting on the strengths and weaknesses of PFM systems. PEFA was developed by seven development partners (European Commission, French Ministry of Foreign Affairs, International Monetary Fund, Norwegian Ministry of Foreign Affairs, State Secretariat of Economic Affairs of Switzerland, U.K. Department for International Development, and World Bank) primarily for

assessing country-level PFM systems. Although initially designed to focus on central governments' financial management performance, the same framework has gradually and successfully been used to assess the financial management quality of cities or other subnational governments, with the addition of one indicator specifically highlighting intergovernmental transfers. The Debt Management Performance Assessment (DeMPA) was developed and is being tested by the World Bank. Whereas PEFA focuses on public financial management, the DeMPA focuses on only one critical segment of PEFA, namely debt management. As outlined in figure 1.3, the MFSA is much broader in scope, content, and intention than the other instruments. PEFA, for example, focuses on only one of the five steps of the MFSA (financial management), so there is very little overlap; in that section, MFSA uses 18 of the 31 PEFA thematic areas so as to foster harmony and consistency between the two tools.

Quid of the Capital Improvement Program and Its Connection with the Urban Audit/Self-Assessment?

A Capital Improvement Plan (CIP) is a planning and fiscal management tool used to coordinate the location, timing, and financing of capital improvements over a multiyear period (Center for Land Use Education 2008)—usually four to six years. Capital improvements refer to major, nonrecurring physical expenditures such as land, buildings, public infrastructure, and equipment. The CIP, typically, includes a description of proposed capital improvement projects ranked by priority, a year-by-year schedule of expected project funding, and an estimate of project costs and financing sources. The CIP is considered to be a working document; it is expected to be reviewed and updated annually to reflect changing community needs, priorities, and funding opportunities.

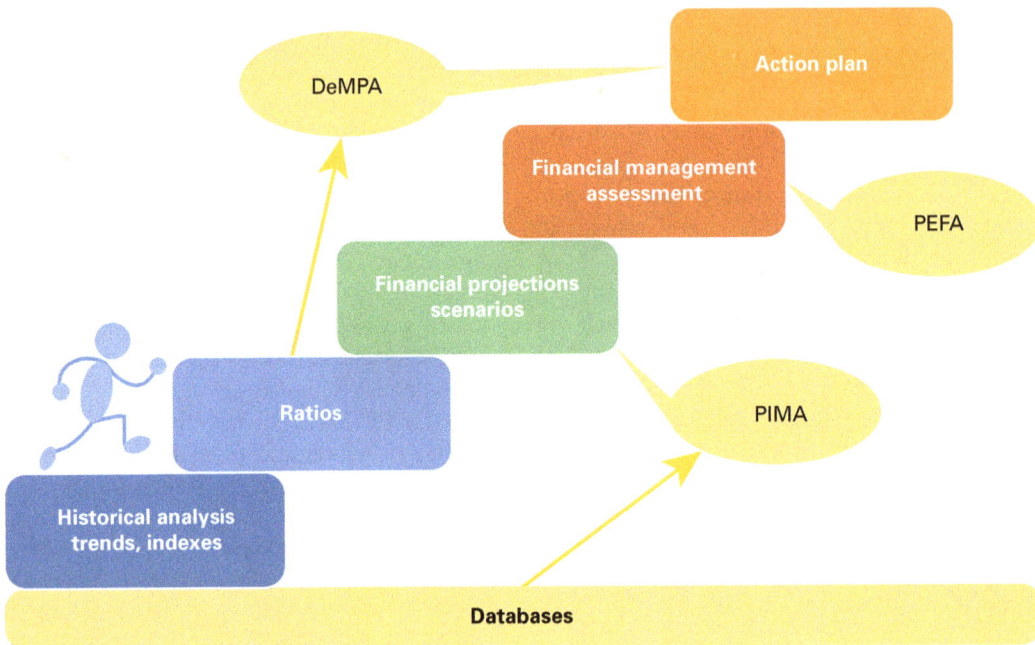

Note: DeMPA = Debt Management Performance Assessment; MFSA = Municipal Finances Self-Assessment; PEFA = Public Expenditure and Financial Accountability; PIMA = Public Investment Management Assessment.

Common categories of capital expenditures include (1) acquisition of land for a public purpose (for example, park, landfill, industrial site); (2) construction, expansion, or major renovation of a public building or facility (for example, school, library, roads, sewage network, treatment plant, building retrofit for energy efficiency); (3) related planning, engineering, design, appraisal, or feasibility studies (for example, architectural fees, certifications); and (4) purchase of major equipment (for example, playground equipment, snow plows, computers).

Although the CIP process works well in cities with dedicated staff, a sound technical capacity, and a long tradition of city planning documentation, it does not work as well in many other cities around the world. The latter cities are mandated to prepare CIPs but do not know where to start or how to produce a meaningful "living" document. For those cities, the UA/SA process will be extremely valuable. Why? Because it will (1) guide them to look for the right information; (2) give them access to a standardized yet customized template, framework, and grid of analysis; (3) help them make sense of the city's trends and spatial patterns; (4) acknowledge the city's specificities; (5) produce a "standardized" yet "customized" analysis of the city's challenges and opportunities; (6) provide a clear definition of rules of the game, criteria, arbitration, and trade-offs in the selection of public investments; (7) outline the key requirements or prerequisites for implementation; and (8) help them do a sound financial measurement of costs with cross-checking and matching of available and potential funding resources using MFSA information.

In short, the MFSA and the UA/SA are changing the way medium-term investment planning, budgeting, and implementation are done by helping cities move away from simple ad hoc or politically driven selection of priority investments to a more fine-tuned citywide programmatic approach.

How Does the Consultation Process Work?

Consultations are a key component of LGSAs. The companion book (*Municipal Finances: A Handbook for Local Governments*) devoted a full chapter (chapter 8, "Achieving Greater Transparency and Accountability: Measuring Municipal Finances Performance and Paving a Path for Reforms") to the importance of consultation, accessibility of data, and citizens' voice in determining the use of public funds. Their voice is equally important in the decision-making process regarding urban investments. It is commonly accepted and recognized that effective citizen engagement is an integral part of good governance. The "ladder of citizen engagement" pioneered in the 1970s and 1980s still pertains today (figure 1.4):

- **Inform**: Provide citizens with balanced and objective information to assist them in understanding the problems, alternatives, opportunities, and solutions.

Figure 1.4 Ladder of Citizen Engagement

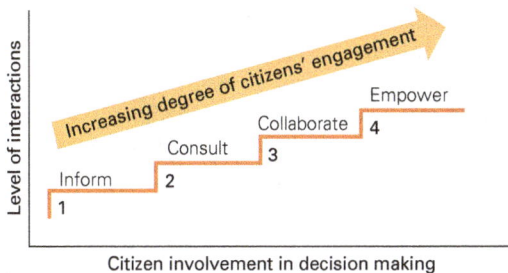

Source: Based on City of Victoria 2017.

- **Consult**: Obtain citizen feedback on analyses, alternatives, and decisions.
- **Collaborate**: Partner with citizens in parts or all of the decision making.
- **Empower**: Include citizens' inputs in final decision making.

This emphasis on citizen engagement, in turn, means that certain key guiding principles must be introduced and respected:

- **Transparency**: The city is open and transparent in how it shares information.
- **Inclusiveness**: The city makes its best effort to reach, inform, and engage all people impacted by the decisions being considered.
- **Welcoming**: The city creates safe, welcoming, and respectful engagement spaces and processes in which everyone feels comfortable sharing feedback.
- **Clear information**: The city provides people with the information they need to participate in a meaningful way.
- **Timely information**: The city provides the community with ample notice of opportunities to participate.
- **Commitment**: The city demonstrates its commitment to engaging the community in a meaningful way, continuously improving practices to remain relevant and effective.
- **Accessibility**: The city works to remove barriers to participation, with the goal of providing all community members with an opportunity for meaningful engagement (adapted from City of Victoria 2017).

As discussed in the following chapters, both the UA/SA and the MFSA aim to integrate these key principles. The process for each tool is very cognizant of the need to include the voice of key stakeholders, including citizens, in the use of taxpayers' money and in the selection of investments that will eventually affect them directly and permanently. Even with the best intentions, however, experience shows that this consultation and participatory approach can be messy for a number of reasons: (1) there is a lack of political will, (2) some of the participatory tools are not effective and pay lip service to the cause, and (3) the increase in citizens' expectations (demand side) falls short of the local government's capacity to respond (supply side). LGSAs can play a balancing act and restore public confidence in municipal action while bringing realism in expectations.

Green Cities, Smart Cities, Compact Cities, Sustainable and Resilient Cities: How Do LGSAs Move the Agenda Forward?

Cities account for about two-thirds of the world's annual energy consumption and about 70 percent of global greenhouse gas emissions (Ostojic and others 2013). In the coming decades, urbanization and income growth in developing countries are expected to push cities' energy consumption and greenhouse gas emissions shares even higher. The number of people living in urban areas in developing countries is expected to double from 2 billion to 4 billion between 2000 and 2030. This massive increase is expected to triple the physical footprint of urbanized areas from 200,000 to 600,000 square kilometers (World Bank 2012). Rapid urbanization has been seen as the major culprit for a heavy carbon footprint and pollution, and cities have therefore become a major focus for addressing climate change issues. Thousands of cities around the world are currently engaged in lessening their environmental impact by reducing waste, expanding recycling, lowering emissions, and increasing density while expanding open space and encouraging the development of sustainable urban lifestyles. LGSAs can help

move the agenda forward in two different ways:

1. The UA/SA can help local officials and decision makers zoom in on issues of key relevance, such as the following:

- the shape of urban development and compact, accessible urban forms
- clean and efficient urban transportation options
- efficient use of energy in buildings and availability of local clean energy
- efficient urban waste management.

The Urban Audit/SA will support the collection of relevant data on urbanization patterns, shapes and trends, densities, and existing coverage and quality of infrastructure and services. Its template is flexible enough to accommodate additional indicators specifically targeted at (1) assessing the current city-level environmental situation, (2) steering policy discussion in the right direction, (3) evaluating the impact of projected investments on the environment, and (4) screening and promoting the inclusion of such projects in the Priority Investment Program. Infrastructure policies are central to green growth strategies, and inertia in infrastructure investments has great potential for regrets.

2. On the financing side, the guiding principles that rule the funding of environmentally sound or smart projects or programs remain very similar at the core to the funding principles of all other projects. In both instances, the city needs to get its finances right, manage its expenditures, mobilize revenues, do proper bookkeeping, and be or become creditworthy to have access to external financing or to issue sector-specific bonds. All these attributes are supported by the MFSA, and we would argue that filling out the MFSA template should be very much part of the practice of any city seeking to improve its

green or smart agenda. In addition, the MFSA can help outline the key fiscal instruments or subsidies that can help either to incentivize the "right" investments or policies or to discourage unwanted practices and behaviors.

Moving along the Social Inclusion and Poverty Reduction Agenda: Can LGSAs Help?

Despite claims that the world has made tremendous progress in reducing extreme poverty—with the percentage of people living in extreme poverty (defined as people living on under US$1.90 a day) falling globally to a new low of 10 percent in 2015 (World Bank 2018)—rates remain stubbornly high in low-income countries and those affected by conflict and political upheaval. In fact, the total number of poor in Sub-Saharan Africa has increased. In 2015, more extremely poor people lived in that region than in the rest of the world combined. Besides extreme poverty, we know that poverty exists everywhere, but data on urban poverty remain very scarce and difficult to capture. How can LGSAs help?

First, the Urban Audit/Self-Assessment includes a spatially based inventory and scoring of the level of infrastructure and services in a city. This process provides an opportunity to locate and map out underserviced neighborhoods, thereby clearly identifying where the city most needs investments and what types of investments are needed. Second, this analysis enables the prioritization of such investments and the documentation of the screening process used to target existing pockets of poverty.

The Importance of Space, Shape, and Form in Public Investment Decisions: Location Matters

Looking at citywide investment needs and priorities spatially is at the core of the UA/SA. Location decisions affect the efficiency,

effectiveness, productivity, and profitability of investments, as well as their environmental and social impacts. Equally important is the need to take into account and understand the spatial impact of financial measures and fiscal policies within a city. The relationship between fiscal policies and urban shape is poorly understood, as is the relationship between land-based revenues and urbanization patterns. The UA and MFSA help connect the dots between financial and fiscal policies and the spatial pattern of city development. The ultimate goal remains a livable city.

Building the Human Capital of City Hall: One City at a Time with LGSAs

LGSAs are built on the concept of "learning by doing," an old adage that is very much an actuality. Indeed, building and improving local governments' capacity are at the core of the LGSAs presented in this book. The premise of *Better Cities, Better World* is that many city governments are very keen to improve their ability to govern and to strengthen their management capacity. Training, however, is not always available and, if available, may not adequately match the specific skill needs of the municipal staff. On-the-job training has proven to be much more effective because it fits better with the day-to-day tasks at hand (in terms of both content and timing). The LGSAs aim to fill the skill gap in financial management, city planning, and investment programming. As mentioned, the first-time LGSA user may need some hand-holding. This hand-holding can occur with the practical use of this handbook, which provides a detailed step-by-step explanation of the process, and of a companion online tool (appendix C). The role of national local government associations is worth mentioning. In the case of the Urban Partnership Program in Southeast Europe, the Regional Association of Local Governments had the foresight to place great emphasis on both face-to-face training and online training and to offer a menu of courses in local languages based on the perceived needs of its constituents. Strengthening the human capital of city hall and enhancing the professionalization of municipal leaders and staff are the only ways to truly put local governments in charge of their present and future.

So What Is New and Innovative about LGSAs?

First, the topics addressed by LGSAs as developed in this book are not new. Investment programming and local finances are actually recurrent issues; what is new is the lens through which we look at these problems. The new lens emphasizes a deep-dive approach into the analysis of the problems and into the identification of concrete solutions and advocates for a long-overdue and missing connection between investments and finances. Second, it promotes a bottom-line, no-nonsense approach to better city management. It does not have thrills and does not get into the fad of the moment but, rather, focuses on bare-bones existential questions for the city. Finally, it provides a standardized yet customized framework of analysis, allowing for an in-depth dive into core issues but also allowing some flexibility with the possibility to add on new layers depending on the focus of interest or the specificities of the city.

Beyond the Nuts and Bolts of LGSAs, What Are Some of the Key Transformative Outcomes Derived from Their Use and Application?

From data curation to policy changes, LGSAs support municipal action over a wide range of applications. Chapter 4 will develop how the tools effectively lead to changes in city management practices, help produce city-based knowledge products, help tell a story and articulate a

position, and sometimes can lead to promising partnerships among various stakeholders, such as central and local governments and the private sector.

References

Acuto, Michele, and Susan Parnell. 2016 "Leave No City Behind." *Science* 352 (6288): 873.

Center for Land Use Education. 2008. "Planning Implementation Tools: Capital Improvement Plan." Center for Land Use Education, University of Wisconsin–Stevens Point. https://www.uwsp .edu/cnr-ap/clue/documents/planimplementa tion/capital_improvement_plan.pdf.

City of Victoria. 2017. "Engagement Framework." Participate Victoria, City of Victoria, Canada.

Farvacque-Vitkovic, Catherine, and Lucien Godin. 2003. *The Future of African Cities: Challenges and Priorities for Urban Development.* Directions in Development. Washington, DC: World Bank.

Farvacque-Vitkovic, Catherine, and Mihaly Kopanyi, eds. 2014. *Municipal Finances: A Handbook for Local Governments.* Washington, DC: World Bank.

International Monetary Fund. 2018. "Public Investment Management Assessment (PIMA)." Fiscal Affairs Department, International Monetary Fund, Washington, DC.

Ostojic, Dejan R., Ranjan K. Bose, Holly Krambeck, Jeanette Lim, and Yabei Zhang. 2013. *Energizing Green Cities in Southeast Asia: Applying Sustainable Urban Energy and Emissions Planning.* Directions in Development. Washington, DC: World Bank.

PEFA Secretariat. 2016. "Supplementary Guidance for Subnational PEFA Assessments." PEFA Secretariat, Washington, DC. https://pefa .org/sites/default/files/SNG%20PEFA%20 guide%20revised%2016-03-10%20edited.pdf.

Science. 2016. "Rise of the City." *Science* 352 (6288): 906–07.

World Bank. 2012. *Inclusive Green Growth: The Pathway to Sustainable Development.* Washington, DC: World Bank.

———. 2015. "Debt Management Performance Assessment (DeMPA) Methodology." World Bank, Washington, DC.

———. 2018. *Poverty and Shared Prosperity 2018: Piecing Together the Poverty Puzzle.* Washington, DC: World Bank.

Additional Readings

Farvacque-Vitkovic, Catherine, and Lucien Godin. 2010. "Decentralization and Municipal Development: Municipal Contracts." Working Paper, World Bank, Washington, DC.

Farvacque-Vitkovic, Catherine, Lucien Godin, and Anne Sinet. 2014. "Municipal Self-Assessments: A Handbook for Local Governments." Working Paper, World Bank, Washington, DC.

Senegal Municipal Development Agency. (multiple years, 2006 onward). "Guide to Cities' Finances." Dakar.

———. 2007. *Atlas des Communes de la Region de Dakar.* Dakar.

World Bank. 2009. "Improving Municipal Management for Cities to Succeed: An IEG Special Study." World Bank, Washington, DC.

———. 2014. "Improving Local Governments Capacity: The Experience of Municipal Finances Self-Assessment in South-East Europe." UPP Program, World Bank, Washington, DC.

———. 2018. "Improving Local Governments Capacity: The Experience of Municipal Finances Self-Assessment in South East Europe." UPP Program, World Bank, Washington, DC.

———. Forthcoming. "Municipal Finances Self-Assessment." Online application. World Bank, Washington, DC.

CHAPTER 2

Making Sense of the City and Sorting Out Investment Needs and Priorities

The Urban Audit/Self-Assessment

The Urban Audit/Self-Assessment (UA/SA), as presented in this book, does not pretend to address every single urban issue. Cities are complex microorganisms, city situations are diverse, city functions may vary, and, consequently, city priorities may not be fully captured in the current version of the UA/SA. What this UA/SA does provide, however, is (1) a "bottom line" analytical grid/framework focusing on essential municipal infrastructure and services; (2) a way of assessing the performance of the city in the delivery of those basic infrastructure and services; and (3) an identification of location-based priority needs leading to a Municipal Investments Program containing both capital projects and maintenance tasks. Those seeking to find solutions to wider challenges may not find them here, although the UA/SA provides a screening mechanism for investment projects and programs, which definitely gives priority to projects that have a positive environmental impact as well as positive social benefits. One of the key objectives of the UA/SA is to promote a "Do No Wrong" approach in investment decisions. The attractiveness of this tool is that additional layers of analysis can be customized and added to the template presented below so as to reflect the specific strategic vision or situation of the city while keeping in the equation the key basic, nonnegotiable, and sometimes unglamorous duties and functions that any urban local government in the world has to perform and for which funding has to be freed.

Objectives and Approach

What Is an Urban Audit/Self-Assessment?

The UA/SA is an analytical framework designed to enable local governments to (1) take stock of their own situation; (2) assess the level of service and infrastructure delivery within their jurisdiction; (3) locate and quantify the gaps; (4) outline the key components of a Priority Investments Program (PIP), and in some cases, of a Priority Maintenance Program (PMP); and (5) provide the foundations for speedy implementation of city and neighborhood-level investments programs, as well as supporting policy change (box 2.1).

What Are the Key Objectives of the UA/SA?

The UA/SA is an analytical framework designed to enable local governments to assess their local socioeconomic situation, citizens' needs, and level of services in a systematic and comprehensive manner. The UA/SA has the following key objectives:

- Ensure that patterns of growth and development and key urbanization challenges are understood and documented by all parties involved in public investment decisions.

- Ensure that investment planning takes a **city-level** spatial programmatic approach rather than a project-based approach.

- Ensure transparency and accountability in the prioritization of key needed capital investments.

- Ensure the timely repair and replacement of aging infrastructure.

- Provide a level of certainty for residents, businesses, and developers regarding the location and timing of public investments.

- Identify the most economical means of financing capital improvements.

Box 2.1
Urban Audit/Self-Assessment Objectives and Preparation

Objectives

- To assess current urbanization trends, existing levels of infrastructure and services, and key challenges in the management of municipal investments
- To support the identification of a municipal program consisting of priority investments and accompanying city management capacity-building measures
- To connect the dots between the big picture (urbanization challenges, sectoral policies) and the technical implementation of brick-and-mortar "construction and maintenance" of the city

Preparation

- The UA/SA is typically conducted in parallel with an MFSA and enables the municipality to match its investment needs with its capacity to finance and maintain its existing and projected infrastructure and services.
- The UA/SA is produced by the municipal services. It is prepared for a period of 5 years and is annually updated.
- The UA/SA is based on the available data that municipal services can collect and curate.

- Provide an opportunity for public input in the budgeting and financing process.

- Eliminate unanticipated, poorly planned, or unnecessary capital expenditures.

- Avoid using sharp increases in tax rates, user fees, and debt levels to cover unexpected capital improvements.

- Balance desired public improvements with the city's financial resources.

Why Is the UA/SA Important?

First, it is important because, in many cases, the local regulatory framework and the planning document requirements have failed local governments. Local governments are often faced with the mandatory production of planning documents that they do not have the capacity to produce. UA/SAs do not aim to replace existing documentation requirements but rather to facilitate their timely completion. UA/SAs constitute an important building block in the planning process and contribute to a complete rethinking of the traditional practice of investment programming because they relink planning with finances and programming and position investment programming in the realm of the "possible" and the "realistic."

Second, the UA/SA contributes to enhanced transparency, participation, and accountability in the decision-making process over what and how priorities should be financed, shedding light on the use of public funds in the municipal space.

Third, the UA/SA brings together several professions and municipal departments that typically do not communicate. Cities that have conducted Urban Audits/SA and Municipal Finances Self-Assessments (MFSAs) have noted this connection as a key benefit.

When Should a UA/SA Be Performed?

Cities of all sizes can benefit from the UA/SA process. Experience shows that capital cities, medium-size cities, and smaller towns that have embarked on UA/SAs have done so with a great level of success. As stated in chapter 1, the starting point will differ greatly depending on the size of the city, the level and skill mix of the municipal staff, and the availability of data (in particular geospatial data). As seen in the previous chapter, the data needed to fill out the UA/SA template are in large part already available but are fragmented in several city departments that may not traditionally collaborate, such as the city planning office, the city's technical department, the utility companies, and the various sectoral agencies in charge of land, housing, economic development, and disaster risk management, not to mention the entity in charge of Capital Improvement Plans, which commonly sits on the other side of the organization chart of city hall. The UA/SA is an opportunity to bring these data together into a cohesive story conducive to decision making and policy dialogue.

Who Should Drive the Process?

Central and local governments and city leaders. They are the primary users and beneficiaries. First, it is crucial to have buy-in upstream from city leaders and policy makers. They need to be aware of the availability, accessibility, and ease of use of such a tool; and they need to understand what it can do for them, for their current agenda, and for their legacy. In many ways, these tools are much more than tools: the key findings will shape policy discussions and support or drive policy reforms and changes. The UA/SA calls for a different set of skills than the ones commonly found in municipal departments. It requires a combination of skills that crosses the boundaries between city planners, municipal engineers, budgeting, and programming and relies on a more integrated, more strategic, less compartmentalized approach to city management, as well as a greater professionalization of municipal staff. The practice of UA/SA can help build the capacity of municipal staff to meet that goal.

Citizens. Obviously, citizen participation is a key component of the Local Governments Self-Assessments (LGSAs), and no LGSA should be conducted without the timely inputs of civil society. Citizens are very engaged in the UA/SA process through a series of consultations and are able to express their voices and concerns regarding the relevance, location, and prioritization of investments that affect them directly as both users and taxpayers. By making data readily accessible and by telling a story that genuinely shows the pros and cons and trade-offs of investment decisions, the UA/SA contributes to greater accountability and transparency in the use of public funds. It goes well beyond the lip service that often prevails when it comes to citizens' input. Clicking on an app to report potholes is great, but being actively engaged in a decision-making process before decisions are made is even better.

Donor/aid community. Multi- and bilateral agencies involved in the urban space have long struggled with a lack of data, a lack of common language, and a sense of "reinventing the wheel" every time they engage in dialogues with central or local governments on urban issues. The analytical grid of the UA/SA can be used for project/program preparation as well as constitute the key components of a lending or assistance program focusing on both investments and capacity building. One key component of the UA/SA is the identification/formulation of an Investment Plan. This Investment Plan is very much like a sophisticated procurement plan, including project data sheets on each selected project and a checklist of key prerequisites for implementation. In addition, the UA/SA and MFSA provide the basis for a companion set of policy actions and capacity-building tasks. Both components constitute valuable foundations for lending or assistance programs with greater prospects for results on the ground and for fast disbursements.

Other financial partners. Private banks and other financial partners are keen to have adequate information for lending purposes and to assess the creditworthiness of a city or to identify "bankable" projects within the urban space. UA/SAs provide that easy access, in one single document, to the type of quality and targeted information that lending institutions would otherwise have to gather from many different sources.

What Are the Key Ingredients of Success?

Sorting out "bad" projects. There is such a thing as a bad project. Examples of so-called white elephants that have made some towns and cities famously unpopular are numerous. Many developing cities are riddled with such projects that made it to the implementation stage because of corruption, political struggle, and one-time financing for capital costs forgoing the long-term operations and maintenance funding needs. For example, one can wonder if building an ice-skating rink in a tropical region is absolutely necessary. The scrutiny of implementation is key in order to prevent the funding of bad projects. The UA/SA provides an evaluation grid to help determine up-front the desirability and feasibility of proposed projects. Is land available for new proposed projects? Does the project meet the social, environmental, and economic scores? If available, where does funding come from and how will its use affect the financial position of the city in the future? Assessing the level of readiness of a project is time well spent because it will likely prevent long delays in implementation down the road.

Focusing on location, location, location. Because the UA/SA is map-based, location matters a great deal in the process as it should in any investment programming exercise. Looking at the world and cities spatially brings a new dimension to decisions on infrastructure investments (box 2.2).

Taking politics out of the equation. The UA/SA process can most certainly minimize the disruptive impact that changes in government leadership can have on investment programs. The UA/SA screening process is fact-based and devoid of politics, and selected programs are vetted publicly through a series of consultations:

Box 2.2
A World of Maps: How Are Urban Maps Created?

Cartography, or more generically, "making maps" is the process of map creation and map design.

To make maps, the cartographer needs two main components:

1. A base map

A base map will serve as an outline of a country or area where data will be plotted. It is rare that one person will create a base map from scratch. Many tools can be used to start a mapping project. One of the main tools is the open-source OpenStreetMap (OSM) with its HOT Export Tool. Natural Earth or GADM are also among the most prominent free data providers.

2. Data to be represented on the map

Data are ultimately composed of three types:

- Points
- Lines
- Polygons

Organized together as layers, they will create the map. Points can represent cities or metro stations; lines can represent rivers, railways, or roads; and polygons can represent lakes, buildings, or areas.

Once the base map has been decided and set, specific project data will need to be added to it. The data can be found in a variety of forms, from Excel spreadsheets collecting poverty indicators to satellite imagery survey results and street addressing data. All of these data will have geographical information that will be laid down on the base map.

Learn your audience: General and thematic maps

One of the key components of making maps is understanding to whom the map is addressed. Because a map will target a specific audience, one map will totally change from one to another. This is the case with general maps, which will display general information for a general audience. A simple metro map will target general metro users, such as commuters and tourists.

Thematic maps portray special themes on maps that will target specific audience. This could be a choropleth map showing access to public transport in minutes, which could be used by city officials when planning urban growth or to modernize a public transport system.

continued next page

Who Is in Charge of Producing Maps, and Where Can I Access Public Data?

Depending on the level of organization of the government, a national statistical agency or geographic information agency is usually in charge of collecting, organizing, and distributing data and sometimes of producing maps. The IBGE in Brazil, the IGN in France, and the USGS in the United States are examples of well-established, historical agencies that are responsible for their countries' geographical data.

In cases where national data are not centrally organized, international development agencies like the Food and Agriculture Organization of the United Nations, the World Bank, or the United Nations Office for the Coordination of Humanitarian Affairs collect, organize, and release public data through their websites, for example, the Humanitarian Data Exchange or Data Catalog. This helps greatly to fill the vacuum where there is a lack of organized and maintained datasets, mainly in low- and middle-income countries.

On a smaller scale for more targeted needs, nongovernmental organizations like the International Union for Conservation of Nature or the World Resources Institute also collect, organize, and publish map data. Protected Planet and Global Forest Watch are among the two most prominent GIS databases freely available.

Which Software Should I Use for Creating Maps?

Open-source software (free of charge)

- QGIS (https://www.qgis.org)
- OSM (https://www.openstreetmap.org)
- Hot Export Tool for OSM (https://export.hotosm.org/en/v3/)
- Google Earth (https://www.google.com/earth/)
- GADM (https://gadm.org)
- World Bank datasets (https://data.worldbank.org)
- Natural Earth (https://www.naturalearthdata.com)
- Leaflet (https://leafletjs.com)
- Color Brewer (http://colorbrewer2.org)
- Geoserver (https://geoserver.org)

Licensed (fee-based) software

- ArcGIS/ArcMap (http://desktop.arcgis.com/en/arcmap/)
- ArcGIS Pro (https://pro.arcgis.com/en/pro-app/)
- MapInfo Pro (https://www.pitneybowes.com/us/location-intelligence/geographic-information-systems/mapinfo-pro.html)
- Mapbox (https://www.mapbox.com)
- CARTO (https://carto.com)
- ArcGIS Server (https://enterprise.arcgis.com/en/)

Source: Bruno Bonansea, Cartographer, the World Bank 2019.

the very public nature of this decision-making process makes it difficult for new incumbents to ignore the legacy of the past and to end or cancel ongoing projects. The municipal contract was designed in large part to circumvent the issue of the dependency of municipal programs on the cycle of political mandates.

Should the UA/SA Be Performed as a Single Task or Complemented with an MFSA?

The UA/SA can be carried out by itself; however, combining it with an MFSA makes it much more compelling because it is then possible to match the PIP with the financial absorptive capacity of the local government. The MFSA will provide a snapshot of the financial position of the city and of its financial projections and will give an assessment of what makes or breaks a municipal investment program. The MFSA will also provide an assessment of the existing financial commitments of the municipality as well as its current borrowing capacity and its potential to attract external funding.

What If the City Is Not Ready, Prepared, or Equipped for a Full-Fledged Urban Audit/SA?

In such a case, the city may choose to follow a simpler path and to use a simplified version of the Urban Audit/SA. The template of this simplified version (Version "Light") can be found in appendix A.

What Is the Process of the UA/SA?

The basic framework of the UA/SA includes three main building blocks and 13 steps (figure 2.1):

- **Block 1: City Profile**

  - Step 1: Spatial and Urban Governance

  - Step 2: Demography and Densities

  - Step 3: Stakeholders and Share of Functions and Responsibilities

Figure 2.1 **Urban Audit/Self-Assessment Framework**

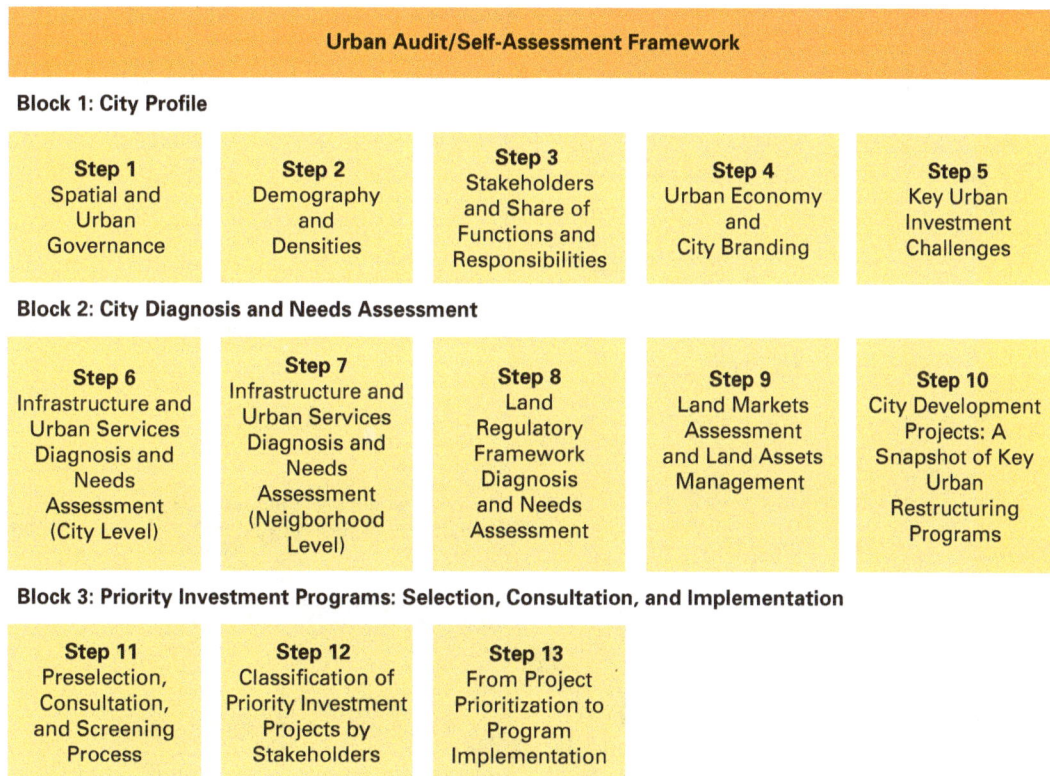

Urban Audit/Self-Assessment Framework				

Block 1: City Profile

Step 1 Spatial and Urban Governance	Step 2 Demography and Densities	Step 3 Stakeholders and Share of Functions and Responsibilities	Step 4 Urban Economy and City Branding	Step 5 Key Urban Investment Challenges

Block 2: City Diagnosis and Needs Assessment

Step 6 Infrastructure and Urban Services Diagnosis and Needs Assessment (City Level)	Step 7 Infrastructure and Urban Services Diagnosis and Needs Assessment (Neigborhood Level)	Step 8 Land Regulatory Framework Diagnosis and Needs Assessment	Step 9 Land Markets Assessment and Land Assets Management	Step 10 City Development Projects: A Snapshot of Key Urban Restructuring Programs

Block 3: Priority Investment Programs: Selection, Consultation, and Implementation

Step 11 Preselection, Consultation, and Screening Process	Step 12 Classification of Priority Investment Projects by Stakeholders	Step 13 From Project Prioritization to Program Implementation

- Step 4: Urban Economy and City Branding

- Step 5: Key Urban Investment Challenges

- **Block 2: City Diagnosis and Needs Assessment**

  - Step 6: Infrastructure and Services Diagnosis and Needs Assessment (City Level)

  - Step 7: Infrastructure and Services Diagnosis and Needs Assessment (Neighborhood Level)

  - Step 8: Land Regulatory Framework Diagnosis and Needs Assessment

  - Step 9: Land Markets Assessment and Land Assets Management

  - Step 10: City Development Projects—A Snapshot of Key Urban Restructuring Programs (urban extensions, inner-city redevelopment, neighborhood or slum upgrading)

- **Block 3: Priority Investment Programs— Selection, Consultation, and Implementation**

  - Step 11: Preselection, Consultation, and Screening Process

  - Step 12: Classification of Priority Investment Projects by Stakeholders

  - Step 13: From Project Prioritization to Program Implementation

Block 1. City Profile

Objectives and Methodology

The objective of the City Profile is to provide a brief overview of the situation of the city. It is a crucial step in the Local Governments Self-Assessment (LGSA) process and should be done as a first step even when the municipality elects to carry out an MFSA alone without necessarily conducting a UA/SA. Doing a City Profile up-front enables the city to (1) brand itself by outlining the key features that characterize its demographic, social, and economic situation; and (2) isolate the most meaningful and measurable indicators for the city in a way that makes the City Profile relevant and informative for potential PIP partners such as banks, private partners, or development agencies. The City Profile should almost be seen as a promotional exercise.

Urban issues and challenges faced by municipalities around the world do have similarities; however, they do not necessarily call for similar solutions. The size of the city and the growth of its population, as well as its administrative status (city government, district within a metropolitan area, small or medium-size city, or metropolitan authority) and its main urban economic features, will all have an impact on its strategic choices and its investment policies.

Institutional framework and organizational structure (functions and responsibilities both

Figure 2.2 City Profile: Key Components

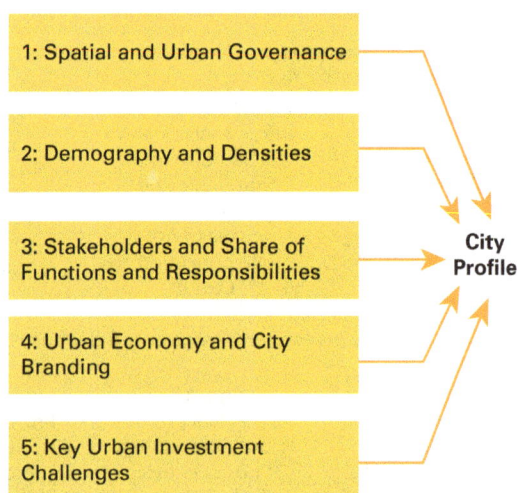

1: Spatial and Urban Governance

2: Demography and Densities

3: Stakeholders and Share of Functions and Responsibilities

4: Urban Economy and City Branding

5: Key Urban Investment Challenges

City Profile

vertically and horizontally) will also have a major influence on the content of municipal investment programs and on the efficiency level of their implementation. Local development has become increasingly complex, even in developing countries, and often involves multiple stakeholders and sophisticated cross-financing mechanisms.

The City Profile includes the following five steps:

- Step 1: Spatial and Urban Governance

- Step 2: Demography and Densities

- Step 3: Stakeholders and Share of Functions and Responsibilities

- Step 4: Urban Economy and City Branding

- Step 5: Key Urban Investment Challenges.

The presentation of the City Profile has been intentionally simplified because each item could clearly generate detailed explanations and many add-ons. In other words, the list provided in figure 2.2 is a "bottom line" list that can be modified, expanded, or customized in order to better reflect the specific circumstances of the city or town.

Step 1: Spatial and Urban Governance

Objective and content. The UA/SA's first step is to clarify the geographical boundaries of the municipality involved in the process. The aim is to identify correctly the spatial area and the level of local government unit responsible for infrastructure and service delivery within those boundaries. The clear definition of the unit of analysis is extremely important for the UA/SA as well as for the MFSA. In order to have a viable benchmark for urban and financial assessments and to propose realistic and accurate recommendations for action and policy reforms, we need to have a common understanding of what it is that we are looking at. For the sake of simplicity, the UA/SA will adopt the commonly recognized typology shown in box 2.3.

Tasks. This section will provide a map of the city's boundaries and a brief explanation of the governance structure. It will state clearly the various tiers of government administration and the legal framework that underlies the governance structure (map 2.1).

Step 3 will address the details on (1) the distribution of functions and responsibilities among the various jurisdictions, (2) the institutional organization, and (3) the channeling of public funds.

Step 2: Demography and Densities

Objective and content. Population trends of the municipality are key indicators to evaluate investment needs. It is very important to

---

Box 2.3
Typology Guidance

- **Type 1**: Municipality as a core individual unit, with no specific autonomous subdivisions
- **Type 2**: City district, which is a subdivision of the city according to strict legal criteria regarding funding resources,

funding obligations, and share of functions and responsibilities
- **Type 3**: Metropolitan entity, including several situations such as intergovernmental entity and authority (Urban Community) and even larger metropolitan unit

---

Map 2.1 Spatial and Urban Governance

a. Capital city level	b. Regional level (8 counties, 1301 LGs)	c. Metropolitan level (20 districts)

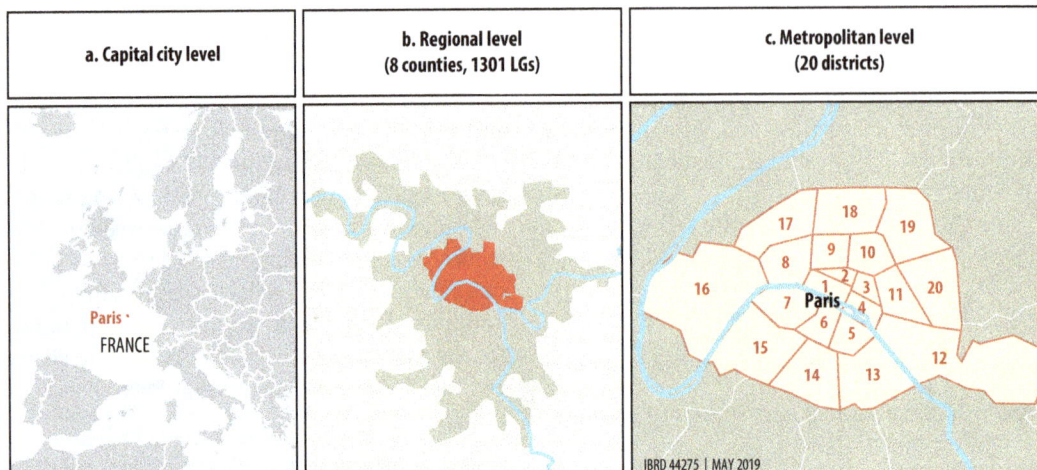

These maps were created using OSM and local data, reprojected in ArcGIS, and refined in Adobe Illustrator.

Note: LG = local government.

understand both the current structure of the population and the projected trends in order to inject relevance and realism in investment programs. Similarly, the current and projected profile of a city's population will determine current and future potentials for tax revenues. An aging population will require investments that are better geared to its needs—such as neighborhood health clinics and community centers, accessible public transportation, maintained sidewalks and street lighting, and accessible administrative services. A younger population will have different needs—such as neighborhood child care centers, schools, sports facilities, and safe open space—and will require serious consideration of the economic development policy of the city with the goal of providing job opportunities and retaining an economic vibrancy. Characteristics of an aging population or a younger population will have an impact on the profile of the current and future tax base.

An additional very important item for analysis is density. Achieving the "right" level of density is a difficult goal, as most experts and practitioners do not agree on what the "right" level of density

might be. The basic concept is to promote an efficient use of land, making the city more compact, limiting peri-urban sprawl, and curbing its high costs on infrastructure and the environment. This is easier said than done, and it entails a high level of fine-tuning and sophistication in the use of land use regulations, fiscal instruments, and incentives. Many cities struggle with underserviced densely populated neighborhoods. The Inventory for the Programming of Services and Infrastructure tool (explained in step 7) will enable an analysis of densities at the neighborhood level. Finally, the world has witnessed the ravages of wars and the displacement of millions of refugees. Some parts of the globe have experienced this issue in dramatic and tragic proportions. The City Profile will look at estimated numbers, the location patterns, and the impact on infrastructure and services of these new migrants in order to customize the response in terms of investments and funding needs.

Tasks. Key items will include the following:

- Provide an overview of city-level population trends and show demographic projections

Figure 2.3 **Demographic Trends**

Population Trends

Year	Cens 1	R	Cens 2	R	N	R	N+5	R	N+10	R	N+15
Municipality Region											

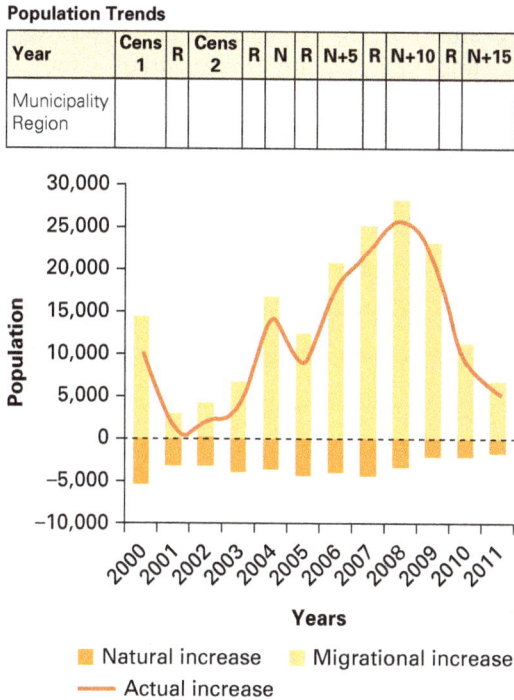

- Natural increase
- Migrational increase
- Actual increase

Note: Cens = census; R = growth rate.

Map 2.2 **Population Densities**

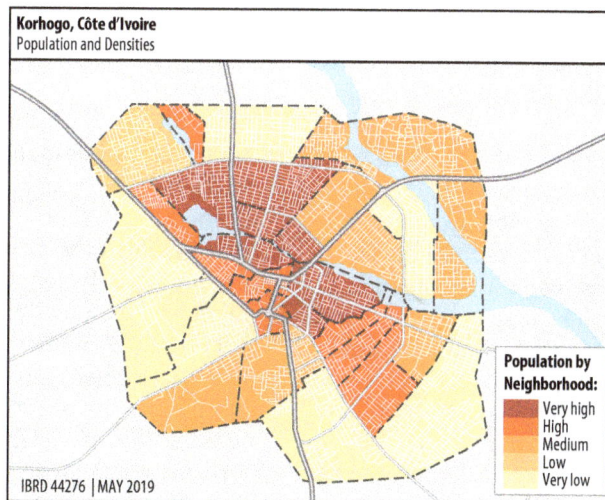

over 5, 10, and 15 years. A distinction will be made between natural growth and growth due to immigration. The population of the municipality will be compared to regional and national population.

- Provide an overview of city-level population profile and composition, including age and gender. State any salient feature with a long-term impact on the city's infrastructure needs.

- Provide a neighborhood-level analysis of densities.

- In case of catastrophic conditions (conditions related to refugee crises or climatic incidents), explain the current situation and provide numbers and locations (maps) of new settlements.

These data will be presented in tables and figures as follows (see below and figure 2.3). Maps will be added to illustrate demographic trends (see map 2.2).

Step 3: Stakeholders and Share of Functions and Responsibilities

Objective and content. Because the municipality does not act alone within its territory, it is essential to outline who is responsible for what at the city level and to provide a clear snapshot of the institutional and organizational structure of the municipality. This understanding will help (1) assess to what extent the municipality is prepared to meet its key core functions and emerging new responsibilities and (2) identify existing needs and gaps in the current structure.

Tasks. Key items will include the following:

1. A summary table indicating key stakeholders in terms of public investments and who is responsible for what. Clarification of the roles and responsibilities for the delivery and maintenance of key infrastructure, utilities, services, and land development seems a no-brainer. In practice and in reality, however, there are many local jurisdictions where such delineation is fuzzy or where functions overlap. Sometimes, for reasons related to lack of proper governance, lack of capacity, lack of confidence, or lack of funding, the central or state government has had to step in to assume delegated functions. Having clarity on the distribution of responsibilities is essential for a number of reasons: (1) it prevents duplication of efforts and improves efficiency in delivery and maintenance; (2) it provides greater accountability to the citizens; and (3) it outlines the funding responsibilities and the channeling of funds. Table 2.1 can be used as a model and adjusted according to specific situations.

2. A matrix showing the roles of stakeholders in the financing of infrastructure, public utilities, services, land development, and real estate (figure 2.4). A clear definition of roles and responsibilities allows for a greater understanding of the funding needs and challenges. The local government finds itself at the crossroads of a mix of financing sources that include (1) transfers from the central to the local government, (2) fiscal revenues (own revenues and shared taxes), (3) private sector financing, and (4) external funding such as donors and banks (borrowing). Understanding what the municipality is responsible for should ideally provide a basis for the volume of transfers and the importance of fiscal decentralization. Because this is not an ideal world, however, everybody finds it ultimately convenient to keep this information in a gray area.

3. A flow chart showing the organizational structure of the municipality (figure 2.5). This organizational structure might change depending on the local situation or context. A constant is that every city will have a financial department in charge of city finances and of keeping the books in order and a technical services department in charge of running the day-to-day management and maintenance of the city's infrastructure and services. The UA/SA should aim to provide an accurate snapshot of the structure of the city government, with the goal to (1) assess if there is a proper match between mandates and departments, skill mix and functions; (2) assess if there is enough coordination between the various departments, in particular between the financial department and the technical department and between the municipal staff in charge of financial projections and those in charge of investments programming; and (3) outline the key deficiencies in the existing structure and the key actions required to improve these deficiencies.

Table 2.1　Share of Responsibilities: Who Is Responsible for What?

		Municipality		State government		Utility companies		Private	
Sectors	Items	New works	Maintenance	New works	Maintenance	New works	Maintenance	New works	Maintenance
1 Infrastructure	Primary roads			O	O				
	Secondary roads	X	X						
	Drainage	X	X						
	Solid waste	X	X	O	O				
	Street lighting	X	X						
2 Utilities	Electricity					X	X		
	Water supply					X	X		
	Wastewater					X	X		
	Urban transport	X	X			X	X		
	Public heating					X	X		
	Others								
3 Services	Education	X	X	O	O				
	Health	X	X	O	O				
	Social	X	X	O	O				
	Culture	X	X	O	O				
	Green spaces	X	X	O	O				
4 Land development	Housing	X	X	O	O			V	V
	Industrial	X	X	O	O			V	V
	Urban renewal	X	X	O	O			V	V

Note: X = municipal level; O = state level; V = private.

Figure 2.4　Financing Mechanisms: A Simplified Matrix

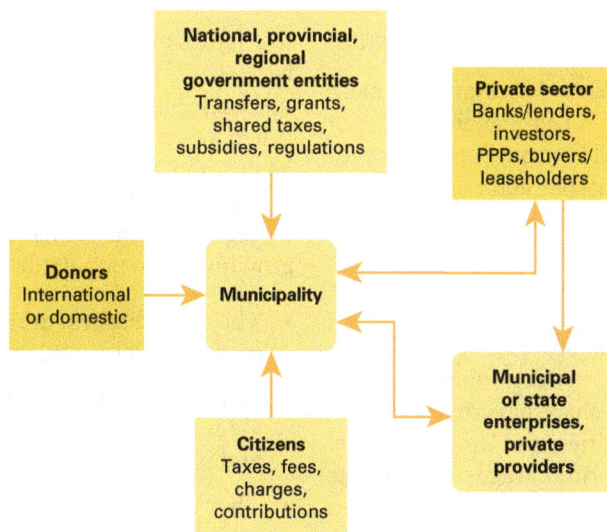

Note: PPP = public–private partnership.

Figure 2.5 Organizational Chart of the Municipality: An Example

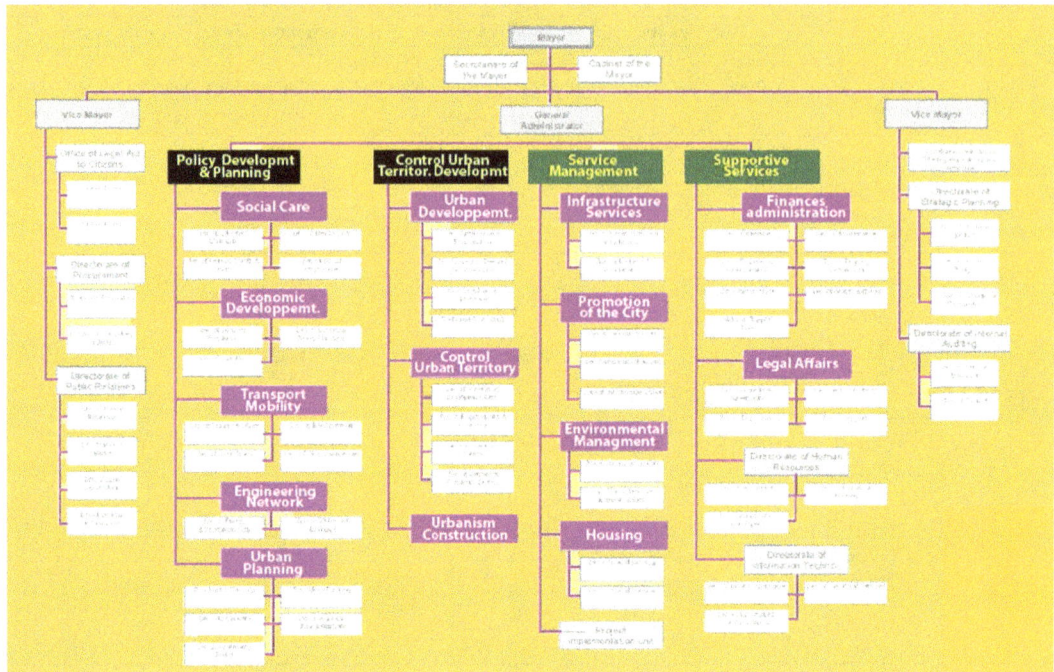

Step 4: Urban Economy and City Branding

Objective and content. Cities are the main creators of economic wealth, generating over 70 percent of the world's gross domestic product (GDP). Most industries and businesses are located in or within the immediate vicinity of urban areas, providing city residents with jobs. Because most employment opportunities are within urban areas, cities attract a large proportion of a country's job-seeking population. This is especially true in developing countries, where an increasing share of economic activities takes place in cities, and the differential between urban and rural wages is growing. These factors cause rapid rural-to-urban migration. Today, urban dwellers make up over 50 percent of the world's population, with

this figure expected to rise to over 65 percent by 2030. If urban economic opportunities do not keep pace with the influx of job seekers, urban poverty can have dire results for the health and well-being of large shares of the population. Governments face a set of economic and financial challenges in dealing with growing urban populations:

- They must harness urban population growth to generate economic prosperity.

- They must pay for infrastructure and services to both accommodate new residents and support the existing population.

- They must facilitate economic growth and job creation that are broad-based and inclusive.

- They must leverage the youth dividend to create a new generation of economic vibrancy. The youth demographics can be an economic strength if youth are empowered to participate in urban life. Globally, there are more people under the age of 25 today than ever before, and it is estimated that as many as 60 percent of all urban dwellers will be under the age of 18 by 2030. Cities of the developing world account for over 90 percent of the world's urban growth, and, consequently, youth constitute a large percentage of those inhabitants.

This section of the UA/SA summarizes steps to measure the key aspects of the city's economy:

- Identify the key components of the local economy and the major factors that affect these different components.

- Identify the "drivers" of the local economy and principal stakeholders involved (public and private, local and outside the region, "modern" and "informal").

- Describe the features and level of urban employment: government, commerce, industry, agriculture, informal activities. Name the major "employers."

- Identify "modern" businesses, such as start-ups and self-employment.

- Estimate scale of informal activities.

- Describe the "brand" and "branding policies" of the city.

Tasks. Key items will include the following:

1. Provide key current economic indicators (use presentation below and see the example in figure 2.6).

Figure 2.6   Key Urban Economic Indicators: Example of Belgrade, Serbia

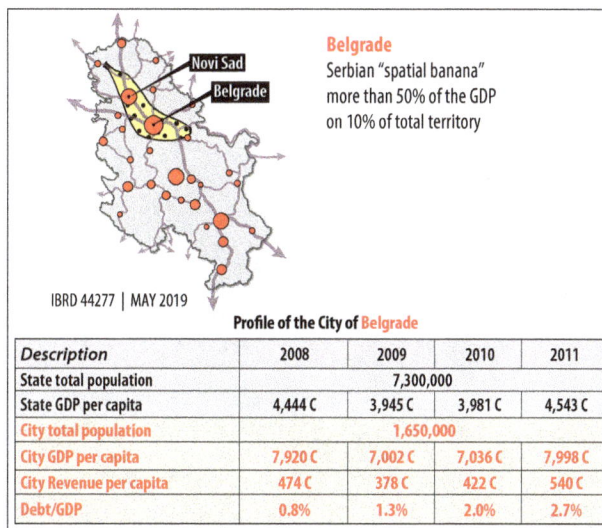

Profile of the City of Belgrade

Description	2008	2009	2010	2011
State total population	7,300,000			
State GDP per capita	4,444 C	3,945 C	3,981 C	4,543 C
City total population	1,650,000			
City GDP per capita	7,920 C	7,002 C	7,036 C	7,998 C
City Revenue per capita	474 C	378 C	422 C	540 C
Debt/GDP	0.8%	1.3%	2.0%	2.7%

This map was created using OSM and local data, reprojected in ArcGIS, and refined in Adobe Illustrator.

Key Urban Economic Indicators

Economy	Year					
GDP per capita (country level)—in U.S. dollars or euros						
City GDP per capita (if available)—in U.S. dollars or euros						
Median disposal annual household income—in U.S. dollars or euros						
Activity rate						
Unemployment rate (% active population)						

2. Describe key economic activities and jobs: Who are the drivers of the economy and the biggest employers? Map them for better visual understanding of location patterns (using the graph below and map 2.3).

Sector of activity	Economic unit	Type of activity	Number of jobs	Location
Industry/ manufacturing				
Commerce/ trade				
Start-up companies				
Agriculture				
Public sector				
Administration				
Self-employment Informal activities				
Other				

3. Describe what is known about the demographic profile (using information from step 2 of the City Profile). What factors will affect the level of employment and the types of jobs that are most needed? One of the key issues in many cities around the world is unemployment among youth. Another important issue will be female-headed households. An important growing trend in

Map 2.3 Drivers of the Local Economy

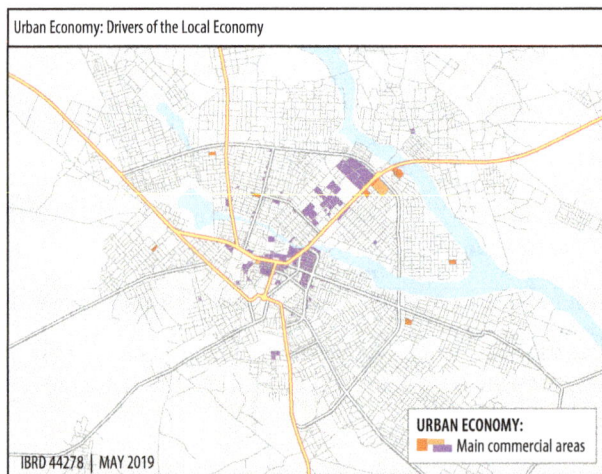

This map was created using OSM and local data, reprojected in ArcGIS, and refined in Adobe Illustrator.

the employment profile of a city is the increase in the number of self-employed people working remotely from home and the impact this has on connectivity issues and mobility. This part of the analysis should reflect the specific characteristics of the city demographics and their implications for the jobs profile of the city.

4. Describe how the city brands itself. Is it known for anything in particular? Is it striving to be known for something in particular? The branding can pertain to a single factor or a combination of factors such as the city's history and cultural heritage, its geographical situation, its cultural scene, its social makeup, its manufacturing or industrial makeup, its universities and places of higher learning, its waterways and waterfront, its food scene, its green spaces or parks, its innovative governance system, its digital systems or smart investments, its social integration schemes, and its progressive transportation systems.

5. Is a major employer present in the city? How many jobs can be attributed to this major employer? Is such a presence shaping the way the city is growing? Is it putting pressure on housing prices and transportation?

6. Outline the structure currently responsible for job creation and economic development in city hall. Is there a dedicated economic development office in the organizational chart of the city? Who are the key champions? What are the key strategic orientations, and what are the key documents supporting the city's vision?

7. Describe the incentives or disincentives to attract companies and create jobs. What are the fiscal incentives, land incentives, services and infrastructure delivery, public transport, and mass transit options?

8. Describe the two or three key economic "deals" that the city has made in the last five years. Describe briefly what mechanisms were put in place to attract the company, how long the negotiations lasted, and how many jobs were created. What fiscal incentives were put in place to close the deal? How are the costs of offsite infrastructure shared?

Step 5: Key Urban Investment Challenges

Objective and content. This section of the UA/SA aims to explain and illustrate the development policy of the municipality and its urbanization challenges in broad terms.

Tasks. Key items will include the following:

- Determine if there is a strategic vision for the development of the city, and outline the supporting documents (strategic plan? city development strategy? long-term development plan? urbanization reviews?). Indicate the date of approval and the status of implementation.

Strategic Vision for the City: Supporting Documents

Document name	Date of approval and timeframe	Key strategic areas	Status of implementation

- Describe briefly the key strategic areas for implementation of the vision, as outlined in the supporting documents.

- If it exists, provide the Capital Improvement Plan (CIP), indicating the list of projects, the time frame for implementation, the costs, and the source of financing.

Capital Improvement Plan

Project name	Time frame	Total costs	Source of financing

Block 2. City Diagnosis and Needs Assessment

Objectives and Methodology

This section of the UA/SA constitutes a crucial milestone of the process. The framework focuses on three key drivers:

1. *Infrastructure and Urban Services Diagnosis and Needs Assessment*: This section is very important because it focuses on the assessment of services and infrastructure at two levels (map 2.4):

   • Infrastructure and services provided at the **city level (sector level)**, with the goal of capturing what is happening at the city level sector by sector.

   • Infrastructure and services provided at the **district or neighborhood level**, with the goal of capturing what is happening within the city and assessing the level and quality of coverage as well as any gaps.

2. *Land Management Diagnosis and Needs Assessment*: This section focuses on two key topics that have a direct impact on urbanization patterns and city shape:

   • Land Development Regulatory Framework Assessment

Map 2.4 Two Levels of City Diagnosis and Needs Assessment

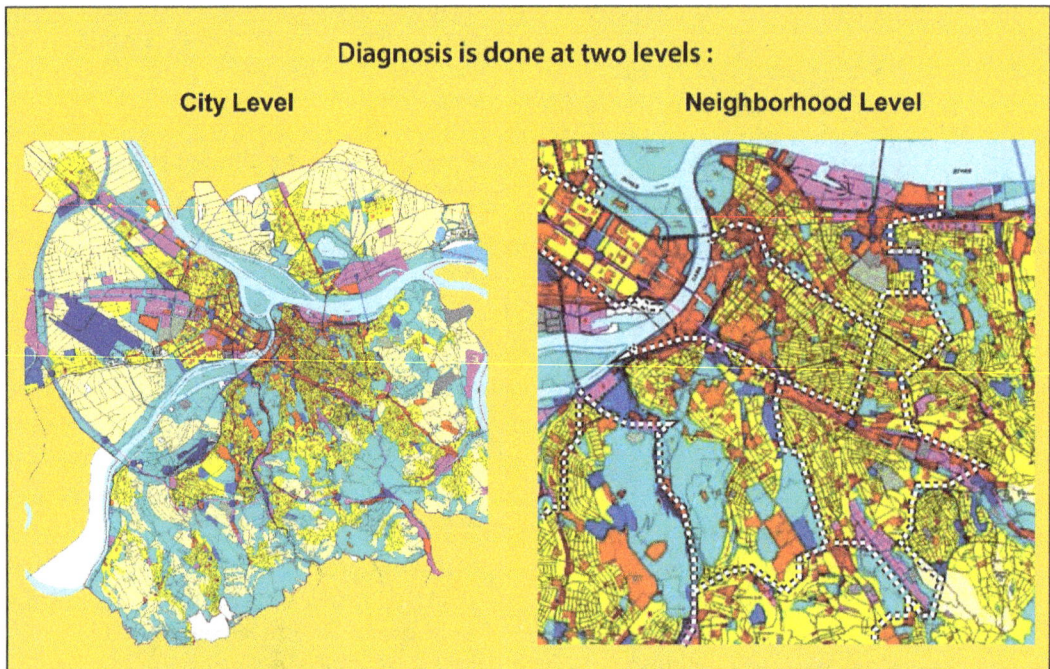

- Land Markets Assessment and Land Assets Management

3. *City Development Projects*: This section provides a snapshot of ongoing or projected citywide programs of significant impact on the economy, population, and finances of the city: (1) urban extensions, (2) inner-city redevelopment, and (3) neighborhood or slum upgrading schemes.

Step 6: Infrastructure and Urban Services Diagnosis and Needs Assessment (City Level)

Objective and content. Although there is a great deal of research on assessing and quantifying global infrastructure needs, very little is actually known at the city level. We know, for example, that an estimated US$93 billion a year is needed to bridge the gap in Africa and that, in the United States alone, US$2 trillion are needed to restore the country's aging infrastructure (ASCE 2017). If we add the pressing need to lower the carbon footprint of global infrastructure, a staggering US$5 trillion is required per year in green investments (box 2.4). These numbers account for an all-encompassing definition of infrastructure that includes energy, bridges, airports, and more. In cities, we know surprisingly little about the gaps and investment needs. This step of the UA/SA is therefore a crucial milestone in the process. It provides an opportunity to do the following:

- Clarify definitions of what urban infrastructure and services are, and which ones fall under the responsibility of the city government;

- Map out and provide a qualitative and quantitative assessment of existing levels of services and infrastructure throughout the city;

Box 2.4
Green Investment Needs for Global Infrastructure

About US$5 trillion in global infrastructure investment is required per year to the year 2030 in various sectors. This investment must be greened to secure future growth.

To support a future global population of 9 billion people, an estimated US$5 trillion per year needs to be invested in global infrastructure (about US$100 trillion over the next two decades). A business-as-usual approach would maintain investment in conventional, emissions-intensive technologies, endangering future growth. A 2012 World Bank report highlighted that the planet is on track for a global average temperature rise of at least 4°C beyond preindustrial levels, which would bring impacts detrimental to growth, includ-ing unprecedented heat waves, severe droughts, and major floods. The McKinsey Global Growth Institute has estimated that rates of environmental degradation are unsustainable for the long-term functioning of the global economy. Existing and future investments, therefore, must be greened to avoid dangerous levels of climate change and adverse environmental impacts that could erode the benefits from new green developments. If nongreen investments continue to grow in parallel with increased investment in green infrastructure, it will not be possible to achieve green growth.

Source: World Economic Forum 2013.

- Map out and clearly identify underserviced neighborhoods and pockets of poverty;

- Outline key priority investment needs to bridge the gap in service delivery; and

- Describe the general situation of each sector and discuss how sectoral entities are performing their tasks. This diagnosis identifies their ability to perform the tasks assigned and their deficiencies. It also suggests solutions to mitigate ongoing challenges.

Tasks. The analysis focuses on the following "bottom line" items that are considered essential deliverables in any municipal government:

Infrastructure:

- Roads and streets (mobility)

- Drainage and sanitation

- Water supply

- Solid waste

- Electricity and public lighting

- Urban heating

- Transport and communications

Services:

- Education

- Health

- Public transportation

- Social and environmental

- Recreation, sports, parks, and public space

1. Provide a general assessment of each sector per the above list. This general assessment will focus on a few key indicators such as service coverage, costs of service, and quality of service providers. The objective is to get a general understanding of the state of affairs and to outline key issues pertaining to scope of coverage and quality of service.

2. Conduct or update an inventory of municipal assets. Asset management is complex and requires both professional and consistent effort. If inventory records do not exist, inventorying capital assets will be the highest priority. Usually, various records exist that can be used as initial sources of data for an inventory. The legal department and the line departments typically have some record of existing capital assets. Often, asset ledgers are also maintained by city accountants. If a street-addressing program has been implemented, it will prove very useful to identify and locate municipal assets. Geographic information systems (GISs) are becoming increasingly affordable for local governments. They help tremendously in the identification of assets as well as provide interactive maps for strategic planning and daily asset management. However, for cities where capacity remains an issue, it is better to start simply: in places where inventory records do not exist, it is wise to start the inventory from a simple Excel spreadsheet that can later be imported into a more advanced database linked to a GIS.

3. Provide a list of municipal assets by sector based on the assets list typically maintained by the line city departments. The first step starts with identifying the key components of the networks and systems to be inventoried. Typical municipal infrastructure will include the following:

- Water systems: distribution lines, transmission lines, water treatment plant, water reservoir, pumping stations, fire hydrants, river, wells

- Wastewater systems: wastewater treatment plant, distribution lines, pumping stations, sludge disposal areas

- Storm drainage systems: canals, ditches, stormwater inlets, flood control reservoirs, erosion protection, dikes

- Solid waste collection: landfill, disposal facilities, collection points

- Streets and roads: roadways, sidewalks, lighting, signage, traffic control devices, bridges, drainage systems.

Additional assets will include municipal land as well as all public municipal facilities such as schools, clinics, administrative offices, community facilities, sports and recreation facilities, parks and gardens, and cemeteries. Many cities own and are responsible for the maintenance of commercial facilities such as markets. Because the city owns and is responsible for a wide range of assets, it is crucial to be able to list them, assess their current state and deficiencies, and value them.

Municipal Assets by Sector: Example of Road Sector Inventory

Description	Property type	Current state	Location/ Address	Size/ right of way	Unit responsible	Date built/ age	Present value
Primary/arterial roads							
Secondary roads							
Asphalt							
Gravel							
Tertiary roads/local							
Asphalt							
Gravel							
Dirt roads							
Total							

Example of a Basic Building Inventory

	Property current function	Address	Cadastre number	Total floor area, sq. m	Land area, sq. m	Year of construc- tion	Building condition	Building book value, thousands, local currency	Current occupancy, %	Notes
1	2	3	4	5	6	7	8	9	10	11
1	Administrative building	Chapichi St, 4	170,477	7,500	2,600	1985	Good	80,670	80	
2	Kindergarten government 1	Sevani St, 2	NA	580	350	1980	Satisfac- tory	3,500	100	
3	Kindergarten government 2	River St, 57	NA	990	690	1964	Bad	NA	33	Repair planned
4	Culture Center	Karmin St, 39	NA	6,500	4,500	1984	Bad	61,732	50	

Note: NA = not available.

4. Reconcile the list of municipal assets with the municipal assets table of the MFSA (table 2.2).

5. Provide maps showing location of existing network for each sector (map 2.5).

6. List recent and ongoing projects in the sector, including projects undertaken by the municipality and projects undertaken by other operators such as utility companies:

- Project proposals in order to reduce or eliminate the gaps or needs (figure 2.7)

- Project outlines, including priorities, category of investment (new construction, rehabilitation), operations and maintenance, preliminary cost estimates, and schedule.

Table 2.2 MFSA Table: Asset Development and Maintenance

Service sectors and functions	Year 1 Develop-ment	Year 1 Mainte-nance	Year 2 Develop-ment	Year 2 Mainte-nance	Year 3 Develop-ment	Year 3 Mainte-nance	Year 4 Develop-ment	Year 4 Mainte-nance	Year 5 Develop-ment	Year 5 Mainte-nance	Growth indexes % develop-ment	Growth indexes % mainte-nance
General administration												
Office buildings												
Other assets (vehicle, equipment)												
Urban services												
Roads and drainage												
Public transport												
Water and wastewater												
Solid waste												
Street lighting												
Fire protection												
Police, crime prevention												
Environmental protection												
Social services												
Health												
Education												
Culture and religion												
Housing												
Recreation and sport												
Social welfare												
Commercial services/ investments												
Parking												
Markets												
Commercial places												
Land development												
Local economic development												
TOTAL EXPENDITURES												

Recent, Ongoing, and Scheduled Projects

	Description	Year	Location	Amount	Financing
Recent					
Ongoing					
Scheduled					

Map 2.5   Examples of Infrastructure and Services Maps

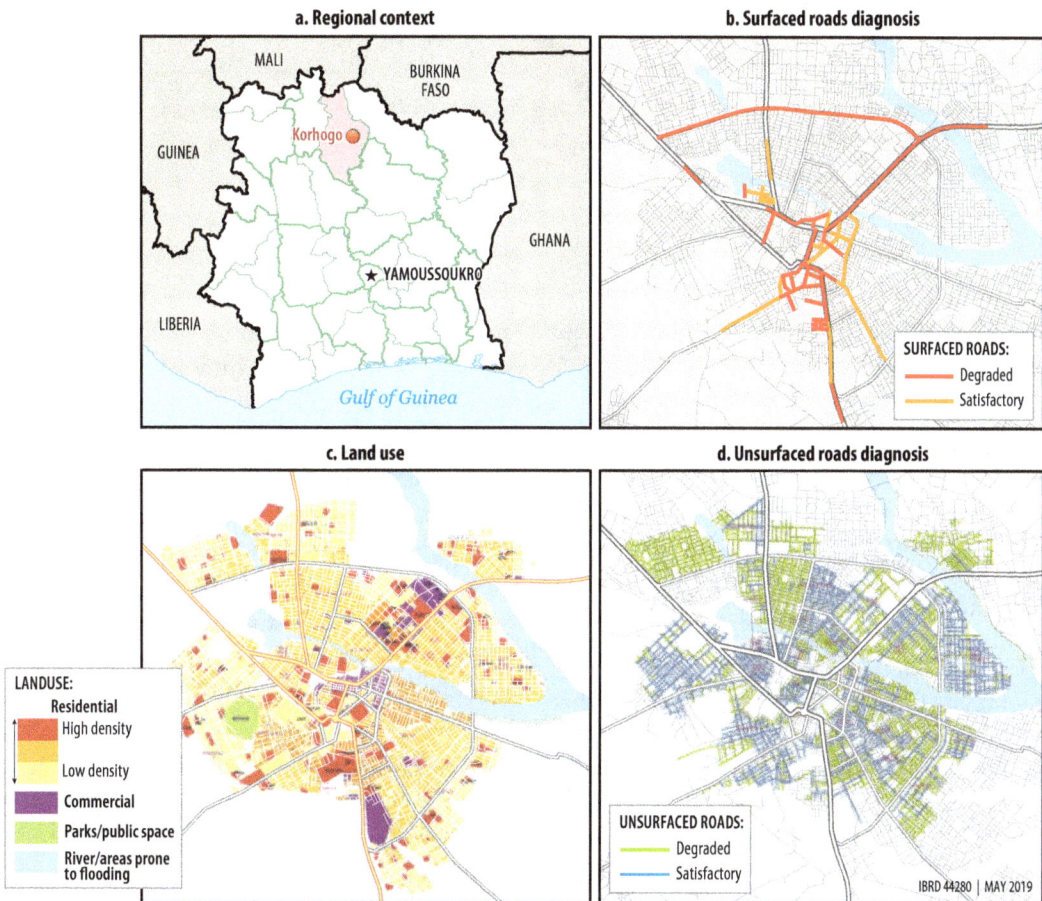

a. Regional context

b. Surfaced roads diagnosis

SURFACED ROADS:
— Degraded
— Satisfactory

c. Land use

LANDUSE:
Residential
High density
Low density
Commercial
Parks/public space
River/areas prone to flooding

d. Unsurfaced roads diagnosis

UNSURFACED ROADS:
— Degraded
— Satisfactory

IBRD 44280 | MAY 2019

These maps were created using OSM and local data, reprojected in ArcGIS, and refined in Adobe Illustrator.

Figure 2.7   **From Diagnosis to Technical Selection**

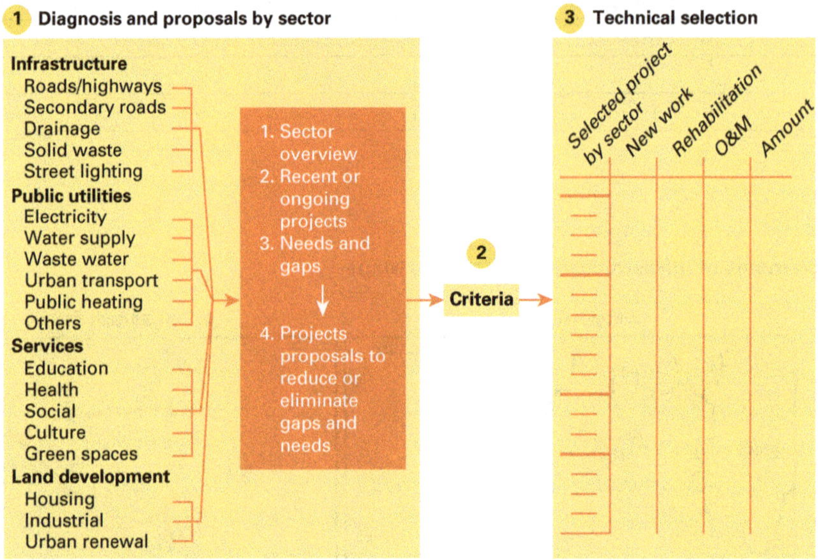

1 Diagnosis and proposals by sector

Infrastructure
Roads/highways
Secondary roads
Drainage
Solid waste
Street lighting
Public utilities
Electricity
Water supply
Waste water
Urban transport
Public heating
Others
Services
Education
Health
Social
Culture
Green spaces
Land development
Housing
Industrial
Urban renewal

1. Sector overview
2. Recent or ongoing projects
3. Needs and gaps
4. Projects proposals to reduce or eliminate gaps and needs

2 Criteria

3 Technical selection

Selected project by sector | New work | Rehabilitation | O&M | Amount

Step 7: Infrastructure and Urban Services Diagnosis and Needs Assessment (Neigborhood Level)

Objective and content. Being able to track and assess the level of services and infrastructure at the neighborhood or district level is very important to understand the spatial diversity within the city. Locating and mapping out pockets of underserviced neighborhoods can help guide political choices and investment programs. With this goal in mind, a template has been developed to do just that. This template is called Inventory for the Programming of Services and Infrastructure (IPSI).[1] IPSI is an aid to decision making. Its purpose is to provide a framework for planning urban projects and to identify priorities. It uses a limited number of inputs to produce indicators and "scores" that convey information about local public services and infrastructure. Thus, it allows neighborhoods to be classified, and priorities to be identified by

neighborhood and type of facility, all in the context of the city as a whole.

Tasks. The document consists of, essentially, three Excel tables (inventory, indicators, and scores) and a set of maps.

1. The **inventory** contains about 50 types of data, for each neighborhood or zone, on population, land occupancy, and services provided by existing infrastructure and facilities. For the most part, these data can be collected from existing sources.

2. The **indicators** (about 30) are calculated and generated automatically. They quantify the characteristics of the neighborhood and the level of public services provided, per inhabitant, by type of existing infrastructure and facilities. To some extent, they also provide some information on the quality of service coverage per neighborhood and for the city as a whole: for example, the number of

public standpipes per 1,000 inhabitants, population densities, and total extent of paved roads.

3. The **scores** are automatically deducted from the indicators, and the results for the neighborhood are compared with numbers for the city as a whole, which will be taken as the average or mean. A neighborhood's score is defined in qualitative terms, as "zero, poor, average, acceptable, or satisfactory," and in quantitative terms, measured on a scale from 0 to 4. These results are weighted by coefficients. The scores indicate the following:

- Zero (rating 0): The neighborhood has no facilities or infrastructure.

- Poor (rating 1): The neighborhood indicator is below the mean.

- Average (rating 2): Services are at the level of the city mean.

- Acceptable (rating 3): The neighborhood indicator falls between the mean and 1.5 times the mean.

- Satisfactory (rating 4): The neighborhood indicator is higher than 1.5 times the mean.

Each scoring line is given a coefficient, for example, 2 for a paved road, or 1.5 for a street with public lighting. Calculating this weight is done by assessing the service or infrastructure's importance to the local population. We have given identical weights to the following sectors: housing, roads, energy (water, electricity), sanitation and environment, and institutional facilities (schools, health centers, and the like).

Maps/cartographic support. The results of the IPSI analysis need to be spatially represented, using maps to locate key findings.

The cartographic documentation is established (at 1:5,000 or 1:10,000 scale) on the basis of recent maps and existing GIS information. The base map is supplemented by various layers of information (the data for which are shown in the inventory table), including the following:

- Site constraints and urbanization trends: (1) major relief features, topographic specificities, direction of water flow, flood-prone areas, no-build zones; and (2) recently settled areas and urban sprawl trends

- Land occupancy: housing, businesses, open spaces (avoid introducing too many types)

- Major facilities and principal neighborhood facilities (for example, markets)

- Roads according to their condition and classification, showing the extent of paved roads, unpaved roads, unimproved roads, and roads with public lighting

- Drainage: main outflow points and runoff channels (with lengths)

- Sanitation and solid waste management: wastewater system, treatment plant, local solid waste transfer points, city landfill

- Potable water supply: water treatment plant, reservoirs, wells, water mains (with lengths), and public standpipes

- Breakdown by neighborhood (data collection by neighborhoods or zones)

- Planned growth corridors

- Priority actions (to be determined by the authorities on the basis of the inventory documents)

A simple tool. IPSI was designed for use by services with modest means at their disposal. This explains why it is presented in the form of simple tables and maps; the number of data items is low but is not intended to be limiting.

The list of data to be collected can be modified and expanded according to the dataset and the level of GISs available. However, it would be better to use the same list across cities so as to make it easier to derive common indicators and make comparisons between cities. The result will be a comprehensive urban database that can be updated and, if possible, enhanced over time.

Implementation. This tool is designed to be implemented by local and central governments. The scheme is not the only one possible, but it is generally appropriate to situations where implementation capacities are satisfactory at the central level but weak at the local level. This may help the sectoral ministry or line ministry to regain a degree of legitimacy that it may have lost over the years, by introducing and updating an effective urban database and helping municipalities develop their own expertise in this area.

Practical aspects. The tool can be used in a rudimentary form at first, and then progressively developed with more sophisticated techniques. The initial stage can be handled with computerized spreadsheets and maps and move toward the use of GISs.

What are the expected outputs of such an exercise? IPSI offers cities the following three benefits:

1. *An urban "snapshot"*: The systematic compilation of data, maps, and indicators will provide an overview that can be used to more clearly assess the problems in a city and its neighborhoods.

2. *Identification of priorities*: Results will allow classification of neighborhoods in terms of their levels of service delivery and will indicate those neighborhoods where upgrading should be given priority. Classification is determined by the total score obtained for each neighborhood. Thus, in the example shown below (figure 2.8), the most poorly serviced neighborhood is District C (with a score of 26), followed by District B (score 36), and finally District A (score 109). The results make it possible to detail the neighborhoods that are most poorly serviced, with respect to each type of infrastructure or facility, and to determine priorities. Thus, District C should have priority for public street lighting, followed by District B.

3. *Ranking of priorities*: Ranking priorities is easy enough with regard to defining target districts: the global score can serve as the reference point. It is more difficult to assign a priority ranking to specific works, particularly if they fall under different headings—roads, energy, sanitation, facilities—since it is hard to arrange these headings in order of importance. However, the first cut will normally be made by comparing the cost of each type of work against the available funding envelope—projects that seem too costly will simply be left for further consideration. The ultimate selection will have to be left to the central or local authorities (and perhaps to arbitration by the funding partner).

Illustrations. The sequence of tables is shown in tables 2.3, 2.4, and 2.5. Table 2.3 provides an example of an inventory template, showing a proposed classification which can be adjusted according to each city's specific situation. Table 2.4 provides a sample template of key indicators, which, again, can be adjusted to specific needs and circumstances. They focus on level of coverage and quality of service. Table 2.5 proposes a sample template for establishing scores for each neighborhood focusing on quantitative and qualitative results. Starting from the inventory table, the indicator and score

Figure 2.8   IPSI Method: From Inventory to Scoring—A Road Map

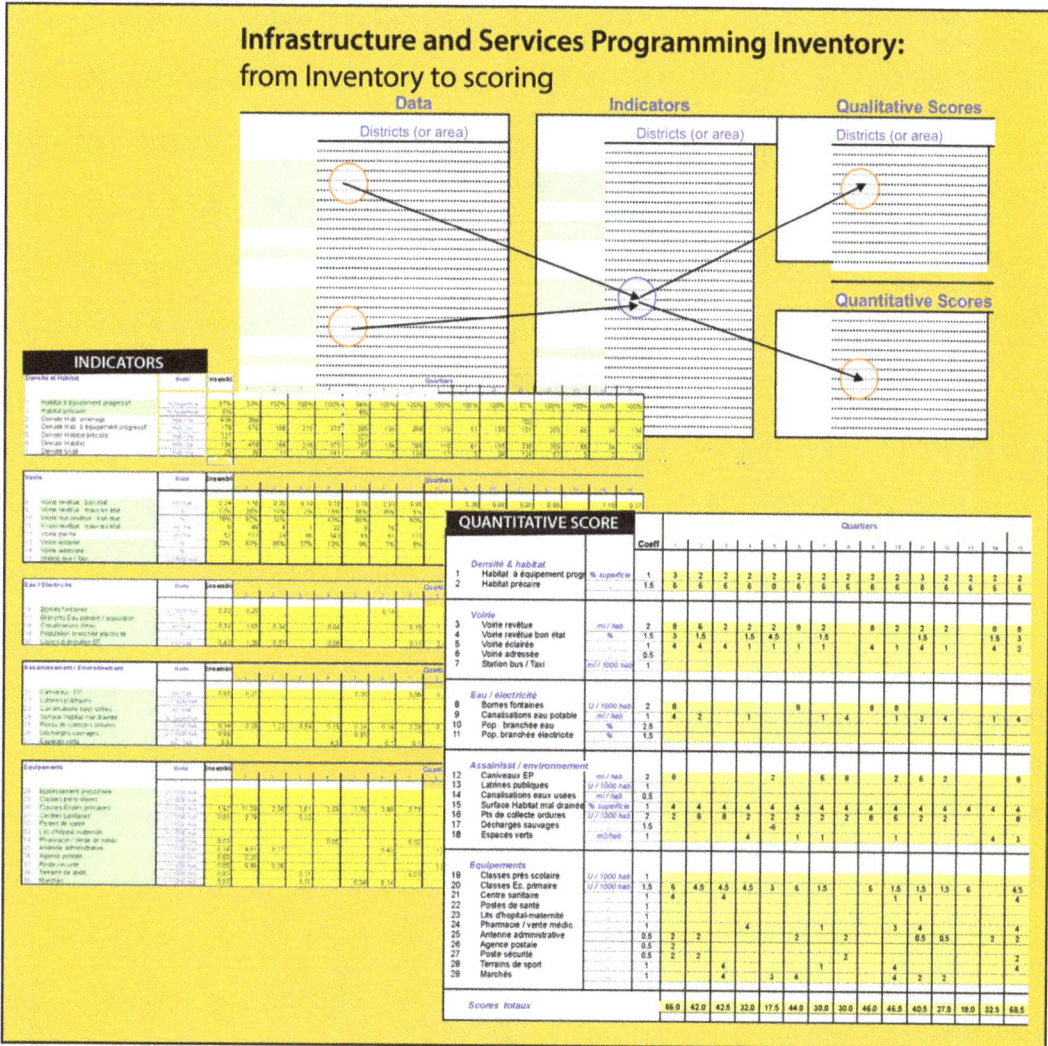

Infrastructure and Services Programming Inventory: from Inventory to scoring

tables can be deduced. The tasks will include the following:

- Comment on the qualitative scores and ranking of districts. Identify underserviced neighborhoods by type of public service.

- Comment on the quantitative scores. Identify deficiencies and gaps by sector.

- Synthesize deficiencies at the level of the whole city and at the district/neighborhood level.

Table 2.3 Inventory for the Programming of Services and Infrastructure (IPSI): Inventory

1. Inventory	Unit of measure	Total	Neighborhoods				
			1	2	3	4	5
Population							
1 Pop. serviced housing	Number of inhabitants						
2 Pop. underserviced housing	Number of inhabitants						
3 Pop. irregular housing	Number of inhabitants						
4 Total population	Number of inhabitants						
5 Residents per household							
Land occupancy							
Housing							
6 Area with serviced housing	Square meters						
7 Area with underserviced housing	Square meters						
8 Area irregular housing	Square meters						
Total area housing	Square meters						
Other							
9 Large infrastructure	Square meters						
10 Economic activities	Square meters						
11 Green space	Square meters						
12 Roads, open areas	Square meters						
Total	Square meters						
Access to infrastructure							
Streets/Urban roads							
13 Paved street (good condition)	Meters						
14 Paved street (poor condition)	Meters						
15 Unpaved street (good condition)	Meters						
16 Unpaved street (poor condition)	Meters						
17 Unimproved street (track)	Meters						
Total streets	Meters						
18 Street with lighting	Meters						
19 Street with an address	Meters						
20 Bus station	Number						
Water/Electricity							
21 Standpipes	Number						
22 Water main	Number						
23 Water connections	Number						
24 Water pipes	Meters						
25 Water reservoir	Cubic meters						
26 Water treatment station	Number						
27 Electricity connections	Number						
28 Electric power station	Number						
29 Low-tension distribution lines	Meters						

continued next page

Table 2.3   Continued

1. Inventory	Unit of measure	Total	Neighborhoods				
			1	2	3	4	5
Sanitation/Environment							
30 Rainwater main outflow	Meters						
31 Rainwater drains	Meters						
32 Public latrines (working)	Number						
33 Public latrines (not working)	Number						
34 Wastewater sewage	Meters						
35 Area not connected to networks	Hectares						
36 Solid waste collection points	Number						
37 Solid waste transfer zones	Number						
38 Informal dumpsites	Number						
39 Authorized landfill	Number						
40 Waste treatment center	Number						
Access to facilities and superstructure							
Education							
41 Preschool facilities	Number						
42 Preschool classrooms	Number						
43 Primary schools	Number						
44 Primary school classrooms	Number						
45 Middle schools and high schools	Number						
Health							
46 Health centers/clinics	Number						
47 Hospital beds	Number						
48 Maternity beds	Number						
49 Health center (good)	Number						
50 Health center (not adequate)	Number						
51 Pharmacies (good)	Number						
52 Pharmacies (not adequate)	Number						
Revenue-earning facilities							
53 Central market	Number						
54 Neighborhood market (good)	Number						
55 Neighborhood market (not adequate)	Number						
56 Bus stations	Number						
57 Commercial centers	Number						
58 Tourism facilities	Number						
59 Slaughterhouse	Number						
Sport/Youth							
60 Stadium/Soccer field	Number						
61 Recreational facility	Number						
62 Sport center	Number						

continued next page

Table 2.3   Continued

1. Inventory	Unit of measure	Neighborhoods					
		Total	1	2	3	4	5
63 Swimming pool/Aquatic center	Number						
Culture/Recreation							
64 Community center	Number						
65 Library/Other	Number						
Administration							
66 Administrative offices	Number						
67 Post office	Number						
68 Police station	Number						

Table 2.4   **Inventory for the Programming of Services and Infrastructure (IPSI): Indicators**

2. Indicators	Unit	Neighborhoods					
		Average total	1	2	3	4	5
Density and housing							
1 Underserviced housing	% area						
2 Irregular housing	% area						
3 Density serviced housing	Inhabitants/hectare						
4 Density underserviced housing	Inhabitants/hectare						
5 Density irregular housing	Inhabitants/hectare						
6 Density housing	Inhabitants/hectare						
7 Density (gross)	Inhabitants/hectare						
Streets and roads							
8 Paved street per inhabitant	Meters/inhabitant						
9 Unpaved street	%						
10 Paved street (good condition)	%						
11 Paved street per hectare	Meters						
12 Total streets per hectare	Meters						
13 Street with lighting	%						
14 Street with address	%						
15 Bus station	Unit/1,000 inhabitants						
Water/Electricity							
16 Standpipes	Unit/1000 inhabitants						
17 Population with water connection	%						
18 Water lines	Meters/inhabitant						
19 Population with electricity connection	%						
20 Low-tension distribution lines	Meters/inhabitant						

continued next page

Table 2.4 **Continued**

2. Indicators	Unit	Average total	Neighborhoods				
			1	2	3	4	5
Sanitation/Environment							
21 Storm drainage	Meters/inhabitant						
22 Public latrines	Unit/1,000 inhabitants						
23 Wastewater sewage	Meters/inhabitant						
24 Area housing poor sanitation	% area						
25 Solid waste collection points	Unit/1,000 inhabitants						
26 Unauthorized dumpsites	Unit/1,000 inhabitants						
27 Green space	Square meters/inhabitant						
Facilities							
28 Preschools	Unit/1,000 inhabitants						
29 Preschool classrooms	Unit/1,000 inhabitants						
30 Primary schools	Unit/1,000 inhabitants						
31 Primary school classrooms	Unit/1,000 inhabitants						
32 Health clinics	Unit/1,000 inhabitants						
33 Hospital/Maternity beds	Unit/1,000 inhabitants						
34 Pharmacies	Unit/1,000 inhabitants						
35 Administrative offices	Unit/1,000 inhabitants						
36 Post office	Unit/1,000 inhabitants						
37 Police station	Unit/1,000 inhabitants						
38 Sport facilities	Unit/1,000 inhabitants						
39 Markets	Unit/1,000 inhabitants						

Table 2.5 Inventory for the Programming of Services and Infrastructure (IPSI): Scores

3. Scores	Unit		Neighborhood				
			1	2	3	4	5
Density and housing							
1 Underserviced housing	% area	1.0					
2 Irregular housing	% area	1.5					
Streets							
3 Paved street	Meters/inhabitant	2.0					
4 Paved street (good condition)	%	1.5					
5 Street with lighting	%	1.0					
6 Street with addresses	%	0.5					
7 Bus station	Unit/1,000 inhabitants	1.0					
Water/Electricity							

continued next page

Table 2.5 **Continued**

3. Scores	Unit	Neighborhood					
			1	2	3	4	5
8 Standpipes	Unit/1,000 inhabitants	2.0					
9 Water mains	Meters/inhabitant	1.0					
10 Pop. with water connections	%	2.5					
11 Pop. with electric connections	%	1.5					
Sanitation/Environment							
12 Storm sewage	Meters/inhabitant	2.0					
13 Public latrines	Unit/1,000 inhabitants	1.0					
14 Wastewater sewage	Meters/inhabitant	0.5					
15 Area not serviced by sewage	% area	1.0					
16 Solid waste collection points	Unit/1,000 inhabitants	2.0					
17 Unauthorized dumpsites	Unit/1,000 inhabitants	1.5					
18 Green space	Square meters/ inhabitant	1.0					
Facilities							
19 Primary schools	Unit/1,000 inhabitants	1.5					
20 Secondary schools	Unit/1,000 inhabitants	1.0					
21 Health clinics	Unit/1,000 inhabitants	1.0					
22 Hospital beds	Unit/1,000 inhabitants	1.0					
23 Pharmacies	Unit/1,000 inhabitants	1.0					
24 Administrative office	Unit/1,000 inhabitants	0.5					
25 Post office	Unit/1,000 inhabitants	0.5					
26 Police station	Unit/1,000 inhabitants	0.5					
27 Sports facilities	Unit/1,000 inhabitants	1.0					
28 Markets	Unit/1,000 inhabitants	1.0					
Total Scores							

Note: This table presents both qualitative and quantitative results.

- Propose projects and programs in order to reduce or eliminate the gaps.

Objective of scoring. The objective is to determine for each type of infrastructure or service the location of underserviced neighborhoods and to outline priorities (see below and figure 2.9). Using the data from the indicators table (see table 2.4), scores are calculated. These scores can facilitate the comparison between neighborhoods and the average at the city level. The score of the neighborhood is defined qualitatively and quantitatively and is given a grade (0 to 4).

Figure 2.9   Urban Audit/Self-Assessment: Urban Services, Using IPSI as Database

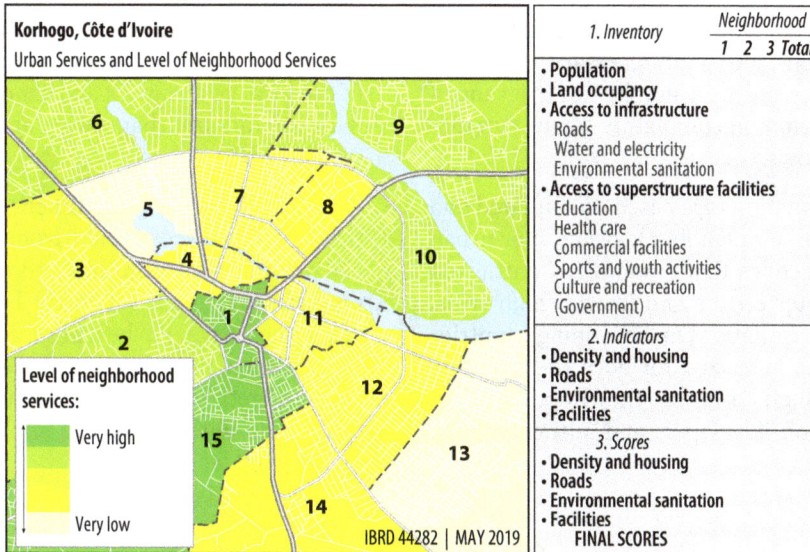

This map was created using OSM and local data, reprojected in ArcGIS, and refined in Adobe Illustrator.

Note: IPSI = Inventory for the Programming of Services and Infrastructure.

List (Non-Exhaustive) of Project Proposals to Reduce or Eliminate Deficiencies

Type	Location/ Address	Priority	New construction	Rehabilitation	Operations and maintenance	Costs
Infrastructure						
• Roads						
• Drainage						
• Sewage						
Amenities						
• Education						
• Health						
• Social						

Step 8: Land Regulatory Framework Diagnosis and Needs Assessment

Objective and content. The key goals of this section of the UA/SA are (1) to produce an objective and accurate diagnosis of key land-related issues and present them in a unified format; (2) to compare performance among cities quantitatively and qualitatively; and (3) to establish common ground for actions to be taken at the national, regional, and local levels. This section of the UA/SA focuses on two key pillars that have a direct, powerful, and lasting impact on future growth, trends, and investments on the city. These are (1) existing urban planning documentation and

(2) key regulations pertaining to zoning/land use, building construction, and permits affecting the development of the city (box 2.5).

Regulations, although necessary and much needed, have led to a number of grievances. The most common complaints can be summarized as follows:

- Most regulations are based on outdated and inappropriate planning legislation or urban planning codes that emphasize centralized public interference and impose high costs. Existing regulations in developing countries have been criticized for both their rigidity and the high costs that they impose on the builder, or developer, and ultimately the purchaser.

- Traditional planning documents such as master plans take too long to prepare and are difficult to enforce. They are often disconnected from the financing capabilities of the local government and cannot keep up with the rate of urbanization and the pressure on land.

- The urban/city planning function has been traditionally disconnected from the financial planning function, and traditional planning has too often set forth development goals that have no bearing on their cost implications. But the reverse is also true in that budgetary exercises frequently have little to do with the spatial implications of investment decisions.

Box 2.5
Land Use Regulatory Framework: Some Definitions

The most common forms of land use regulation and control are (1) zoning, (2) subdivision regulations, (3) building regulations, and (4) urban planning. They regulate such things as the shape, volume, density, and placement of buildings; height limitations; setback requirements; and requirements for open space, amenities, and utilities.

- **Zoning** is the demarcation of a city by ordinances and the establishment of zones in which certain activities are prohibited and others are allowed and covers use, location, plot ratio, and height. Zoning is an eminently political process that may be the most important municipal function in many cities.
- **Subdivision regulations** govern the development of raw land for residential or other purposes and prescribe standards for lot sizes, layout, street improvements, and procedures for dedicating private land for public purposes. The importance lies in the fact that these regulations enable the community to force the developers to pay for some of the infrastructure related to the project.
- **Building regulations** limit or define the way new structures are to be built and the materials to be used. Building regulations are among the oldest and most common methods for controlling land development.
- **Urban/City planning** is the process by which decisions are made regarding the global configuration of a city and its projections for expansion. The plan is the reference framework that is used for the application and the use of the regulatory instruments mentioned above.

Source: Farvacque-Vitkovic and McAuslan 1992.

- In many cities around the world, getting a building permit or any kind of development permit can be a challenge. Studies have been done and papers have been written on the whole issue of lengthy procedural nightmares involving many segments of the public administration and numerous steps to get a building permit approved.

- Cumbersome procedures have led, in some cases, to the rise of informal land use activities and the erosion of the rule of law.

In Malaysia, for example, a 1992 World Bank study already showed that approval procedures were time-consuming and fraught with uncertainties. Some 18 to 20 departments participated in the approval cycle of urban plans, and the final approval could take between one and seven years, depending on the particular state or local authority. The Kuala Lumpur Structure Plan of the 1980s is a case in point. Plan preparation began in 1978, the plan was released to the public in September 1982, and it was finally gazetted in June 1984, almost six years later. The unofficial estimated cost was US$3 million. The administrative process of receiving, reviewing, and deciding on applications for conversion or subdivision could take between two and seven years. Building permits were generally approved faster and were more readily understood; however, some 16 to 20 departments were involved in the process. In the case of Malaysia, improvements have been made. The 2017 Doing Business ranking showed Malaysia in 24th position for overall ranking and in number 11 out of 190 in ease of getting a building permit (see map 2.6 and box 2.6 for more information on the Doing Business Index).

So, what does it mean? Things are changing in some parts of the world. City planning is no longer the realm of stodgy planners left in the dusty corner of city hall. City planners have become in many places very vocal voices for change. In many ways, the urbanization trends and unprecedented urban growth of the last 20 years have created a state of urgency for renewal, an impetus for change. In addition, the incredible leap in technology has also enabled cities to have access to and appetite for spatial data and to start developing, with many shades of success, GISs. New thinking has also occurred on the function of city planning. No longer seen as a reactive function, city planning is perceived at the front and center of city management. New planning techniques aim to (1) provide proactive guidance and orientations for future urbanization; (2) take into account new technologies and smart ideas to address environmental concerns; (3) embrace social inclusion challenges; (4) foster and support city "branding"; (5) listen to the various stakeholders, including citizens; and (6) play a new role of "broker" between public and private interests. In addition, the growing number of climate change–related events has shown that regulations are much needed to prevent human occupation of disaster-prone areas and that city planning has a major role to play in preventing floods, landslides, and other natural disasters.

Tasks. Key tasks for this section include the following.

1. Conduct an urban/city planning assessment:

   - List major existing planning documents, from general urban master plan and land use plan to layouts developed for specific land development areas, by name, date of approval, scope (section 1.a and section 1.b in table 2.6).

   - Assess the process from preparation to approval as well as costs (section 1.c in table 2.6).

Map 2.6   Subnational Doing Business around the World

83 locations in OECD
high-income economies

84 locations
in Europe and Central Asia

30 locations
in the Middle East
and North Africa

46 locations
in South Asia

76 locations
in East Asia
and the Pacific

82 locations
in Sub-Saharan Africa

109 locations
in Latin America
and the Caribbean

Economies with one subnational or regional study
Economies with more than one subnational or regional study

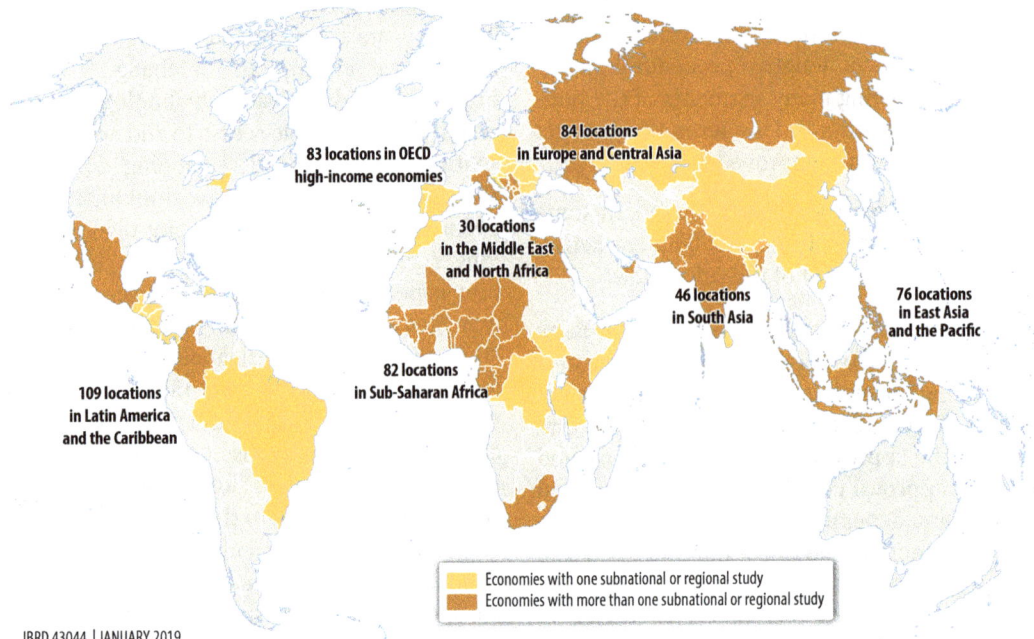

IBRD 43044 | JANUARY 2019

Box 2.6
The World Bank's Ease of Doing Business Index

The Ease of Doing Business Index developed by the World Bank includes "dealing with construction permits" as one of the 10 indicators highlighted as having an impact on business development. Economies are ranked on their ease of doing business on a scale between 1 and 190. A high Ease of Doing Business ranking means that the regulatory environment is more conducive to the startup and operation of a local firm. The Index is updated for 190 countries and economies, and 438 subnational entities (cities) have been benchmarked in 65 economies since 2005.

- Assess the process of consultation with all stakeholders and citizens.

- Highlight the key orientations of the master plan; outline proposed investments and main recommendations (insert map).

2. Assess the existing land use regulations and building standards (table 2.7).

3. Assess the potential correlation between city planning and investment programming (table 2.8).

4. Assess to what extent existing planning and land use regulations affect the illegal occupation of land (table 2.9).

5. Map out existing land use in the city (map 2.7 and map 2.8).

Table 2.6 Urban/City Planning Assessment: City Planning Process

City_____
Population: City_____ Municipality _____
Land area: City_____ Municipality _____
Date _____
Section 1. City Planning Process
Section 1.a Legal framework

Type and level of plan (provide *name of plan*)	Duration of validity of plan
National …	
Regional …	
Citywide general …	
Subcity detailed …	
Others …	

Section 1.b Preparation and approval process

Name of plan	Which level of government is responsible for preparation of plan (Name department)?		Which level of government is responsible for approval of plan?		Notes and comment
	Central/regional	Local	Central/regional	Local	
National …					
Regional …					
Citywide general …					
Subcity detailed …					
Other					

continued next page

Table 2.6 Continued

Section 1.c Factual progress, number of plans, and coverage

Name of plan	How many plans of this type have been done in your city?	Start and end year of the plans	Part of the territory covered by the plan (% or hectares)	Approval date	Who actually did the preparation work? (municipal department, consultants, or central government)
National …					
Regional …					
Citywide general …					
Subcity detailed …					
Other					

Section 1.d Implementation progress, actors, costs

	Cost of plan preparation	Sources of funding for implementation (municipal budget, central government, private developers, donors)	Limiting factors for completing/ updating the plans, if any		Notes/ remarks, including issues related to transfer of land ownership
National …					
Regional …					
Citywide general …					
Subcity detailed …					
Other					

Section 1.e Public participation in city planning

- Does the law describe the process of public participation in planning? _____ Yes or No _____
- At what time or at what stage in the procedure is the plan published or made available for public review?
  _____
- Method of public notice and publication?
  _____
- Procedure and time period for review and comment?
  _____
- Requirement for public hearing, public meeting, or seminar?
  _____
- How is the response given to the public comments?
  _____
- Does your city provide more opportunities for public participation in addition to those required by law?
  _____ Yes or No _____

Table 2.7 Land Use Regulations and Building Standards

Section 2. Construction standards and land use parameters						
Permitted land use or site characteristics	City center			Peri-urban area		
	Residential	Commercial	Industrial	Residential	Commercial	Industrial
1. Permitted land uses						
Indicator on land uses						
2. Parceling Minimum plot size Minimum width of street/ road front						
3. Construction require- **ments**						
a. Maximum floor-to-area ratio (total floor area divided by plot area)						
b. Land coverage (area of a building footprint divided by the plot area), %						
c. Number of floors						
d. Maximum height						
e. Type of buildings						
f. Horizontal regulation						
Min. distance from building to plot front (street) boundary (i.e., between construction line and regulatory line)						
Min. distance from building to side boundaries of plot						
Min. distance from building to back boundary of plot						
Min. distance from other buildings						
Min. distance between two buildings on plot						
4. Beautification of open **space on plot** Min. mandatory green area, %						
Indicator on land use *parameters: the total* *number of requirements in* *categories 2–4*						
Other requirements Underground space – permit- ted or not Rainwater drainage						

Table 2.8 Potential Correlation between City Planning and Investment Programming

Section 3. Does a link exist between land development planning and estimating the cost of public infrastructure needed for the planned development? and Does the link exist between the planning process and the decision-making process on key investments in the city?

Title and level of each required plan (those listed in section 1.a)	Are cost estimates for land acquisition, engineering studies, and onsite and offsite infrastructure calculated and included?	Notes
1	Yes / No	
2	Yes / No	
3	Yes / No	

Instruction: Provide answer for each plan listed in Column 1

To what extent is the planning process influencing the decision-making process on key infrastructure and services investments in the city?

- **Greatly**
- **Moderately**
- **Not at all**

Table 2.9 Effect of Existing Planning and Land Use Regulations on the Illegal Occupation of Land

Section 4. Selected indicators on informal and illegal construction

Does informal/illegal construction exist on the territory of your city/municipality?

Types of informal/illegal construction present in your city/municipality	Present?	How significant is this type in your city/municipality?	What kind of construction is present in this type?	Notes
1. **Construction on land owned by occupants, and in areas zoned for construction; the construction conforms to official land use and building requirements; but occupants do not have proper documents and / or did not pay required charges (*e.g., land development fee*)**	Yes / No	• Common or dominating case • Sometimes • Rare	• Individual houses • Multiunit apartment buildings • Commercial or industrial property • Public (government) buildings • Public infrastructure (roads, pipelines, power lines, etc.)	

continued next page

Table 2.9 Continued

Section 4. Selected Indicators on informal and illegal construction				
Does informal/illegal construction exist on the territory of your city/municipality?				
Types of informal/illegal construction present in your city/municipality	Present?	How significant is this type in your city/municipality?	What kind of construction is present in this type?	Notes
2. Construction on land owned by occupants, and in areas zoned for construction; but construction does not conform to official land use and building requirements and deviates from documentation if such exists		• Common or dominating case • Sometimes • Rare	• Individual houses • Multiunit apartment buildings • Commercial or industrial property • Public (government) buildings • Public infrastructure (roads, pipelines, power lines, etc.)	
3. Construction on land owned by occupants, but on territory not zoned for construction		• Common or dominating case • Sometimes • Rare	• Individual houses • Multiunit apartment buildings • Commercial or industrial property • Public (government) buildings • Public infrastructure (roads, pipelines, power lines, etc.)	
4. Construction on public or private land, zoned for construction, but occupied/built by squatters/illegal tenants		• Common or dominating case • Sometimes • Rare	• Individual houses • Multiunit apartment buildings • Commercial or industrial property • Public (government) buildings • Public infrastructure (roads, pipelines, power lines, etc.)	
5. Construction on public or private land, not zoned for construction and occupied/built by squatters		• Common or dominating case • Sometimes • Rare	• Individual houses • Multiunit apartment buildings • Commercial or industrial property • Public (government) buildings • Public infrastructure (roads, pipelines, power lines, etc.)	

continued next page

Table 2.9 **Continued**

Section 4. Selected Indicators on informal and illegal construction

Does informal/illegal construction exist on the territory of your city/municipality?

Types of informal/illegal construction present in your city/municipality	Present?	How significant is this type in your city/municipality?	What kind of construction is present in this type?	Notes
6. **Roma settlements** (slum or low-quality durable housing)		• Common or dominating case • Sometimes • Rare		
7. **Other (specify)**		• Common case • Sometimes • Rare		

If the previous answer is "yes," please classify according to the typology in the table below.

What is the estimated share of the area under the informal/illegal construction and settlements in the total urban territory of the city?_____%

What is the estimated share of illegally built housing units in overall housing stock on the city/municipal territory? _____%

If informal/illegal construction is still effective, what is the estimated share of informal housing construction in the total housing production in year 11? _____

If the informal construction has stopped, what was the reason?_____
_____

Existence of national and local regulations related to legalization (Yes / No):

   a. Within the general planning regulations_____

   b. As a special legalization legislation_____

What is the relation between the fees paid under the regular development procedure and the fees to be paid in the legalization process:

   Are the costs the same? Yes/No

   Is the legalization cheaper or more expensive than the regular development? (provide a commentary, including special incentives, discounts for lower-income households, etc.)

Is eminent domain used appropriately?_____

Map 2.7   Urban Audit/Self-Assessment: Land Use Map

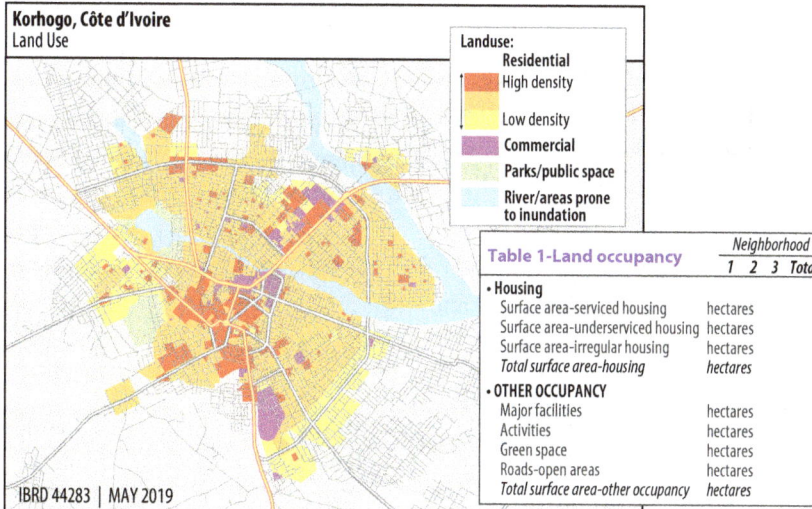

Korhogo, Côte d'Ivoire
Land Use

Landuse:
Residential
High density
Low density
Commercial
Parks/public space
River/areas prone to inundation

Table 1-Land occupancy	Neighborhood			
	1	2	3	Total
• Housing				
Surface area-serviced housing				hectares
Surface area-underserviced housing				hectares
Surface area-irregular housing				hectares
Total surface area-housing				*hectares*
• OTHER OCCUPANCY				
Major facilities				hectares
Activities				hectares
Green space				hectares
Roads-open areas				hectares
Total surface area-other occupancy				*hectares*

IBRD 44283 | MAY 2019

This map was created using OSM and local data, reprojected in ArcGIS, and refined in Adobe Illustrator.

Map 2.8   Land Use Map: Sample from the Municipality of Gazi Baba, North Macedonia

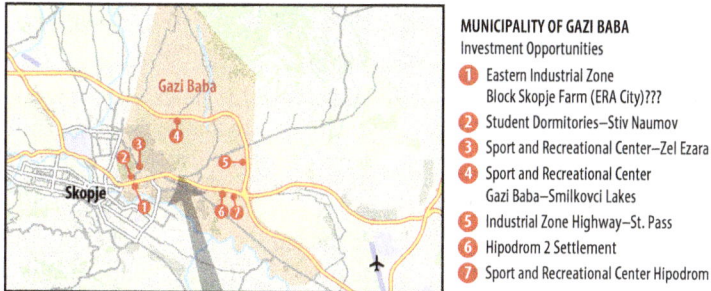

MUNICIPALITY OF GAZI BABA
Investment Opportunities

1 Eastern Industrial Zone
  Block Skopje Farm (ERA City)???
2 Student Dormitories–Stiv Naumov
3 Sport and Recreational Center–Zel Ezara
4 Sport and Recreational Center
  Gazi Baba–Smilkovci Lakes
5 Industrial Zone Highway–St. Pass
6 Hipodrom 2 Settlement
7 Sport and Recreational Center Hipodrom

AGRICULTURAL LAND	LAND RE-ZONED AND PLANNED FOR DEVELOPMENT	LAND WITH OFF-SITE INFRASTRUCTURE	BUILT-UP PROPERTY (BUILDINGS AND LAND)
3 Euro/m³	25 Euro/m³	325 Euro/m³	1250 Euro/m³
Who?	Government and municipalities	Those who build infrastructure	Developer
Who?	Government and municipalities	Those who build infrastructure	Developer
Who?	Government and municipalities/ or developer	Tax payers, tariff payers, and/or developers	Developer and their buyers
Who?	Those who can build here, legally	Future buyers/users of real estate	Developer, their buyers, and users of property and space

These maps were created using OSM and local data, reprojected in ArcGIS, and refined in Adobe Illustrator.

Step 9: Land Markets Assessment and Land Assets Management

This step focuses on two crucial components of the land management agenda. These tasks are hugely important for any city. Some cities may have all the systems in place and up-to-date data readily available. Others might be in the process of compiling such information in their existing GIS systems. Some may not be there yet and may require more time and support to monitor land prices in their jurisdiction and inventory and value their assets. Whatever the situation might be, what follows are commonly accepted guiding principles on best practices for data collection and analysis.

Land Markets Assessment

Objectives and Methodology. The land markets assessment aims to provide data on land prices, the supply of serviced land, and current and projected land projects (Dowall 1995). It provides foundational knowledge for defining appropriate strategies to improve land market performance and to support governmental planning and decision making, evaluation of government policies and actions, private sector investment and development decisions, structuring of land-based taxation systems, and shaping of various land-based infrastructure financing tools. One of its primary objectives is to answer the following questions (tables 2.10 and 2.11):

- Is the supply of urban serviced land expanding to meet growing population and employment needs?

- Which land uses are growing the fastest?

- Where is urban land conversion taking place?

- Where is urban land conversion outstripping the supply of serviced land?

- Are land prices increasing faster than the overall rate of inflation?

- Where are land prices the highest, and where are land prices increasing the fastest?

- How much land is being provided with the minimum services needed for future urban development?

- Is there enough urban land to accommodate urban growth for the next five years?

- Are the price and affordability of housing and commercial and industrial space changing?

- Which segments of the population do not have access to housing from the formal private sector?

- What is the impact of large infrastructure investments, such as public transit systems, on land values?

- How can land value be captured for infrastructure financing?

- What can the geography of land values tell us about the patterns of urbanization and development both for the city center and peri-urban areas?

- Is the current land market pricing out some segments of the population?

- Is the current land market changing the face of the city, and in what ways?

- Is land being used wisely, keeping in mind the overall objectives of a livable city, a socially inclusive city, and a green city?

A full-fledged land market assessment requires time, resources, and a multiskilled team. Typically, LMA data are collected from primary and secondary sources such as census data, land price surveys, household surveys, and interviews with developers and real estate agents, as well as GIS data. Doing household

Table 2.10 Basic Land-Use and Population Data

For each geographic zone, data on land use and population attributes should be collected for at least two points in time — a base year and the current year. Ideally, the two years should span a period of 5 to 10 years

	Base year	Current year
1. Zone identification number		
2. Size of zone, in hectares		
3. Total urbanized land, in hectares		
4. Total residential land area		
5. Total housing units		
6. Commercial land area		
7. Industrial land area		
8. Institutional land area		
9. Vacant land area		
10. Vacant land area with infrastructure		
11. Change in urbanized land, in hectares		
12. Change in residential land area		
13. Change in total housing units		
14. Change in commercial land area		
15. Change in industrial land area		
16. Change in institutional land area		
17. Change in vacant land area		
18. Change in vacant land area with infrastructure		
19. Population in base year		
20. Change in population		
21. Population density		
22. Change in population density		

Table 2.11 Land Values

Land values (based on appraisals) can be tabulated by type of land. All land values should be expressed in constant prices.

	Base year value (per square meter)	Current year value (per square meter)	Median
1. Serviced residential plots in city center			
2. Office space in city center			
3. Commercial plots in city center			
4. Land near mass transit systems			
5. Industrial plots			
6. Vacant plots in city center			
7. Serviced plots in peri-urban areas			
8. Unserviced plots in peri-urban areas			

surveys or any type of surveys is beyond the scope of the Urban Audit/SA; however, a great deal of data is available from various sources, and UA/SA users just need to know where to look. Property transactions records, local property valuation rolls, street addressing databases, and interviews with real estate professionals are all useful entry points to get access to valuable data that can be collected and mapped with less cost and effort than full-fledged surveys. There are some key guiding principles (An Introduction to Land Market Assessment in Complex Urban Settings OLC e-course) that will help outline a roadmap for action.

Tasks:

1. Define up front the "study zone" or location in order to get a balanced and representative sample.
2. Adhere to commonly accepted indicators, which are as follows:

- Population density per hectare

- Changes in population density at 5 to 10 years

- Land value or mean price of land based on the distance from the city center and in different zones of the study area

- Average annual increase in urbanized land (or land converted to urban use)

- Area of vacant land inside the built-up area

- Correlation between income and supply

3. Compute key indices:

- Land affordability: This indicator measures land price per square meter over annual household income. It assesses the extent to which some segments of the population might be affected by land values and priced out of the market. It will provide markers for the supply side of the housing stock as well as for the types of services and infrastructure needed.

- Land Developer Multiplier: This indicator measures the median price of serviced land per square meter over underserviced but subdivided urban land per square meter.

- Land conversion multiplier: This indicator measures the median price of unserviced land in urban areas per square meter over median price of land in rural areas per square meter.

- Density gradient: This indicator is used to measure the level of suburbanization or urban sprawl and to describe the population density patterns of a city according to the distance from the city center.

Market value is not an exact science and is a rather abstract concept. There are several ways to appraise market value, among which the following three prevail: sales comparison, income capitalization (for commercial real estate), and mass appraisal. It is important to keep in mind why the exercise is being done: not only to assess the performance of the land market but, more importantly, to better understand how the land market affects, positively or negatively, the vibrancy, the social and economic fabric, and the diversity and livability of the city.

Land Assets Management

Objective and content. Most municipalities do not know what they own, where their assets are located, or how much those assets are worth. Land is often the most valuable asset of local governments, which implies that the quality of land assets management is especially important. This section of the UA/SA reviews the status of public land in the city and aims to assess the needs in terms of its inventory. If the city does not have a proper registry of land assets, the UA/SA will not be able to fill this gap, but it will be able to guide the city in the right direction and give more visibility to this issue. If the city does have a land assets registry, the UA/SA can be used to update it, map it, monitor it, and analyze it. Again, if the municipality has an updated street addressing system, the database and maps attached to this street addressing will be extremely valuable (see box 2.7).

Tasks. This section will assess the inventory of land assets owned by the municipality or available on the market for urban development. The assessment will include the following tasks:

- Review or jump-start an inventory of land owned by the municipality: area, location, developed or not, and estimated value.

- Map location of land owned or controlled by the municipality (map 2.9).

- Outline methods used for the allocation of municipal land.

- Identify developers' complaints: number, frequency, and type.

Main Land Assets

	Property type	Unit	Price	Area	Location/Address
• Plots owned by the munici-pality					
• Plots con-trolled by the munici-pality					
• Buildings owned by the munici-pality					
Total					

Box 2.7
The Importance of Street Addressing: A Precious Ally

The importance of street addressing cannot be overlooked. Although many cities around the world take it for granted, the lack of street addresses is vast and problematic. It is estimated that 4 billion citizens worldwide do not have an address. This problem needs to be taken seriously and tackled with care.

What Is Street Addressing?

- Technique shifts emphasis from plot level demarcation and registration titling to occupancy units at the street level and from property rights to occupancy status.
- A system that allows the identification of a building or plot of land based on the identification of a street and an entrance number.
- Includes installing street signs, numbering doorways, mapping, street indexing, and database management.

Why Is Street Addressing Important?

It has multiple applications related to municipal management and municipal services:
- Civic identity
- Urban information systems
- Land and land assets management
- Service delivery: road maintenance, solid waste removal, concessionary services, and utilities
- Local taxation
- Slum upgrading
- Emergency response: fire and ambulance services
- Epidemic prevention and disaster recovery
- Mail, ecommerce, and economic development

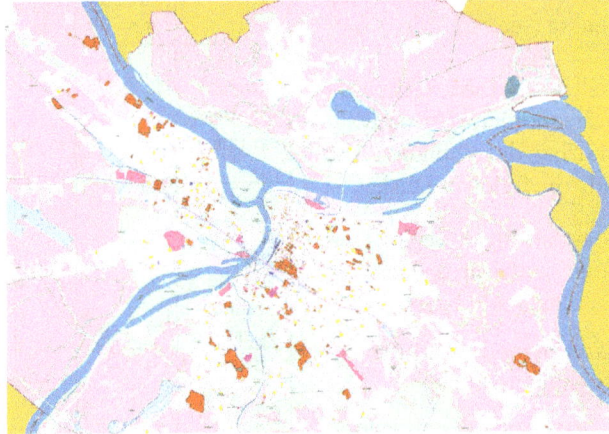

Step 10: City Development Projects: A Snapshot of Key Urban Restructuring Programs

Objective and content. This section of the UA/SA reviews the current urban development growth patterns in the city and takes a more holistic approach to citywide programs. It, therefore, focuses on the following three key items: (1) urban extension areas for residential or economic activity uses (typically located in the outskirts of the municipality), (2) city redevelopment/reuse/renewal projects (typically located in the inner city), and (3) slum or irregular neighborhood upgrading.

Tasks. This section of the UA/SA identifies and analyzes the ongoing and contemplated urban development projects (see table 2.12 for an example). Step 10 is very important because it takes a look at large infrastructure or development projects that will have a "structuring" or "branding" impact on the city. These projects can range widely in terms of scope, location, partnerships, funding, and operating arrangements. They may include waterfront redevelopment: many cities

located on waterways are reclaiming land on waterfronts, transforming them into mixed-use residential and touristic destinations. Others are doing Greenfield redevelopment, turning rural, agricultural, or vacant land into sustainable peri-urban areas. Large former industrial tracts are also being turned into land development projects. City center renovation and inner city renewal programs have enabled many declining cities to revamp their images and their economies. Large upgrading programs have also, with more or less success, attempted to integrate large, densely populated, and underserviced neighborhoods into the city's urban fabric. Last, but not least, are other large infrastructure projects, such as public transit systems as well as large primary road network extensions or new construction, that have a tremendous impact on mobility, shape, density, land values, housing prices, and urban residents. The Urban Audit/SA wants to know everything there is to know about these large structuring projects, including the following:

- Location

- Land ownership status

Table 2.12 Example: Land Development Project

Objectives	Quantitative indicator	Definition and comments
Social office project	31%	% of housing FVIT has 140 000 Dh (slums) and social has 200 000 Dh (others)
Resorption of slums	10 000	Number of slum households affected
Impacts on adjoining or adjacent areas	(1)+(2)+(3)	(1) Improvement of the built environment, (2) Infrastructure contribution, (3) Opening of the urbanization zone, (4) Integration with the existing outcome, (5) Other (to be specified)
Social mobility	69%	% of households expected as slum and prevention
Other		Activities (including industries)

Designation	Number of units	Unit area (in m²)	Total area (in m²)	Induced Housing	Induced Housing
1– Lots of resettlement (total)					
with lots equipped in ZAP					
2– Lots of prevention					
3– Collective lots (R + 3 and more)					
4– Other promoted lots					
5– Lots of Partnership (AMI)	132	41 041	5 417 451	54 270	
with social housing & FVIT				16 700	31%
6– Lots of activities including industries					
7– Socio-collective equipments	29		131 913		
for Health					
for Education					
for Green Spaces					
Total	**161**	**41 041**	**5 549 364**		
Roads and others (places, streams…)			2 850 636		
General Total	**161**	**41 041**	**8 400 000**	**54 270**	
COS–Coefficient for ground use			**66%**		

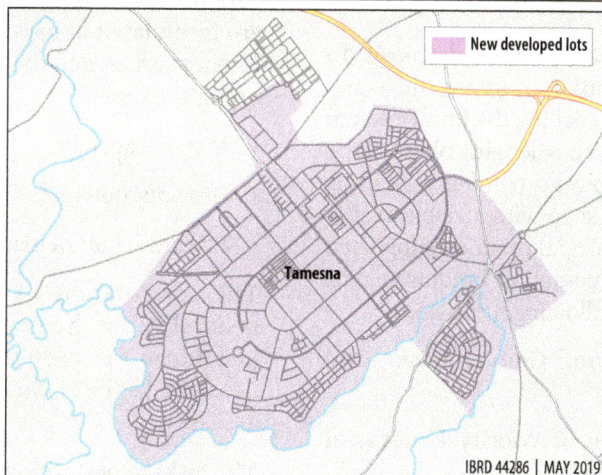

New developed lots

Tamesna

IBRD 44286 | MAY 2019

This map was created using OSM and local data, reprojected in ArcGIS, and refined in Adobe Illustrator.

- Planning documentation and approval process
- Consultation process
- Feasibility studies
- Status of technical studies
- Environmental, economic, and social evaluations
- Costs and financing agreements (total and detailed, onsite and offsite)
- Institutional arrangements (dedicated authority, if any)
- Population expected to be served
- Implementation schedule
- Land sales proceeds and other revenues expected

Block 3. Priority Investment Programs: Selection, Consultation, and Implementation

Objective and Methodology

Block 3 is moving away from diagnosis to actual implementation. It outlines the various steps involved in reaching the final product. In a sense, it is the most challenging phase of the UA/SA, because it involves screening, validating, and arbitrating to come up with a viable, realistic, and desirable municipal program supported by concrete implementation requirements. Block 3 includes the following three steps:

Step 11: Preselection, Consultation, and Screening Process

Step 12: Classification of Priority Investment Projects by Stakeholders

Step 13: From Project Prioritization to Program Implementation

The chapter ends with a note of wisdom and advice: it is important for cities to get ahead of the game with sound procurement practices and procedures that will help them ultimately speed up the physical implementation of their municipal programs while enhancing the quality of public works and the transparency in the use of public funds.

Step 11: Preselection, Consultation, and Screening Process

Objective and content. This phase of the process is extremely important because it provides an opportunity to put the pieces of the puzzle together and to take into account the social, technical, and highly political features of investment programming.

Tasks. Key tasks in this phase include the following.

1. **Estimating the "demand" for projects**

   Block 2 of the UA/SA provided a diagnosis that helped identify gaps and needs as well as propose investment orientations to mitigate or eliminate them. But other projects are formulated in parallel coming from different sources, and these sources have to be brought to light:

   - Mayor's agenda
   - Citizens' demands
   - Private sector demands

   The formulation of these demands is generally not homogeneous. Some are just ideas for projects; others are well described, but their costs are not assessed.

   The tasks to perform will be the following:

   - To identify and detail specific projects included in the mayor's agenda and not necessarily listed in the previous diagnosis conducted by the municipal departments;

- To inform and consult citizens and the private sector through public hearings, consultation of private investors, chamber of commerce, and so on (table 2.13); and

- To present these projects in the same format (project fact sheet). The most important information is the following: a brief description, location, summary of cost estimates, financial participation, responsibility, and impacts.

2. Setting up the consultation process

Cities may have their own consultation processes. Some municipalities may also request feedback from their citizens on a regular basis or on a project basis. Table 2.13 (Taking the Pulse of the City: Perception of the City by its Citizens) presents an example of a simple questionnaire designed to determine how the city is

Table 2.13   Taking the Pulse of the City: Perception of the City by its Citizens

Taking the Pulse of the City: Perception of the City by its Citizens								
Name of the City –>			Replies			Sample answer		
			1	2	3	4	5	6
			Bad	Fair	Good	Bad	Fair	Good
1	Urban site	Urban design	X					
2		Downtown area	X					
3		Image of the city	X					
4		Neighborhood life		X				
5	Risks	Floods			X	> 25% of the city flooded		< 5% of the city flooded
6		Seismic risk			X	Some strong earthquake		Little or no risk
7		Climate change	X			High vulnerability		Low vulnerability
8		Other: industrial risk, landslides...		X		High risk		Low risk
9	Environment	Natural heritage	X			Few natural heritage		Signficant heritage
10		Green spaces	X			Insufficient green spaces		Vast green spaces
11		Air pollution	X			Very polluted city		No significant pollution
12		Water pollution		X		Widespread water pollution		No significant pollution
13	Land tenure	Land availability			X	Little developable land		No problem urban expansion
14		Tenure security			X	Informal > 25%		Informal: < 5%
15	Economy	Economic vibrancy	X			Economic stagnation		Growth
16		Growth factors		X		Weak economic foundation		Diversified base

continued next page

Table 2.13 Continued

Taking the Pulse of the City: Perception of the City by its Citizens								
Name of the City —>		**Replies**			**Sample answer**			
		1	2	3	4	5	6	
		Bad	Fair	Good	Bad	Fair	Good	
17		Home business	X			No incentive		Incentives
18		Unemployment	X			Unemployment rate: > 40%		Unemployment rate: < 10%
19		Informal employment	X			Majority share of informal		Almost non-existent informal
20	Housing	Housing provision		X		Insufficient		Exceeds demand
21		Housing prices			X	Prohibitive for middle classes		Accessible to middle class
22	Urban services	Water supply			X	Unsatisfactory		Satisfactory
23		Wastewater	X			Unsatisfactory		Satisfactory
24		Electricity		X		Unsatisfactory		Satisfactory
25		Street lighting	X			Lighting: < 50% of quarters		Lighting: in all neighborhoods
26		District heating	X			Unsatisfactory		Satisfactory
27		Information technology	X			Uncommon internet access		Widespread internet access
28		Solid waste		X		Unsatisfactory		Satisfactory
29		Security			X	Insecurity		No security problem
30	Roads, mobility, transport	Road network			X	Heavy congestion in the center		Low congestion in the city center
31		Quality of road network	X			Roads in poor condition: > 70%		Roads in poor condition: < 10%
32		Public transportation		X		Poor system		Efficient system
		Mobility for all						
		- Bikes						
		- Pedestrians						
		- Challenged mobility						
33	Amenities/ Public facilities	Schools		X		Poor		Good
34		Health centers			X	Poor		Good
35		Leisure, culture, and sport	X			Poor		Good

	Number of replies (example)				
	Bad	1,700	47%		
Results	**Fair**	1,000	28%		
	Good	900	25%		
		3,600	100%		

Note: Information on the age group, gender, and years of residence in the city of each respondent will be useful to draw further conclusions as to how to use the results.

doing and how it is perceived by its citizens. The questionnaire covers many aspects of city life and city services and will provide a "quick and dirty" subjective evaluation of how citizens see their cities and their urban environment. Covering topics from housing prices to traffic congestion to quality of roads and schools, this simple questionnaire can produce valuable inputs on key pressure points, offer a formal outlet for citizens' voices, and provide city leaders with food for thought.

The consultation process for the UA/SA proposes a three-step approach:

2.1 An "information/consultation" phase before the UA/SA process starts. This information session aims at (1) presenting the process and explaining how it is going to be conducted and (2) gaining early buy-in from various stakeholders.

2.2 A "reinstatement/consultation" phase upon completion of the analysis: (1) the first findings are presented along with a list of projects whose cost is compatible with the initial funding envelope and that addresses the stated deficiencies and needs; (2) any project proposals brought up during consultation are listed.

2.3 A "consultation/validation" discussion stage after the costs and feasibility of all the projects have been assessed. This "long list" of projects is examined, discussed, and filtered through a set of criteria (see the next section, "Setting criteria for project preselection"). The consultations are followed by discussion as needed to decide which projects are PIP-eligible.

If the UA/SA is conducted in parallel with the MFSA, the discussion will focus on the key question of availability of funding. If all the prerequisites and criteria for selection are met, the remaining key questions include the following:

- Is funding available?

- What are the cost implications on the existing and projected tax burden?

- What is the likelihood of partnering with private operators?

- Does the inclusion of the project in the investment program preclude the financing of other priority projects?

Regardless of the type, format, scope, and duration of these consultations, there are a number of principles that govern the process and, when applied, make it effective (World Bank 2013):

- *Openness*: The process is open. By calling a consultation, the city is prepared to be influenced when making decisions and open to the input from citizens; citizens' contributions will be taken into account.

- *Access to information*: Citizens need access to all relevant information in advance. This principle applies to information on the consultation process as well as materials that would help citizens to provide informed opinions on the subject of consultation. Information should ideally be customized and made available as needed.

- *Accountability*: The input and feedback from each citizen are collated and assessed, shared back with citizens, and brought to the attention of decision makers. In a consultative process, the city is accountable for the outcome of the consultation and for how citizens' input has informed and helped decision making.

- *Transparency*: The consultation process is transparent. Information is available to citizens about relevant aspects of the process, citizen engagement, citizen input, consultation outcomes, and how citizen input is used.

- *Visibility*: All those who may be impacted by a decision or are interested in participating in a consultation process need to be made reasonably aware of the process. This means making an effort to reach all impacted groups, including persons from vulnerable groups. Citizens should be informed of proposed consultations through social media, media, press releases, advertisements, newsletters, and so on.

- *Accessibility*: Citizens must have reasonable access to the process. The methods chosen for the consultation must be suitable for all citizens. Additionally, the information provided to citizens should be reasonably easy to comprehend.

3. **Setting criteria for project preselection**

   Setting up criteria for preselection and checking the boxes is not a futile exercise because it forces decision makers to (1) realistically assess the technical and financial feasibility of a project and (2) provide some strategic orientations on choices and priorities. Some of the key criteria to consider will include confirmation of the following:

- That the proposed project/program falls under the responsibility of the local government or follows established multijurisdictional arrangements;

- That it will bring a structural benefit to the city;

- That it will have an impact on a large share of the population;

- That it will favor rehabilitation of existing assets whenever possible;

- That it will promote a balanced densification of urban areas;

- That it meets all the technical, financial, economic, environmental, and social conditions required for a smooth execution.

- Some of the key questions to ask are:

- Is the land available and land tenure/ownership worked out?

- Does the proposed new facility conform to central government mapping (schools, health centers)?

- Are both the equipment and staffing secured so that the facility does not sit empty after completion?

- Is funding available?

- Has it been cross-checked with MFSA findings?

- What external sources of funding have been secured?

- Is the private sector involved in the implementation and maintenance of the proposed program?

- Are the proposed financing and institutional arrangements acceptable?

- Does the project make sense environmentally?

- How green is the proposed investment?

- Does it contribute to social inclusion?

Figure 2.10 and figure 2.11 illustrate the criteria and process for preselection.

The project fact sheet is an essential tool that will be updated throughout the selection process and finalized for attachment to the PIP at the end of the process.

Figure 2.10 Criteria Selection and Validation

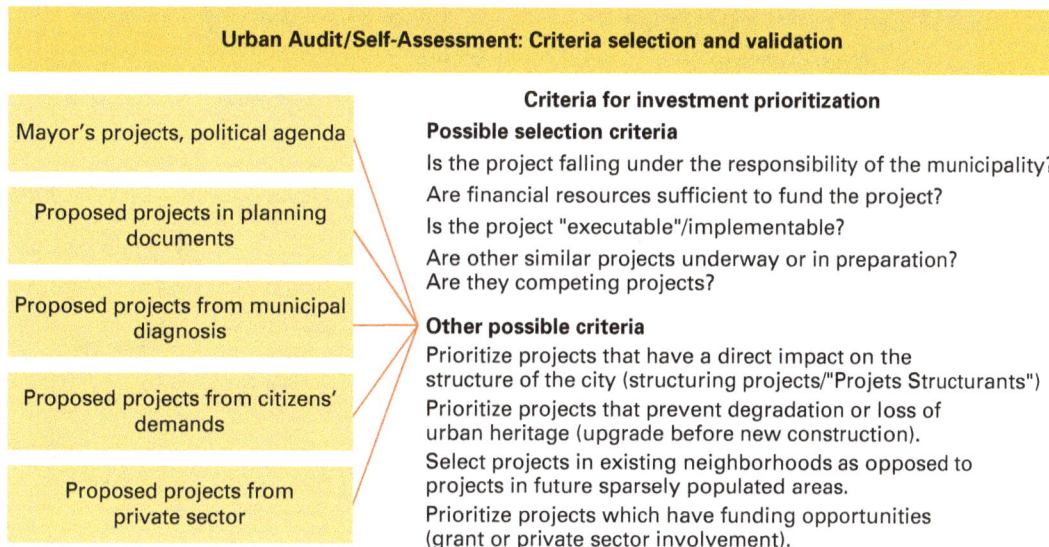

Urban Audit/Self-Assessment: Criteria selection and validation

Mayor's projects, political agenda

Proposed projects in planning documents

Proposed projects from municipal diagnosis

Proposed projects from citizens' demands

Proposed projects from private sector

Criteria for investment prioritization

Possible selection criteria

Is the project falling under the responsibility of the municipality?
Are financial resources sufficient to fund the project?
Is the project "executable"/implementable?
Are other similar projects underway or in preparation? Are they competing projects?

Other possible criteria

Prioritize projects that have a direct impact on the structure of the city (structuring projects/"Projets Structurants")
Prioritize projects that prevent degradation or loss of urban heritage (upgrade before new construction).
Select projects in existing neighborhoods as opposed to projects in future sparsely populated areas.
Prioritize projects which have funding opportunities (grant or private sector involvement).

Figure 2.11 Criteria and Process for Preselection of Municipal Investments

a. Example of preselection criteria

Example of investments preselection criteria

1. To prioritize rehabilitation of existing assets rather than new assets construction
2. To prioritize projects that deliver basic services in under-equipped areas
3. To prioritize projects that impact a larger population
4. To prioritize projects whose feasibility is confirmed (land tenure, implementation schedule, complexity)
5. To prioritize projects with funding opportunities (target grants or private sector involvement)
6. To prioritize projects with strong potential environmental impact

Proposed project	1	2	3	4	5	6	Final score
Project A	X		X	X		X	4
Project B		X					1
Project C					X		1
Project D		X	X				2
Project E	X				X	X	3
Project F	X		X	X		X	4
Project G		X					1
Project H							0
Project I			X		X		2
Project J							0

Criteria

Figure 2.11 Continued

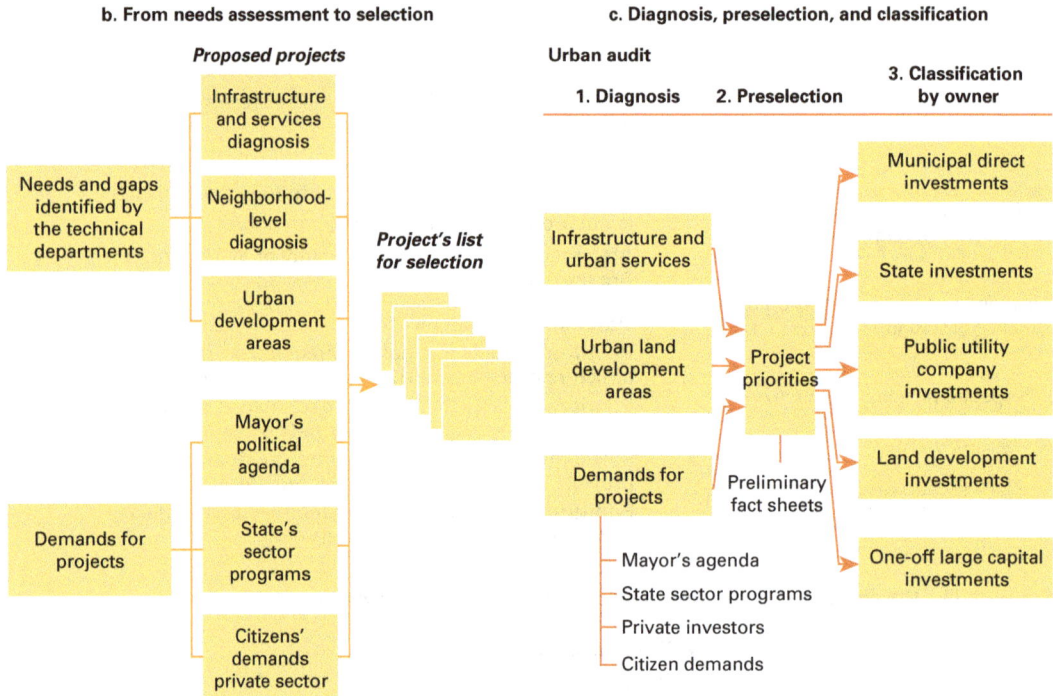

b. From needs assessment to selection

Proposed projects

c. Diagnosis, preselection, and classification

Urban audit

1. Diagnosis   2. Preselection   3. Classification by owner

Step 12. Classification of Priority Investment Projects by Stakeholders

Objective and content. This step consists of classifying the preselected investment projects according to the key stakeholders responsible for financing. This step is particularly crucial because it distributes responsibility for implementation and financing, and it emphasizes the need for coordination in terms of implementation schedule, share of responsibility, and possible cross-financing.

Tasks. Table 2.14 lists stakeholders typically involved in the selection and implementation of municipal investment projects.

Each stakeholder involved in the urban project investment selection and implementation has

its own rules and financing strategy. The classification will give an overview of the scope of the program, the institutional arrangements to put in place, and the spread of the financing charges. Types of project ownership include the following:

- **Municipality**: Municipal direct investment projects, owned and conducted directly by the municipality. Their financing refers to fiscal capacity of the municipality, which is assessed in parallel through the Municipal Finances Self-Assessment.

- **Public utility company**: Generally, in charge of all the basic services such as water supply, sewage and drainage, electricity, urban heating, and others. Their financing comes from tariff proceeds and

Table 2.14 Classification of Priority Investment Projects by Category and Financing Source

Name of project sector	Proposed by	PRIORITY	Direct municipal investment — Urban roads, street lighting, solid waste, drainage, schools, health, culture	Public utility company investment — Water supply, wastewater, urban transport, heating...	Land development investment — Housing, industrial and logistics, urban renewal	One-off investment — Urban expressway, subway, tramway
				Key financing sources		
			Municipality credit-worthiness	Costs recovery and tariff policy	Land sales (or leases) PPP	Intergovernmental finance—PPP
Project A... (Culture)	Mayor's agenda					
Project B... (Roads)	Municipal diagnosis					
Project C... (Street lighting)	Municipal diagnosis					
Project D... (Primary school)	Mayor's agenda					
Project E... (Roads)	Municipal diagnosis					
Project F... (Greening)	Planning documents					
Project G... (Water supply)	Citizens' demand	1				
Project H.... (Water supply)	Citizens' demand					
Project I... (Drainage)	Municipal diagnosis					
Project J... (Housing)	Private sector					
Project K.... (Solid waste)	Municipal diagnosis					
Project L... (Culture)	Mayor's agenda					

continued next page

Table 2.14 Continued

Name of project sector	Proposed by	PRIORITY	Direct municipal investment (Urban roads, street lighting solid waste, drainage, schools, health, culture) — Municipality credit-worthiness	Public utility company investment (Water supply, wastewater, urban transport, heating...) — Costs recovery and tariff policy	Land development investment (Housing, industrial and logistics, urban renewal) — Land sales (or leases) PPP	One-off investment (Urban expressway, subway, tramway) — Intergovernmental finance – PPP
					Key financing sources	
Project M... (Housing)	Private sector					
Project N... (Trade)	Private sector					
Project O... (Street lighting)	Municipal diagnosis					
Project P... (Elementary school)	Mayor's agenda					
Project Q... (Industry)	Private sector	2				
Project R... (Roads)	Citizens' demand					
Project S... (Sewage)	Municipal diagnosis					
Project T... (Water supply)	Municipal diagnosis					
Project U... (Water supply)	Mayor's agenda					
Project V... (Transport)	Planning documents					
Project W... (Transport)	Municipal diagnosis	3				
Project X... (Solid waste)	Mayor's agenda					
Project Y... (Trade)	Private sector					
Project Z... (Culture)	Citizens' demand					

Note: PPP = public–private partnership.

the capacity of the company, through these proceeds, to recover the costs (cost recovery or full cost recovery). The level of performance will determine the capacity of the utility company to invest by itself (self-financing and debt) or to get support from the municipality or higher level of government through a subsidy or loan guarantee.

- **Land developer**: Land development (see the three categories defined above—housing, industrial, and urban renewal—in the UA/SA) is generally assumed by the specific agency allowed to sell or lease the land and to account for proceeds generated by this activity. Consequently, investment projects related to urban development will be attributed to these specific stakeholders. In the MFSA, specific financial analysis will be conducted at the project level and as corporate-based analysis to assess the ability of the stakeholder to carry out the project with or without support from the municipality.

- **One-off project with complex institutional and financial arrangements**: The idea is to differentiate "exceptional" projects from the other projects listed in the UA/SA. These exceptional projects generally involve the state level and the private sector in complex contractual arrangements (public–private partnerships). They have several owners. The objective of the classification will, in this case, be to list them in the municipal investment program, but also to evaluate the role of the municipality in the implementation of these projects.

Step 13: From Project Prioritization to Program Implementation

Objective and content. The final step of the UA/SA addresses the "So what?" question.

After a deep dive into the analysis of the various components of what makes a city a city, it is crucial to bring some closure and to determine what it means in terms of next steps.

Tasks. Looking forward, the next steps will include the following:

- Create a list of potential actions/reforms on (1) the regulatory framework on the basis of what we have learned on city planning/land development/land use regulations and practices; (2) capacity building of local municipal staff to better perform their tasks; and (3) connecting the dots with the financial capacity of the municipality to assume a coherent financing base for its future investments (including maintenance needs) through own revenues, loans, or public–private partnerships.

- Outline a clear, realistic Priority Investment Program (PIP), which will include three key features: (1) maintenance, (2) rehabilitation, and (3) new investments (table 2.15 and table 2.16). The temptation is always to focus on development and new investments. However, there is a great deal to say about "conservation," especially in environments where one has to be mindful of financial constraints, physical limitations, and the environmental footprint. Hence, in many cases, taking a good look at what the municipality owns (its assets) and the great advantages of a central location will outweigh more costly alternatives of new development in peri-urban areas. The Project Fact Sheet shown in table 2.14 is an additional working document that enables decision-makers to concretize the justification, description, cost, and implementation arrangement of each project or program selected in the PIP.

PIP: Allocation and Schedule of Investments. The final step is the allocation of investments according to priorities and the

Table 2.15 Priority Investment Program

	Type of investment	Order of priority	Estimated amount			
			Maintenance	Rehabilitation	New projects	Total
1	*Infrastructure*					
	Primary roads					
	Secondary streets					
2	*Education and health care facilities*					
	Subtotal education					
	Subtotal health care					
3	*Community facilities*					
4	*Government and municipal technical facilities*					
	Subtotal government					
	Subtotal municipal technical					
5	*Commercial facilities*					
6	*Environmental facilities*					
7	*Historical assets*					
	Total					

Table 2.16 Project Fact Sheet

1	**Project type and eligibility**
1.1	Investment category:
1.2	• Location:
1.3	• Beneficiaries:
1.4	Special conditions and eligibility
	• Eligibility:
	• Agreement reached:
	• Assumption of responsibility for maintenance:
2	**Justification**
2.1	• Priority level:
2.2	• Social impact:
2.3	• Financial/economic analysis:
2.4	• Environmental impact:
3	**Description of project**
3.1	Number of buildings and/or m2 to be built:
	• Description:
	Development of access roads:

continued next page

Table 2.16 Continued

3.2	Project preparation status • Availability of technical documents: • Cost basis: • Dates of meetings with beneficiaries:
3.3	Constraints related to implementation • Land ownership status: • Deed of land ownership or assignment: • Slum clearance: • Utilities to be relocated: • Easements:
3.4	Practical terms of startup:
3.5	Execution deadlines • Studies: • Work:
3.6	Site drawing Implementation plan
3.7	Other graphics:
4	**Costs**
4.1	Cost of work:
4.2	Recurring expenses:

schedule of implementation over a three-year period. Forecasts beyond three years are not realistic because they leave too much room for slippage and delays.

Investments in facilities and infrastructure should be allocated according to priorities, the nature of the work (rehabilitation, new work, and so on), and the amount of the investment (table 2.17).

Getting Ahead of the Game: Good Procurement Matters

The topic of procurement should not be overlooked. The ability of the local government to procure is a key factor in the efficient, speedy, and cost-effective implementation of its Priority Investments Plan. As the Urban Audit/Self-Assessment moves from diagnosis to program implementation, it is essential that cities and local governments

quickly progress from project identification to project implementation. Identifying the right contractors, getting quality work at the right price, keeping the schedule of works under control, and having in place a proper monitoring system for the supervision of public works will enhance the ability of a city to get things done while ensuring transparency and accountability in the use of public funds.

To be able to meet those objectives, cities and local governments should assess and strengthen the quality and effectiveness of their procurement systems. This assessment goes beyond the scope of the UA/SA. The topic is, however, of importance and should not be sidelined. Accordingly, although the UA does not include a specific section on procurement self-assessment, what follows can provide a level of guidance to cities and municipalities around the world seeking to improve their current procurement practices.

Table 2.17 Priority Investment Program Implementation Schedule

	Type of investment	Year 1	Year 2	Year 3	Total
1	*Infrastructure*				
2	*Education and health care facilities*				
	Subtotal education				
	Subtotal health care				
3	*Community facilities*				
4	*Government and municipal technical facilities*				
	Subtotal government				
	Subtotal municipal technical				
5	*Commercial facilities*				
6	*Environmental facilities*				
7	*Historical assets*				
	Total				

Since cities and local governments worldwide follow national procurement regulations, they should, in principle, be able to rely on existing assessments carried out at the national level. In 2004, under the auspices of a partnership between the World Bank and the OECD-DAC Procurement Round Table, which included most multilateral and bilateral donors and more than 30 partner countries, a Methodology for Assessing Procurement Systems (MAPS) was developed to measure the systems' strengths and weaknesses. MAPS has been carried out in more than 60 borrowing and client countries. The number of countries that use MAPS is likely to be even higher today, but no global monitoring has taken place since 2011.

A revised version of MAPS was launched in 2017; it is a universal tool that can be used by all countries, irrespective of income level and development status. The revised version reflects a modern understanding of public procurement. Although MAPS II is still in a pilot phase, two of its modules are very relevant to cities and towns. These modules are:

- **Sector-Level Assessment:** This assessment is intended to provide a harmonized tool for assessing the functioning and performance of the public procurement system and market conditions at the sector level. It provides an overall functioning and performance of public procurement and understanding of the business environment. It also assesses the trust and capacity of the private sector to access and respond to public procurement. This assessment provides for an analytical foundation for the overall planning and budgeting in the sector; it also informs cities of public procurement risks, including institutional shortcomings in terms of expenditure, competition, environmental impact, and socioeconomic issues. This, in turn, will shape the procurement strategy, planning, and packaging that will enable procurement methods to be optimally designed to achieve value for money as well as effective capacity building of both public institutions and the private sector.

- **Agency-Level Assessment:** This assessment is intended to provide a harmonized tool for assessing the procurement arrange-ments and performance of individual agencies (procuring entities). It offers an opportunity to assess the capacity of the entity to assume procurement functions and to take full charge of its role as a contract manager. In the case of the city, it will be important to assess items such as (1) the pro-curement arrangements, namely whether there is a dedicated and qualified procure-ment team in line with the nature and vol-ume of procurement to be carried out; (2) the procurement practices (for example, compliance with obligations that include policies, filing systems, data collection, and performance measurement); (3) strengths and weaknesses of the procurement system; and (4) management capacity. Normally, this assessment is heavily depended on the MAPS core assessment; accordingly, a comprehensive MAPS at the national level is recommended before the Agency-Level Assessment is carried out.

The key guiding principles and require-ments for good procurement at the city level are very much in tune with the key objectives of the UA/SA and are worth mentioning again:

- **Value for Money:** Reflecting the basic goal of any procurement system to provide goods, works, and services in an economical, efficient, effective, and sustainable way.

- **Transparency:** Reflecting the basic and commonly agreed-upon goal of disclosure of policies and information related to decisions on contract awards and complaints to the public in a comprehensible, accessible, and timely manner.

- **Fairness:** Reflecting the ambition that the public procurement process should be free from bias to ensure equal treatment of bidders.

- **Good Governance:** Recognizing that pro-curement is a critical part of the broader governance system within which it operates and that poor procurement processes, bad policies, and secondary procurement goals can have a negative impact on that system.

The "So What?" Question: Beyond Investments, A Solution Package of Supporting Measures

After the analysis is done, after the needs assessment is completed, and after the various pieces of the puzzle have been put together, comes the time of reckoning. So What? What do we do with this information? How is it going to impact the way a city conducts its business? Is it just another short-lived intellectual exer-cise that will be put on the shelf once com-pleted? Experience shows that the last step of the Local Governments Self-Assessments (both the Urban Audit/SA and the MFSA) is the most difficult because it involves deci-sion making and strategic choices. However, it is also the most crucial phase, and the "So What?" question should be at the front and center of it all.

Like the MFSA, the UA/SA ends with a concrete set of actions that translate into (1) a Priority Investment Plan, including capital investments, rehabilitation, and maintenance and (2) a set of measures to improve the capacities of local govern-ments to do their jobs better. The Priority Investments Program, as discussed in this chapter, is a straightforward product with defined steps and a process that is screened and validated along the way. The support-ing and accompanying measures are more difficult to map out and more challenging to implement and monitor, but they are equally essential, because they aim to build the capacity of local governments and their propensity to provide services and infrastructure for current and future urban residents. Among these supporting measures, the following list, organized in clusters of actions and activities, is likely to come up most often. This list is by no means exhaustive and will be tailored to city-specific findings and situations. Some may require time and political endorsements; others may have costs attached to their implementation; but most need to be on the critical path of the change agenda of cities and towns.

Cluster 1: Improving the Functioning of Municipal Departments

As seen previously, the Urban Audit/SA is an opportunity to map out the existing governance structure and organizational framework of the local government and may lead to specific follow-up actions, such as:

- Reviewing and stabilizing the organizational framework.

- Clarifying city and governance structure. A very important item is to clearly define the tasks and decision-making procedures within the correct spatial jurisdictional boundaries.

- Reviewing skills and capacity needs. We talked previously about the need to professionalize municipal staff and strengthen their skills so that they are better equipped to address the ever-increasing set of complex issues faced by cities around the world. Beyond the actual capacity-building of individuals lies the looming and unresolved issue of incentives and recognition (civil servants' status and salary matrix). Follow-up actions on this topic require

major political and legislative measures that go beyond the scope of this exercise but may be an opportunity to open the policy dialogue.

- Breaking the silos within the various departments. One key challenge to effective governance is the lack of coordination among various departments within a given city. Two simple ways to start addressing this issue are to conduct regular staff meetings between financial and technical departments and to entice collaboration across the board on specific projects.

Cluster 2: Improving Urban Investments Planning

The Urban Audit/SA will help the municipality shed light on its current city planning practices and its land regulatory environment as well as unbundle the strengths and weaknesses of the existing systems. Follow-up actions may include the following:

- Taking action on the city planning assessment carried out during the UA/SA with regard to planning documentation, approval time, key planning documents, connectivity between planning and financing. It is important to assess whether the city is equipped in terms of planning documentation, programming tools, and staff skills to produce the right regulatory environment conducive to effectively addressing the urbanization challenges of the city, both current and future.

- Exploring new avenues for developing a preventive rather than reactive regulatory environment. There are several innovative urban planning documents that aim at guiding the programming of urban investments and outlining the major development options. These "anticipatory" documents serve as references to guide new land development projects and housing and business activities as well as major road networks.

- Reviewing improvements to be made to the CIP process or similar processes, such as linking projects to budgeting.

- Using transportation investments and policy as guiding forces.

The Urban Audit/SA also sheds light on the need for local governments to get a grasp of their municipal properties (land and buildings), as well as these properties' value. Land markets and land assets management are big-ticket items and cannot be fully resolved within the scope of the Urban Audit/SA. Here are a few follow-up suggestions:

- Assess the state of affairs: registry or no registry.

- Use pricing and taxation instruments.

- Connect with urban transport and public transit.

Cluster 3: Improving the Quality and Level of Urban Services

Follow-up actions might include:

- Review existing contracting arrangements with service providers.

- Improve maintenance efforts and responsiveness, including:

   ○ Implementing an annual maintenance plan

   ○ Adhering to a bottom-line maintenance expenditure commitment (see Service Sustainability ratio).

   ○ Reviewing ongoing maintenance contracts.

Cluster 4: Improving City Information: The Three "Cs"

Follow-up actions might include:

- **Collection:** Gather and organize the urban information needed to improve the management of cities, such as databases and GIS systems.

- **Curation:** The text-based and cartographic data generated by the Urban Audit/SA may be organized to create a municipal atlas or a city brochure with the goal of presenting and promoting the city's salient features.

- **Communication:** Communication and awareness-raising activities are an essential thread to any capacity-building program. Cities need to do more and better to make their agenda known and understood by their many constituents.

Note

1. IPSI was originally designed by Lucien Godin (Groupe Huit / Allnext). The initial template of IPSI is included in the toolkit of another World Bank publication, *The Future of African Cities: Challenges and Priorities for Urban Development,* by Catherine Farvacque-Vitkovic and Lucien Godin.

References

ASCE (American Society of Civil Engineers). 2017. "Infrastructure Report Card and Failure to Act" Series. ASCE, Reston, VA.

Dowall, David E. 1995. "The Land Market Assessment: A New Tool for Urban Management." Urban Management Programme Discussion Paper No 4. World Bank, Washington, DC.

Farvacque-Vitkovic, Catherine, and Lucien Godin. 2003. *The Future of African Cities: Challenges and Priorities for Urban Development.* Directions in Development. Washington, DC: World Bank.

Farvacque-Vitkovic, Catherine, and Patrick McAuslan. 1992. *Reforming Urban Land Policies and Institutions in Developing Countries.* Washington, DC: World Bank.

Glaeser, Edward, and Joshi-Ghani Abha, eds. 2015. *The Urban Imperative.* Oxford, UK: Oxford University Press.

Mitrić, Slobodan. 2018. "World Bank's Engagement with Transport in Cities: The Early Years." World Bank, Washington, DC.

World Bank. 1989. "Malaysia Housing Sector Study." World Bank, Washington, DC.

———. 1992. "Housing Sector Study, 1989–1992." World Bank, Washington, DC.

———. 2012. *Inclusive Green Growth: The Pathway to Sustainable Development.* Washington, DC: World Bank.

———. 2013. *Planning, Connecting, and Financing Cities Now: Priorities for City Leaders.* Washington, DC: World Bank.

———. 2013. "Consultation Guidelines." World Bank, Washington, DC. https://consultations .worldbank.org/Data/hub/files/documents /world_bank_consultation_guidelines _oct_2013_0.pdf.

———. 2017. "Open Learning Campus (OLC): E-course Introduction to Land Markets Assessment in Complex Urban Settings." World Bank, Washington, DC.

———. "Republic of Senegal Urban Development and Decentralization Program, Project Appraisal Document and Implementation Completion Report, World Bank, Washington, DC.

———. "Republic of Guinea Third Urban Development Project, Project Appraisal Document and Implementation Completion Report," World Bank, Washington, DC.

World Economic Forum. 2013. "The Green Investment Report: The Ways and Means to Unlock Private Finance for Green Growth." World Economic Forum, Geneva. http://www3 .weforum.org/docs/WEF_GreenInvestment _Report_2013.pdf.

Additional Readings

Bertaud, Alain. 2018. *Order Without Design: How Markets Shape Cities.* Cambridge, MA: MIT Press.

de Blij, Harm. 2012. *Why Geography Matters More than Ever.* New York: Oxford University Press.

Center for Land Use Education. 2008. "Planning Implementation Tools: Capital Improvement Plan." Center for Land Use Education, University of Wisconsin–Stevens Point. https://www.uwsp .edu/cnr-ap/clue/documents/planimplementa- tion/capital_improvement_plan.pdf.

Deininger, Klaus, Harris Selod, and Anthony Burns. 2012. *The Land Governance Assessment Framework: Identifying and Monitoring Good Practice in the Land Sector.* Washington, DC: World Bank.

Farvacque-Vitkovic, Catherine, and Lucien Godin. 2006. "Decentralization and Municipal Development: Municipal Contracts." Working Paper, World Bank, Washington, DC.

Farvacque-Vitkovic, Catherine, Lucien Godin, Leroux Hugues, Roberto Chavez, and Florence Verdet. 2005. *Street Addressing and the Management of Cities.* Washington, DC: World Bank.

Farvacque-Vitkovic, Catherine, Lucien Godin, and Anne Sinet. 2014. "Municipal Self-Assessments: A Handbook for Local Governments." Working Paper, World Bank, Washington, DC.

OECD-DAC. 2011. "Strengthening Country Procure- ment Systems: Results and Opportunities."

———. 2017. "Draft Methodology for Assessing Procurement Systems (MAPS): Supplementary Module Agency Level Assessments."

———. 2018. "Draft Methodology for Assessing Procurement Systems (MAPS): Supplementary Module Sector Level Assessment."

Senegal (Republic of). 2008. "Municipal Develop- ment Agency: Canevas de l'Audit Urbain et Cane- vas de l'Audit Financier et Organisationnel."

Universal Postal Union (UPU). 2012. "Addressing the World, An Address for Everyone." UPU, Bern.

CHAPTER 3

Getting the Finances in Order
The Municipal Finances Self-Assessment

Objectives and Rationale

Cities are tasked with increasingly complex and expensive functions as well as an ever-growing agenda. In this fast-urbanizing world, the infrastructure gap, the delivery of basic services, and maintenance needs are key challenges for city managers and policy makers. Meanwhile, in most low- and middle-income countries, local taxation accounts for a mere 3 to 5 percent of all tax revenues. As stated in previous chapters, this situation has induced a sense of urgency and an impetus for change. Business as usual cannot any longer be the name of the game. In this context of skewed and centralized resources and increasing pressure on investments, it is essential that local governments (1) gain a better understanding of their financial position—past, present, and

future; (2) identify the key bottlenecks in their financial systems; and (3) outline a road map for solutions and actions.

The Municipal Finances Self-Assessment (MFSA) aims to help municipal officers analyze the financial situation of their municipalities in a systematic manner and in ways that are accessible and compelling to their main or potential partners (investors, banks, developers, private service providers, or rating agencies), including indicators or ratios those partners are able to understand and use to assess the financial situation.

Traditionally, local and national legislation and financial reporting regulations often stipulate a long list of reporting tables or templates the municipalities must fill out yearly, quarterly, or monthly. These regulations also rule that the municipalities should submit these financial reports to higher government tiers, such as finance, local government, or line ministries as well as to the office of auditor general for compliance audits (Muwonge and Ebel 2014; Shah 2007; Venkateswaran 2014). The central government entities typically review the reports to verify accuracy and compliance with rules and may aggregate them into national-level municipal databases. However, the regulations rarely require municipalities to analyze their data and assess the financial health or project future trends in order to uncover issues or induce corrective measures ahead of problems.

The MFSA, therefore, represents a drastic departure from traditional practices. It provides a quantum leap in data analysis and promotes a new culture of self-assessment with a purpose. In short, the MFSA helps municipalities move from plain bookkeeping to analysis, diagnosis, and action. While doing so, it promotes the following mutually reinforcing objectives:

- *Accountability*: To promote financial self-assessment at the municipal level as part of the management change process in local public administrations.

- *Visibility in the use of public funds*: To encourage local governments to share information with other municipalities and to inform central government, local government associations, and citizens about their current situation.

- *Prioritization*: To encourage financial and other relevant municipal departments—asset management, urban and strategic planning, and the mayor's cabinet—to work together on municipal investment programs securely anchored in financial feasibility and realism.

- *Efficiency and transparency*: To monitor the financial situation and act on a set of

key initiatives to improve the mobilization of local resources, rationalize public expenditures, and improve financial management practices.

- *Access to external funding*: To agree on a common set of concepts, methodologies, and internationally accepted indicators, and to improve communications and negotiations with banking institutions, private partners, and donors (bilateral and international). This is a very important point because local governments will not be able to rely solely on their own revenues and will, therefore, need to seek innovative partnerships with the private sector as well as show their creditworthiness for accessing external funding.

Connecting the dots with urban investments: Adopting sound investments programs is key. The MFSA provides an opportunity to assess the absorptive capacity of a local government. Matched with the key findings of an Urban Audit/Self-Assessment (UA/SA), the MFSA becomes even more relevant because it will provide the municipality with a sense of "Deal or No-Deal" and a picture of where it needs to go and what partnerships it needs to seek in order to bridge its infrastructure and service delivery financing gaps.

Technical notes: The MFSA analysis discussed in this chapter requires specific and detailed methodology for completing some steps. Some readers/users may need help in completing specific calculations or using software applications such as Excel to calculate results or establish trends. To help those users, the MFSA analysis section includes technical notes (technical details, or TD) marked with numbered signs—for example, TD1, TD2, and so on—and presented in numeric order in appendix B, "Detailed Methodology and Procedures to Help Calculate Specific Results in MFSA." Users who are familiar with the methodology may omit these notes and focus rather on the analysis of the results as presented in this chapter.

Participation and collaboration in municipal self-assessments: The MFSA is inherently a self-assessment instrument geared toward local financial officers and municipal decision-making bodies, and it provides critical links and opportunities for using relevant results to inform and involve citizens and other stakeholders (see also Bahl, Linn, and Wetzel 2013). The connection with other city departments in charge of city planning, service delivery, infrastructure, and maintenance is another important opportunity facilitated by the MFSA process. As seen before, this connection is often missing although extremely important for good city management.

MFSA online application: In order to facilitate and scale up the use of the MFSA, the authors have developed an online application. The concepts, methodology, and steps are the same as the ones presented in this book.

MFSA Methodology

The MFSA builds on regular financial reports, but also adds on and suggests institutionalizing additional reports/tables beyond regular budgets to strengthen the situation analysis. The MFSA focuses on and supplements mandatory financial reports with detailed analysis of the financial health of the municipality. The municipal financial diagnosis is performed in six steps (see also figure 3.1):

- Step 1: Setting Up Core Databases
- Step 2: Historical Analysis
- Step 3: Ratio Analysis
- Step 4: Financial Projections
- Step 5: Financial Management Assessment
- Step 6: MFSA Action Plan

Figure 3.1   **Main Steps of MFSA Analysis**

The MFSA analysis also requires following a *generic financial framework*, which is a specific structure of the municipal budgets or financial reports that segregates *current (recurrent)* and *capital revenues* and *current* and *capital expenditures* (figure 3.2 depicts the generic financial framework). This segregation enables defining important balances such as current balance, capital balance, and financing balance that are often overlooked or left unnoticed in regular municipal reports, which more often than not include only a balance total. One of the most important lessons figure 3.2 suggests is that a healthy city is able to generate operating surplus beyond the amount of operating expenditures and create a self-financing source for the capital budget. A negative operating balance would indicate that a city is not sustainable because it uses up its capital to cover expenditures required for regular operations.

Figure 3.2 **Generic Financial Framework**

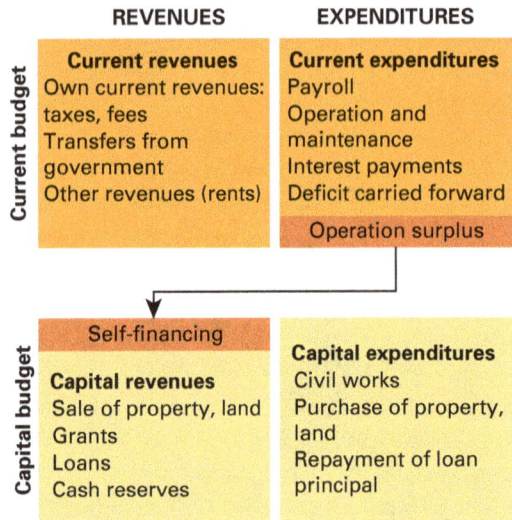

	REVENUES	EXPENDITURES
Current budget	**Current revenues** Own current revenues: taxes, fees Transfers from government Other revenues (rents)	**Current expenditures** Payroll Operation and maintenance Interest payments Deficit carried forward
		Operation surplus
Capital budget	Self-financing **Capital revenues** Sale of property, land Grants Loans Cash reserves	**Capital expenditures** Civil works Purchase of property, land Repayment of loan principal

Source: Farvacque-Vitkovic and Kopanyi 2014.

Figure 3.3 **MFSA Framework**

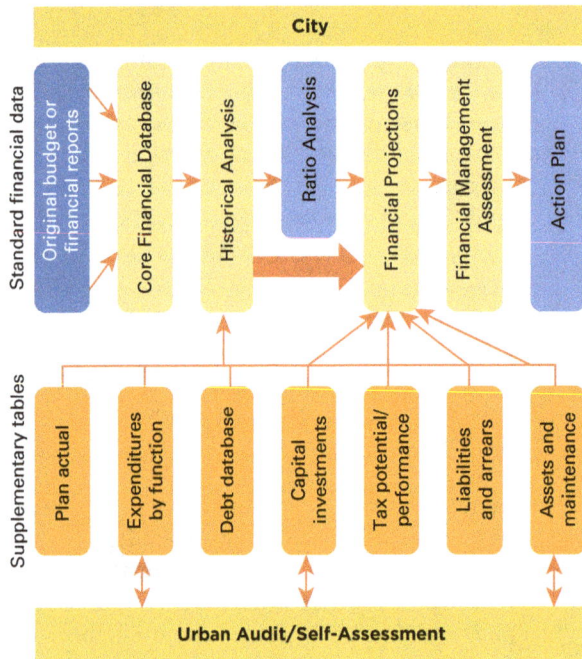

City

Standard financial data: Original budget or financial reports → Core Financial Database → Historical Analysis → Ratio Analysis → Financial Projections → Financial Management Assessment → Action Plan

Supplementary tables: Plan actual | Expenditures by function | Debt database | Capital investments | Tax potential/performance | Liabilities and arrears | Assets and maintenance

Urban Audit/Self-Assessment

Note: MFSA = Municipal Finances Self-Assessment.

Transforming the local data into the MFSA and into the generic financial framework requires some level of flexibility because the level of details, and the size of the original financial tables may depend on the size of the municipality, on the national financial reporting regulations, and on the local situation, for example, if urban services are provided directly by the municipality or instead via municipal enterprises or by private partners.

The MFSA includes two sets of tables, called core databases:

1. Standard financial data, which are generated directly from the regular financial reports and regular municipal budgets

2. Supplementary tables, which are outside the regular budgets or financial reports, although some municipalities may record them in different departments and different formats (figure 3.3 summarizes the framework of the MFSA and shows its interaction with the UA/SA).

Figure 3.3 includes standard financial tables and supplementary tables, but also indicates that it is useful to distinguish "core databases" and "derivative databases." The standard financial database and the supplementary databases constitute the MFSA core databases to be filled with external data obtained from outside the MFSA. In contrast, several tables and data are generated from the core databases during MFSA analysis and summarized in "derivative" tables, such as the financial snapshot, financial projections, and financial ratios.

The set of supplementary tables includes items that are not recorded within the regular budgets or financial reports (for example, list of loans, liabilities, and assets); these are also known as "under the line" or "memorandum" items. Most of these supplementary tables can be developed with moderate workload, and many may exist in various municipal departments and various levels of sophistication. It is important to bring these tables into the spotlight of the MFSA analysis: because most national regulations exclude or do not make these tables mandatory, many local governments ignore or fail to record these additional data in a timely or consistent fashion. Developing these tables under the MFSA requires close cooperation across various municipal departments or entities, and this cross-fertilization is an added benefit of the MFSA process.

The supplementary tables are particularly important for the MFSA because they provide key clarifying information and data to the budgets (for example, stock and accrual items); they support financial projections, budget analysis, and planning; and they provide critical links to the UA/SA (see the MFSA framework in figure 3.3). These additional data also help cities communicate with stakeholders about the city's services, financial issues, and underpinning plans. MFSA users need to approach these tables with flexibly to fit into the local situation. For instance, cities that are prohibited from borrowing or taking debt in any other form clearly will not have the debt database, but the liabilities and arrears table that summarizes the unpaid or overdue bills remains very critical for them to develop and analyze. Cities may develop many more supporting tables, but this second set of tables contains the most important sources of supplementary data.

The MFSA can be performed step by step as depicted in figure 3.4. Detailed explanations of these steps are summarized in the sections below. Figure 3.4 also indicates the rationale behind each step and outlines the actions required to complete them. The figure depicts the process of MFSA analysis step by step, but

Figure 3.4 **MFSA Framework**

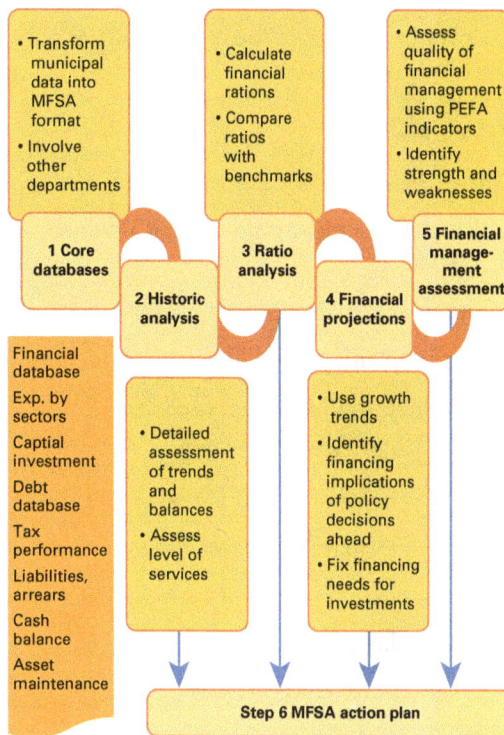

Note: PEFA = Public Expenditure and Financial Accountability.

also indicates that the Action Plan should define transformative actions from the results of the four critical preceding steps: Historic Analysis, Ratio Analysis, Financial Projections, and Financial Management Assessment (discussed in detail later in "Step 6: MFSA Action Plan").

Step 1: Setting Up Core Databases

Objective: Before starting the MFSA analysis, it is important to set up and populate core databases that include the core Financial Database and the supplementary databases. The first and most important is the core Financial

Database, but as previously indicated, there are many supplementary databases important for proper analysis of the city's financial position and services.

The MFSA core databases (core tables) are as follows:

Core Financial Database

- This is the most fundamental database in the MFSA.

Supplementary databases

- Actual/plan financial database
- Expenditures by sectors database
- Debt database
- Capital investments database
- Tax performance database
- Liabilities and arrears database
- Cash balance database
- Asset maintenance database

Many of these datasets are quite simplified and not at all new to municipal finance practitioners; many may already exist in different forms, although some may not be relevant in a given city. The recommended forms of these templates reflect international practices, and we suggest using them in the MFSA in order to ensure consistency and comparability of MFSA results. Experience shows that finance officers engaged in MFSA understand and appreciate the use of these supplementary tables that help provide a standardized and deeper analysis and communication of the city's situation and financial health. Officers in many cities have introduced or institutionalized these supplementary tables that have been overlooked before and may use them on a regular basis beyond the MFSA analysis.

Core Financial Database

Objective: The MFSA requires transforming the city's original budget or financial data into a relatively short, standardized MFSA core *Financial Database* that reflects the logic of the generic financial framework explained earlier (figure 3.2). The reason for using the standardized format is that accounting systems and classifications are very different across countries (Berger and Heiling 2013; Venkateswaran 2014). Local financial reports can be different in two ways: (1) cities may follow different accounting or budgeting systems (cash-based, partial, or full accrual accounting, line item or fund-based budgeting, and so on); and (2) the level of detail can be very different among cities. For the purpose of the MFSA analysis, which aims to be used comparably across continents and in developed or developing countries alike, the core Financial Database is short and consistent with cash-based accounting, while the supplementary tables provide additional information such as accruals, arrears, liabilities, or assets.

Tasks: The MFSA requires transforming the "raw" municipal reports into a standardized MFSA financial database to help easy and automated generation of subsequent tables, analysis of the results, and comparison of the results across cities within countries (Kopanyi 2018). The first and most important step for users of the MFSA is therefore to review and get familiar with the standard MFSA Financial Database and build a bridge between this database and their local/municipal financial report tables. Experience suggests that, in most cases, automated links can be developed between the original local tables and the MFSA database by simple programming steps. These simple steps would not only make the transformation of data to the MFSA platform easier but also substantially reduce the risk of numeric errors that may occur when data are transformed manually. Thus, programmed transformation of local data is recommended.

The core MFSA Financial Database should include actual figures because huge differences often occur between the budget plans adopted before the beginning of a fiscal year and the closing budgets reported in the final accounts at the end or soon after the closing of the fiscal year. Municipalities often adopt a revised budget during the fiscal year; these revised budgets are even ruled as mandatory if the actual figures diverge substantially from the planned. The revised budgets, therefore, are often in better harmony with the closing accounts, but the actual figures remain the most important for the MFSA analysis. We recommend establishing also a supplementary financial table that compares the *initial plan* with the *actual data* annually, in order to draw lessons on budget realism, identify issues and areas that repeatedly cause variances between initial plans and actuals, and support informed corrective measures to improve budget realism.

MFSA Core Financial Database—Revenues
The *revenue* template of the core Financial Database structures total revenues into three main categories: current revenues, capital revenues, and financing transactions (table 3.1). For illustrative purposes, we filled out all templates discussed below with numbers generated from a city's financial reports to help explain specific issues and challenges based on real numbers and results. We will call this city "our city" or "sample city" in the sections below.

Current revenues include revenues received from higher government tiers, own-source revenue (OSR), and other revenues. We recommend adding unspecified other revenues to the OSR because there might be revenues that do not fit the proposed categories, but these other revenues should be small in size.

Revenues from higher government tiers (also called grants) are broken down into three categories for the sake of simplicity: shared taxes, unconditional operation transfers, and conditional or earmarked operation transfers. Sometimes there are no clear boundaries between these three categories, but MFSA users can apply the following rules:

- *Shared taxes* are municipal revenues from specific taxes collected by the national government and shared in proportion of the volume collected in the municipality's jurisdiction (for example 10 percent of personal income tax, 6 percent of value added tax, and so on). Some finance officers may consider the shared taxes as OSR, but we recommend not doing so unless the municipality receives the amount collected in its jurisdiction (for example, 90 percent of some local taxes collected truly on behalf of the municipality with a 10 percent fee retained by the collecting national agency). Property tax in Rwanda is OSR because the Rwanda Revenue Authority collects it, retains a 5 percent collection fee, and returns 95 percent of the proceeds to the cities on a monthly basis (Kopanyi 2015a).

- *Unconditional transfers/grants* are municipal revenues provided by the national government according to formulas, ad hoc, or against other allocation criteria without attaching usage conditions to them. Governments may commit a portion of various taxes for sharing with the local government sector on the basis of a national allocation formula. These are grants and not shared taxes, although they might be called transfers from shared tax revenues because the transferred amounts do not correspond to the volume collected in the municipalities' jurisdictions.

- *Conditional transfers/grants* are municipal revenues received from national governments or entities and that have attached specific conditions to them; therefore, they can be spent exclusively for specific purposes, areas, or projects. These grants are

Table 3.1   MFSA Core Financial Database—Revenues (*ShS million*)

	Year 1	Year 2	Year 3	Year 4	Year 5
	Actual	Actual	Actual	Actual	Actual
Total revenues	**62,955**	**58,735**	**68,131**	**73,511**	**80,250**
I Current revenues	**41,999**	**41,214**	**48,636**	**52,743**	**65,821**
Revenues from central/higher government	**30,300**	**25,162**	**26,120**	**29,933**	**35,984**
1 Shared taxes	24,053	22,255	22,747	26,915	35,631
2 Unconditional operation transfers	6,192	2,613	3,076	2,865	0
3 Conditional/earmarked operation transfers	55	294	297	153	353
Own current revenues	**11,700**	**16,053**	**22,516**	**22,810**	**29,837**
1 Local taxes and levies	**4,235**	**4,818**	**6,212**	**7,548**	**8,037**
Property tax	2,688	3,119	3,979	4,466	4,759
Business tax	1,443	1,590	2,111	2,952	3,146
Other local taxes	104	108	122	130	132
2 Fees and charges	**2,496**	**4,389**	**5,571**	**5,397**	**12,347**
Fees on urban services (city fee, utility charges)	2,402	4,310	4,640	5,289	11,747
Licenses, permits, fines, other	93	79	931	108	600
3 Revenues from assets	**4,969**	**6,847**	**9,778**	**8,723**	**8,989**
Interests received	317	674	268	463	540
Revenues from leasing/renting assets	4,652	6,173	9,510	8,260	8,449
Other revenues	0	0	0	0	0
4 Revenue from municipal enterprises	**0**	**0**	**955**	**1,142**	**464**
Dividends, profit shares	0	0	955	1,142	464
Cash transfers received from enterprises	0	0	0	0	0
5 Other revenues	0	0	0	0	0
II Capital revenues without loans and reserves	**12,756**	**9,697**	**9,303**	**8,220**	**7,407**
Capital grants from central/higher government	0	0	0	145	324
Own capital revenues	12,724	9,607	8,938	7,904	7,078
Proceeds from sale of assets	887	645	546	443	1,354
Land development fee	11,668	8,893	8,333	7,413	5,604
Participation of firms and individuals	169	69	59	48	120
Donations/grants from persons or nongovernment organizations	32	90	365	171	5
III Financing proceeds from reserves and debts	**8,200**	**7,823**	**10,192**	**12,548**	**7,022**
Cash reserves from previous years	4,978	2,867	0	0	0
Sale of financial assets	0	0	0	0	0
Proceeds from domestic loans and bonds	0	883	4,619	2,546	862
Proceeds from foreign borrowing	3,222	4,074	5,573	10,002	6,160
Planned total revenues (from initial plan)	60,000	65,000	70,000	75,000	80,000
Actual/Plan variations (%)	104.9	90.4	97.3	98.0	100.3

Note: MFSA = Municipal Finances Self-Assessment; ShS (shillings) is a notional name of the currency of the sample city.

often called *earmarked grants;* they may finance specified functions, such as grants to pay teachers' salaries, provide welfare support (cash benefits), or they may subsidize water supply in poor areas (slums). Conditions can be more general, such as with grants for cultural, sporting, or historic events or generally for capital investment expenditures.

Own current revenues include four clear categories: taxes, fees, revenues from assets, and revenues from municipal enterprises (box 3.1). Some revenues may not fit well into these four groups and thus can be put into the "other revenues" category. Examples include small donations (such as for training or for cultural or sporting events), security deposits from contractors, and the like; but these "other revenues" should represent a negligible portion of the own revenues. The vast majority of own current revenues should fit into the first four categories. Should a financial report include a substantial share (over 10 percent of total revenues) as unspecified "other revenues,"

there might be some classification issue that deserves clarification and correction.

- *Local taxes* vary country by country and city by city, and so the property or the business tax marked in the revenue template may not represent the two most substantial local revenues in some municipalities. Should a municipality collect substantial revenues from a source not specified in the template, it can be added either as a new subline or to replace a subline that is not relevant in that municipality. For instance, a city may collect substantial rental income tax and tourism tax but insignificant or no property tax. In this case, the tax revenue sublines should be renamed to reflect the three most significant own tax revenues and all other smaller taxes should be put in the line of "other local taxes."

- *Local fees and charges* should include the fees and charges on services provided by municipal departments and accounted for through the municipal budget. In contrast, fees collected by independent entities, whether owned by the municipality or by

---

Box 3.1
Beware of Classifications!

Some taxes are legislated as fees, such as the "business license fee," "traffic congestion fee," or "commuter fee" often collected in fact as taxes; such taxes provide for substantial revenue in Kampala, Uganda (Kopanyi 2015b). Fees that are excessive compared to the cost of service or administration should be accounted for as taxes regardless of their name. Finally, not all fees are current revenues; for example, developers often need to contribute to the trunk infrastructure and pay a "development fee." We recommend classifying a development

fee as capital revenue because (1) it is a one-time, nonrecurrent revenue, and (2) the reason for charging it is to finance infrastructure. The Municipal Finances Self-Assessment (MFSA) aims for and promotes honest self-assessment, so users need to make personal judgments to ensure classifying the local revenue categories for the best use of the MFSA. Reclassifications for MFSA purposes, if any, do not require changing the standard reports of the municipality, but they are very important for optimizing the results of the MFSA.

others, are not part of municipal revenues and should be excluded from the budget report. Should any of these independent entities channel some revenue back to the municipal budget, those revenues should be accounted for in the fourth section "revenue from municipal entities."

- *Revenues from assets* (also called asset proceeds) include recurrent revenues generated as *interest proceeds* from financial assets (daily deposit of excess cash, treasury bills, loans to employees), renting or leasing fixed assets (residential units, shops, office spaces), or other petty cash received in relation to assets. In contrast, revenues from selling or long-term lease of land, office buildings, or big structures, as well as proceeds from selling financial assets should be accounted for as capital (nonrecurrent) revenues.

- *Revenues from municipal enterprises* or entities may include dividends, ad hoc transfers, license fees, or interest paid for loans the municipality has provided to them. In short, it is important to clearly include all types of money transaction from the municipal entities.

Consolidated statements: The MFSA core Financial Database does not capture the budgets or financial statements of the independent municipal entities (for example, the water company); however, it puts emphasis on money movements between the municipality and its entities. The MFSA also promotes and includes supplementary tables for each independent entity to create a better and more realistic picture of the services, their development, and other financial implications. Some municipalities prepare two financial statements at the end of the year: one is the *final account of the municipality*, and the other is a *consolidated report* that includes the results of the municipality and the municipal entities on consolidated bases by netting out cross-transactions to avoid double accounting. This option is beyond the scope of the current MFSA.

Capital revenues are presented in two groups: direct *capital revenues* and *financing proceeds*. These two groups of resources together form the revenue side of the capital budget (see table 3.2, copied from the MFSA database, table 3.1), which includes capital

Table 3.2 Capital Revenues (*ShS million*)

II Capital revenues without loans and reserves	**12,756**
Capital grants from central/higher government	0
Own capital revenues	12,724
Proceeds from sale of assets	887
Land development fee	11,668
Participation of firms and individuals	169
Donations/grants from persons or nongovernment organizations	32
III Financing proceeds from reserves and debts	**8,200**
Cash reserves from previous years	4,978
Sale of financial assets	0
Proceeds from domestic loans and bonds	0
Proceeds from foreign borrowing	3,222

Note: ShS (shillings) is a notional name of the currency of the sample city.

grants from government, own capital revenues, and financing proceeds that are composed of cash reserves from previous years and proceeds from domestic or foreign debt.

Capital grants from central/higher government are revenues provided for the municipality with conditions to use them exclusively for capital/infrastructure development. Examples include capital block grants provided as general budget support for development and earmarked or project grants provided for specific development projects such as building roads, or a specific school or a water network.

National government entities such as ministries or development agencies may support municipalities by direct financing and direct management of construction of infrastructure facilities that are handed over after completion of construction projects. These types of projects are also known as *in-kind support* to local governments and are not accounted for in the local budgets because their costs are neither transferred nor reported to the municipality; therefore, this type of support should not be included among capital revenues. The municipality does, however, need to account these items in the asset inventory and should finance proper operation and maintenance of these assets in years ahead. Thus, in-kind projects have substantial implications for operating budgets in the medium to long term but are excluded from standard financial reports.

Own capital revenues include proceeds from asset sales, land development fees, and participation of firms or individuals. It is important to account for all of these revenues in the capital budget not only because they all should serve development of municipal assets and services but also because they are nonrecurrent revenues.

- *Sale of assets* should be a strategic action of the municipality (for example, sale of a piece of land to finance building a school or road,

or for debt repayment) because municipalities have limited numbers or volume of sellable assets. In addition, the proceeds should be returned to the assets to ensure that the wealth of the municipality remains the same or even improves eventually. There may be crisis situations when the proceeds from an asset sale are used to cover urgent operating costs (pay salaries), but these cases should be truly exceptional and temporary measures. In short, the proceeds from asset sale by default should be accounted for in the capital budget.

- *Land development fees* are fees collected from developers (under various names) to involve them in financing trunk infrastructure. In some countries, it is common to charge developers according to the value of the development or as a negotiated levy without specific connection to the improvement of the nearby infrastructure. For instance, Nairobi charges developers a 1.25 percent fee levied on the cost estimates of the private project, a condition of approval of the development application (Kopanyi and Muwonge, forthcoming). The supporting argument is that the municipality develops the infrastructure continuously, so the developer needs to contribute regardless of whether the specific project requires expansion of the trunk infrastructure in the neighborhood. Some question this practice, because the fee is often unregulated and some proceeds may be used for covering operations (Southeast Europe). We do recommend accounting development fees in the capital budget as own capital revenue.

- *Participation of firms and individuals*: Municipalities often collect contributions or charges (such as hook-up charges or betterment levies) from the property owners who benefit from a specific infrastructure project to finance specifically a portion of the project cost. In this case, impacted property owners (not only the new developers) are identified and charged, and the fee is often regulated as a portion of the well-calculated cost of the municipal infrastructure project. For instance, in Turkey up to 50 percent of the municipal infrastructure project cost can be collected from the beneficiary property owners provided that the charge is not greater than 2 percent of each property's taxable value (Kopanyi 2015c). Participation charges should be accounted for as development budget revenues.

Financing proceeds are part of the capital budget, but it is important to segregate them to better reflect the financing situation of the municipality. These proceeds include surplus or cash reserves accumulated over the years, proceeds from the sale of financial assets, proceeds from domestic debt, and proceeds from foreign debt, if any.

- *Cash reserves*: Municipalities often generate cash reserves on purpose (like debt service reserve fund) or just accumulate reserves from annual cash balances to use on "rainy days," that is, in years when expenditures appear to be greater than current year revenues for one reason or another. Accumulated reserves are easy to measure by reconciliation of bank accounts at the end of the fiscal year; however, because they are apparently not recurrent revenues, it is better not to count them as current revenues of the following fiscal year. Thus, we recommend accounting them in the financing section of the capital budget, despite the fact that the municipality may use a portion of reserves to cover operating expenses on rainy days.

- *Sale of financial assets* is a strategic option of the municipality that may purposely invest into financial assets and divest them later as it deems necessary. For instance, a municipality

issues a bond and obtains cash of ShS8 billion that will be used for road development over four years. It is wise to invest the excess cash immediately into treasury bills and government bonds with one- to three-year terms and then sell parts of this financial investment portfolio annually according to estimated need for said road construction. The annual interest on financial assets can be accounted for as current revenues form assets, and the proceeds from selling financial assets should be accounted for in the financing section of the financial report.

- *Domestic debt* includes proceeds from loans or bonds. It is important to clarify that only the amount disbursed altogether from various loans during a fiscal year should be accounted for here, not the total amount of loan contracted in the year. Should a municipality sell a bond in a particular fiscal year, however, then the proceeds of the bond sale should be accounted for in full in this line as a one-time income for that year. Often, a good portion of these bond sale proceeds may move to financial investments or cash reserves for the next fiscal year because the municipality manages to use up only a part of the bond proceeds in the same fiscal year. Loans that are originated by foreign development partners (such as the World Bank or other international or bilateral banks) that lend money to the national government for on-lending to municipalities should be accounted here as domestic debt.

- *Foreign debt* should be accounted only if the municipality managed to mobilize funds directly from foreign markets—for example, if Turkish cities sold Euro-bonds in Europe or borrowed in euros or dollars from foreign banks. Compared to domestic debts, foreign debt liabilities behave differently because they are exposed to foreign currency variations; therefore, it is important to reflect them in separate lines in a fair financial report like the MFSA financial database.

MFSA Core Financial Database—Expenditures

The second main section of the MFSA core Financial Database focuses on *total expenditures* under three subsections (table 3.3): current expenditures, capital expenditures, and financing items corresponding to the revenue sections discussed above. The MFSA database follows the economic classification of expenditures, whereas a recommended supplementary table reflects functional classification of the expenditures. Both classifications are extremely important for analyzing and communicating the health and performance of a municipality. The *economic classification* helps create key ratios and balances. The *functional classification* reflects how the municipality finances public functions. This classification helps plan functions and communicate achievements with citizens or other stakeholders (for example, how much was spent on schools, roads, water, or culture).

Current expenditures (*recurrent expenditures*) constitute the *current budget*. These expenditures include costs of regular services and operation of the municipality and are also called *operating expenditures*. In fact, two cost items do not come from operation: interest and borrowing costs; they make the difference between operating and current expenditures. Some analysis requires calculating operating expenditures separately, which can be easily completed from this basic expenditure table by excluding line number 3 in table 3.3.

Capital expenditures and *financing* together represent *capital budget expenditures*. Capital expenditures include expenses spent for developing infrastructure or other capital costs, such as capital transfers to municipal entities. *Current* and *capital* expenditures should be clearly distinguished, even if the country's accounting forms do not make such difference. Usually, expenditures are considered *capital* expenditure when they contribute to expand the public assets of the municipality.

Financing includes expenditures associated with financial transactions, namely debt principal repayment or purchasing of financial assets. These are both inherent parts of the capital budget, because the loan proceeds are in-advance financing of assets from external sources that are internalized by the repayment of the principal. Municipalities may also purchase financial assets (bonds, treasury bills, or shares) to set aside funds for future use with gains above regular bank deposits. These investments should be accounted for in the capital budget because they are not related to operations and are a form of assets.

Classification of current expenditures is self-explanatory, but the explanation below provides some quick guidance:

- *Labor costs* include not only salaries for regular staff and wages for other paid workers but also the taxes and levies the municipality may be obliged to pay on labor costs. The classification is plain, easy, and available in most cases. One issue deserves attention though, namely that development projects also include labor costs besides the cost of material, machinery, or energy. Those labor costs, however, should be counted under the development or infrastructure item, so this labor is part of the projects thus classified as capital expenditures and should be accounted for as part of the capital budget expenses. The reason behind this classification is that these labor costs are part of the investments: they are one-time, nonrecurrent costs. Investments completed by and paid out to contractors are naturally accounted for as capital expenditures regardless of the fact that cost plans include labor costs. Some investments are completed by a unit of the municipality like the department of public

Table 3.3 MFSA Core Financial Database—Expenditures (ShS million)

	Year 1	Year 2	Year 3	Year 4	Year 5
	Actual	Actual	Actual	Actual	Actual
Total expenditures	**60,088**	**62,546**	**70,872**	**75,848**	**84,702**
I Current expenditures	**33,818**	**38,286**	**41,883**	**46,060**	**59,105**
1 Labor (wages,salaries,taxes and charges)	6,592	7,635	8,141	9,075	10,034
– Administrative staff					
– Technical,service,and other staff					
2 Goods and services	13,008	14,151	14,199	16,209	18,984
– Office supply	0	0	0	0	0
– Electricity	0	0	0	0	0
– Fuel and gas	0	0	0	0	0
– Repair and maintenance	2,956	3,234	2,813	3,472	3,940
– Other goods and services	10,052	10,917	11,386	12,737	15,044
3 Interest and borrowing costs	321	502	695	1,450	2,212
4 Current subsidies to service entities	7,606	6,023	9,134	8,612	11,242
5 Current grants and transfers	3,128	5,466	4,582	5,549	11,577
6 Social care/welfare support	1,946	3,274	3,827	3,774	3,492
7 Other current expenditures	1,217	1,236	1,305	1,392	1,563
II Capital expenditures	**25,845**	**23,770**	**28,222**	**29,100**	**22,614**
1 Purchase/development of assets/ infrastructure	18,901	21,005	24,040	26,903	20,584
2 Capital subsidies to PU/PUC	3,437	1,491	3,207	1,295	987
3 Capital transfers to other level of government	3,507	1,275	974	902	1,043
4 Investments or lending	0	0	0	0	0
III Financing	**425**	**490**	**768**	**687**	**2,982**
1 Debt principal repayment	425	490	768	687	2,982
2 Purchase of financial assets					
IV Balance total with loan proceeds	**2,867**	**–3,812**	**–2,741**	**–2,337**	**–4,452**
Planned total expenditures (initial plan)	60,000	65,000	70,000	75,000	80,000
Actual/Plan variations (%)	100.1	96.2	101.2	101.1	105.9

Note: MFSA = Municipal Finances Self-Assessment; PU/PUC = public utility/public utility company; ShS (shillings) is a notional name of the currency of the sample city.

works that may complete new roads, new buildings, or other structures. These projects should be and often are approached as projects with dedicated budget, and hence the total costs of material and labor together should be accounted for as capital investment in the capital budget. Finally, separating the labor costs for administrative staff and direct staff of services provides for useful insight about the cost of labor. A high share of administrative staff costs may signal careless hiring of those staff.

- *Cost of goods and services* is often the single largest item among the expenditures, because municipal services require procurement of a large volume of goods or services. It is both useful and important to account the four main expenditure subcategories clearly as follows: office supply, electricity, fuel and gas, and repair and maintenance (R&M), and then account all the rest under "other goods and services." MFSA users may add more sublines to capture large expenditure items such as telecommunications or travel if those appear to be substantial. This classification also focuses on goods and services associated with municipal functions. It is better to exclude goods and services used under investment projects—for example, material, machinery, or transport or construction services that are part of the investment projects' budgets.

  Under *goods and services,* R&M is part of the operating expenditures that deserve attention. There are two main challenges: (1) R&M activities also require procurement of goods or services, but it is vital to account these activities as independent projects and account the required goods and services under the R&M rather than among general goods or services; and (2) R&M activities inherently overlap with investments in two ways. First, R&M may be accounted for as investments because of unclear accounting guidelines or procedures. Second, although the municipality receives development grants, R&M is assumed to be financed from the operating budget. There is even a third reason, namely that R&M is often postponed/deferred for several years and eventually can be corrected only with a major investment. For instance, a road may deteriorate so much that simple repair of potholes would be more expensive than rebuilding the road.

- *Interest and borrowing costs* are straightforward categories. Users need to make sure to account for all interest and additional charges paid for loans or other liabilities. Borrowing costs are not interest; instead they may occur during preparation of a new loan or other debt instrument paid to the agent who structures the debt. These costs can be substantial, so it is important to account for them in this line item.

- *Current subsidies to service entities* include any kinds of financial support the municipality may provide for entities to help operation by subsidizing the tariffs or service charges in support of specific beneficiary groups or more general customers. Subsidies could be defined as a share of tariff, as a general annual support in lieu of tariffs, or as a transfer to fill the budget gap, often understood as a result of low tariffs. All kinds of operating support linked to tariffs, fees, or charges should be accounted here, regardless of the fact that some of these may not be called or accounted for under the line of subsidies. Table 3.3 illustrates that the sample city spends a very substantial amount as current subsidies to municipal entities or other subordinated entities.

- *Current grants and transfers* include various forms of support provided without connections to the tariffs, fees, or charges (investments' support should be in the capital budget!). The support may be formalized as a performance grant, could be ad hoc to support a specific action or general annual allotment, or could be a grant to cover entities' deficit at the end of the fiscal year (bad practice, but should be clearly accounted in the MFSA). Some transfers are provided as payment to a third party, often to pay an electricity company, on behalf of service entities that have no budget to pay. MFSA users should reclassify these kinds of support and account these as grants or transfers to entities, instead of hiding them among "goods and services."

- *Social care/welfare support* includes various items the municipality may provide to specific disadvantaged groups as subsidies and social assistance programs (cash to the poorest of the poor, cash or food allowance for school attendance, support to people with disabilities or to vulnerable minorities, and so on). These supports can be voluntary actions by a municipality or funded by the central government via earmarked grants.

- *Other current expenditures*: There are many small other current expenditures, and we recommend reporting them together under the *Other* category not only to simplify the financial database but also to ensure accounting accuracy (that is, not to leave out any expenses). However, should current expenditures appear to be a substantial amount (for example, over 10 percent of total expenditures), the classification of entries deserves revision and entries reclassified or a new line opened to ensure clarity of uses of money and to reduce the share of "other" expenditures to a small residual amount.

Capital budget expenditures include direct capital expenditures and financing items that together should be financed from the capital budget (table 3.4 is an excerpt from the expenditure budget to help close correspondence between the budget and the issues discussed below).

- *Purchase or development of physical assets or infrastructure* is the most important line and often the single most significant part of the capital budget. This category should include

Table 3.4   Capital Budget Expenditures (*ShS million*)

II Capital expenditures	25,845
1 Purchase/development of assets/ infrastructure	18,901
2 Capital subsidies to PU/PUC	3,437
3 Capital transfers to other level of government	3,507
4 Investments or lending	0
III Financing	**425**
1 Debt principal repayment	425
2 Purchase of financial assets	0

Note: PU/PUC = public utility/public utility company; ShS (shillings) is a notional name of the currency of the sample city.

all kinds of transactions that constitute capital development or physical asset acquisition, including but not limited to purchasing land, buildings, and equipment; developing land (offsite and onsite land development); and developing buildings. As noted earlier, there is a fine line between development of infrastructure and R&M of assets. MFSA users can generally follow the regular accounting classifications unless outstanding items occur. A useful technical classification option to follow is that R&M on existing assets should be the default classification option and should be accounted for as current expenditure. In contrast, major rehabilitation of roads, buildings, or equipment that aims to substantially restore or even increase the value (new engine to a truck, major rehabilitation of an office building typically with upgrading) and expand the useful life of the assets should be accounted for as investment. Because major rehabilitations are often made under specific projects with a dedicated project budget, they are easy to identify.

- *Capital subsidies to public utilities (PUs) or public utility companies (PUCs)* are special forms of municipal investments justified by legal arrangements, namely if some municipal services are rendered by legally independent entities outside the municipal budget. Municipalities often provide these PUs/PUCs with capital subsidies to expand networks or otherwise develop the municipal services and reduce the burden of customers (that is, to reduce the fees or charges the PUC would need if investment were financed from its revenues) and support affordability. These subsidies are indirect investments made on behalf of the municipality, so they should be accounted for in the capital budget. Accounting for these subsidies in capital budgets also improves comparability of MFSA financial reports across municipalities or countries, because services (such as solid waste or water) rendered directly under municipal departments are more comparable to those (waste or water) services that are rendered by legally independent entities. Table 3.4 shows that the sample city uses a substantial part of the capital budget for providing PUCs with capital subsidies (also known as capital expenditure, or CAPEX, subsidies).

In-kind support to PUCs could be considered as subsidies in cases when the municipality pays for infrastructure (for example, by extending the water network) and then hands over the assets after project completion. Such investments are accounted for under the line of purchase/development of assets/infrastructure. This support is equivalent to capital subsidies from the perspective of the municipality, but it will be accounted for only in the balance sheet of the PUC/water entity without having effects on its cash flow. In contrast, a municipality may provide subsidy in the form of land that has no effect on the municipality's cash-based budget; rather it should be accounted for in the asset register and on the balance sheet (if the latter is prepared). This is a delicate issue from the MFSA perspective because,

on one hand, this is a capital subsidy, but, on the other hand, it is not a cash transaction by the municipality. Thus, for consistency purposes, we recommend reflecting transfers of already-owned physical assets only in the asset supplementary tables of MFSA, if those transfers are not paired with financial transactions (land, building, equipment).

- *Capital transfers to other levels of government* are transactions in which funds for capital investments are transferred to either lower or higher government tiers from a municipality. Transfers can move up to county or province governments to contribute to specific joint investment projects, or down to districts, towns, villages, or wards that operate somewhat independently under a municipality. The downward transfers are often parts of incentive-based supports in which part of a project is financed by the municipality, whereas the other part is financed, and the project is executed, by the lower governing tier. Should these kinds of transfers be irrelevant in a municipality, the subject line should be left empty or filled with zeros.

- *Investment or lending* may include actions when a municipality forms a joint venture with another municipality or a private partner and invests into a joint company the agreed share of capital. Investment may be combined with lending to the same entity under conditions to turn the loan to capital if repayment fails according to the agreed time and conditions (subordinated loan). Municipalities may lend money to municipal companies instead of providing them with subsidy or investments. These loans should be accounted for in this line. Municipalities may lend money to staff such as for housing loans. In short, all of these forms of expenditures should be accounted for in the capital budget.

This also implies that decisions in comparing options between investments and lending, between lending and joint venture, or between company A and company B should be made using the analysis of the net present value of these investments.

Financing that includes repayment of debt principal and a financial investment is also an important part of the capital budget and can turn out to be very substantial in specific years.

- *Debt repayment* is typically considered a small amount; however, it can jump when various loans coincide, and repayment could become very substantial (30 percent or more of the capital budget in some year in the sample city, as we discuss later in the chapter). Likewise, a bond may provide a convenient amount of money the first year, requiring a moderate amount of expenditure by paying only the annual interest (coupon) for several years; but it may trigger a large balloon payment the last year when the municipality must repay the total volume of the principal amount by repurchasing the bond. Monitoring debt service expenditures, and particularly forecasting with realism the potential burden in the years ahead, is a vital part of managing the capital budget.

- *Financial investments* are justified by the fact that a municipality often needs reserves or may unintentionally generate extra income when an asset sale transaction results in income much greater than expected or greater than the volume of money needed in a particular year. Prudence demands that finance managers and mayors should not invest these resources immediately into physical assets, which will cause them to lose flexibility in future spending because it is far more difficult to transfer physical

assets than financial assets back into cash. Nevertheless, financial investments are investments and should always be compared with physical asset investment alternatives and should be accounted for in the capital budget.

Balance total with loan proceeds: This line is important to monitor and to ensure consistency between the MFSA financial table and the original/official financial reports of the municipality. Discrepancies between the two balances suggest entry or numeric errors; users might have failed to upload all due original data to the MFSA or might have misclassified some entries. We strongly advise users to double-check the entries and correct errors until these two balances (the city's original financial report and the MFSA Financial Database in tables 3.1 and 3.3) appear equivalent.

Supplementary Databases

The supplementary tables are particularly important for the MFSA because they provide key clarifying information and data to the cash-based budgets (for example, stock, and accrual items); they support financial projections, budget analysis, and planning; and they provide for critical links to the UA/SA (figure 3.3). These additional data also help cities communicate with stakeholders about the city's services, financial issues, and underpinning plans.

Finally, the set of supplementary tables also serves as a sort of bridge across the various accounting, budgeting, and financial reporting systems (for example, cash or accrual accounting). The supplementary tables support clear comparability of municipal financial situations across various municipalities and systems. MFSA users need to approach these tables flexibly to fit into the local situation. For instance, cities that are prohibited from borrowing or taking debt in any other form will not have the debt database, but the liabilities and arrears table that summarizes the unpaid or overdue bills remains critical for them. Cities may develop many more supportive tables, but the tables presented include the most important sources of supplementary data.

Actual/Plan Analysis

Objective: The objective is to analyze the quality and reliability of the budget and the quality of budget planning and execution by comparing the actual revenue and expenditure data by each budget line and identify areas that need attention and deserve corrective measures. These corrective measures will be outlined in the Action Plan, which constitutes the final step of the MFSA. This is why it is important to get it right.

Actual/Plan table: It is useful to generate a new table from the core Financial Database to monitor budget performance by comparing the budget actuals reported in the closing accounts of the fiscal year and the initial budget plans adopted at the beginning of a fiscal year. It is further advisable to monitor the actual/plan (A/P) ratio year by year and measure tendencies and areas of concerns. Using the MFSA

repeatedly year by year, it is advisable to fill out the *Plan* columns at the beginning of the fiscal year and add the *Actuals* only at the end of the fiscal year (see table 3.5). Some municipalities prepare similar tables but add also a column for "revised plans" or similar names. In this case the table's headings would include *Plan*, *Revised Plan*, and *Actual*. This is a very useful practice that provides for more insights about the budget planning and execution process. It is advisable, however, to use the initial plans from the beginning of the year for A/P analysis if the municipality wants to use only two columns: *Plan* and *Actual*.

A/P analysis: It is important to monitor the actual/plan performance (A/P % in table 3.6) not only for the total budget but also for each line and year by year, in order to identify the specific areas that cause deviations between plans and actuals. Improving budget reality by getting the total plans and actuals closer together can only be done by corrective measures on the areas that cause the main differences between the total plans and total actuals. Table 3.6 shows that the sample city has low predictability in planning conditional and

Table 3.5 **Supplementary Database Actual/Plan Analysis** *(ShS million)*

	Year 1		
	Plan	**Actual**	**A/P%**
Total revenues	**60,000**	**62,955**	104.9
I Current revenues	**42,400**	**41,999**	99.1
Revenues from central/higher government	**30,200**	**30,300**	100.3
1 Shared taxes	23,000	24,053	104.6
2 Unconditional operation transfers	7,000	6,192	88.5
3 Conditional/earmarked operation transfers	200	55	27.4
Own current revenues	**12,200**	**11,700**	**95.9**
1 Local taxes and levies	**4,600**	**4,235**	92.1
Property tax	3,000	2,688	89.6
Business tax	1,500	1,443	96.2
Other local taxes	100	104	103.8

Note: A/P = actual/plan; ShS (shillings) is a notional name of the currency of the sample city.

Table 3.6 Actual/Plan Analysis Measured by Average Absolute Deviation

	Year 1 A/P%	Year 2 A/P%	Year 3 A/P%	Year 4 A/P%	Year 5 A/P%	Average absolute deviation from 100%
Total revenues	104.9	90.4	97.3	98.0	100.3	3.9
I Current revenues	99.1	85.6	99.7	98.1	102.0	3.9
Revenues from central/higher government	100.3	83.3	91.6	101.5	104.3	6.2
1 Shared taxes	104.6	92.7	94.8	107.7	118.8	8.7
2 Unconditional operation transfers	88.5	43.5	76.9	71.6	0	43.9
3 Conditonal/earmarked operation transfers	27.4	147.0	59.4	30.6	70.6	51.8
Own current revenues	95.9	89.5	110.9	94.1	99.3	6.4
1 Local taxes and levies	92.1	86.0	88.7	100.6	95.7	7.6
Property tax	89.6	89.1	99.5	99.2	91.5	6.2
Business tax	96.2	79.5	84.4	118.1	104.9	12.6
Other local taxes	103.8	107.9	24.3	26.0	66.1	39.1
2 Fees and charges	104.0	107.0	132.6	98.1	123.6	13.8
Fees on urban services (city fee, utility charges)	104.5	107.7	116.0	105.8	123.8	11.6
Licenses, permits, fines, other	93.3	79.1	465.4	21.6	120.0	98.3
3 Revenues from assets	101.4	85.2	132.1	85.6	84.8	15.6
Interests received	105.7	96.3	89.5	92.6	108.0	7.1
Revenues from leasing/ renting assets	103.4	85.3	135.9	86.1	84.5	16.7
Other revenues	0	0	0	0	0	0
4 Revenue from municipal enterprises	0	0	86.8	113.1	45.9	56.1
Dividends, profit shares	0	0	95.5	114.2	46.4	54.5
Cash transfers received from enterprises	0	0	0	0	0	0
5 Other revenues	0	0	0	0	0	0
II Capital revenues without loans and reserves	114.0	86.9	83.1	73.1	87.7	16.7
Capital grants from central/ higher government	0	0	0	289.8	161.9	110.3
Own capital revenues	113.9	86.5	80.5	71.2	86.3	17.9
Proceeds from sale of assets	177.4	64.5	54.6	44.3	1353.7	293.5
Land development fee	110.4	88.9	83.3	74.1	70.1	18.8
Participation of firms and individuals	169.1	69.4	59.2	48.2	120.5	42.5

continued next page

Table 3.6 Continued

	Year 1 A/P%	Year 2 A/P%	Year 3 A/P%	Year 4 A/P%	Year 5 A/P%	Average absolute deviation from 100%
Donations/grants from persons or nongovernment	319.8	180.1	730.3	171.0	9.6	218.3
III Financing proceeds from reserves and debt	127.9	137.3	101.9	125.5	100.3	18.6
Surplus or cash reserves from previous year	100.0	106.7	0	0	0	61.3
Sale of financial assets	0	0	0	0	0	0
Proceeds from domestic loans and bonds	0	176.5	92.4	127.3	86.3	45.0
Proceeds from foreign borrowing	226.6	163.0	111.5	125.0	102.7	45.7

Note: Values highlighted in yellow show extremely high deviation. A/P = actual/plan.

unconditional transfers, but also in planning property tax collection (and because of that planning local taxes and levies), because the actual figures are beyond the ± 5 percent range of plans.

Absolute deviation: The deviation of total revenues from 100 percent is very low (3.9 percent), which suggests good planning and revenue management practices in total volumes (TD5 in appendix B). However, table 3.6 shows that some revenue sources (highlighted) show extremely high deviation calculated as five-year averages (for example, proceeds from sale of assets, capital grants from higher government, and licenses and permits). Because these are five-year average deviations, the city should consider them as persistent and serious planning problems that deserve attention and may trigger corrective measures. The table also suggests that the city uses asset sales to fill revenue gaps, which results in high volatility of asset sales. This could be a rational behavior, but this high deviation also suggests multiple weaknesses in revenue and expenditure planning.

Publishing of the planned figures side by side with the actual and calculating the A/P ratios are mandatory in many countries. Municipalities do it, although they often apply some cosmetics, that is, they publish a revised budget with figures close to the actual and then calculate A/P ratios from the revised budget. This practice compromises the main objective of the A/P analysis because the real issue is how good the initial revenue and expenditures plans are when compared to the final closing accounts. Differences between plans and actuals may occur for various reasons, including inflation and natural disasters; but more often bad planning, budgeting, or accounting practices are the real underlying causes.

Bad or questionable practices: Some municipalities opt to hide bad practices, such as if the revenue and expenditure sides of the budget are prepared independently and remain disconnected till the very last phase of the budgeting process. Officers then put artificial revenue figures, like unspecified "other" revenues, land sale, or unrealistic tax or fee revenues (for example, inflated by plans to collect huge old arrears), to formally balance the budget. They do this because the expenditure side is more sensitive: cutting expenditures down to the level of conservative revenue budget would require cutting the budget of various entities or departments. This practice might lead to another bad practice, namely to allow spending according to the initial budget plans despite the fact that the "inflated" revenue figures become apparently unrealistic during the year and the growing gap between revenues and expenditures can only be financed by unpaid expenses (arrears) often rolled over year on year.

Good practices: Several elements of good practices include the following: (1) make the A/P analysis honestly and provide the best information to the council, mayor, and respective departments; (2) avoid cosmetics and include the initial plans or initial, revised, and actual results side by side; (3) identify areas of persistent deviation between plans and actuals; and (4) propose corrective measures to improve planning reality.

Expenditures by Functions

Objective: The objective is to measure and monitor over time the composition of the functional classes of expenditures and use results for planning, budgeting, and communicating the coverage and costs of municipal services and functions.

Expenditures by functions: This supplementary table is very important, because it helps monitor the municipality's performance on various services and public functions. Table 3.7 is based on the Classification of Functions of Governments (COFOG) initiated by the United Nations and widely used by the Organisation for Economic Co-operation and Development, International Monetary Fund, and World Bank (IMF 2014; OECD 2011). The MFSA has introduced one remarkable difference in the grouping of expenditures, namely, that the category of *Commercial services* in

this table is limited to the services that are beyond the mandatory local government functions and therefore can be rendered by private entities. Some COFOG classifications name all fee-based services (water, solid waste) also as "commercial." We believe the structure in table 3.7 better serves municipal planning and MFSA analysis.

Structuring data as in table 3.7 is a powerful way to communicate results and plans with citizens or other major stakeholders of a municipality, because the categories are self-explanatory and people easily understand them. Current and capital expenditures should be accounted together in this classification to show the total funds the municipality has spent on the functional areas. Many municipalities use financial reports with this functional classification. It is a bigger challenge but doable if users need to collect the respective expenditure items from various ledgers or municipal units to consolidate expenditures by these functions and services. The results are quite useful for planning, comparison, control, and communication purposes. Finally, it is worth mentioning that COFOG classification makes it difficult to establish various balances or conduct ratio analysis and assess the financial health of the municipality. In contrast, the economic classification used in the core Financial Database is more suitable for financial analysis and assessment of financial health issues.

Analysis of the functional classification of expenditures is useful for measuring the service performance over time and across municipalities within the same country with some level of caution. Intergovernmental fiscal systems show great differences and variations depending on the level of decentralization and allocation of functions across government tiers. For instance, social services, especially education and health, are central government functions in many countries. Meanwhile, within the same country, some urban services

Table 3.7 Expenditures by Functions

	Year 1	Year 2	Year 3	Year 4	Year 5
	Actual	Actual	Actual	Actual	Actual
General administration					
Urban services					
Roads and drainage					
Public transport					
Water and wastewater					
Solid waste					
Street lighting					
Fire protection					
Police, crime prevention					
Environmental protection					
Social services					
Health					
Education					
Culture and religion					
Housing					
Recreation and sport					
Social welfare					
Commercial services					
Parking					
Markets					
Commercial places					
Land development					
Local economic development					
Total expenditures					

Source: Based on OECD 2011.

can be rendered by independent entities or even by private providers outside the municipal budget in one city and by the municipality and inside the budget in another city. Such differences are often greater and more apparent across countries. Analyzing the share of expenditures spent on various functions, and particularly comparing years and measuring trends with annual growth indexes, is one important way to measure the municipalities' performances and inform strategy decisions. Again, the UA/SA will help clarify the expenditures functions and mediate prioritization of expenditures.

Consolidated reports on services can also be generated in another similar table in which the expenditures are consolidated from all kinds of service providers in the municipal jurisdiction. The consolidated expenditures report would be very useful to build a more realistic picture on the level, coverage, and costs of public services in the municipality's jurisdiction. Consolidation means including all kinds of service providers but netting out cross-transactions, like subsidies and transfers the municipality has provided to or received from any of these entities to avoid double accounting. Consolidation should cover direct municipal expenditures, expenditures by independent (off-budget) municipal entities (such as water, waste management, or transport companies), service entities from higher government tiers (national or regional water company owned by the higher tiers of governments), and even private providers.

Debt Database

Objective: The objective is to draw a complete and consistent picture of the municipal debts, and to monitor, plan ahead, and consolidate the annual payments on principal and interest and the outstanding debt liabilities. A good debt database supports medium- to long-term planning, budget planning, and execution by providing reliable data for policy decisions.

Debt database: This database may include two related tables: the summary list of debts (table 3.8) and the aging list of debt (table 3.9). These tables can be filled out from the various debt documents (such as loan agreements and any supplementary document like subsequent modification of loan terms and conditions). Municipalities do have all these data, but they may not maintain and update a database similar to the suggested tables for several reasons, including lack of computerized financial management system and/or lack of a dedicated debt management team. Therefore, these supplementary tables are useful instruments because they improve debt management by clearly and consistently recording the true data on debts, regardless of whether users aim to fill them out for the purpose of an MFSA analysis or to improve and institutionalize a good debt database.

The summary list of debts (table 3.8) is useful for drawing a picture of the various debt forms, sources, and main conditions such as loans from higher government tiers (national/central, provincial, or county); loans from commercial banks; municipal bonds; and indications of short-term debt facilities if they are contracted (Freire 2014). These tables should be filled out from the loan agreements and other important documents and should capture all key terms and conditions until the final repayment of a particular debt item.

The aging list of debt table summarizes each debt instrument (loan, bond) over the years from the first disbursement year to the final repayment. Table 3.9 provides an example of an aging list of loans with detailed data on outstanding principal at the end of the year, loan amortization (principal repayment installments by year and interest payments by year), actual figures between year 1 and year 5, and forecasted figures five years ahead to year 10. It is advisable to expand the debt amortization table until the end of the last year of each loan (table 3.9 is shortened to year 10 for simplicity). Finally, users should reconcile the actual year figures of this table (the total debt, total principal amortization, and interest paid) with respective accounting or financial reports of the municipality, and they should also ensure harmony with the *Finance* section of the core Financial Database. The table also needs specific or annual updates, because the effective repayment of debts may occur differently from the original loan agreement because of either faster or delayed payment of some dues. The table may include a line to reflect the actual disbursement of loans yearly, for control and consistency purposes.

Filling out the aging list of debt table: The best rules to follow include (1) entering actual figures by using data from real transactions and accounting ledgers (not from loan agreements), because actual principal or interest payments may differ from the loan agreement; (2) forecasting

Table 3.8 Summary List of Debts and Terms (ShS million)

List of debts	Bank or institute	Year of the loan subscription	Initial amount	Duration	Currency	Maturity	Grace period	Interest rate (fixed, variable)	Rate %
1 Loan/onlending from central government	IBRD	2001	7,500	18 year	local	2019	5 year	Fixed	4.25
	ADB	2013	11,000	20 year	local	2033	3 year	Fixed	3.00
2 Direct loans									
– Commercial bank	Credit Bank	2011	4,500	8 year	local	2019	2 year	Floating	13.8
– State development bank, municipal fund									
3 Municipal bond									
Short-term debt									
1 Treasury facility from state									
2 Loan/overdraft from commercial bank									

Note: ADB = Asian Development Bank; IBRD = International Bank for Reconstruction and Development (World Bank); ShS (shillings) is a notional name of the currency of the sample city.

Table 3.9 Aging List of Debt (ShS million)

Items	Conditions	Year 1	Year 2	Year 3	Year 4	Year 5	Year 6	Year 7	Year 8	Year 9	Year 10
		Actual	Actual	Actual	Actual	Actual	Projected				
1 IBRD Water development 2001–2018	Fixed 4.75%										
– Outstanding		**3,045**	**3,580**	**3,667**	**3,091**	**2,822**	**2,216**	**1,696**	**1,084**	**1,096**	**1,108**
– Principal repayment		425	490	537	531	591	591	622	636	643	650
– Interest charge		151	190	157	150	159	102	72	49	37	28
2 ADB Road development 2013–2033	Fixed 3.00%										
– Outstanding						**1,670**	**3,503**	**10,615**	**10,467**	**10,206**	**9,678**
– Principal repayment						0	0	0	367	371	350
– Interest charge						0	45	203	318	272	268
Credit Bank (domestic)											
3 Markets/Malls 2011–2019	Floating rate 13.8%										
– Outstanding				**3,757**	**4,523**	**3,733**	**2,828**	**1,924**	**1,019**	**115**	**13**
– Principal repayment				0	0	790	905	905	905	102	13
– Interest charge				0	517	507	449	328	214	100	14
Several loan lines are ommitted from display for simplicity											
Total											
– Outstanding debt		**8,599**	**13,820**	**24,705**	**37,320**	**45,295**	**47,428**	**55,215**	**51,229**	**49,181**	**47,614**
– **Principal repayment**		**425**	**490**	**768**	**687**	**2,982**	**4,084**	**4,423**	**5,039**	**5,309**	**7,198**
– **Interest charge**		**321**	**502**	**695**	**1,450**	**2,212**	**2,144**	**2,213**	**2,187**	**1,849**	**1,661**
Debt service		**746**	**992**	**1,464**	**2,138**	**5,194**	**6,228**	**6,636**	**7,226**	**7,158**	**8,859**
Borrowing disbursement		3,197	5,645	11,375	13,383	8,662	5,115	11,871	438	2,991	3,741

Note: ADB = Asian Development Bank; IBRD = International Bank for Reconstruction and Development (World Bank); ShS (shillings) is a notional name of the currency of the sample city.

payments five years ahead based on loan agreement data, or covering the entire debt amortization period, using data from *loan agreements* (maybe 10–15 or 20 years); (3) noticing that loans borrowed from foreign currency origins (such as Asian Development Bank and World Bank) may show moving interest payments despite fixed rates because of exchange rate fluctuation of local currency; (4) being aware that loans with floating interests (domestic bank loan in table 3.9) show changing rates in actual figures; (5) noting, as signaled by table 3.9, that the volume of interest payments in the beginning years depends mutually on the gradual disbursement of the loan and the repayment of the principals, and on the grace period if any; and (6) including bonds in the debt table and typically including the annual interest payments (coupon) until the last year when the total principal amount becomes due and should be planned and accounted for (sample city did not issue a bond).

Forecasting of debt service five years ahead should be based on loan agreements that may include annuity or debt amortization information and list of installments. This means that *debt forecasting should not use trend or other simple calculations of annual growth of debt stock or debt payments* (as opposed to other forecasts in MFSA). Forecasting interest payments ahead with fixed rates can be calculated using the forecasted debt stock and repayments, if they are not included in the loan agreement. Forecasting interest charges on floating rate loans can be done using forecasted benchmark rates from the central bank or referred international capital market information. Forecasting floating interest rates and payments should be revised annually to improve accuracy and capture changing trends on floating rates.

Capital Investment Plan

Objective: The overarching objective of developing a capital investment plan (CIP) is to put the municipality's development plans into a medium-term perspective, that is, to move away from shortsighted annual planning (a common practice in cities in the developing world) to a systematic analysis of options and finances and setting plans for the medium term. The objective of using CIP in MFSA is to support medium-term planning, investment financing, and communication with stakeholders, and to inform budgeting on capital investments for the coming fiscal years, embedded in a medium-term vision or plan.

Capital investment plan (also known as capital improvement plan): CIPs have become best-practice instruments in well-run cities. In many cities, however, CIPs remain an unachievable requirement imposed by central governments to local governments that do not have the capacity or tradition of interdepartmental coordination to prepare a meaningful and realistic CIP. The CIP is based on strong (and often absent) cooperation and connection between the technical departments in charge of infrastructure investments and service delivery and the planning, budget, and finance departments. It is also subject to political pressure to include the mayor's agenda (see Urban Audit/Self-Assessment). It is therefore recommended that cities carry out the UA/SA, which will provide an excellent building block and platform to develop a CIP.

As described in chapter 1, the CIP includes a procedure that starts with creating an initial list of possible projects received from department proposals; evaluation of the preliminary salient project features (technical, social, and financial); engaging in detailed discussions with stakeholders; and adoption of a scoring and selection procedure to create a short list of priority projects from the initial list (Kaganova 2011). The CIP may include a substantial amount of supporting documentation such as maps and pictures, simple technical summaries, and initial financial estimates. A CIP is typically prepared for a three- to five-year time horizon on a rolling basis; this means that, every year, there should be a final review and approval of the selected projects for the upcoming year. These projects go to the budget after the due approval process during budgeting and move out from the CIP; another year is then added to the scope of the revised CIP to cover five years ahead again (table 3.10).

The added value of going through the process of a UA/SA process can be summarized as follows: (1) instead of having a list of "atomized projects," the UA/SA will lead to a citywide municipal investment program taking into account the many specificities of the city's urbanization patterns; (2) the Priority Investment Program (PIP) derived from the UA/SA will also include a maintenance and a rehabilitation component that pays attention to the financing needs of the existing stock as much as of the new investments needs; (3) the map-based process of the UA/SA ensures that the right investments go to the right location; and (4) the consultation, validation, vetting, screening, and prioritization of the PIP is such that it will ensure both that investment decisions have been widely and rigorously vetted and that implementation problems have been anticipated. Key questions behind investment prioritization, as stated in chapter 2, remain the following: Are we doing things right? Are we doing the right things?

Table 3.10 shows a *possible* financial summary of a CIP report that provides for an easy direct link to the budgeting and financial planning processes also important in the MFSA. A CIP is good if the stakeholders strongly own and support it, but the quality of the financing plans and projections determines its value and usefulness. A plan with vague financing ideas is not a plan; it is a wish list. Lacking CIP data and practices, MFSA

users may prepare a simpler list of projects structured into three categories: ongoing, well prepared, and preliminary; but creating a CIP table is preferable. Again, the UA/SA can greatly help this process (see table 2.15 in chapter 2).

Tax Performance Database
Objective: The objective of this database is to monitor and forecast tax revenues and measure tax performance by major tax revenue sources, and then eventually support informed decisions for corrective measures (some will be outlined and addressed in the MFSA Action Plan).

The tax performance database (table 3.11) is one possible supplementary table outside the budget or regular mandatory financial reports. Its content reflects general practices, but MFSA users might include different taxes to reflect the context of their own city. The adequate list should include local taxes preferably in order of significance (volume of generated revenues), which depends on the intergovernmental fiscal relations' revenue assignments, the national tax legislation, and most important the quality of local revenue collection systems, procedures, and actions. This table is a very simplified summary of tax performances, and MFSA users may use their own systems if they have better and more detailed tax registers and reports that provide a solid basis for measuring tax performance and forecasting future tax revenues.

More detailed taxation information would be useful but would require substantial analysis and data collection, which can be done as self-standing actions periodically (every five years, for instance). Specific investigations may include measuring tax potential by calculating the potential tax revenues if all tax payers were captured in the tax base; measuring the scope of tax exemptions and the magnitude of revenue losses they cause; analyzing the effectiveness of

Table 3.10 Capital Investment Plan Summary, Year 6–Year 10 (ShS million)

No.	Project name/description	Status	Budgeted Year 5	CIP Expenditure Plan					Total by projects
				Year 6	Year 7	Year 8	Year 9	Year 10	
1	Road	Ongoing	13,584	6,000	3,000	3,000	3,000	3,000	18,000
2	Water extension and connection	Ongoing	4,000		5,000	4,000	4,000	3,000	16,000
3	Compactor trucks/vehicle	Plan approved and budgeted		5,000					5,000
4	Shopping arcade	Plan approved and budgeted	3,000	4,000	3,000				7,000
5	Housing development	Draft plans			2,000	2,000	2,000	2,000	8,000
6	Water network development	CAPEX subsidy to water PUC	987		1,000	1,000	1,000	1,000	4,000
7	Support districts and wards	Transfers for roads	1,043		1,000	1,000	1,000	1,000	4,000
8	Fleet expansion	Implemented by the transport PUC	3,000	3,000	2,000				5,000
9	**Total expenditures**		**25,614**	**18,000**	**17,000**	**11,000**	**11,000**	**10,000**	**67,000**
10	**Source of financing**								
11	Budget own-source		15,268	11,500	7,000	7,500	7,500	7,500	41,000
12	Budget - Grants		324	1,500	1,000	1,500	1,500	500	6,000
13	Loan		7,022	2,000	7,000	1,000	1,000	1,000	12,000
14	PUCs fund		3,000	3,000	2,000				5,000
15	Private		–	0		1,000	1,000	1,000	3,000
16	**Total sources by years**		**25,614**	**18,000**	**17,000**	**11,000**	**11,000**	**10,000**	**67,000**
17	**Total budgeted expenditures**	Financed from budget	**22,614**	**15,000**	**15,000**	**10,000**	**10,000**	**9,000**	**59,000**

Note: CAPEX = capital expenditure; CIP = Capital Investment Plan; PUC = public utility company; ShS (shillings) is a notional name of the currency of the sample city.

Table 3.11 Tax Performance Database (*ShS million*)

	Year 1	Year 2	Year 3	Year 4	Year 5
I Property tax - households (Rate 6%)					
1 Tax base (amount billed)	1,526	1,650	1,800	2,000	2,200
2 Tax collected	1,075	1,248	1,592	1,786	1,903
3 Tax performance % (2/1)	**70.5**	**75.6**	**88.4**	**89.3**	**86.5**
4 Stock of arrears	3,000	3,200	3,300	3,250	3,120
5 Arrears collected	280	300	250	300	250
6 Tax performance % (5/4)	9.3	9.4	7.6	9.2	8.0
II Property tax - business entities (Rate 8%)					
7 Tax base (amount billed)	1,650	1,900	2,400	2,700	3,000
8 Tax collected	1,613	1,872	2,388	2,680	2,855
9 Tax performance % (7/6)	**97.7**	**98.5**	**99.5**	**99.2**	**95.2**
10 Stock of arrears	153	170	168	140	130
11 Arrears collected	25	30	40	30	30
12 Tax performance % (10/9)	16.3	17.6	23.8	21.4	23.1
III Business tax (Rate 3%)					
13 Tax base (amount billed)	1,500	1,600	2,150	3,000	3,200
14 Tax collected	1,443	1,590	2,111	2,952	3,146
15 Tax performance % (17/16)	**96.2**	**99.4**	**98.2**	**98.4**	**98.3**
16 Stock of arrears	40	43	33	42	30
17 Arrears collected	10	20	30	20	15
18 Total tax billed	**4,676**	**5,150**	**6,350**	**7,700**	**8,400**
19 Total tax collected	**4,131**	**4,710**	**6,090**	**7,418**	**7,905**
20 Stock of arrears total	**3,193**	**3,413**	**3,501**	**3,432**	**3,280**
21 Total arrears collected	**315**	**350**	**320**	**350**	**295**

Note: ShS (shillings) is a notional name of the currency of the sample city.

the billing and collection system; and exploring the magnitude of arrears and the effectiveness of systems and procedures to collect revenues from past tax arrears. These analyses may lead to the adoption of a Revenue Enhancement Program (Kopanyi 2015b). MFSA users will include some of these actions in the MFSA Action Plan.

Tax performance issues for users' attention: Table 3.11 is self-explanatory. Here are a few highlights:

• The scope of this table depends on the available information, and it is advisable to make substantial efforts to collect data

and populate this table accurately. The table may only include three to four taxes, provided that they cover a very substantial share, say about 75 percent of total local tax revenues.

• Separate property tax tables for households and for businesses are advisable, because taxes are often charged with different rates for households and businesses. The collection rate is often higher for businesses because tax collection is easier to enforce.

• Measure tax performance (collected/billed or levied) on the tax collection yields on an annual basis in order to signal any worsening of performance, because tax collection can deteriorate unless it is kept tight and disciplined, and unless sufficient resources are allocated to maintain or improve performance.

- Separate collection of taxes due in a year from collection of tax arrears that have been accumulated over years and some recovered during a year. It is important not to mix arrears collection with regular tax revenues to avoid showing sharp increase of tax revenues without any improvement in collection of regular taxes in a specific year.

- There are several other taxes related to properties, some charged as proportion of the property tax: stamp tax, inheritance tax, or transfer tax. The tax on transfer of properties can be significant, particularly if property tax collection is low, because transfer tax is easier to collect, because, in most countries, the transfer is not registered or approved until the transfer tax is paid. Thus, transfer tax can be reported as a single separate line item if it is substantial (it may, however, be a national tax). Should it be less important, then it can be reported together with the stamp duties and taxes on gifts and inheritances.

- Many municipalities collect business tax in various forms and under various names. Business tax can be levied on the basis of net turnover, business revenues, or labor charges, or in the form of block levies universal by size clusters of businesses (for example, ShS50,000 for small businesses, ShS200,000 for medium-sized businesses, and turnover-based for large businesses). A business license fee is one popular form of block levies collected from businesses annually; but, because the charge is far higher than an administrative fee, this levy is often a massive and substantial tax, not a fee. MFSA users are recommended to include the business license fee in the tax performance table either under the title of business tax or replacing the business tax title, if there is no other form of business tax collected locally.

- Rental income tax can be significant depending on the tax rate and the size of the local house rental market.

- Hotel tax, also known as tourism tax, is becoming increasingly popular for cities with strong tourism markets. This tax is easy to collect from hotels or other organized renters, and it is often collected by adding a small charge (one or two U.S. dollars or equivalent per day) to the guest's bill and paid into the municipal budget daily or weekly. The supporting argument is that tourists burden the cities with waste, water, traffic, and noise, and therefore need to contribute to improve the urban environment and better urban services.

- A communal tax or communal fee may be collected as a self-standing tax of one government layer or as a substitute for the property tax that is not collected for one reason or another. It has a simplified tax base that often resembles property taxation (and uses a basis like proxies of property values). Should your city levy some tax that has a different name but can be considered a variation of a communal tax or fee, then it is important to include it in the tax performance database.

- It is useful to attach comments to the taxes in order to help MFSA readers understand underlying issues and specific situations. Such information may include changes of tax rate, tax base (rules on taxable properties), tax value (revaluation), and exemptions, and change of rules for collecting arrears or tax penalties. Tax base or policy information is especially important when this table is used for projecting future revenues.

Liabilities, Arrears, and Cash Reserves

Objective: The objective of this supplementary table is to prepare a reliable and clear list of payments due by the local government and build a more realistic picture of the financial health of the municipality at the end of the fiscal year.

Financial liabilities and arrears: Financial liabilities include all kinds of bills or valid demands for payments left unpaid at the end of the fiscal year. A good part of these liabilities is unpaid for technical or legal reasons; for instance, because there are national regulations that allow time to verify and question validity or to complete due transactions, it is legal to pay within 45 days after receiving an invoice, bill, or demand note. Thus, liabilities that are unpaid but are within the country's legal payment limits are *regular liabilities* and are a natural part of business, whether municipalities or private firms pay, because a number of bills are received in the last months, days, and minutes of the fiscal year. These liabilities may not be paid within the same fiscal year, and thus remain unpaid liabilities. In contrast, liabilities that are overdue and whose delay for payment is beyond the legally accepted payment time period are considered overdue liabilities, often called *arrears*.

Financial liabilities: Table 3.12 includes a sample of unpaid dues to municipal entities, like water bills, wages or salary bonuses, leasing fees for cultural facilities, and so on. Typically, the largest volume of financial liabilities are payments due to contractors or suppliers, because the municipality receives their bills at the very end of the fiscal year. MFSA users may develop a more detailed list by indicating each liability separately under these main categories. In short, it should include all bills the city received from partners that were left unpaid at the end of the fiscal year.

It is important to supplement cash-based financial reports with a detailed list of liabilities (both regular and overdue) to build an honest picture of the financial health of the municipality. This is also mandatory in many developing countries; for instance, local governments in Kenya are supposed to maintain debtors and creditors ledgers, although none of them have obeyed this rule since devolution (Kopanyi and Muwonge, forthcoming). The table includes a line that indicates the cash reserves at the end of the fiscal year that can be filled out from bank deposit records. Table 3.12 shows that our sample city owns much less in cash reserves than the volume of liabilities

Table 3.12 Total Financial Liabilities—City Dues, End of the Fiscal Year (*ShS million*)

	Year 1	Year 2	Year 3	Year 4	Year 5
Public stakeholders (city dues to entities)					
– Water PUC	1,000	1,200	1,300	1,400	1,500
– Solid waste PUC	500	800	900	1,000	1,100
– Transport PUC	800	1,000	1,100	1,200	1,300
– Schools	50	–	120	140	160
– Kindergartens	10	10	10	10	10
– Culture or sport entities	500	550	600	650	700
Private contractors (city dues to private)	2,700	3,000	3,400	3,800	4,000
Labor (wages, salaries)	500	400	550	600	650
Total liabilities (city dues)	6,060	6,960	7,980	8,800	9,420
Cash reserves end of fiscal year	4,300	2,980	2,500	2,400	2,300

Note: PUC = public utility company; ShS (shillings) is a notional name of the currency of the sample city.

Table 3.13 Arrears—Overdue Financial Liabilities (ShS million)

	Year 5	Year 6	Year 7	Year 8	Year 9	Growth indexes (%)
Public stakeholders						
– Water PUC	200	220	260	230	210	1.2
– Solid waste PUC	50	50	50	50	50	0
– Transport PUC	100	110	120	130	140	8.8
– Schools						
– Kindergartens						
– Culture or sport entities						
Private contractors (city dues to private)	1,100	1,200	1,300	1,400	1,500	8.1
Labor arrears (wages, salaries)						0
Total arrears	1,450	1,580	1,730	1,810	1,900	7.0

Note: PUC = public utility company; ShS (shillings) is a notional name of the currency of the sample city.

(ShS2,300 vs. ShS9,420 in year 5) and this gap is growing. This gap signals financial management and financial health problems and suggests that the municipality regularly uses up for the current year a portion of the upcoming year's revenues, because the bills need to be paid in the first weeks or months of the coming fiscal year. It is also a signal of hidden budget deficits or imbalances.

Arrears: Arrears are parts of the total liabilities, but it is wise to indicate them separately. Table 3.13 shows a case when shortage of funds results in overdue liabilities in relation to private contractors or suppliers. Mayors or finance officers may put some bills in drawers and wait until the partners send reminders but do not act unless the partners strongly demand payments or unless there is sufficient cash in hand to pay. The appearance of arrears and their trends over time is an important signal of the municipality's self-discipline, financial health, and creditworthiness. Arrears of the sample city have grown at a 7 percent annual pace.

Accounting liabilities: Accrual accounting systems capture and reflect all kinds of liabilities, and account costs immediately at the time an invoice is received. In contrast, many

municipalities and the MFSA core financial tables follow cash-based accounting rules and do not include liabilities. Leaving liabilities unnoticed or unaccounted for severely distorts the financial picture of the municipality. The MFSA supplementary tables on liabilities are therefore vital for drawing a realistic picture of the financial health of a municipality, but also indicating liabilities for each creditor (detailed list of creditors).

Contingent liabilities: Contingent liabilities are liabilities that may be incurred by the municipality depending on the outcome of a future event such as the inability of the PUC to repay a loan (OECD 2006). Table 3.14 shows liabilities that do not appear in the form of bills or payment requests, at least not on a regular basis; rather, the liabilities are included in various contracts, such as loan agreements on the city's commitments to pay in case of the PUC's default. The table shows that the transport PUC borrowed ShS5,000 million with a guarantee by the municipality; the amount of the guarantee reduces year by year as the PUC repays a portion of the loan principal. A detailed assessment of the contingent liabilities is beyond the scope of the MFSA, but it is important to shed light on a number of lessons: (1) a municipality

Table 3.14   Contingent Liabilities (*ShS million*)

	Year 5	Year 6	Year 7	Year 8	Year 9
Public stakeholders					
– Water PUC paying electricity bill	900	800	800	700	700
– Solid waste PUC					
– Transport PUC loan guarantee	5,000	4,000	3,000	2,000	1,000
– Culture or sport entities					
Total contingent liabilities	5,900	4,800	3,800	2,700	1,700

Note: PUC = public utility company; ShS (shillings) is a notional name of the currency of the sample city.

may provide financial guarantee to support borrowing of various independent municipal entities like transport PUCs; and (2) a guarantee could be attached also to a supplier or developer's contract signed by the entity, but countersigned by the municipality as guarantor (CABRI 2017; Sirtaine 2014).

The guarantees are explicit contingent liabilities, but there also are often less obvious implicit liabilities. For instance, the municipality is generally responsible for all kinds of losses or dues (such as unpaid electricity bills) by the municipal entities (PUCs, schools, and so on) because it is the sole owner of these entities. This is an implicit liability that may trigger payments, but it is hard to quantify ahead without specific evidence and so need not be accounted in advance (OECD 2006). Table 3.14 includes payments based on historical data showing that the water company has been repeatedly failing to pay its electricity bills and that the municipality has repeatedly been stepping in on behalf of the water company; Turkish municipalities suffer from such burdens (Kopanyi 2015c). These payments might be accounted eventually (that is, when a guarantee is called or the electricity bill paid) among municipal expenditures as a simple purchase of goods and services, a transfer, a subsidy, or a loan, which obscures the real reasons behind them. It is useful to list the contingent liabilities in a supplementary table under the MFSA to further improve the

reality of the financial picture of the municipality. These contingent liabilities are not part of the regular financial reports, and calculating their present values requires further analysis, which is beyond the scope of MFSA.

Monthly Cash Balances
Objective: The objective of this supplementary table is to prepare a reliable and clear list of cash movements on a monthly basis, document liquidity, and document the payment ability of the municipality.

Monthly cash balances (table 3.15) are results of various movements and actions, including cash inflow from various revenue sources such as taxes, fees, and asset proceeds; but they also include disbursements of longer-term investment loans previously contracted, and cash received from short-term liquidity loans, overdrafts, or lines of credit. The MFSA user will need to enter cash receipts and cash payments, then calculate cumulative inflow, outflow, and finally the stock of cash at the end of the month and year.

The cumulative inflow should start with the cash reserves carried over from the previous fiscal year and should correspond to the bank reconciliations. Likewise, the stock of cash should be calculated within this table but also be reconciled with bank deposit reports, especially at the end of the fiscal year. Modern computerized financial management systems

Table 3.15 Monthly Cash Balance (*ShS million*)

Fiscal year 5	Cash receipts	Cash payments	Cumulative inflow	Cumulative outflow	Stock of cash
Carried over from previous fiscal year	0	0	1,234	0	1,234
January	3,456	2,560	4,690	2,560	2,130
February	2,800	4,600	7,490	7,160	330
March	4,300	3,800	11,790	10,960	830
April	5,120	4,330	16,910	15,290	1,620
May	4,500	4,100	21,410	19,390	2,020
June	7,230	4,500	28,640	23,890	4,750
July	3,800	4,700	32,440	28,590	3,850
August	3,300	4,500	35,740	33,090	2,650
September	4,600	4,700	40,340	37,790	2,550
October	2,500	3,900	42,840	41,690	1,150
November	3,800	3,950	46,640	45,640	1,000
December	5,300	4,000	51,940	49,640	2,300

Note: ShS (shillings) is a notional name of the currency of the sample city.

provide cash balance reports on a daily basis to help better cash management and support timely corrective actions. MFSA users can use those automated reports without generating this table. Short-term liquidity loans should be repaid during the same fiscal year; however, these loans or overdrafts may show negative balances at the end of the fiscal year that distort the cash balance report and should be reported as a memo item under the cash balances table.

Asset Investment and Maintenance
Objective: The objective of this supplementary table is to prepare a reliable and clear picture of the investment and maintenance expenditures by the main functional categories of assets to help planning, communication, and implementation of investments, maintenance, and management of assets. This table follows the COFOG classification introduced in table 3.7.

Asset management and asset registers: Asset management is a vital function of municipalities but is often poorly done, is fragmented, and lacks data, rules, and procedures. In many cases, cities do not know what they own or where. Various entities (such as transport, public works, health, or housing departments) perform some asset management functions, albeit often in silos and beyond the vision of the municipal finance officers who are supposed to oversee and consolidate asset management at the municipal level. Asset registers are often incomplete, unreliable, or nonexistent; and establishing and populating them would require enormous work and substantial investment (Kaganova and Kopanyi 2014, Kopanyi and Muwonge, forthcoming). Thus, MFSA users may benefit from well-developed asset management systems if those exist; if they do not exist, one should not underestimate the complexity of setting up an asset register with detailed technical, financial, and asset value data, which can obviously not be done as part of the MFSA process. The MFSA has a more moderate goal, namely to introduce a consolidated report on annual investments and asset maintenance expenditures. Should a municipality be also engaged in a UA/SA, the UA/SA may be the first step in identifying, locating, and registering municipal assets and developing reliable asset registers and inventories.

Asset investment and maintenance: Table 3.16 is a very simple template whose structure is based on the functional list of current expenditures (see table 3.7). Many of these data are also parts of the budget plans and execution reports, but they might be structured somewhat differently. The table includes a long list of functional areas; some of these may seem irrelevant if the respective functions are not local mandates of an MFSA user. Even in these cases, however, information about the investments by third parties (national government, companies, or private providers), if available, is useful to draw a detailed picture of the municipal service provision and to reflect the trends over time.

The table helps to calculate and document the breakdown of expenditures by main functional areas (urban, social, and commercial services or activities) or within each of these areas (for example, road, waste, or fire protection in urban services). The table is also a powerful instrument to communicate results and development plans and progress to the citizens, who are more interested in these issues than in specific financial ratios or balances.

There are often blurred lines between investments and R&M. MFSA users may follow one of the next two rules: (1) account everything the way it is presented in various asset ledgers or financial reports, or (2) request the various departments to more precisely identify what actions should be considered as investments and what as repair or maintenance. Users would then fill out table 3.16 accordingly. Should the table reflect an extreme situation, like very small amounts accounted as "maintenance" expenditures, the MFSA users

may ask partners to revise their data and more precisely define expenditures on maintenance. The low level of maintenance expenditure, however, may simply reflect the ground reality and poor maintenance practices.

Step 2: Historical Analysis

Step 2 focuses on the practice of historical analysis of data on municipal finances and services. Historical analysis is a very useful procedure and a big step in the right direction. Typically, national regulations do not stipulate historical analyses and, instead, often instruct municipalities to prepare set formats in a timely fashion and to submit to higher governments financial reports of the completed fiscal year only. In some cases, some national regulations and supporting documentation may include presenting results of the previous year or planned figures alongside the final outcomes ("Actuals") of a completed fiscal year without guiding or demanding an analysis beyond Actual/Plan variations.

The MFSA, by contrast, puts high emphasis not only on the analysis of results by looking at the composition of revenues and expenditures of the last year or comparing structures with other years, but also on drawing lessons from historic trends. For these reasons, we strongly recommend that users collect data for at least the last completed five years or that they even keep expanding the data series by adding new years later without dropping previous years. MFSA helps to draw valuable lessons even from very short two- to three-year data series, but the statistical power and reliability of analyses and forecasts are better if they are based on longer data series. The following examples include historical data (actual figures) for five consecutive years.

Objective: The overarching objective of the historical analysis is to systematically analyze municipal data uploaded into the MFSA core

Table 3.16 Municipal Assets—Investment and Maintenance (*ShS million*)

Service sectors and functions	Year 1		Year 5		Growth indexes (%) development	Growth indexes (%) maintenance
	Development	Maintenance	Development	Maintenance		
General administration						
Office buildings						
Other assets (vehicle, equipment)						
Urban services						
Roads and drainage						
Public transport						
Water and waste water						
Solid waste						
Street lighting						
Fire protection						
Police, crime prevention						
Environmental protection						
Social services						
Health						
Education						
Culture and religion						
Housing						
Recreation and sport						
Social welfare						
Commercial services/investments						
Parking						
Markets						
Commercial places						
Land development						
Local economic development						
Total expenditures						

Note: ShS (shillings) is a notional name of the currency of the sample city.

financial tables and supplementary tables, explore trends, and quantify growth indexes or other ratios for future projections.

Tasks:

Main tables and results: The historical analysis is based on the core financial tables and the supplementary tables generated in Step 1, but it also introduces some new summary tables to communicate results. Most of the summary tables can be easily generated or populated from the MFSA core Financial Database, and the supplementary tables can be analyzed without changing or repeating them. Historical analysis includes 12 tables and sets of tasks in two groups—core summary tables and supplementary tables—as follows:

Core summary tables

- Financial Position Snapshot

- Main Revenue Sources

- Main Current Expenditures (line items)

- Capital Investment Financing

Supplementary tables

- Actual/Plan Analysis

- Expenditures by Function

- Indebtedness Situation

- Capital Investment Plan (CIP)

- Tax Potential and Performance

- Liabilities and Arrears

- Cash Balances

- Municipal Assets Maintenance

Historical Analysis: Financial Position Snapshot

Objective: The main objective of the Financial Position Snapshot is to exhibit and help communicate the financial position and some financial trends of a municipality from the perspective of financial managers and financial or capital market players (banks, investors, rating agencies, or developers). It is also important, however, to present this snapshot to the city council, to the finance committee, and (in a further simplified form like lines 1, 2, 7, 12, and 15 of table 3.17) to the citizens.

Task: Fill out the table and analyze the financial position of your municipality in a brief summary report that would be suitable to inform the council's finance committee, the mayor, the council, or the key external stakeholders (investors, banks, and citizens). The numeric examples below aim to help the analysis, drawing specific lessons, and drafting of a report.

Financial position: Table 3.17 is a standard summary of the *financial positions* that can be generated automatically from the core Financial Database or filled out from original annual closing financial reports. This is the shortest format in which the municipality's financial situation can be summarized and communicated. The first two lines compare operating revenues and expenditures that establish the *gross operating margin/balance* in line 3 (otherwise known as the operating surplus or margin), which is the most important health test of a municipality as explained in the generic financial framework shown in figure 3.2. A substantial operating margin shows financial strength; in contrast, a low or especially a negative operating margin would signal serious financial illness and unsustainable operation of a municipality. A strong operating margin is a key creditworthiness ratio that will be of great interest to creditors or investors. The *current margin* is a balance after the interest payment (interest is current but not operating expenditure), which jumped in year 5. By deducting from the *current margin* the repayment of debt principals (which also jumped in year 5 presumably because of the expiration of grace periods of loans), we get the net margin (line 7).

Table 3.17   Financial Position Snapshot (*ShS million*)

Items	Calculation/ source	Year 1 Actual	Year 2 Actual	Year 3 Actual	Year 4 Actual	Year 5 Actual
1 **Current revenue**		**41,999**	**41,214**	**48,636**	**52,743**	**65,821**
2 **Operating expenditure**		**33,498**	**37,785**	**41,187**	**44,610**	**56,893**
3 **Gross operating margin/ balance**	(1–2)	**8,501**	**3,430**	**7,449**	**8,132**	**8,927**
4 Interests and borrowing costs		321	502	695	1,450	2,212
5 **Current margin/balance**	(3–4)	**8,181**	**2,928**	**6,753**	**6,682**	**6,715**
6 Debt principal repayment		425	490	768	687	2,982
7 **Net margin - net current balance**	(5–6)	**7,756**	**2,438**	**5,985**	**5,995**	**3,733**
8 **Capital revenues**	(9+10+11)	**17,734**	**12,564**	**9,303**	**8,220**	**7,407**
9 Own capital revenues		12,724	9,607	8,938	7,904	7,078
10 Investment grants and donations		32	90	365	316	329
11 Cash reserve from previous years	bank reconciliation	4,978	2,867	0	0	0
12 **Capital investment expenditures**		**25,845**	**23,770**	**28,222**	**29,100**	**22,614**
13 **Investment balance before loan**	(7+8–12)	**–355**	**–8,768**	**–12,933**	**–14,886**	**–11,474**
14 Loan proceeds (disbursed)	actual	3,222	4,956	10,192	12,548	7,022
15 **Overall closing balance with loans**	(13+14)	**2,866**	**–3,812**	**–2,741**	**–2,337**	**–4,452**

Note: ShS (shillings) is a notional name of the currency of the sample city.

Self-financing investments: The net margin plus the capital revenues provide funds for self-financing of investments; subtracting *capital investment expenditures* (line 12) of the sum of these revenues establishes the *investment balance* (line 13). Investment balance is often negative if investments are financed partly from debts. The third balance, however, namely the *overall closing balance with loans* (line 15) should be zero or positive. However, it also shows a growing negative trend in the sample city; this is a problem for the city because the budget is supposed to be balanced with debt financing. The key lesson of this table is that the municipality is running well in terms of financing operations, but it has overinvested before and is presumably overly indebted, which has led to deficit budget. The finance subcommittee of a municipal council and eventually the council itself should discuss the financial snapshot and may decide on further inquiries and corrective measures.

Historical analysis of financial position: It is important to analyze the financial position in two ways: (1) analyzing the trends, that is, the change of key indicators over time; and (2) comparing the composition of the financial position lines between the first and the last years.

Evaluating the results: First, we need to summarize the results and draw lessons, and then discuss methodology and guide MFSA users on how to complete historical analyses, while addressing different local situations and different nature (behavior) of data. What are some of the key results in table 3.18 based on the analysis of growth indexes, comparing year 1 and year 5 results, and comparing ratios and benchmarks?

- *The growth indexes* show how the data on various line items grew from year 1 to year 5 and offer important lessons (the striking results are highlighted). Key findings include the following: (1) operating expenditures grew faster than current revenues (14.2 percent vs. 11.9 percent), and as a result and not surprisingly, the operating margin grew only by 1.2 percent; (2) both interest and principal payments jumped (growing over 60 percent per year on average); (3) cash reserves disappeared; (4) negative investment balances skyrocketed (growing by 138.4 percent annually); (5) loan proceeds grew faster than revenues; and (6) the overall closing balance turned from positive to negative. These findings underline the need for the city council to discuss these results and seek options for reversing some alarming trends. One obvious option to consider would be increasing own revenues substantially, which, however, requires time and specific efforts.

- *Comparing year 1 and year 5*: The last two columns of table 3.18 show the following most visible changes: (1) the net margin dropped down by two-thirds (from 18.5 percent to 5.7 percent share of current revenues); (2) the share of operating expenditures increased; (3) capital revenues dropped by three quarters (from 42.2 percent to 11.3 percent); and (4) cash reserves disappeared. These changes suggest that the city has overinvested and faces heavy debt burden challenges in the years ahead.

- *Ratio Analysis* is the third analysis beyond the above two analyses, and it is very important

for drawing a detailed and complete lesson from the Financial Snapshot. For example, the creditworthiness ratio (that is, operating margin over current revenues) was 20.2 percent in year 1 but fell to 13.9 percent in year 5. This drop suggests weakening creditworthiness, because both of these ratios are well below the 30 percent benchmark commonly accepted (Farvacque-Vitkovic and Sinet 2014) and the ratio shows a downward trend. Key financial ratios will be discussed later in Step 3, "Ratio Analysis."

Methodologies and procedures for analyzing tendencies: The MFSA analysis approaches tendencies by using *geometric average/mean* to calculate annual growth indexes, and *linear trends* to establish trends for analysis and forecasting. TD1 in appendix B summarizes the detailed methodologies and compares options for trend analysis. We recommend that readers who feel they lack statistical knowledge visit appendix B and read TD1 and other technical and methodological explanations.

Historical Analysis: Main Revenue Sources

Objective: The purpose of the historical analysis of main revenue sources is to summarize and comment on the main lessons learned from the revenue source data. Users may analyze the principal sources of municipal financing by looking at the share of main sources in total revenues and then draw lessons from growth indexes. Below we summarize some lessons from table 3.19.

Task: Fill out the table and analyze the main revenue sources of your municipality in a brief summary report that would be suitable to inform the council's finance committee, the mayor, or the council. The examples below aim to help the analysis and the reporting, following the same logic and procedures.

Table 3.18   Historical Tendencies in Financial Position (*ShS million*)

Items	Year 1 Actual	Year 2 Actual	Year 3 Actual	Year 4 Actual	Year 5 Actual	Growth indexes (%)	Structure (% of current revenues)	
							Year 5	Year 1
1 Current revenue	41,999	41,214	48,636	52,743	65,821	11.9	100.0	100.0
2 Operating expenditure	33,498	37,785	41,187	44,610	56,893	14.2	86.4	79.8
3 Gross operating margin/balance	8,501	3,430	7,449	8,132	8,927	1.2	13.6	20.2
4 Interests and borrowing costs	321	502	695	1,450	2,212	62.1	3.4	0.8
5 Current margin/balance	8,181	2,928	6,753	6,682	6,715	-4.8	10.2	19.5
6 Debt principal repayment	425	490	768	687	2,982	62.7	4.5	1.0
7 Net margin - net current balance	7,756	2,438	5,985	5,995	3,733	-16.7	5.7	18.5
8 Capital revenues	17,734	12,564	9,303	8,220	7,407	-19.6	11.3	42.2
9 Own capital revenues	12,724	9,607	8,938	7,904	7,078	-13.6	10.8	30.3
10 Investment grants and donations	32	90	365	316	329	79.0	0.5	0.1
11 Cash reserve from previous years	4,978	2,867	0	0	0	-100.0	0.0	11.9
12 Capital expenditures	25,845	23,770	28,222	29,100	22,614	-3.3	34.4	61.5
13 Investment balance before loan	-355	-8,768	-12,933	-14,886	-11,474	138.4	-17.4	-0.8
14 Loan proceeds (disbursed)	3,222	4,956	10,192	12,548	7,022	21.5	10.7	7.7
15 Overall closing balance with loans	2,866	-3,812	-2,741	-2,337	-4,452		-6.8	6.8

Note: ShS (shillings) is a notional name of the currency of the sample city.

Table 3.19 **Main Revenue Sources (ShS million)**

Items	Year 1 Actual	Year 2 Actual	Year 3 Actual	Year 4 Actual	Year 5 Actual	Average annual growth index (%)	% Structure (total revenue)
Total current revenue	**41,999**	**41,214**	**48,636**	**52,743**	**65,821**	11.9	82.0
1 Revenues from central/higher government	**30,300**	**25,162**	**26,120**	**29,933**	**35,984**	4.4	44.8
– Shared taxes	24,053	22,255	22,747	26,915	35,631	10.3	44.4
– Unconditional transfers	6,192	2,613	3,076	2,865	0	–100.0	0
– Conditional transfers	55	294	297	153	353	59.4	0.4
2 Own revenue	**11,700**	**16,053**	**22,516**	**22,810**	**29,837**	26.4	37.2
– Local taxes and levies	4,235	4,818	6,212	7,548	8,037	17.4	10.0
– Local fees, charges	2,496	4,389	5,571	5,397	12,347	49.1	15.4
– Local asset revenues	4,969	6,847	9,778	8,723	8,989	16.0	11.2
– Revenues from municipal enterprises	0	0	955	1,142	464	n.a.	0.6
– Local other revenues	0	0	0	0	0	n.a.	0
Total noncurrent revenue without loan	**17,734**	**12,564**	**9,303**	**8,220**	**7,407**	–19.6	9.2
1 Capital grants from central/higher government	0	0	0	145	324		0.4
2 Own nonrecurrent revenues	12,724	9,607	8,938	7,904	7,078	–13.6	8.8
Asset sales' proceeds	887	645	546	443	1,354	11.1	1.7
Land development fee	11,668	8,893	8,333	7,413	5,604	–16.8	7.0
Participation/transfers of individuals	169	69	59	48	120	–8.1	0.2
3 Donation	32	90	365	171	5	–37.7	0
4 Financing	**8,200**	**7,823**	**10,192**	**12,548**	**7,022**	–3.8	8.8
Surplus or cash reserves from previous years	4,978	2,867	0	0	0	–100.0	0
Sale of financial assets	0	0	0	0	0	n.a.	n.a.
Loans/bonds' proceeds (disbursements)	3,222	4,956	10,192	12,548	7,022	21.5	8.8
Total revenue	**62,955**	**55,778**	**67,766**	**73,340**	**80,245**	6.3	100.0
1 State transfers/grants	30,300	25,162	26,120	30,078	36,308	4.6	45.2
2 Own revenues	29,434	25,660	31,454	30,714	36,915	5.8	46.0
3 External revenues	3,222	4,956	10,192	12,548	7,022	21.5	8.8

Note: n.a. = not applicable; ShS (shillings) is a notional name of the currency of the sample city.

Methodology and procedure: The main methodology advice is to focus on the *large items and substantial movements* and to draw a big picture of the revenue sources rather than to analyze every single line of this table. We recommend that users focus on those items that decision makers should be aware of or would be interested to learn about. There are two procedures to follow: first, illustrate the structure of revenues by calculating the share of each revenue source as a percentage of the total revenues; second, show the revenue tendencies by calculating the growth indexes.

Revenue structure: First, take the *total revenue* as the basis for calculating the revenue shares, then pick the largest items (highlighted). Here are some lessons: (1) first, look at the section on total revenues, which shows that the sample city generates largely equal share of own revenues (46 percent) and transfers (45.2 percent) received from higher government, which signals solid reliance on own revenues; (2) external revenues are substantial (8.8 percent); (3) revenues from shared taxes (44 percent) are greater than the own current revenues (37 percent); and (4) nonrecurrent own revenues are substantial and largely generated by land development fee, which has been volatile because of economic factors beyond the control of the municipality.

Revenue tendencies: The growth indexes indicate interesting tendencies: (1) revenues from higher government grew a mere 4.4 percent annually, far below the growth of current revenues (11.9 percent), thus the municipality is increasingly reliant on own revenues; (2) the shared taxes grew nicely (10.3 percent), but failed to compensate for the lost unconditional transfers; (3) local fees jumped in year 5, maybe because of a change in revenue base or rate (this requires further inquiry to see if it was a one-time movement or if it is a sign of long-term increase of fee revenues); (4) local taxes and levies grew much faster than the total current revenues, which is a good tendency and should

be continued; (5) land development fees show a steep decline that affects the own nonrecurrent revenues, which is a very worrisome trend; (6) surplus and cash reserves have vanished and signal growing underlying budget imbalances, which need immediate attention from higher management; and (7) external revenues (loan disbursement) show a strong increase over the last five years albeit declining in year 5, which may signal that the municipality has exhausted its borrowing capacity.

Historical Analysis: Main Current Expenditures

Objective: The purpose of the historical analysis of main current expenditures is to briefly summarize and comment on the lessons learned from the expenditure data. Users may analyze the expenditures by looking at the share of main expenditures in total current expenditures and then draw lessons from growth indexes and trends that underscore measures for improving expenditure management (Morell and Kopanyi 2014).

Task: Fill out table 3.20 and analyze the main expenditure items of your municipality in a brief summary report that would be suitable to inform the council's finance committee, the mayor, or the city council. The example below aims to help you carry out your own analysis as well as draft your own report, using the same logic and methodology.

Methodology and procedure: The main methodology advice is again to focus on the large items and substantial movements and draw a big picture of the current expenditures rather than to analyze every single line of this table.

Expenditure structure: What does table 3.20 tell us about current expenditures in the case of the sample city? Lessons are highlighted: (1) the municipality spends a moderate amount on labor and goods and services (17.0 percent and 32.1 percent, respectively); and (2) the service expenditures are low because municipal entities

Table 3.20 Main Current Expenditures (*ShS million*)

Items	Year 1 Actual	Year 2 Actual	Year 3 Actual	Year 4 Actual	Year 5 Actual	Average annual growth index (%)	% Structure (total revenue)
Operating expenses	**33,498**	**37,785**	**41,187**	**44,610**	**56,893**	14.2	96.3
1 Labor (wages, salaries, taxes and charges)	6,592	7,635	8,141	9,075	10,034	11.1	17.0
– Administrative staff							0
– Technical, service, and other staff							0
2 Goods and services	13,008	14,151	14,199	16,209	18,984	9.9	32.1
– Office supply							0
– Electricity							0
– Fuel and gas							0
– Repair and maintenance	2,956	3,234	2,813	3,472	3,940	7.4	6.7
– Other goods and services	10,052	10,917	11,386	12,737	15,044	10.6	25.5
3 Current subsidies to service entities	7,606	6,023	9,134	8,612	11,242	10.3	19.0
4 Current grants and transfers	3,128	5,466	4,582	5,549	11,577	38.7	19.6
5 Social care/welfare support	1,946	3,274	3,827	3,774	3,492	15.7	5.9
6 Other current expenditures	1,217	1,236	1,305	1,392	1,563	6.5	2.6
Interest and borrowing costs	321	502	695	1,450	2,212	62.1	3.7
Current expenses total	**33,819**	**38,286**	**41,883**	**46,061**	**59,105**	15.0	100.0

Note: ShS (shillings) is a notional name of the currency of the sample city.

seem to provide many services outside the budget, but in turn the municipality is burdened with subsidies and grants provided to municipal entities (19.0 percent and 19.6 percent, respectively). Controlling these two line items is vital for sustainable expenditure management.

Expenditure tendencies: The growth indexes indicate interesting tendencies: (1) current grants and transfers to municipal entities not only represent a high share of revenues but also show a steep 38.7 percent annual increase over the last five years, which is a very worrisome tendency (in part because typically these grants are less regulated than other expenditures); (2) interest and borrowing costs show a steep 62.1 percent annual increase that needs city management's attention, because debt service

might be difficult and may constrain investment capacity in coming years; and, finally, (3) social/welfare support shows dynamic 15.7 percent annual increase and creates substantial burden. Social/welfare supports are typically financed by earmarked conditional grants in many countries, but the sample city needs to finance them from shared taxes or own-source tax or fee revenues because it gets only miniscule conditional transfers/grants.

Historical Analysis: Capital Investment Financing

Objective: The purpose of the historical analysis of capital expenditures and financing is to summarize and comment on the lessons learned from the expenditure data trends. Users may analyze the expenditures by looking at the share of main expenditures in total capital expenditures and then draw lessons from growth indexes. Some lessons are shown in table 3.21.

Task: Fill out the table and analyze the main expenditure and financing items of your municipality in a brief summary report that would be suitable to inform the council's finance committee, the mayor, or the council. The example below aims to help users analyze and draft reports, using the same logic and methodology. The main methodology advice is again to focus on the large items and substantial movements and draw a big picture of the capital expenditures rather than to analyze every single line of this table.

Structure of capital expenditures and financing: What is table 3.21 telling us? The main lessons are highlighted: (1) the purchase or development of capital assets is the single largest item among capital expenditures (91.0 percent); (2) the debt service became a substantial part of capital expenses in year 5 and requires attention from management; (3) development was financed by roughly equal shares of capital revenues, self-financing, and loans; and (4) the

Table 3.21   **Capital Expenditures and Financing (*ShS million*)**

Items	Year 1 Actual	Year 2 Actual	Year 3 Actual	Year 4 Actual	Year 5 Actual	Average annual growth index (%)	% Structure (total revenue)
Capital investment expenditure	**25,845**	**23,770**	**28,222**	**29,100**	**22,614**	−3.3	100.0
Purchase/development of assets/infrastructure	18,901	21,005	24,040	26,903	20,584	2.2	91.0
Capital subsidies to PU/PUC	3,437	1,491	3,207	1,295	987	−26.8	4.4
Capital transfers to other level of government	3,507	1,275	974	902	1,043	−26.2	4.6
Investments/Lending	0	0	0	0	0		0
Financing	**28,711**	**19,958**	**25,480**	**26,763**	**18,162**	−10.8	100.0
Capital transfers/grants from government	0	0	0	145	324	n.a.	1.8
Capital grants (international/other)	32	90.	365	171	5	−37.7	0
Capital revenue (sales of assets, etc.)	12,724	9,607	8,938	7,904	7,078	−13.6	39.0
Self financing (Net margin)	7,756	2,438	5,985	5,995	3,733	−16.7	20.6
Cash reserve from previous years	4,978	2,867	0	0	0	−100.0	0
Sale of financial assets	0	0	0	0	0	n.a.	0
Loan/bond proceeds (disbursement)	3,222	4,956	10,192	12,548	7,022	21.5	38.7
Financing gap after loan proceeds	−2,866	3,812	2,741	2,337	4,452	n.a.	24.5

Note: n.a. = not applicable; PU/PUC = public utility/public utility company; ShS (shillings) is a notional name of the currency of the sample city.

financing gap became substantial and worrisome in year 5, which also requires immediate management attention (note: in this line, positive figures are gaps, and the negative amount in year 1 is surplus).

Tendencies in capital expenditures and financing: The growth indexes indicate interesting tendencies: (1) capital investment expenditures show strong volatility and a slightly declining trend (–3.3 percent); (2) capital subsidies and capital transfers from city to entities show a sharp decline (over 26 percent per year), a tendency that needs management attention in line with the fast-growing operating subsidies to PUCs; (3) capital financing available shows a steady decline (10.8 percent per year) largely because of the declining revenues from asset sales (13.6 percent annual decrease). These findings together suggest that the municipality should revise its capital development and financing strategy urgently because its development seems nonsustainable and because chronic budget imbalances have emerged and are likely to remain in force in the medium term.

Historical Analysis: Supplementary Tables

It is important to analyze the historical trends of the supplementary tables in the same way we did for the core financial tables. There are understandable differences due to the special structure of some tables. The historical analysis is not only important to see the results in the supplementary tables, but some of these results also provide vital information for forecasting the core financial tables, which thus cannot be completed without proper analysis of supplementary tables. The same procedures, logic, and structure apply as those used for core financial tables.

Actual/Plan Analysis—Historical Trends

Objective: The objective of this analysis is to measure the quality or predictability of the budget plans by comparing planned figures with actuals. The lessons from A/P analysis are important to take into account during the forecasting of revenues and expenditures for the next five years. It is also useful to prepare a list of A/P results in percentage performance for the last five years and estimate from them average deviations to measure the changes in budget planning and execution results over time. The average absolute deviations for five years would clearly show the areas where persistent differences occur between the plans and actual figures.

Task: Generate a historic trend table from the A/P table (table 3.22) that indicates only the A/P% figures, and calculate average absolute deviations from the 100 percent benchmark on A/P% over five years.

Good budget planning and execution: Good budget planning can be witnessed if the planned and actual figures are in the range of plus/minus 5 percent of 100 percent (95 percent < A/P < 105 percent). The following steps need to be completed: (1) list or mark the outstanding lines, especially those that show over 20 percent differences, and propose analysis of the possible underlying causes; and (2) initiate comprehensive corrective actions regarding expenditures that are persistently outstanding for several years or if differences show a growing tendency in some line items.

The sample city has performed well in terms of budgeting and controlling expenditures in total volume (*total expenditures* in first line), exemplified by the 2.4 percent absolute deviation from 100 percent (see TD2 in appendix B); however, there are wide variations of expenditure performance behind the scene. For example, current subsidies and current grants and transfers to municipal entities show over 35 percent absolute deviation (lines 4 and 5 in table 3.22), which signals not only that the city spends a substantial amount on subsidizing entities but also that the subsidy system seems to be unregulated

Table 3.22   Actual/Plan Analysis—Expenditures

Expenditures	Year 1 A/P%	Year 2 A/P%	Year 3 A/P%	Year 4 A/P%	Year 5 A/P%	Average absolute deviaton from 100%
Total expenditures	100.1	96.2	101.2	101.1	105.9	2.4
I Current expenditures	103.9	114.8	104.2	107.7	123.2	10.8
1 Labor (wages, salaries, taxes and charges)	106.3	109.1	101.8	113.4	111.5	8.4
– Administrative staff	0	0	0	0	0	n.a.
– Technical, service, and other staff	0	0	0	0	0	n.a.
– Other	3296.0	2545.1	1628.1	1814.9	2006.8	n.a.
2 Goods and services	103.6	95.6	86.1	98.2	116.5	8.0
– Office supply	0	0	0	0	0	n.a.
– Electricity	0	0	0	0	0	n.a.
– Fuel and gas	0	0	0	0	0	n.a.
– Repair and maintenance	84.5	71.9	56.3	69.4	98.5	23.9
– Other goods and services	5026.0	2183.4	2277.2	2547.4	3008.8	n.a.
3 Interest and borrowing costs	106.9	100.3	99.3	96.7	100.5	2.3
4 Current subsidies to service entities	108.7	150.6	152.2	123.0	140.5	35.0
5 Current grants and transfers	104.3	136.7	131.7	138.7	165.7	35.4
6 Social care/welfare support	97.3	128.9	85.0	82.3	77.6	17.3
7 Other current expenditures	81.1	247.2	130.5	116.0	156.3	53.8
II Capital expenditures	95.7	76.3	97.3	92.4	78.0	12.1
1 Purchase/development of assets/infrastructure	94.5	83.7	96.2	96.1	79.2	10.1
2 Capital subsidies to PC/PUC	98.2	49.7	106.9	51.8	49.3	31.6
3 Capital transfers to other level of government	100.2	42.5	97.4	90.2	104.3	14.9
4 Investments/Lending	0	0	0	0	0	n.a.
III Financing	97.7	96.1	94.9	97.8	99.3	2.8
1 Debt principal repayment	100.0	98.0	96.0	98.2	99.4	1.7
2 Purchase of financial assets	0	0	0	0	0	n.a.

Note: A/P = actual/plan; n.a. = not applicable; PU/PUC = public utility/public utility company; ShS (shillings) is a notional name of the currency of the sample city.

and presumably burdened with ad hoc grants. Capital subsidies to PUs/PUCs show over 30 percent deviation that may signal weaknesses also in capital investment planning and the project selection process.

Expenditures by Functions—Historical Trends
Objective: The overarching objective is to analyze tendencies and highlight outstanding moves in the way the municipality spends money to provide various core and non-core services over time. The average growth indexes can be calculated by using the methods explained in previous sections.

Should the municipality use legally independent entities for service provision, then table 3.23 can be supplemented by a table that would include consolidated expenditures of

Table 3.23 Historical Analysis—Expenditures by Functions

	Year 1 Actual	Year 2 Actual	Year 3 Actual	Year 4 Actual	Year 5 Actual	Average annual growth index	Structure (% of total expenditures)
General administration							
Urban services							
Roads and drainage							
Public transport							
Water and wastewater							
Solid waste							
Street lighting							
Fire protection							
Police, crime prevention							
Environmental protection							
Social services							
Health							
Education							
Culture and religion							
Housing							
Recreation and sport							
Social welfare							
Commercial services							
Parking							
Markets							
Commercial places							
Land development							
Local economic development							
Total expenditures							

the municipality and of the service entities. Consolidation means adding line items of city and entities together but netting out items that would cause double accounting such as current or capital transfers that the municipality has provided to these entities.

Debt Stock and Debt Service—Historical Analysis

Objective: The objective of this analysis is to explore underlying tendencies in the movement of debt stock and debt service indicators.

The historical analysis of the indebtedness level should follow a procedure completely different from the growth index, trend, or other historical analyses used above. The reason is that municipalities typically borrow (procure debt) for the medium to long term for investment purposes. Thus, in a year of analysis and forecasting, the key debt figures, such as due interest payments, principal repayments, grace period, bond maturities, and so on, are largely known four to five years ahead or even longer.

Procedure: Looking ahead to the next five-year period requires precise knowledge of each debt, including the aging list of debts and estimating the future events (debt service). New loans or bonds may emerge during the forecasting period, but those cannot be derived from trend analysis, rather they require information from borrowing plans. Structuring debts often takes years, so a new investment loan or bond cannot appear by surprise. In short, trends and general growth indexes can be calculated, but they are largely not relevant to analyze and forecast debt movements by each loan item.

Analysis: It is useful to calculate and communicate to higher-level bodies (city council, finance committee, mayor) the growth indexes or tendencies of the total indebtedness figures, including debt stock, principal and interest payments, and total debt service calculated by adding together the projected annual figures derived from actual payments or loan agreements. Table 3.24 shows interesting tendencies, the most important among them is that the debt stock has grown by over 50 percent annually, while the annual debt service and the payment of interest grew by over 60 percent annually between year 1 and year 5. This growth indicates that the debt service has increased dramatically and is likely to eat up a substantial part of funds that would be available for investments in the coming years. The growth indexes calculated over the time period of year 1 through year 10 indicate that these indexes will drop radically in projected years unless new loans are incurred. Principal repayment burden, however, will remain high (36.9 percent annual growth over 10 years) even without new loans.

Tax Potential and Performance—Historical Analysis

Objective: The overarching objective is to explore the tendencies of various tax revenues, unfold shift or volume change from one to another tax revenue, and quantify the trends in tax performance and in collection of arrears in order to support strategic decisions on tax policy and administration. There is much useful literature discussing objectives, implications, and methods of assessing and reforming local tax and fee revenue systems (Bird 2010, 2013; Freire and Garzon 2014; Kelly 2013; Slack and Bird 2015; Stiglitz and Rosengard 2015).

Tasks: Calculate the share of the main tax revenue sources as a percentage of total tax revenues. It is wise to calculate these shares for both the first and last years of the time period under analysis and to highlight main changes and outstanding items. Calculate growth indexes for each line to explore underlying tendencies of billing, collection, collection performance, and arrear collection.

Analysis: It is important to analyze each line of table 3.25 because the core financial reports often include only one summary line of tax revenues and leave out the key underlying changes in composition of revenues or collections of various taxes. Small or no change in tax base, collection, or arrears signals lack of improvement and maybe lack of taxation strategy, policy, or procedures; so these results should be identified and adequately communicated to higher levels of city management. Specific attention should be paid to the accumulation of arrears (for example, if the growth indexes on stock of arrears are greater than the growth indexes of tax base or tax collection).

Table 3.25 shows that property tax is the most substantial own-source revenue (OSR) of the sample city; the revenues from households and businesses combined generate over 60 percent of tax revenues. The taxes billed have increased in all three main taxes but most on businesses (21 percent per year), a good sign; but the city is rolling over a huge stock of arrears on household property tax with low collection and stagnant total volume. This suggests a need for further analysis to help policy

Table 3.24 Historical Analysis of Debt Stock and Debt Service (*ShS million*)

Items	Year 1	Year 2	Year 3	Year 4	Year 5	Year 6	Year 7	Year 8	Year 9	Year 10	Growth index year 1–year 5	Growth index year 1–year 10
	Actual	Actual	Actual	Actual	Actual			Projected				
1 IBRD water development												
– Outstanding	3,045	3,580	3,667	3,091	2,822	2,216	1,696	1,084	1,096	1,108		
– Principal repayment	425	490	537	531	591	591	622	636	643	650		
– Interest charge	151	190	157	150	159	102	72	49	37	28		
2 ADB road development												
– Outstanding					1,670	3,503	10,615	10,467	10,206	9,678		
– Principal repayment					0	0	0	367	371	350		
– Interest charge					0	45	203	318	272	268		
Credit bank (domestic)												
3 Markets/Malls												
– Outstanding			3,757	4,523	3,733	2,828	1,924	1,019	115	13		
– Principal repayment				0	790	905	905	905	102	13		
– Interest charge			0	517	507	449	328	214	100	14		
Several loan lines are ommitted from display for simplicity												
Total												
– **Outstanding debt**	**8,599**	**13,820**	**24,705**	**37,320**	**45,295**	**47,428**	**55,215**	**51,229**	**49,181**	**47,614**	51.5%	20.9%
– **Principal repayment**	**425**	**490**	**768**	**687**	**2,982**	**4,084**	**4,423**	**5,039**	**5,309**	**7,198**	62.7%	36.9%
– **Interest charge**	**321**	**502**	**695**	**1,450**	**2,212**	**2,144**	**2,213**	**2,187**	**1,849**	**1,661**	62.1%	20.1%
Debt service	**746**	**992**	**1,464**	**2,138**	**5,194**	**6,228**	**6,636**	**7,226**	**7,158**	**8,859**	62.5%	31.6%
Borrowing disbursement	3,197	5,645	11,375	13,383	8,662	5,115	11,871	438	2,991	3,741	28.3%	1.8%

Note: ADB = Asian Development Bank; IBRD = International Bank for Reconstruction; ShS (shillings) is a notional name of the currency of the sample city.

Table 3.25 Historical Analysis of Tax Revenues and Tax Performance (ShS million)

	Year 1	Year 2	Year 3	Year 4	Year 5	Growth indexes (%)	Share (%) in year 5
I Property tax - households (Rate 6%)							
1 Tax base (amount billed)	1,526	1,650	1,800	2,000	2,200	9.6	26.2
2 Tax collected	1,075	1,248	1,592	1,786	1,903	15.3	24.1
3 Tax performance % (2/1)	**70.5**	**75.6**	**88.4**	**89.3**	**86.5**	5.3	n.a.
4 Stock of arrears	3,000	3,200	3,300	3,250	3,120	1.0	95.1
5 Arrears collected	280	300	250	300	250	−2.8	84.7
6 Tax performance % (5/4)	9.3	9.4	7.6	9.2	8.0	−2.8	n.a.
II Property tax - business entities (Rate 8%)							
7 Tax base (amount billed)	1,650	1,900	2,400	2,700	3,000	16.1	35.7
8 Tax collected	1,613	1,872	2,388	2,680	2,855	15.3	36.1
9 Tax performance % (7/6)	**97.7**	**98.5**	**99.5**	**99.2**	**95.2**	−0.7	n.a.
10 Stock of arrears	153	170	168	140	130	−4.0	4.0
11 Arrears collected	25	30	40	30	30	4.7	10.2
12 Tax performance % (10/9)	16.3	17.6	23.8	21.4	23.1	4.7	n.a.
III Business tax (Rate 3%)							
13 Tax base (amount billed)	1,500	1,600	2,150	3,000	3,200	20.9	38.1
14 Tax collected	1,443	1,590	2,111	2,952	3,146	21.5	39.8
15 Tax performance % (17/16)	**96.2**	**99.4**	**98.2**	**98.4**	**98.3**	0.5	n.a.
16 Stock of arrears	40	43	33	42	30	−6.9	0.9
17 Arrears collected	10	20	30	20	15	10.7	5.1
18 **Total tax billed**	**4,676**	**5,150**	**6,350**	**7,700**	**8,400**	15.8	n.a.
19 **Total tax collected**	**4,131**	**4,710**	**6,090**	**7,418**	**7,905**	17.6	n.a.
20 **Stock of arrears total**	**3,193**	**3,413**	**3,501**	**3,432**	**3,280**	0.7	n.a.
21 **Total arrears collected**	**315**	**350**	**320**	**350**	**295**	−1.6	n.a.

Note: n.a. = not applicable; ShS (shillings) is a notional name of the currency of the sample city.

setting and defining corrective measures, such as a special program to collect and radically reduce stock of arrears and in general improve collection efficiency of annual taxes.

These actions can be supplemented with a more detailed analysis of the tax bases that include data about the number of tax payers, exemptions, and the number of bills issued compared to number of bills paid. This information is available in advanced computerized tax administration systems, but it might require specific inquiry and data collection when such information is not collected on a regular basis. The latter case is outside the scope of MFSA, but a target tax base analysis can be included in the MFSA Action Plan as one priority action for the medium term.

Liabilities and Arrears—Historical Trends

Objective: The objective is to develop a clear and reliable picture of liabilities by listing all financial liabilities and separating the regular and overdue liabilities. This is particularly important when the adopted accounting system is cash based and financial reports exclude/ignore accrued liabilities. By including a clear picture of financial liabilities, the financial situation and health of a municipality can be realistically analyzed and assessed (see template table 3.26).

Tasks: Fill out table 3.26 as precisely and honestly as possible, and make sure to include all kinds of financial obligations incurred but left unserved/unpaid at the end of the fiscal year. Complete the following analysis: (1) include the cash reserves from bank reconciliations; (2) calculate the ratio between the cash reserves and the financial liabilities; (3) include the overdue financial liabilities (they are part of the total, but report them also in a separate section of the table); (4) calculate the growth indexes; and (5) it is wise to generate one more table and report the contingent liabilities such as guarantees or other financial obligations like minimum payment commitments to private service providers (landfill or water charges). These indirect financial liabilities do not appear in the form of bills

at the end of the year; instead, they are buried in financial or service contracts, but they may become very real financial obligations if the guarantees are called or minimum fees are due. Write a short report for higher management based on the analysis that follows.

Analysis: First, compare the cash reserves available with the total financial liabilities. Should the cash reserve appear greater than the total financial liabilities, then the liabilities can be considered a technical issue because they can be fulfilled from the cash reserves in due course. In contrast, table 3.26 shows that the financial liabilities of the sample city appear two to three times greater than the cash reserves, which signals financial weaknesses because the liabilities cannot be fulfilled from the available cash even if the liabilities are only technical in nature (within due payment period). Second, the tendency of the *cash reserves over total liabilities* ratio over time is an indicator of the severity of the financial situation if the reserves are below the liabilities (index is less than 100 percent). Not only were the sample city's cash reserves

Table 3.26   Financial Liabilities and Arrears (*ShS million*)

	Year 1	Year 2	Year 3	Year 4	Year 5	Growth indexes (%)
Public stakeholders (city dues to entities)						
– Water PUC	1,000	1,200	1,300	1,400	1,500	10.7
– Solid waste PUC	500	800	900	1,000	1,100	21.8
– Transport PUC	800	1,000	1,100	1,200	1,300	12.9
– Schools	50	–	120	140	160	33.7
– Kindergartens	10	10	10	10	10	0
– Culture or sport entities	500	550	600	650	700	8.8
Private contractors (city dues to private)	2,700	3,000	3,400	3,800	4,000	10.3
Labor (wages, salaries)	500	400	550	600	650	6.8
Total liabilities (city dues)	6,060	6,960	7,980	8,800	9,420	11.7
Cash reserves end of fiscal year	4,300	2,980	2,500	2,400	2,300	−14.5
Cash reserves/Total liabilities %	71	43	31	27	24	−23.4

Note: PUC = public utility company; ShS (shillings) is a notional name of the currency of the sample city.

Better Cities, Better World

below financial liabilities, but the gap has also quickly increased at an annual pace of 23.4 percent. Thus, the financial situation seems unsustainable and requires attention and corrective measures by higher management and governing bodies. Third, the growth indexes of the various liabilities provide further insights on the most problematic areas and the severity of the problems. The volume of liabilities grew faster than revenues or expenditures in several critical areas like schools and PUCs. Needless to say, chief officers are often aware of unpaid bills and financial distresses, but the MFSA helps more precisely quantify the factors and highlight specific problem areas.

Contingent liabilities: Analysis of the contingent liabilities requires a more complex financial analysis and projections of the net present values of those liabilities and thus is beyond the scope of MFSA. Users can, however, make a big step in the right direction by merely listing the contingent liabilities in face value. Table 3.27 depicts the situation of a city and helps MFSA users to better understand the nature of contingent liabilities.

What can we learn from this table? Lessons include the following: (1) paying the electricity bill may not even appear in any contract, but it is the legal, moral, and political responsibility of the owner municipality to pay on behalf of the water company to avoid interruption of the electricity service and suspension of water services; and (2) loan guarantee is an explicit contingent liability, which means that the municipality has committed itself, by contract, to step in and honor debt service if the company fails to do so. The city has a solid situation because guarantees have not been called, so contingent liabilities can be projected to decrease in line with repayment of guaranteed loans and phase out entirely in year 10. In sum, taking into account contingent liabilities is a wise procedure and also part of the inquiry by rating agencies, so it is advisable to include it in the MFSA as a supplementary table.

Municipal Assets (Investments and Maintenance)—Historical Trends

Objective: The main objective is to draw a detailed, realistic, and reliable picture of the asset development and maintenance expenditures and their movements over time.

Task: Fill out table 3.28 that lists assets by sector or function. This entails the following: (1) make sure to separate the expenditures on development or investments and on maintenance of the various asset groups (the borders between development and maintenance might be blurred and thus require an expert judgement or just follow the way they are accounted); (2) calculate the growth indexes separately for development and for maintenance by each line and the total; (3) write a short note about the

Table 3.27 **Contingent Liabilities (*ShS million*)**

	Year 6	Year 7	Year 8	Year 9	Year 10	Growth indexes (%)
Public stakeholders						
– Water PUC paying electricity bill	900	800	800	700	700	–6
– Solid waste PUC						
– Transport PUC loan guarantee	5,000	4,000	3,000	2,000	1,000	–33
– Culture or sport entities						
Total contingent liabilities	5,900	4,800	3,800	2,700	1,700	–27

Note: PUC = public utility company; ShS (shillings) is a notional name of the currency of the sample city.

Table 3.28 Asset Inventory and Maintenance

Items	Tentative assets Inventory in current year	Year 5		Year 6		Year 7		Growth index	
		Development Actual	Maintenance Actual	Development Actual	Maintenance Actual	Development Actual	Maintenance Actual	Development Last/First yr	Maintenance Last/First yr
Roads, streets (km²)									
Paved roads km									
Unpaved roads km									
Public lighting (number of lighting posts)									
Water network km									
Water treatment plants (m³ total capacity)									
Sewer network km									
Wastewater treatment plants and pumping stations (number)									
Solid waste management trucks (number)									
Solid waste facilities: transfer stations (number)									
Solid waste facilities: landfill (number)									
Other public infrastructure and equipment (parks, cemeteries, parking and garage, etc.) (m²)									
Educational facilities (number of class or m²)									
Health care facilities (m²)									
Administrative facilities (m²)									
Cultural facilities (m²)									
Sport facilities (number)									
Commercial facilities (m²)									
Environmental facilities (number)									
Public housing									
Number of units									
Total m² of units									
Cultural heritage (number)									
Vacant municipal land hectare									
Urban land									
Agricultural, forest, nonurban land									

Note: km² = square kilometer; m² = square meter; m³ = cubic meter.

main lessons learned, following the analysis below. Insert a short summary on the asset composition and management. Provide a short description of how maintenance activities are carried out: directly by municipal staff, by municipal enterprises, by private contractors, and by the residents themselves.

Analysis of results: It is good to start the analysis with the total expenditures and discuss the general growth of investments and of maintenance, calculating the share of maintenance compared to investment expenses over time. The sample city has not yet filled out the asset and maintenance database. Should results indicate very low levels or low growth of maintenance expenditures, the note may propose specific inquiry to find the real underlying causes. Underlying causes may include (1) accounting and expenditure classification challenges, (2) real imbalance between development and maintenance and danger of neglecting existing assets, (3) neglecting specific areas of assets (roads or water networks), and (4) a general policy that allocates insufficient resources for maintenance. Comparing the growth indexes across service sectors and functions may reveal strong priorities in some areas and negligence in others. Highlighting and measuring by indexes the disparities across sectors or service functions is very important because, although high-level decision makers may allocate skewed resources on what they perceive as priority sectors, a comprehensive picture and numeric results would provide solid ground for a more substantial and integral policy dialogue and a more informed decision-making process.

Stock of assets: Discussion on stock of assets would be a useful part of the short MFSA note, but it is only possible if the municipality has developed a comprehensive asset register or a reliable asset inventory from which the main results can be included in the historical analysis of asset development and maintenance. Most municipalities in the developing world have not yet developed asset registers; in such situations, the MFSA report should be very brief or silent on the stock, composition, or value of assets, because data collection would be overwhelming. However, establishing and gradually populating a reliable asset register can be included among the medium-term priority actions in the MFSA Action Plan. The first step in the right direction would be to fill out table 3.28 with preliminary but reliable information on stock of most critical assets, to indicate the underlying stock of assets against the annual development and maintenance figures. As stated earlier, the asset inventory can also be started as part of the UA/SA.

Step 3: Ratio Analysis

Objectives: The objectives of the ratio analysis are (1) to get familiar with and to adopt *municipal finance benchmarks*, (2) to foster greater understanding of a municipality's financial position compared with the world or with other cities in the region (Kopanyi 2018), and (3) to highlight its potentials and key gaps. The ratios and benchmarks presented in table 3.29 are based on international standards and are in harmony with ratios used by rating agencies (Farvacque-Vitkovic and Sinet 2014). The ratios outlined in table 3.29 are indicative and not mandatory targets.

MFSA users may feel the ratios set standards that are too high, and some may suggest applying different ratios for different groups of countries with different levels of development. We tend to disagree and recommend using the same ratios regardless of the development or income level of a country or of a municipality because (1) these ratios convey important messages for immediate, medium-term,

Table 3.29   Key Financial Ratios

Indicator (definition)	Comparative index (benchmark)	Actual Year 1	Year 2	Year 3	Year 4	Year 5
1 Creditworthiness						
Operating savings before interests/Current revenue	> 30%	20%	8%	15%	15%	14%
Net operating surplus (after debt service)/Current revenue	> 20%	19%	7%	14%	13%	10%
Investment balance before loan/Total revenue	> –15%	–1%	–16%	–22%	–24%	–16%
Financing gap after loan proceeds/Total revenue	> –5%	5%	–7%	–5%	–4%	–6%
2 Indebtedness						
Debt outstanding/Operating surplus (capacity to clear its debt)	< 10 years	1	4	3	5	5
Debt service/Total current revenue	< 10%	2%	2%	3%	4%	8%
Debt outstanding/Budget total	< 60%	14%	24%	36%	51%	56%
Borrowing/Current revenues	< 15%	8%	14%	23%	25%	13%
Operating margin/Interest payment	> 15	27	7	11	6	4
Debt outstanding/Total current revenue	< 100%	20%	34%	51%	71%	69%
3 Fiscal autonomy						
Own (taxes + fees + unconditional grants)/Total current revenue	> 80%	85%	93%	93%	94%	99%
4 Capital investment effort						
Capital investment expenditure/Current revenue	> 40%	61%	56%	56%	54%	30%
Capital investment expenditure/Total expenditure	> 30%	43%	38%	40%	39%	25%
Current margin/Capital investment expenditure	> 25%	32%	13%	25%	24%	34%
Capital investments from earmarked grants/Total investment expenditure	< 50%	0%	0%	1%	1%	1%
5 Level of service sustainability						
Maintenance works expenditure/Operating expenditures	> 15%	9%	9%	7%	8%	7%
Taxes collected/Taxes levied	> 90%					
Fees collected/Fees billed	> 90%					
6 Quality of operations						
Salaries and wages/Operating actual expenditures	< 40%	20%	20%	20%	20%	18%
Number of municipal employees/1,000 citizens	< 25	22	22	22	22	23
Actual revenue/Planned revenue	95%<A/P<105%	105%	90%	97%	98%	100%
Arrears amount/Net cash (end of the year)	< 1	34%	53%	69%	75%	83%
Financial resources (cash+cashlike)/Financial obligations (due liabilities + arrears)	> 1	71%	43%	31%	27%	24%

or long-term recommendations; (2) should a municipality meet most of these benchmark ratios, it is proof of good financial health and creditworthiness; and (3) setting separate ratios for groups of countries would therefore compromise comparability and would create space for subjective judgements.

The vast majority of these ratios can be calculated from the core financial tables discussed above, although some require additional information like the population of the municipality for each analyzed year or national averages of the per capita revenue and expenditure indicators that can be obtained from finance ministries or from websites of bureaus of statistics. The ratio analysis tables can be generated automatically by linking respective cells of the discussed core and supplementary tables if users generate those in Excel (other platforms or other accounting instruments can be used, too). Finally, Excel also makes it easy to generate charts and figures (see figures 3.5, 3.6, and 3.7) to showcase the tendencies of these ratios over the time period under analysis. Figures and charts are powerful instruments for communicating the results of the ratio analysis to key stakeholders such as city officials, investors, or other strategic partners.

Tasks: The specific tasks include the following: (1) fill out or generate automatically the key financial ratios table (table 3.29); (2) draw lessons from the ratios, and write a short note on ratio analysis results by covering each ratio area and focusing on specific outstanding items; and (3) generate charts on key ratios and use them to support findings in your ratio analysis note. In the analysis, try to relate various ratios and draw joint lessons across ratios.

Analysis: Table 3.29 includes real results from the sample city and shows the following key features:

Creditworthiness ratios

Creditworthiness is a complex subject that depends on various quantitative and qualitative factors, but in simple ratio form it is measured by the ratio between the operating savings and the current revenues in gross and net form. Investors are also interested in whether investment balances and financing gaps are under control.

The sample city achieved positive operating savings over this time period, which is a good sign of creditworthiness; however, the

Figure 3.5 Operating Savings/Current Revenues

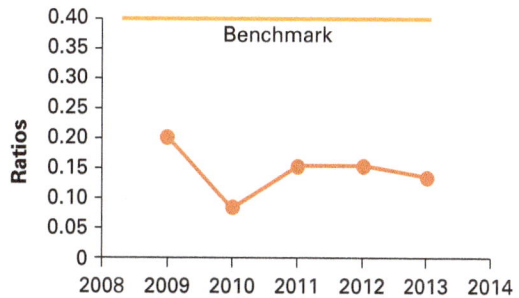

Figure 3.6 Capital Investment Expenditure/Current Revenue

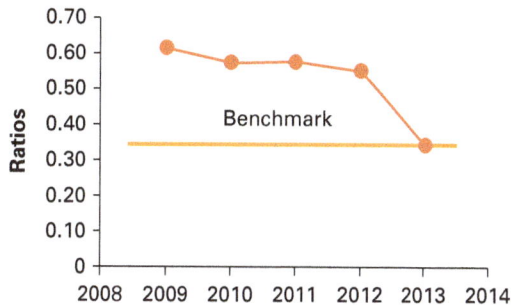

Figure 3.7 Maintenance Expenditure/Current Revenue

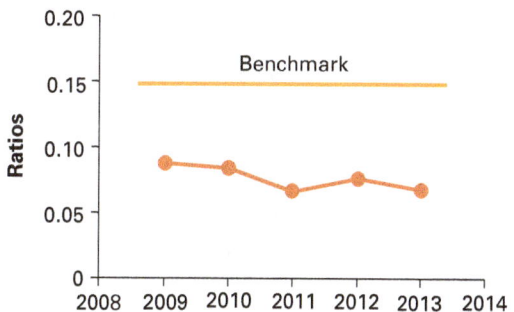

savings are well below the benchmarks (figure 3.5 and table 3.30). This suggests that the city is on the right track but has medium creditworthiness and needs improvement in order to support borrowing on the private

Table 3.30 Creditworthiness Ratios

	Benchmarks	Year 1	Year 2	Year 3	Year 4	Year 5
Operating savings before interests/Current revenue	> 30%	**20%**	8%	15%	15%	14%
Net operating surplus (after debt service)/Current revenue	> 20%	**19%**	7%	14%	13%	10%
Investment balance before loan/Total revenue	> –15%	–1%	–16%	–22%	–24%	–16%
Financing gap after loan proceeds/Total revenue	> –5%	5%	–7%	–5%	–4%	–6%

Table 3.31 Indebtedness Ratios

	Benchmarks	Year 1	Year 2	Year 3	Year 4	Year 5
Debt outstanding/Operating surplus (capacity to clear its debt)	< 10 years	1	4	3	5	**5**
Debt service/Total current revenue	< 10%	2%	2%	3%	4%	**8%**
Debt outstanding/Budget total	< 60%	14%	24%	36%	51%	**56%**
Borrowing/Current revenues	< 15%	8%	14%	23%	**25%**	13%
Operating margin/Interest payment	> 15	27	7	11	6	4
Debt outstanding/Total current revenue	< 100%	20%	34%	51%	**71%**	69%

debt market. Is the 30 percent of current revenues too high a benchmark? No. Cities that are able to finance current expenditures from 70 percent or less of current revenues (or 80 percent with debt service) show a strong foundation for borrowing (that is, strong creditworthiness and creditors would consider a loan to them as "investment grade debt"). Many cities in the world invest when savings are low, but they finance investments from target grants rather than from markets. The sample city gradually weakened investment balances, which fell below the benchmark, whereas the financing gap is by and large under control.

Indebtedness ratios

Indebtedness ratios include six different benchmarks: the first two lines of table 3.31 measure debt repayment capacity; the second two lines of ratios are also known as regulatory rules applied in many countries.

The sample city's indebtedness position is strong (table 3.31). The city could repay all outstanding debt from 5-year operating surplus (against the 10-year benchmark). Likewise, the outstanding debt stock is low: the highest was 71 percent of current revenues in year 4. The debt service has been increasing, however, and reached 8 percent of current revenues (vs. 10 percent benchmark) in year 5. The city's outstanding debt has grown quickly in the period and came close to the 60 percent regulatory benchmark (56 percent) in year 5 (figure 3.8); however, the annual borrowing far exceeded the 15 percent current revenues benchmark in year 3 and year 4. This high borrowing is a red flag in the eyes of regulators, rating agencies, or market partners. The operating margin shrank to 4 percent of interest payments, which is also a red flag and deserves action.

Fiscal autonomy ratio

The fiscal autonomy ratio captures the issue of financial sovereignty of the city by measuring what share of local funds is dependent on local decisions or discretions. Lenders, investors, or other market partners look into not only the main revenue figures but also the power of the local decision makers.

The sample city shows strong spending sovereignty (table 3.32) with over 80–90 percent. It is worth mentioning that fiscal autonomy is more dependent on intergovernmental finance systems and legislation than on local decisions, nevertheless boosting own-source revenues increases sovereignty. Finding a low ratio does

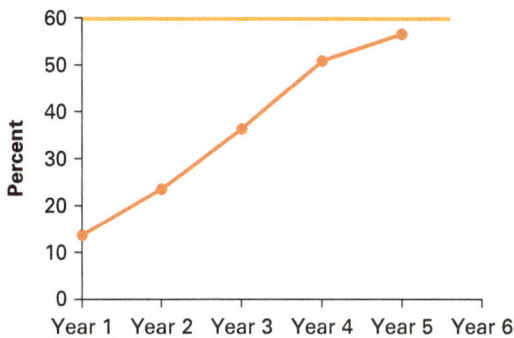

Figure 3.8 Debt Stock/Budget Total

not aim to blame a city; however, it is among indicators the market is interested in.

Capital investment efforts ratios

Financial health can also be measured by capital investment efforts, because capital investments around the benchmarks signal not only financial health but also good investment policies. In contrast, low capital investments signal that a city manages financing operations but fails to generate revenues sufficient to fund the benchmark (40 percent) level of capital investments. The two ratios focus on two aspects: (1) total investment efforts, measured by capital investments against current revenues, against total expenditures, and against current margins; and (2) investments financed from earmarked grants, which are attributed more to national government than to the city.

The ratios of the sample city show strong investment performance, well over 40 percent in some years, and negligible reliance on earmarked investment grants (figure 3.6 and table 3.33). This is a robust result from the market players' perspectives. The figures also show that the extreme investment level gradually went down to the normal range, which

Table 3.32 Fiscal Autonomy Ratios

	Benchmarks	Year 1	Year 2	Year 3	Year 4	Year 5
Own (taxes + fees + unconditional grants)/ Total current revenue	> 80%	85%	93%	93%	94%	99%

Table 3.33 Capital Investment Efforts Ratios

	Benchmarks	Year 1	Year 2	Year 3	Year 4	Year 5
Capital investment expenditure/Current revenue	> 40%	61%	56%	56%	54%	30%
Capital investment expenditure/Total expenditure	> 30%	43%	38%	40%	39%	25%
Current margin/Capital investment expenditure	> 25%	32%	13%	25%	24%	34%
Capital investments from earmarked grants/ Total investment expenditure	< 50%	0%	0%	1%	1%	1%

signals attention from and good reactions by the city's higher decision-making bodies. Finally, the city has not relied on earmarked capital grants, and thus had high sovereignty in selecting priority projects and deciding investments.

Level of service sustainability ratios

This set of ratios aims at capturing the service sustainability from both the expenditure and the revenue sides.

The sample city has stayed well below the benchmark in maintenance expenditures (table 3.34), a common practice that signals high emphasis on investments, low priority on maintenance, or both in many developing countries.

The mere fact that the city has not measured the revenue performance in fees (direct source of service costs) or all taxes (a general source) signals financial management gaps and weaknesses, and a lack of focus on service sustainability. Potential lenders or investors would consider these to be substantial

weaknesses that are likely to reduce creditworthiness scores regardless of the level of other ratios, despite the city's robust and increasing own-revenue collection.

Quality of operation ratios

A set of ratios signal the quality of city management and city operation via numeric figures (table 3.35).

- *Salaries and wages over operating expenditures* is an important sign of expenditure composition and good management.

  The sample city shows robust results with ratios well below the benchmark, which means that the city spends much less on labor costs than the benchmark. It also means that the city saves money this way and can spend proportionately more on services and development. One caveat, however, is that the labor expenditures also depend on the service arrangements, namely whether the main services are provided by independent legal entities (public utilities or private

Table 3.34 **Level of Service Sustainability Ratios**

	Benchmarks	Year 1	Year 2	Year 3	Year 4	Year 5
Maintenance works expenditure/Operating expenditures	> 15%	9%	9%	7%	8%	7%
Taxes collected/Taxes levied	>90%					
Fees collected/Fees billed	>90%					

Table 3.35 **Quality of Operations Ratios**

	Benchmarks	Year 1	Year 2	Year 3	Year 4	Year 5
Salaries and wages/Operating actual expenditures	< 40%	20%	20%	20%	20%	18%
Number of municipal employees/1,000 citizens	< 25	22	22	22	22	23
Actual revenue/Planned revenue	95%<A/P<105%	105%	90%	97%	98%	100%
Arrears amount/Net cash (end of the year)	< 1	34%	53%	69%	75%	83%
Financial resources (cash + cash-like)/Financial obligations (due liabilities + arrears)	> 1	71%	43%	31%	27%	24%

providers), and thus the respective employees are not on the wage list of the municipality. Other data discussed in the historical analysis suggest that this is indeed the case for the sample city and that the city spends less on labor cost but provides for very substantial operating subsidies and transfers to other entities. Rating agencies would take note of this issue.

- *Number of employees per thousand citizens* is a good comparative indicator that does not have direct financial implications, but it is still one signal of good management and service efficiency.

  The sample city performs well on this ratio because it is steadily below the benchmark, although the above-mentioned caveats should be taken into account.

- *Actual revenue over planned revenue* is a very important ratio that signals the quality of revenue management.

  The sample city performs well on this ratio despite the fact mentioned before that it does not clearly measure the collection efficiency of either fee or tax revenues. Another important aspect of this ratio is that total revenue also depends on the predictability of central government transfers, which are apparently stable in the case of this sample city. Finally, as mentioned before, some revenue sources appeared to be volatile and unpredictable and the city counterbalanced those by selling assets or increasing some other revenues, which is a good policy and financial management practice.

- *Arrears over net cash (end of the year)*: This ratio signals the financial strength of a city if the ratio is below one, which means arrears accumulated are less than the cash reserves available. This condition is not a very demanding one, because overdue liabilities should be small, but it signals serious financial troubles if the ratio is greater than one, meaning that the overdue liabilities exceed cash reserves. The sample city has performed well according to this ratio because the ratio remained below one. The ratio has shown an alarming tendency, however, because it has moved from 34 percent to 83 percent over the past five years. Potential lenders, investors, or rating agencies would note this as a potential risk factor.

- *Financial resources over financial obligations*: This ratio indicates good financial health; if it is greater than one, it means that financial resources (cash and cash-like instruments) exceed the total financial liabilities and that the city can pay out all obligations from cash reserves. We should notice not only that the sample city has cash reserves that are too low, well below financial liabilities, but also that this ratio worsened from 71 percent down to 24 percent over the past five years, which undermines the creditworthiness regardless of possible good results on other ratios.

Comparison ratios

There are important ratios beyond the discussed financial ratios, namely ratios that measure the per capita financial results of a city. Table 3.36 summarizes the key comparison ratios of the sample city. These ratios are useful for comparing the city's performance in light of the national averages or in comparison to other cities. The comparison ratios are easy to calculate and provide a platform for comparing cities with their peers. Calculating these per capita ratios in local currency is the commonly accepted approach and useful for national comparisons, but these calculations can easily be transformed into common currencies for broader international comparison purposes.

Table 3.36 Key Comparison Ratios

Comparison ratios in local currency	National average	Year 1	Year 2	Year 3	Year 4	Year 5
Total revenue per capita	32	27.2	24.6	27.7	29.0	30.9
Total expenditure per capita	31	25.9	26.2	28.8	29.9	32.6
Current actual revenue per capita	22	18.1	17.3	19.8	20.8	25.3
Debt outstanding per capita	10	3.7	5.8	10.0	14.7	17.4
Capital investment expenditures per capita	9	11.1	10.0	11.5	11.5	8.7
Comparison ratios in Euros						
Total revenue per capita	4.6	3.9	3.5	3.9	4.1	4.3
Total expenditure per capita	4.4	3.7	3.7	4.1	4.2	4.5
Current actual revenue per capita	3.1	2.6	2.4	2.8	2.9	3.5
Debt outstanding per capita	1.4	0.5	0.8	1.4	2.1	2.4
Capital investment expenditures per capita	1.3	1.6	1.4	1.6	1.6	1.2
Exchange rate		7.00	7.05	7.10	7.15	7.18

Analysis: The first and most common analysis is to compare the city's results with the national average ratios to assess the city's position among municipalities in a country. The sample city is close to the national average in terms of per capita revenues and expenditures. In contrast, it has reached a much higher level of per capita outstanding debt and a remarkably higher level of per capita investment expenditures as compared to the national average. These last two ratios reinforce each other and signal that the city is trying to catch up on infrastructure investments and to use debt financing.

Summary of ratio analysis

Using the results of the sample city, here is an example of key lessons and policy recommendations that can be also included in the MFSA Action Plan. First, the creditworthiness ratios should be improved by expanding own current revenues. This improvement is critical: the city's development depends on savings and borrowing, because it receives no development grants from higher government. Second, the management of fees and taxes should be improved, and revenue administration, capacities, and performances should be analyzed to find options for boosting own revenues. Third, asset maintenance needs better management and increased budget because the levels of expenditures are far below benchmarks and because the recent new investments will further expand the need for maintenance. Finally, improving information on tax and fee arrears and increasing collection is a vital precondition for increasing tax and fee revenues.

Step 4: Financial Projections

Objective: The overarching objective of the financial projections is to support a preliminary analysis of the future financial situation of a municipality, identify main driving factors and challenges, and identify corrective policy measures for the next five years.

Financial Projections: Key Principles and Framework

Principles of projections: The fundamental principles of good financial projections include the following: (1) complete an honest analysis of data and options; (2) account known or foreseen policy decisions into assumptions; (3) use explicit assumptions and avoid implicit assumptions; (4) insert known data into the projections first and then use trends or growth factors to project financials; (5) make conservative estimates for projections; (6) screen and test for consistency after the first complete set of projections; (7) prepare projections in separate conservative and optimistic scenarios; (8) project the sublines first and then calculate the main lines from the results, rather than simply projecting the aggregate main revenue or expenditure lines; (9) use external data from reliable national sources (statistical bureau, ministry of finance or industry) rather than making subjective proxies on national economic factors; and (10) it is wise to start the projections with supplementary tables, then factor in key results to the core financial tables before starting projections of core financial line items. Figure 3.9

summarizes the key building blocks of and framework for the financial projections.

Procedure: Making financial projections requires a procedure with several key steps built upon each other, and largely relies on the results of the historical analysis and ratio analysis. It is advisable to follow the sequence of steps as explained below and summarized in figure 3.9:

1. *Socioeconomic environment:* It is useful to start with collecting a few data and writing a very short note on the socioeconomic environment, including demographic trends (education, age, and growth of the city's population); economic trends such as gross domestic product (GDP) growth and inflation indexes in the country and in the specific sectors active in the city (construction, manufacturing, or agriculture) often available from the statistics office or ministries; and change of the economic environment in the city (such as the growth of firms and job opportunities).

Figure 3.9 Financial Projections Framework

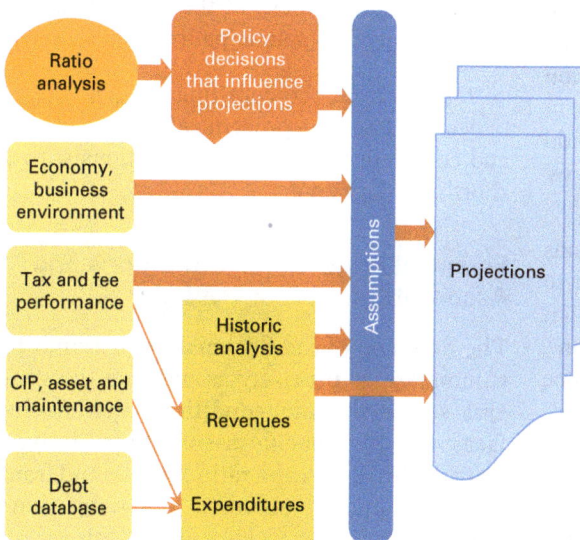

Note: CIP = capital investment plan.

2. *Tax performance:* List the key lessons learned from the tax performance analysis, and take into account factors that may change the future volume of tax or fee revenues (like change of tax or fee base—the number of payers, revaluation of properties or other tax bases, if these have been seriously planned); note the change date/year if those changes have been decided and are likely to happen in the projection period.

3. *Asset management (CIP and maintenance):* If your city has adopted a CIP or is undergoing a UA/SA for the projection period, the results should be accounted into the respective capital expenditure lines on financial

projection tables instead of using trend forecasts. Maintenance may not be clearly accounted in CIP; thus, maintenance expenditures may be projected by trends, unless specific policy decisions are known at the time of the projections.

4. *Debt database*: Include the results (disbursements, principal, interest, and debt service total) projected for the next five years in the debt database directly to the respective financing or expenditure lines of the financial projections. Do not use simple trend projections for disbursement or debt service, because the debt database and CIP should be precise in projecting future debt service commitments for the coming five years.

5. *Ratio analysis*: Select key results from the ratio analysis, and propose or assume policy decisions that will influence the financial projections at some specific points in the projection period. Include these among the critical assumptions and account them in at least one of the projection scenarios.

6. *Policy decisions*: Prepare a short list or bullet points on policy decisions that substantially and directly influence the financial projection in the coming five years, and include them in the list of assumptions. These decisions could be approved plans for revaluing properties, changing fees, and so on.

7. *Assumptions*: Prepare a list of assumptions before starting the financial projections to ensure using well-defined and explicit assumptions during financial projections. Explicit assumptions are vital to convince readers of financial projections and authenticate results. In contrast, should readers realize the application of multiple hidden or implicit assumptions, they would downgrade the presented results, maybe more deeply than would be justified.

8. *Historical analysis of core financial tables*: Select the key lessons learned in the historical analysis of the core financial tables, and include lessons among the assumptions if lessons point to factors that would trigger divergence of data from the historical trends.

9. *Projections*: Complete the projections by factoring in all the respective results mentioned above. Examples are provided using data from the sample city.

10. *Analysis of the financial projection results*: It is important to analyze the results of the financial projections and to test the consistency, reality, and feasibility of the results. MFSA users may need to revise some projections to improve reality or feasibility. For example, final results may project a large and persistent financing gap or budget deficit that could be balanced only with extensive borrowing that would violate borrowing rules or limits, or they are unlikely to happen. In such a case, a careful revision of both revenue and expenditure projections is important to achieve a feasible scenario (less budget deficit) of the future financial situation of the municipality.

Task: Fill out the core financial projection tables. Follow the procedure recommended, and complete the financial projections with a short summary note.

Financial Projections: Conditions and Assumptions

The first step of the financial projection is to summarize as precisely as possible the general socioeconomic conditions that a city faces and the specific assumptions derived from the historical and ratio analysis and from various known or assumed policy decisions that are projected to have direct impact on the financial situation in the next five years.

Conditions and assumptions regarding the sample city

In this section, we summarize socioeconomic conditions and assumptions that impact the financial projections for the sample city to help MFSA users get familiar with the details, challenges, and practices and to understand and apply the procedure for their municipalities. We use the results from the sample city discussed in the previous sections to illustrate the work and guide MFSA users through the maze of financial projection. Many lessons listed below are usable as *explicit assumptions* when filling up the core financial projection tables.

- *Socioeconomic environment*: The sample city is among the largest of the country, with strong economic power (exemplified also by the high volume of shared taxes), steady but moderate population growth, a strong labor market, and a well-educated labor force; it also hosts a strong manufacturing industry and transport hub. Inflation was 7.3 percent per year in the year 1 through year 5 period and projected to fall to about 3 percent. The real GDP growth of the country was a moderate 0.7 percent per year (with a negative growth in year 2) but was expected to improve to above 2 percent in the projected period of year 6 through year 10. In sum, the socioeconomic trends and factors, along with its historical growth rates, suggest steady growth of the city, and even better in some areas. The city's economic growth outperforms the country: the core economic sectors active in the city's metropolitan area grew by 3 percent per year as compared with the 0.7 percent per year national GDP growth in the year 1 through year 5 period.

- *Tax performance and fee revenues*: The fact that the city has no detailed and reliable tax database is a sign of substantial weaknesses in the financial management system

that deserve both attention and corrective measures by higher decision-making bodies. With the lack of specific tax performance data, the historical trends are the only instruments to project future tax revenues. The city has no reported detailed fee revenue database, so again the historical trends are the only useable instruments; however, fee revenues jumped from about ShS5,000 to ShS12,000 in year 5, and this fact deserves further investigation because the high growth rate (49 percent per year in the past five years) calculated using this jump will not be realistic over the coming five years. Thus, an *adjusted projection* is recommended, using the growth rate of the first four years but starting future projections from the level of the year 5 fee revenue results, unless extensive collection of fee arrears has caused a one-time jump of fee revenues. Should the latter be the case, a historical trend from the first four years should project the fee revenues until year 10.

- *Capital investment plan*: The city has adopted a CIP, so estimated budget expenditures can be used.

  The data suggest a radical reduction of capital expenditures as compared to the last five years, exemplified by the year 5 data (table 3.37). The planned capital expenditures are particularly low in the last three years of the projection, which might signal preliminary data and may trigger future upward revision. It is wise to use these capital investment figures in financial projections as conservative estimates, and a more optimistic scenario can be tested later. We should note that the CIP also includes investments funded by the public utility company and by the private sector (see table 3.10); the volume of planned capital investments is therefore somewhat higher, but only the budgeted figures can be included in financial projection tables.

Table 3.37   Capital Investment Plan—Summary (*ShS million*)

	Actual	CIP Expenditure Plan					Total five-year plan
	Year 5	Year 6	Year 7	Year 8	Year 9	Year 10	
Expenditures financed from budget	22,614	15,000	15,000	10,000	10,000	9,000	59,000

Note: CIP = capital improvement plan; ShS (shillings) is a notional name of the currency of the sample city.

- *Debt database*: The city has a debt database with an aging list of debt that provides solid figures for financial projections and should be used instead of trend-line projections.

  The aging list of debts clearly shows the amount the city owes in principal repayment, in interest payment, and in total debt service in year 6 through year 10. These are still projected figures, because effective debt service might differ (for instance, if the city wants early repayment, or "amortization," of some debts, or fails to serve some debt because of budget shortage). In sum, these figures should be included in the core financial projection table. We should also note that the city has experienced an extreme growth of debt (51.5 percent per year!) with the peak of debt stock in year 7; as a result, the city also faces extreme growth of debt service (over 60 percent increase per year in the first five projected years, and over 30 percent annual increase over a 10-year time period—see growth indexes in table 3.38). This underscores the conservative CIPs for the projected time period.

- *Ratio analysis*: The ratio analysis of the city offers key lessons for policy dialogue and corrective measures. In the absence of evidence of such policy dialogue and for training purposes, we will use some assumptions from the ratio analysis summary: (1) database and management of taxes will be improved with additional growth effects in the last three years of the projections; and (2) expenditures on asset maintenance will

increase above the historical growth rates or trend lines to double in five years.

- *Policy decisions*: In the absence of concrete information and for training purposes, we take into account a number of policy decisions and select them on the basis of the historical analyses and lessons learned during the above discussions: (1) control indebtedness and debt benchmark ratios; (2) ensure timely and uninterrupted debt service; (3) improve creditworthiness by increasing own revenues; (4) put more emphasis on asset maintenance; and (5) follow the conservative CIP in projecting capital expenditures, and project more ambitious plans in an optimistic scenario.

Summary of core assumptions

- *Assumptions* are the following: (1) use historical trend projections in financial projection tables unless there are direct data or approved policy decisions; (2) revenues will grow along with historical trends; (3) expenditures will grow along with historical trends as base scenario; (4) some lines require specific assumptions that will be made explicit as memo items; (5) linear trends will be used as instruments for projecting the financial data years ahead; and (6) historical analyses of core financial tables and supplementary tables are the bases for financial projections.

Financial Projections: Sample City's Data

Financial projections of the sample city: In this section, we will complete financial

Table 3.38 Debt Service Summary — Excerpt from Debt Database (*ShS million*)

Items	Year 1 Actual	Year 2 Actual	Year 3 Actual	Year 4 Actual	Year 5 Actual	Year 6	Year 7	Year 8 Projected	Year 9	Year 10	Growth index year 1–year 5 (%)	Growth index year 1–year 10 (%)
– Outstanding debt	8,599	13,820	24,705	37,320	45,295	47,428	55,215	51,229	49,181	47,614	51.5	20.9
– Principal repayment	425	490	768	687	2,982	4,084	4,423	5,039	5,309	7,198	62.7	36.9
– Interest charge	321	502	695	1,450	2,212	2,144	2,213	2,187	1,849	1,661	62.1	20.1
Debt service	**746**	**992**	**1,464**	**2,138**	**5,194**	**6,228**	**6,636**	**7,226**	**7,158**	**8,859**	**62.5**	**31.6**
Borrowing disbursement	3,197	5,645	11,375	13,383	8,662	5,115	11,871	438	2,991	3,741	28.3	1.8

Note: ShS (shillings) is a notional name of the currency of the sample city.

projections based on the set assumptions and the data of the sample city in order to help MFSA users get familiar with the procedures, challenges, and instruments. As mentioned, we first need to insert into the projection tables the financial data borrowed from supplementary tables, and then project the other lines by using linear trends. We will list the explicit assumptions as memo items under each projection table. We will complete the financial projections in two sections: (1) operating revenues, expenditures, and gross margin; and (2) debt service, capital expenditures, capital financing, and overall balance.

Projecting Current Revenues, Operating Expenditures, and Gross Operating Margin

In this section, we will go through the effective projection table of the sample city and highlight and explain findings and specific procedures in important lines. We offer one simple procedure or simple solution, but we admit and emphasize that there are always other and more sophisticated solutions MFSA users may consider (see table 3.39).

General assumptions: Let's first summarize some general assumptions applied all over the financial projections:

- Use historical linear trend projections in financial projection tables unless there are direct data (for example, debt service) or approved policy decisions.

- Revenues will grow along with historical trends.

- Expenditures will grow along with historical trends.

- Some lines require specific assumptions that will be made explicit as memo items.

Projecting Debt Service, Capital Expenditures, and Capital Financing

Projecting debt service, capital expenditures, and capital financing will follow the same procedures as discussed for current revenues and expenditures, but this process should start by inserting data from supplementary tables (see summary in table 3.40). Again, we use the data of the sample city to illustrate best practices and procedures.

Assumptions: General assumptions remain the same as before, and we will use specific assumptions and procedures in some lines marked again as memo items with continued numbering (*8) onward.

*Debt service (*8)*: The debt service projections should be made in the supplementary tables by using the aging list of debts (loans/bonds). Should your municipality fail to prepare an aging list of debts (usually a relatively small table), then the debt service might be projected with trends but should not be considered reliable. Municipal investment loans and loan amortizations should be well known and well documented five years ahead and even longer (till the end of the maturity, that is, the repayment period). New loans might appear during a five-year projection period, but they are under preparation often for one or two years ahead and may include a grace period; they are thus likely to cause only some minor increase of interest payment in the projection period.

Furthermore, should the CIP indicate new borrowing with the effective disbursement and debt service for the projection period, that should first be included in the debt service projections among the aging list of debts. In sum, include in the debt service section the projected figures from the aging list of debts, and avoid trend projections (lines 24–32 in table 3.40). Please note that signing a loan agreement does not immediately change the

Table 3.39 **Projection of Current Revenues, Operating Expenditures, and Gross Operating Margin—Conservative Estimates Scenario (ShS million)**

Items	Year 1 Actual	Year 2 Actual	Year 3 Actual	Year 4 Actual	Year 5 Actual	Assumptions, formulas	Year 6 Projection	Year 7 Projection	Year 8 Projection	Year 9 Projection	Year 10 Projection
	1	2	3	4	5	serial number of years (x)	6	7	8	9	10
A Total current revenue	41,999	41,214	48,636	52,743	65,821	sum lines 1+6	69,588	75,633	83,209	93,118	97,398
1 Transfers from higher government	30,300	25,162	26,120	29,933	35,984	sum lines (7,10)	35,032	37,859	40,686	43,513	46,340
2 – Shared taxes	24,053	22,255	22,747	26,915	35,631	$y=2781.6x+17975$	34,665	37,446	40,228	43,009	45,791
3 – Unconditional transfers *4	6,192	2,613	3,076	2,865		$y=6588.6-1213.2$ USE zero!	0	0	0	0	0
4 – Conditional transfers	55	294	297	153	353	$y=45.565x+93.67$	367	413	458	504	549
5 Own revenue	11,700	16,053	22,516	22,810	29,837	sum lines (2,5)	34,556	37,774	42,523	49,605	51,058
6 – Local tax revenues *1	4,235	4,818	6,212	7,548	8,037	$y=1033.4x+3069.6$	9,270	10,303	11,337	12,370	13,404
7 – Local fees and charges *2	2,496	4,389	5,571	5,397	12,347	$y=988.63x+1991.6+5412$	13,335	14,324	16,844	21,697	20,921
8 – Local asset revenues	4,969	6,847	9,778	8,723	8,989	$y=991.61x+4886.3$	10,836	11,828	12,819	13,811	14,802
9 – Local mixed revenues *3			955	1,142	464	$y=204x-108.84$	1,115	1,319	1,523	1,727	1,931
B Total operating expenditure	33,498	37,784	41,187	44,610	56,893		59,274	65,115	71,054	77,102	83,273
10 Labor (wages, salaries, taxes, charges)	6,592	7,635	8,141	9,075	10,034	$y=832.38x+5798.2$	10,792	11,625	12,457	13,290	14,122
11 – Administrative staff											
12 – Technical, service, and other staff											
13 Goods and services	10,052	10,917	11,386	12,737	15,044	$y=1180.3x+8486$	15,568	16,748	17,928	19,109	20,289
14 – Office supply											
15 – Electricity											
16 – Fuel and gas											
17 – Repair and maintenance *5	2,956	3,234	2,813	3,472	3,940	$y=(220.62x+2621.1)*1.1$	4,339	5,040	5,838	6,745	7,774
18 – Other goods and services											
19 Current subsidies to service entities *6	7,606	6,023	9,134	8,612	11,242	$y=986.19x+5564.9$	11,482	12,468	13,454	14,441	15,427
20 Current grants and transfers *7	3,128	5,466	4,582	5,549	11,577	$y=1698x+966.46$	11,154	12,852	14,550	16,248	17,946
21 Social care/welfare support	1,946	3,274	3,827	3,774	3,492	$y=359.18x+2185$	4,340	4,699	5,058	5,418	5,777
22 Other current expenditures	1,217	1,236	1,305	1,392	1,563	$y=84.93x+10878$	1,597	1,682	1,767	1,852	1,937
C Gross operating saving (A − B)	8,502	3,430	7,449	8,133	8,928		10,315	10,517	12,155	16,016	14,126

Note: Empty cells in lines 11, 12, 14, 15, 16, and 18 reflect missing data (only aggregate figures were available); ShS (shillings) is a notional name of the currency of the sample city.

Table 3.40 Projecting Debt Service, Capital Expenditures, and Capital Financing—Conservative Scenario (ShS million)

		Year 1	Year 2	Year 3	Year 4	Year 5	Assumptions, formulas	Year 6	Year 7	Year 8	Year 9	Year 10
D	Debt service *8	746	992	1,464	2,138	5,194	All data from debt	6,228	6,636	7,226	7,158	8,859
23	– Interest charge	321	502	695	1,450	2,212	database, no plan	2,144	2,213	2,187	1,849	1,661
24	– Loan principal repayment	425	490	768	687	2,982	for new borrowing	4,084	4,423	5,039	5,309	7,198
E	Net saving (C – 30)	4,799	(795)	3,172	2,523	(207)	lines C-30	4,086	3,881	4,929	8,858	5,266
F	Capital expenditure without debt service *9	25,845	23,770	28,222	29,100	22,614	from CIP	15,000	15,000	10,000	10,000	9,000
G	Balance after capital expenditure (E – F)	(21,046)	(24,566)	(25,049)	(26,577)	(22,821)		(10,914)	(11,119)	(5,071)	(1,142)	(3,734)
H	Investment financing (F – E) Need	21,046	24,566	25,049	26,577	22,821		10,914	11,119	5,071	1,142	3,734
I	Investment financing available (capital rev) *13	17,734	12,564	9,303	8,220	7,407		10,467	15,923	19,866	19,677	26,555
25	Capital transfers				145	324	y=79.25–144.01	620	699	778	857	937
26	Investment grants/donations	32	90	365	171	5	y=2.66x+124.63	141	143	146	149	151
27	Own capital revenues	12,724	9,607	8,938	7,904	7,078	sum lines 37+38+39	5,352	4,052	2,753	1,454	1,287
28	– Proceeds from nonfinancial assets	887	645	546	443	1,354	y=73.16x+555.57	995	1068	1141	1214	1287
29	– Development fees and contributions *12	1,837	8,962	8,392	7,461	5,724	y=12593–1372.6x (R2=0.94)	4,357	2,985	1,612	240	0
30	– Proceeds from financial assets	0	0	0	0	0		0	0	0	0	0
31	Cash reserves from previous years *11	4,978	2,867	0	0	0	Actual or projected balance	0	0	16,675	15,232	21,526
32	Debt financing *10	3,222	4,956	10,192	12,548	7,022	From debt database	5,115	11,871	438	2,991	3,741
J	Overall closing balance (A+I) – (B+D+F)	2,867	(3,812)	(2,741)	(2,337)	(4,452)	(A+I) – (B+D+F)	4,669	16,675	15,232	21,526	26,563

Note: ShS (shillings) is a notional name of the currency of the sample city.

debt service or the debt financing figures! Debt financing means and should reflect the amount disbursed in a specific year; likewise, the debt service should only include the amount paid on a loan in forms of either interest or principal repayment in each year.

Memo items: See the discussions and explanations for table 3.40. General assumptions:

- Use historical linear trend projections in financial projection tables unless there are direct data (for example, debt service) or approved policy decisions.

- Expenditures will grow along with historical trends.

- Some lines require specific assumptions that will be made explicit as memo items.

*Capital expenditures (*9)*: Capital expenditures might be listed in a CIP as in the case of our sample city. In such case, the capital expenditure figures should be borrowed from the CIP if it exists or from the PIP of the UA/SA if it is available, and they should only include expenditures the CIP indicates as financed from or through the city budget, such as borrowing or disbursement of a loan in a year. With the lack of an adopted CIP, a list of priority projects might help in projecting capital expenditures, but with less reliable figures. Making trend projections for capital expenditures can be the last resort. We used CIP figures in table 3.40.

*Debt financing (*10)*: Should your municipality have debt or plan borrowing, please first calculate debt financing in the aging list of debt, which may include the projected amount of debt disbursed in years ahead. Municipal loan financing investments often cover 5–10 years or longer and include gradual disbursement of the contracted loan proceeds in 2–3 years or longer, a grace period for repayment of loan principal, and a corresponding payment of interest. MFSA users should understand and follow the fact that the amounts disbursed in years are the historical figures and the amount that will be disbursed (not the loan amount contracted!) should be included in the projection period. Experience shows that disbursements from a new loan do not follow linear trends; they are often moderate in the first year because of the preparation and slow start of the respective infrastructure project, and then disbursement scales up in the second and third year or so. In sum, please use realistic data from disbursement plans for projecting debt financing of infrastructure in the budget, and avoid using trends even if there is no aging list of debts and disbursement plans approved.

*Surplus from previous years (*11)*: Surpluses may accumulate over years and dry up quickly on rainy days or because of increased investments or debt service. For these reasons, MFSA users should use bank reconciliation figures for the years in the historical analysis, but also for careful calculation of budget surpluses for the future years. Do not use trend projections for the surpluses!

*Development fees (*12)*: Development fees are a substantial source of revenues in the sample city; however, experience shows that they depend on economic cycles and thus tend to be volatile. In the case of the sample city, there is a solid and predictable downward sloping trend in development fees (trend predictability appears to be high: $R^2 = 0.94$), which would end with negative development fees in year 10. We therefore calculate a linear trend in projections, but obviously should project zero revenue instead of negative in year 10. City managers may inform the finance department about the change of a trend and suggest projecting solid positive revenues for the coming years, and this can be taken into account. We followed the linear trend with the lack of information that questions this trend. However, we calculated an optimistic scenario discussed below where we assumed that the development fees remain flat in the range of ShS5,000 million for the entire projection period.

Investment financing (*13): The investment financing line includes funds available for financing investments beyond net savings: capital transfers (line 25), investment grants (26), own capital revenues (27), surplus from previous years (31), and debt financing (line 32).

Overall closing balance: The overall closing balance (line J) is the difference between investment financing need (H) and investment financing available (I). This amount should be calculated from the sums of projected revenues and expenditures rather than projecting balance with trends.

Financial Projections: An Optimistic Scenario

Optimistic scenario: There is ample room for projecting more optimistic but still reasonable scenarios (table 3.41). Options are summarized below, based on three policy assumptions: (1) the tax administration improvements increase tax revenues more substantially and double the volume of annual tax revenues from year 5 to year 10; (2) the development fee revenues will stabilize after year 5 and generate ShS5,000 million in revenues per year; (3) the city can borrow against the increased revenue and generated surpluses and thus increase investments to the tune of ShS20,000 million per year (table 3.41 summarizes the results of an optimistic scenario). Some may recommend that the city plan to cut operating subsidies to municipal entities (water or solid waste companies); this is a wise approach, but we should note that it is only justified if there are reasonable plans for implementing those expenditure cuts. We have not included these possible cuts on current subsidies, despite the fact that we would support those measures.

The optimistic scenario is a dangerous proposition: It is wise to compute and show higher decision-making bodies not only a realistic conservative scenario that is most likely to happen come rain or shine but also an optimistic scenario in parallel. MFSA users should be aware, however, that this optimistic scenario is a dangerous proposition because higher decision-making bodies may love to hear better scenarios but projecting and achieving more revenues also requires them to approve respective decisions (for example, voting for increasing fee or tax rates,) and budget to improve tax administration without which the projected revenue increases remain groundless. In addition, an optimistic scenario may convince higher decision-making bodies that the higher revenues or lower expenditures require approval of unpopular policies and budgets for revenue administration improvements. Let's see the results and draw some lessons from table 3.41. We follow the sequence of memo item numbering starting with (*14).

Local tax revenues (*14): We assume that the local tax revenues will increase more substantially after two years of reform preparation and add to trend projections ShS1,000 million, 2,000 million, and 3,000 million in annual revenues from year 8 onward, respectively. This would result in an overall doubling of annual tax revenues by year 10 as compared to the year 5 base year (see line 2 in table 3.41). International experience suggests that doubling tax revenues in five years is ambitious but possible.

Development fees and contributions (*15): As said, the trend of development fees follows a solid downward sloping route that would end up with negative revenue in year 10. The optimistic scenario is that these revenues will be stabilized and generate about ShS5,000 million in revenues per year between year 6 and year 10. This provides for a major improvement of budget balances and room for higher development.

Debt financing (*16): On the basis of the robust increase of revenues in the optimistic

Table 3.41 Projection of Current and Capital Budgets and Balances—Optimistic Scenario (ShS million)

Items	Year 1 Actual 1	Year 2 Actual 2	Year 3 Actual 3	Year 4 Actual 4	Year 5 Actual 5	Assumptions, formulas serial number of years (x)	Year 6 Projection 6	Year 7 Projection 7	Year 8 Projection 8	Year 9 Projection 9	Year 10 Projection 10
A Total current revenue	**41,999**	**41,214**	**48,636**	**52,743**	**65,821**	sum lines 1+6	69,588	75,633	84,209	95,118	100,398
1 Own revenue	11,700	16,053	22,516	22,810	29,837	sum lines (2,5)	34,556	37,774	43,523	51,605	54,058
2 – Local tax revenues *14	4,235	4,818	6,212	7,548	8,037	$y=1033.4x+3069.6$	9,270	10,303	12,337	14,370	16,404
3 – Local fees and charges *1	2,496	4,389	5,571	5,397	12,347	$y=988.63x+1991.6+5412$	13,335	14,324	16,844	21,697	20,921
4 – Local asset revenues	4,969	6,847	9,778	8,723	8,989	$y=991.61x+4886.3$	10,836	11,828	12,819	13,811	14,802
5 – Local mixed revenues *3			955	1,142	464	$y=204x-108.84$	1,115	1,319	1,523	1,727	1,931
6 **Transfers from higher government**	30,300	25,162	26,120	29,933	35,984	sum lines (7,10)	35,032	37,859	40,686	43,513	46,340
7 – Shared taxes	24,053	22,255	22,747	26,915	35,631	$y=2781.6x+17975$	34,665	37,446	40,228	43,009	45,791
8 – Unconditional transfers *4	6,192	2,613	3,076	2,865		$y=6588.6-1213.2$ USE zerol					
9 – Conditional transfers	55	294	297	153	353	$y=45.565x+93.67$	367	413	458	504	549
B Total operating expenditure	**33,498**	**37,784**	**41,187**	**44,610**	**56,893**		59,274	65,115	71,054	77,102	83,273
10 Labor (wages, salaries, taxes, charges)	6,592	7,635	8,141	9,075	10,034	$y=832.38x+5798.2$	10,792	11,625	12,457	13,290	14,122
11 – Administrative staff											
12 – Technical, service, and other staff											
13 Goods and services	10,052	10,917	11,386	12,737	15,044	$y=1180.3x+8486$	15,568	16,748	17,928	19,109	20,289
14 – Office supply											
15 – Electricity											

continued next page

Table 3.41 Continued

Items	Year 1 Actual 1	Year 2 Actual 2	Year 3 Actual 3	Year 4 Actual 4	Year 5 Actual 5	Assumptions, formulas serial number of years (x)	Year 6 Projection 6	Year 7 Projection 7	Year 8 Projection 8	Year 9 Projection 9	Year 10 Projection 10
16 – Fuel and gas											
17 – Repair and maintenance *5	2,956	3,234	2,813	3,472	3,940	y=(220.62*x+2621.1)*1.1	4,339	5,040	5,838	6,745	7,774
18 – Other goods and services											
19 Current subsidies to service entities *6	7,606	6,023	9,134	8,612	11,242	y=986.19x+5564.9	11,482	12,468	13,454	14,441	15,427
20 Current grants and transfers *7	3,128	5,466	4,582	5,549	11,577	y=1698x+966.46	11,154	12,852	14,550	16,248	17,946
21 Social care/welfare support	1,946	3,274	3,827	3,774	3,492	y=359.18x+2185	4,340	4,699	5,058	5,418	5,777
22 Other current expenditures	1,217	1,236	1,305	1,392	1,563	y=84.93x+1087.8	1,597	1,682	1,767	1,852	1,937
C Gross operating saving (A – B)	8,502	3,430	7,449	8,133	8,928		10,315	10,517	13,155	18,016	17,126
						Assumptions, formulas	2014	2015	2016	2017	2018
D Debt service *8	746	992	1,464	2,138	5,194	All data from debt database, no plan for new borrowing	6,228	6,636	7,226	7,158	8,859
23 – Interest charge	321	502	695	1,450	2,212		2,144	2,213	2,187	1,849	1,661
24 – Loan repayment	425	490	768	687	2,982		4,084	4,423	5,039	5,309	7,198
E Net saving (C – D)	7,756	2,438	5,985	5,995	3,733	lines C – D	4,086	3,881	5,929	10,858	8,266
F Capital expenditure without debt service *18	25,845	23,770	28,222	29,100	22,614	from CIP	15,000	20,000	20,000	20,000	20,000
G Balance after capital expenditure (E – F)	(18,089)	(21,332)	(22,236)	(23,105)	(18,881)		(10,914)	(16,119)	(14,071)	(9,142)	(11,734)

continued next page

Table 3.41 Continued

Items	Year 1 Actual 1	Year 2 Actual 2	Year 3 Actual 3	Year 4 Actual 4	Year 5 Actual 5	Assumptions, formulas serial number of years (x)	Year 6 Projection 6	Year 7 Projection 7	Year 8 Projection 8	Year 9 Projection 9	Year 10 Projection 10
H Investment financing (F – E) Need	18,089	21,332	22,236	23,105	18,881		10,914	16,119	14,071	9,142	11,734
I Investment financing available (capital rev) *17	17,734	12,564	9,303	8,220	7,407		11,870	18,781	14,226	11,375	13,350
25 Capital transfers				145	324	$y=79.25-144.01$	620	699	778	857	937
26 Investment grants/donations	32	90	365	171	5	$y=2.66x+124.63$	141	143	146	149	151
27 Own capital revenues	12,724	9,607	8,938	7,904	7,078	sum lines 37+38+39	5,995	6,068	6,141	6,214	6,287
28 – Proceeds from nonfinancial assets	887	645	546	443	1,354	$y=73.16x+555.57$	995	1,068	1,141	1,214	1,287
29 – Development fees and contributions *15	11,837	8,962	8,392	7,461	5,724	$y=12593-1372.6x$ (R2=0.94)	5,000	5,000	5,000	5,000	5,000
30 – Proceeds from financial assets											
31 Cash reserves from previous years	4,978	2,867				actual or projected balances			2,662	155	2,233
32 Debt financing (actual or need in projections) *16	3,222	4,956	10,192	12,548	7,022	From debt database	5,115	11,871	4,500	4,000	3,741
J Overall closing balance (A+I) – (B+D+F)	2,867	(3,812)	(2,741)	(2,337)	(4,452)	(A–I)–(B+D+F)	956	2,662	155	2,233	1,616

Note: ShS (shillings) is a notional name of the currency of the sample city.

scenario, the city may decide to borrow or disburse faster and increase the development funding available substantially. There is no need for large sums: the scenario presented in table 3.41 includes increasing borrowing or loan disbursement in year 8 by ShS4,000 (from ShS438 to ShS4,500), and in year 9 increasing planned disbursement by a mere ShS1,000 (from ShS2,990 to ShS4,000).

*Investment funding available (*17)*: With these changes, the funding available increases dramatically and development investments can be increased substantially while maintaining overall budget balances. Projecting budgets with negative balances should be ruled out!

*Capital development expenditures (*18)*: The optimistic projection scenario would enable the city to maintain capital investments in the range of ShS20,000 million, which would remain below the 40 percent of current revenues (between 20 and 30 percent) but at least would enable moderate but steady development. Important to note is that the CIPs also include investments by municipal entities and even moderately by the private sector, with which the investments will exceed 30 percent of current revenues. Unfortunately, the analyzed scenarios and the projected numbers do not support more ambitious investment plans, unless more radical improvements of the revenues or some remarkable savings in current expenditures create room for greater development funding. This is an important lesson the higher decision-making bodies should be aware of.

Financial Projections: Lessons Learned

Summary lessons from the conservative financial projections

We should note that the overall closing balance has improved and shows robust surpluses due to the increased revenues and the very conservative CIPs in the conservative scenario. This suggests that the city can revise CIPs and use cash reserves directly or borrow against cash reserves and increase capital investments substantially even in the conservative scenario.

Summary lessons from the optimistic financial projections

The optimistic scenario assumes demanding but possible changes in tax revenues, a more optimistic economic scenario that supports generating substantial revenues from land development fees, and enables additional borrowing to finance substantially greater development while maintaining a balanced budget (a key obligation for municipalities).

Gradual changes: The analysis of the two scenarios has also revealed that changes in total revenues, expenditures, and capital finances are very gradual even when strong political support is assumed (which is not always the case), because it is difficult to change large numbers even over a five-year time period.

Financial Ratios in Projections

MFSA users may calculate the main financial ratios for the projected time period. This has been done for the sample city, and results are summarized in table 3.42. This is also an important communication tool to engage the city's higher decision-making bodies in substantial policy dialogue based on real and solid numbers instead of simple revenue or development plans.

Creditworthiness: Operating savings over current revenues show marginal improvements in the base scenario; numbers get closer to the 20 percent range in the optimistic scenario. Thus, the city presumably faces some risk premium in case of debt financing.

Indebtedness: All indebtedness ratios remain stable even in the optimistic and higher investment scenario with increased borrowing. This suggests that there is room for debt financing, although the city should and indeed has started to approach external funding outside debt.

Table 3.42 **Financial Ratios in Conservative Projection Scenario**

Indicator (definition)	Comparative index (benchmark)	Actual					Projections				
		Year 1	Year 2	Year 3	Year 4	Year 5	Year 6	Year 7	Year 8	Year 9	Year 10
1 Creditworthiness											
Operating savings before interests/ Current revenue	> 30%	20%	8%	15%	15%	14%	15%	14%	15%	17%	15%
Net operating surplus (after debt service)/Current revenue	> 20%	19%	7%	14%	13%	10%	6%	5%	6%	10%	5%
Investment balance before loan/Total revenue	> −15%	−1%	−16%	−22%	−24%	−16%	−14%	−12%	−6%	−1%	−4%
Financing gap after loan proceeds/Total revenue	> −5%	5%	−7%	−5%	−4%	−6%	6%	21%	18%	23%	27%
2 Indebtedness											
Debt outstanding/Operating surplus (capacity to clear its debt)	< 10 years	1	4	3	5	5	5	5	4	3	3
Debt service/Total current revenue	< 10%	2%	2%	3%	4%	8%	9%	9%	9%	8%	9%
Debt outstanding/Budget total	< 60%	14%	24%	36%	51%	56%	63%	69%	59%	51%	48%
Borrowing/Current revenues	< 15%	8%	14%	23%	25%	13%	7%	16%	1%	3%	4%
Operating margin/Interest payment	> 15	27	7	11	6	4	5	5	6	9	9
Debt outstanding/Total current revenue	< 100%	20%	34%	51%	71%	69%	68%	73%	62%	53%	49%

continued next page

Table 3.42 Continued

Indicator (definition)	Comparative index (benchmark)	Actual					Projections				
		Year 1	Year 2	Year 3	Year 4	Year 5	Year 6	Year 7	Year 8	Year 9	Year 10
3 Fiscal autonomy											
Own (taxes + fees + unconditional grants)/Total current revenue	> 80%	85%	93%	93%	94%	99%	99%	99%	99%	99%	99%
4 Capital investment effort											
Capital investment expenditure/Current revenue	> 40%	61%	56%	56%	54%	30%	22%	20%	12%	11%	9%
Capital investment expenditure/Total expenditure	> 30%	43%	38%	40%	39%	25%	19%	17%	11%	11%	9%
Current margin/Capital investment expenditure	> 25%	32%	13%	25%	24%	34%	54%	55%	100%	142%	138%
Capital investments from earmarked grants/Total investment expenditure	< 50%	0%	0%	1%	1%	1%	3%	4%	5%	6%	6%
5 Level of service sustainability											
Maintenance works expenditure/Operating expenditures	> 15%	9%	9%	7%	8%	7%	7%	8%	8%	9%	9%
Taxes collected/Taxes levied	> 90%						60%	60%	70%	80%	80%
Fees collected/Fees billed	> 90%						60%	60%	70%	80%	85%
6 Quality of operations											
Salaries and wages/Operating actual expenditures	< 40%	20%	20%	20%	20%	18%	18%	18%	18%	17%	17%

Capital investment efforts: The capital investment efforts ratios reflect a clear policy goal to stabilize indebtedness and ensure solid and timely debt service. As a result, the capital investments are projected to remain below the 40 percent target because of long-time effects of the high investments in the year 1 through year 5 time period. Capital investments are substantially larger in the optimistic scenario, but still leave the city's ratios below 30 percent. These results also underscore the importance of seeking external funding by both municipal enterprises and the private sector.

Repair and maintenance: The ratios on repair and maintenance show a marginal increase in both scenarios, despite the fact that the plans include doubling the annual repair and maintenance expenditures by year 10 as compared to year 5. This is an obvious effect that the overall revenues will also increase in the projected time period. In addition, however, the doubling of an initially low level of maintenance expenses may appear insufficient because the large capital investments completed and assets installed/built during the year 1 through year 5 time period will increasingly pressure repair and maintenance needs in the forecasted five years ahead.

Takeaway lessons

The short summary of the projections results underscores that the most important role of an MFSA analysis is not only to support extensive and substantive policy dialogue in and across various levels of local government executives and policy makers but also to promote the approach that policy dialogues should be based on numbers, clear assumptions, and careful analysis of the results rather than wishful thinking.

MFSA is a policy analysis tool: Finally, it is important to emphasize that the MFSA is not a budget planning tool and that decisions on short or medium terms remain on the shoulders of the persons and bodies responsible for budget planning and execution. The MFSA helps to systematically analyze and explore underlying tendencies, identify feasible and realistic options, and support decisions for corrective measures. These are the subject of the final step of the MFSA, namely the MFSA Action Plan, which builds on key findings of the previous steps.

Financial Projections: Creditworthiness and Borrowing Capacity

Creditworthiness

Creditworthiness is a well-used term, but it is a softer term than some people would expect. The MFSA results help us (just like investors, creditors, or ministries) to assess a city's present and future creditworthiness. The financial ratios provide a solid basis for creditworthiness assessment; however, it is still more a qualitative than a quantitative measurement, because creditworthiness is on a continuum and cannot be captured by one single number. It is, therefore, better to assess creditworthiness in ranges, such as *weak, medium,* or *strong* creditworthiness, and using several years rather than one particular year. Another issue to bear in mind is that historical figures on creditworthiness may be used if there is no projection, but they signal creditworthiness in the past; however, investors are interested more in the projected future creditworthiness that signals capacity for repaying new debts. Finally, there are several indicators that may signal different levels of creditworthiness, so the final assessment is a combination of various signals, explained below with the results of the sample city.

The sample city has medium creditworthiness (as opposed to weak or strong). The *operating savings* are substantial (table 3.43), but the ratios stay in the median between zero and the high creditworthiness level in both the past and the future medium term. They show some improvement in projections but remain

Table 3.43 Creditworthiness Analysis

Indicator (definition)	Comparative index (benchmark)	Actual					Projections				
		Year 1	Year 2	Year 3	Year 4	Year 5	Year 6	Year 7	Year 8	Year 9	Year 10
Operating savings before interests/ Current revenue	> 30%	20%	8%	15%	15%	14%	15%	14%	15%	17%	15%
Net operating surplus (after debt service)/ Current revenue	> 20%	19%	7%	14%	13%	10%	6%	5%	6%	10%	5%
Investment balance before loan/Total revenue	> –15%	–1%	–16%	–22%	–24%	–16%	–14%	–12%	–6%	–1%	–4%
Financing gap after loan proceeds/Total revenue	> –5%	5%	–7%	–5%	–4%	–6%	6%	21%	18%	23%	27%

far from the 30 percent investment grade ratio. The net operating savings ratio is projected to drop from above 10 percent to below 10 percent, which signals substantial weakening of creditworthiness in the projected period. In contrast, both the investment balance and the financing gap ratios show strong positions and good improvements in projected years. Thus, it is fair to say the city has medium creditworthiness.

Borrowing, credit, or debt capacity

Borrowing capacity means how much a city can borrow, that is, what amount of new debt can be procured at a specific point in time. Borrowing, credit, and debt capacity therefore have the same meaning in this context, so we will use the term debt capacity for the sake of simplicity. It is a vital indicator for city governments, and it should be estimated in real numbers (as opposed to qualitative creditworthiness measures). There are several indicators, however, that may induce different numbers in estimating the debt capacity of a city. Estimating debt capacity requires combining results from ratios,

revenues, and debt databases; thus, calculating debt capacity is inevitably more complicated than assessing creditworthiness. Some may use creditworthiness and borrowing capacity terms as synonyms, but for the MFSA analysis it is vital to distinguish these two terms. Table 3.44 shows six ratios, two of which are also known as regulatory ratios: *Debt outstanding / Budget total [<60%]* and *Borrowing / Current revenues [<15%]*. The other four ratios indicate specific financial aspects of credit capacity.

Regulatory ratios are being used in many developed countries (for example, in Europe) and are increasingly popular in the developing world. The advantage of these ratios is that they are easy to measure by both the city and the ministries because they require obtaining only two numbers, such as debt stock and total revenues (or total budget). They have serious shortcomings, however, which include the following. First, a city with low creditworthiness (operating savings are negligible) can still be assessed to have huge debt capacity if its *Debt outstanding / Budget total* is far below 60 percent. The

Table 3.44 Ratios for Debt and Borrowing Capacity Analysis

Indicator (definition)	Comparative index (benchmark)	Actual					Projections				
		Year 1	Year 2	Year 3	Year 4	Year 5	Year 6	Year 7	Year 8	Year 9	Year 10
Debt outstanding/ Operating surplus (capacity to clear its debt)	< 10 years	1	4	3	5	5	5	5	4	3	3
Debt service/Total current revenue	< 10%	2%	2%	3%	4%	8%	9%	9%	9%	8%	9%
Debt outstanding/ Budget total	< 60%	14%	24%	36%	51%	56%	63%	69%	59%	51%	48%
Borrowing/Current revenues	< 15%	8%	14%	23%	25%	13%	7%	16%	1%	3%	4%
Operating margin/ Interest payment	> 15	27	7	11	6	4	5	5	6	9	9
Debt outstanding/ Total current revenue	< 100%	20%	34%	51%	71%	69%	68%	73%	62%	53%	49%

flip-side is that a city may have robust operating savings, and good debt service capacity, but the 60 percent limit constrains its new debt.

The ratio of *Borrowing / Current revenues* again is easy to calculate, but it may be misleading. A city may become overindebted (although in compliance with the indebtedness ratio) if it borrows about 15 percent of current revenues repeatedly in each of several consecutive years. In contrast, a city with strong repayment capacity would be able to service a larger loan that may violate this 15 percent rule in one particular year but plans no borrowing in the next two to three years, so, on average it would comply with this regulation. The combination of these two ratios provides better control over indebtedness, because they control both stock and flow indebtedness ratios. Finally, there are vague enforcement rules attached to these ratios in many countries; as a result, cities may violate these rules without serious consequences. In practice, these guiding regulatory ratios are useful despite their said limitations, so cities

may use them as signals even if there are no such national rules in effect.

The sample city has launched a major investment program with fast-growing debts in the past five years; as a result, it will violate the 60 percent rule in the first two projected years and will have reasonable room for new debt only in the last two projected years from the perspective of this ratio. This suggests that the city can reach debt stock of ShS74 billion, against the ShS47 billion projected debt stock (data from table 3.9 and table 3.38), that is, its capacity to procure new debts will be ShS27 billion in year 10. In the context of the MFSA, borrowing means disbursement of debt in a particular year. The city will exceed the 15 percent of current revenue over borrowing limit in year 7, but it will stay well below after that. In year 10, the city can disburse an additional 11 percent of current revenues beyond the plans (data from table 3.9 and table 3.38), that is, ShS10.8 billion beyond the planned ShS3.7 billion. We will see that some other ratios indicate lower borrowing capacity.

Debt and borrowing capacity based on debt service capacity ratios

The other four ratios in table 3.44 aim to measure debt or borrowing capacity according to the city's ability to service old and new debts in the future. They signal the size of debt a city can procure in addition to its existing debt stock, using benchmarks established by creditors or rating agencies. These ratios provide more precise measures for debt capacity; however, they require more complicated calculations.

Debt outstanding over operating surplus: This ratio requires that a city should be able to clear all debts from operating surplus within 10 years. The sample city's ratios are well below 10 years; it can clear its debts in 5 years or fewer. This ratio suggests that in year 10 the sample city can procure new debt up to the level that its outstanding debts can be cleared within 10 years as opposed to the projected level of 3 years. The sample city is projected to have ShS14.1 billion of operating savings (table 3.39) and ShS47.6 billion of outstanding debt at the end of the five-year plan (table 3.38). According to this ratio, the city can raise its debt stock up to ShS141 billion (10 times the amount of operating savings). Thus, the capacity to procure new debt is ShS93.4 billion in the year 10 planned year. We should note, however, that this ratio does not capture how much of the operating savings is required to service the existing debts.

Debt service over total current revenue: This benchmark suggests that a city can use up to 10 percent of its current revenue for debt service in order to remain a stable debtor. The sample city is projected to nearly exhaust this debt capacity, because the projected ratios will move up to the range of 8–9 percent in the planned period. Calculating the capacity for procuring new debts in the projected year 10 requires a certain procedure and key data.

- The sample city will have a projected current revenue of ShS97.4 billion (table 3.39), which allows ShS9.74 billion debt service according to this ratio.

- The debt service capacity also depends on the debt terms, such as interest rate and maturity (number of years to repay). The existing debt stock of the sample city indicates various interest rates (table 3.8); let's assume a 5 percent rate for debts will be available with a 15-year maturity investment loan to be procured in year 10.

- The city will have high debt service of ShS8.6 billion in year 10 (table 3.38), and thus will have room for additional debt service up to ShS1.14 billion (9.74 billion – 8.6 billion).

- The annuity and present value calculation (see TD4 in appendix B) suggests that the sample city will have the capacity to procure ShS11.83 billion of new debt while complying with the said debt service ratio in year 10; this amount is much less than the other ratios would allow, although it is still substantial.

Operating margin over interest payment: This ratio suggests that, for secure debt management, the operating margin should be 15 times greater than the annual interest payment. The ratios in table 3.38 indicate that the sample city is in trouble, because the combination of debt services (results of interest rates, maturity, and grace period) will overburden the city budget with debt service around year 10. Thus, the city has no borrowing capacity in the planned five years according to this measure, because the operating margin will be only nine times greater than the due interest payments in year 10 (table 3.38 and table 3.39). The city may still procure debt, however, if lenders and regulators do not measure this ratio, or if it receives credit enhancement support (the latter is beyond the scope of MFSA).

Table 3.45 Debt Capacity of Sample City in Year 10

	Capacity to procure new debt
Ratios to project debt capacity	ShS billion
Debt outstanding/ Budget total	27.0
Debt outstanding/ Operating surplus	93.4
Debt service/Total current revenue	11.8
Operating margin/ Interest payment	0
Debt outstanding/ Total current revenue	49.8

Note: ShS (shillings) is a notional name of the currency of the sample city.

Debt outstanding over current revenues: This ratio provides a good cushion for additional debt, because it is projected to be 49 percent, against the 100 percent benchmark. The sample city is projected to have ShS97.4 billion of current revenues in the projected year 10 (table 3.39), so it can reach a debt stock of ShS97.4 billion. It will, however, already have an ShS47.6 billion debt stock from previous years (table 3.38). Thus, the capacity for procuring new debts is estimated to be ShS49.8 billion in the planned year 10.

Summary of estimated debt capacity

The summary table 3.45 offers several lessons. Estimating debt capacity is a complicated business and requires clever judgments and assumptions. The various financial ratios suggest very different levels of debt capacity, meaning different amounts of possible new debt for the sample city ranging from zero to ShS93 billion. Lenders or potential investors most likely would calculate these or similar ratios to estimate how much the sample city can borrow given the present and conservatively projected financial scenarios. Depending on its policy, a lender may remain conservative and estimate ShS11.8 billion new debt capacity in normal terms; however, it may go beyond that amount by attaching a higher risk premium or requesting some credit enhancement or securitization of debt. The list of estimated debt capacity suggests, however, that lenders would likely stay somewhere within the ShS11.8 billion and 27.0 billion range. The city, however, may still need to meet the regulatory rules and limit borrowing (disbursement of loans) below ShS10.8 billion in the last planned year.

Financial projections in optimistic scenarios: The sample city has completed financial projections also in a somewhat optimistic scenario (table 3.41). Readers may test their knowledge and lessons learned by estimating the debt capacity using the optimistic scenario and following the procedures explained above. Lenders and investors, however, would carefully assess assumptions for any optimistic scenario before starting estimation of higher debt/credit capacity of the same city under such scenarios.

Debt capacity based on financial reports: The above assessments of debt capacity reflect the debt capacity of the sample city based on the assumption that the new debts would be paid back exclusively from the city's budgets. In practice, however, there are more options to consider; the most important among these are instruments that help substantially expand either current or capital revenues and thus expand both debt and development capacities. These require detailed investigation, planning, and adoption of specific actions in the MFSA Action Plan, such as asset/liability management or debt policy or project financing policy reforms.

Expanding Credit and Borrowing Capacity: Think Outside the Box

The MFSA not only helps users estimate development funding capacities systematically through detailed analyses of historical results and trends, but it also encourages users to seek options outside their regular box and gain additional funding. Users should test scenarios by assuming more radical improvement of current or capital revenues above the historical trends and adopt medium-term CIPs expanded with additional funding that the city has not used before, and that thus do not show historical trends. Such revenue sources or instruments include land value capture (LVC). LVC, or land-based financing, refers to various instruments that are used to tap into the private gains of land owners, developers, or the general community that resulted in public infrastructure development or in smart strategic planning or zoning (Peterson 2008). The best-known instruments are detailed in chapter 4.

Development capacity can be expanded also by advanced *project financing* policies or procedures that are beyond the scope of the MFSA, although they are core subjects in good CIP planning and clever consideration of financing alternatives (Freire 2014; Freire and Kopanyi 2018). Many such alternatives aim to finance new investments outside the budget of a municipality (off-budget financing), including ring-fenced project financing or public–private partnership.

Step 5: Financial Management Assessment

The MFSA includes two analysis approaches as depicted by figure 3.4. earlier in the chapter: (1) detailed analysis of the financial data and historical analysis of the present and future with projections completed in the above sections; and then (2) a qualitative assessment of the condition of the financial management system. The results of the financial data analysis indicate the health and financial challenges in numeric terms; however, the underlying causes behind financial challenges are often embedded in the financial management framework and system, and issues and solutions can be traced only via a detailed qualitative assessment. A version of this type of assessment is known as the Public Expenditure and Financial Accountability assessment (PEFA), which can be completed in several months by a team of external specialists in cooperation with the municipal staff (PEFA Secretariat 2016a).

Objective: The objective of the financial management assessment (FMA) is to analyze the quality of the financial management system, procedures, and practices of a local government and identify specific areas of concerns, weaknesses, and possible options for improvement.

Methodology: The FMA methodology is very different from the PEFA in three ways. First, the self-assessment modality requires transforming the questions into a multiple choice test format with prefabricated alternatives, from which the users can select those that are most relevant or that most correctly reflect the local situation. Second, the MFSA financial assessment that is supposed to be completed before the FMA provides for a solid ground of financial information useful for selecting the relevant answers; thus, it saves a lot of time in the course of the FMA. Third, the self-assessment modality requires strong self-discipline on the part of users to reduce the subjectivity effects.

Subjective judgments are unavoidable during the self-assessed FMA, but MFSA users should be cautious about these challenges and should aim to reduce the subjectivity effects. Answering the questions or selecting the most relevant alternatives with close correspondence to the financial results and ratios is the best practice to mitigate the subjectivity. For instance, some may say that 60 percent tax collection efficiency is not only realistic in developing countries but also seems reasonable. A closer look at the FMA questions, however, suggests that (1) the answer requires revisiting the financial reports to see the effective local ratio; and (2) 60 percent or below is the lowest score (D) in the FMA assessment. Thus, we strongly encourage that users, before answering the FMA questions, read and consider the financial results related to the financial performance. Should a user fill out this FMA without careful consideration, the results would likely mislead rather than guide the local government and thus will not serve the main objective of identifying issues and specific areas for improvement.

The MFSA is a combination of quantitative (financial) and qualitative assessments (called FMA) that has been developed following the models and methodology of assessments introduced by multinational organizations to review the quality and guide improvements in areas of public financial management for better sustainability. These assessments have grown out of the standard financial analyses and audits that analyze largely numeric results of national accounts and public sector entities (figure 3.10). In contrast, these qualitative assessments aim to explore and expose the underlying legal–institutional framework, organizational, and management factors and capacities that eventually determine the performance of the public sector because the financial results cannot be improved without improving financial management. The four assessments follow the same methodology, supplement, and interlink each other with more emphasis on one or other particular subject area (see figure 3.10 that shows the interlinks in callouts).

Figure 3.10   Systems and Models for Assessing Public Financial Management Performance

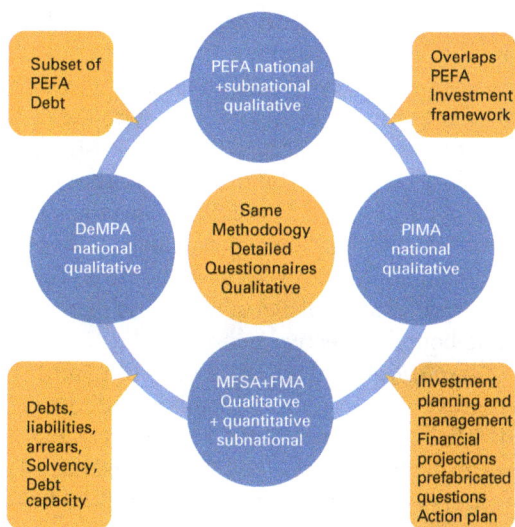

Note: DeMPA = debt management performance assessment; FMA = financial management assessment; MFSA = Municipal Finances Self-Assessment; PEFA = Public Expenditure and Financial Accountability; PIMA = public investment management assessment.

Public Expenditure and Financial Accountability (PEFA) Assessment

The PEFA is a methodology for assessing public financial management performance and reporting strengths and weaknesses to improve financial sustainability. Seven development partners introduced PEFA primarily for assessing country-level systems (European Commission, International Monetary Fund, World Bank, French Ministry of Foreign Affairs, Norwegian Ministry of Foreign Affairs, State Secretariat of Economic Affairs of Switzerland, and U.K. Department for International Development). One PEFA modality applies to cities or other subnational governments, with one additional indicator to assess the transfers from higher government tiers (PEFA Secretariat 2016d). The PEFA assessment uses detailed questionnaires and scoring methodology in 31 thematic areas, and it requires several weeks of work by a dedicated expert team, as explained in the *PEFA Handbook* (PEFA Secretariat 2016a). PEFA results are summarized in a very detailed and long report that helps beneficiaries adopt corrective actions after PEFA. There are also similar assessments

(AECOM 2015), but PEFA has become the main-stream approach worldwide.

The FMA under the MFSA has been modeled after and has greatly benefitted from the PEFA methodology in the *PEFA Handbook*, Volumes I, II, and III (PEFA Secretariat 2016a, 2016b, 2016c,) and in *Supplementary Guidance for Subnational PEFA Assessments* (PEFA Secretariat 2016d). There are substantial differences, which include the following. First, the PEFA requires very extensive fieldwork and data gathering that takes several weeks of expert work for data collection and analysis. Second, the PEFA uses a book-size list of extended guidance and templates for methodology, information gathering, and scoring the results. The extended guidance is meant to apply in all cases no matter the assessment modality. It aims at guaranteeing the same level of objectivity. Specific guidance has been developed for subnational entities. Third, the PEFA ends up with a very detailed report with a series of annexes. Finally, the PEFA report is submitted to a rigorous quality review process involving peers, endorsed by the *PEFA Check* (PEFA Secretariat 2017). In contrast, the MFSA FMA (step 5) is designed to (1) be a self-assessment by one city officer or a small team of municipal officers; (2) be completed in a few hours, rather than several weeks; (3) be completed with the very short list of guidance presented in this section; and (4) result in a final FMA report that is short and aims to signal key challenges and outline solutions to be included in the MFSA Action Plan.

Debt Management Permanence Assessment (DeMPA)

The debt management performance assessment (DeMPA) framework, tool, and methodology introduced by the World Bank emulates and supplements the PEFA (World Bank 2015). DeMPA is fully consistent with and focuses on only one critical segment of PEFA, namely debt management. DeMPA uses the same

methodology—that is, detailed questionnaires and scoring to support aggregate results on strength and weaknesses. Many DeMPA indicators are essentially more detailed drill-downs of PEFA indicators; interlinks between the two assessments include areas such as audit, fiscal planning, and coordination with macroeconomic policies.

Public investment management assessment (PIMA)

Public investment management assessment (PIMA) is an International Monetary Fund tool for assessing infrastructure governance over the full investment cycle and supporting institution building (IMF 2018). PIMA identifies and assesses 15 *institutions* in three groups: planning, allocating resources, and implementing investments. PIMA summarizes the strengths and weaknesses of country public investment processes, and sets out a prioritized and sequenced reform action plan. PIMA overlaps with PEFA in the area of public investment systems and frameworks, and it overlaps with DeMPA in areas of debt management in the public investment context. The PIMA methodology is very similar to the PEFA and DeMPA with detailed questionnaire and scoring; however, PIMA uses multiple-choice questions instead of the open-ended questions used in PEFA to help quick and seamless completion of questionnaires. Unlike PEFA and DeMPA, PIMA also leads to and supports preparation of a detailed Action Plan with time-bound corrective measures.

The MFSA, and within it the MFA, aims to improve financial sustainability and quality of local governance just like the three other assessment systems, but MFSA exclusively focuses on local governments. MFSA has benefitted from and is fully consistent with both the substance and the methodology of the three other systems. FMA covers 18 of the 31 PEFA thematic areas, all that are applicable at the local government level, and uses detailed questionnaires and scoring similar to PEFA, but tailored to self-assessment modality. The MFSA introduces procedures for data and qualitative assessment of local debt management, in harmony with DeMPA modality at the local level on areas such as detailed analysis of debt, contingent liabilities, arrears, and forecasting of debt capacity, as well as quality of expenditure management, audits, planning, and financial structuring. The MFSA covers PIMA areas such as capital investment planning, forecasting, financial management of investments, and expenditure control, but it also uses PIMA methodology with prefabricated questions to help self-assessment modality and puts strong emphasis on forming a time-bound Action Plan with funding projections based on quantitative and qualitative results.

MFSA–FMA Thematic Areas

The FMA covers four thematic areas, each with four or five sets of questions: (1) Intergovernmental Relations; (2) Planning, Budgeting, and Budget Implementation; (3) Financial Management Systems and Practices; and (4) Financial Reporting, Disclosure, and Transparency. These areas constitute the main underlying causes of the good or weak financial performance of a local government. These are the thematic areas where the identified weaknesses deserve attention and thus corrective measures can be included later in the MFSA Action Plan. For instance, the low level and poor collection of local tax revenues is a financial fact, but that does not indicate how to increase revenues or improve revenue collection. The FMA may point correspondingly to the fact that the city does not even have a reliable tax database, without which improving revenues seems impossible.

In the next section we will discuss each thematic area by the respective questions and address some critical challenges in marking the right answers by using the example of the sample city discussed in all other sections of this Handbook.

MFSA–FMA Analysis and Scoring

FMA scoring is a simple and straightforward procedure. The questions of each thematic area are listed in four separate tables. Each table includes four or five questions each with four prefabricated answers, developed by experts using international experience and PEFA practices.

Tasks: The user of the FMA template needs to read the four answers very carefully and select/mark the one he or she feels the most precisely reflects the local situation. It should be noted, however, that the answers often include several conditions and each of these conditions should be sufficiently met in the local situation in order to support a specific scoring.

The scores are ranked and marked with A, B, C, or D. This means that the B score should be granted if all but at least one condition for a score of A are met. For instance, the A answer to predictability of transfers reads: *"There is a mature and robust framework for the local government sector with clear definition of transfers. Any changes are made at a deliberate and predictable pace. Transfers are stable and predictable, regulated, timely transmitted, no ad hoc grants."* Only a B score should be given if said transfers are transmitted with delays, despite all other conditions being met. This sort of rigorous reading and scoring requires not only attention but also discipline by the FMA user.

The scores can be summarized by thematic area: should the scores include C, B, C, and D in a thematic area, then the user may give an aggregate score of C. The short summary report should also address the lowest scores in each area and may propose corrective actions to the Action Plan. Because improvements are always possible and justified in many areas, users need to select eventually the most important issues that can be corrected in the short or medium term. Below we introduce and analyze the scoring tables with information from the sample city to score; we mark the score selected by a local officer with highlighting. The complete FMA questionnaire is presented in appendix B (see TD5).

Intergovernmental Relations

The intergovernmental relations thematic area includes five questions: predictability of transfers, intergovernmental mandate, debt regulations, own revenue self-confidence, and expenditure spending flexibility. This section assesses how the national legal and regulatory framework impacts the quality of local financial management. On one hand, it is a bit of challenge for local finance officers to judge the national framework; on the other hand, the officers are very well aware of these framework issues and run into respective challenges frequently. Thus, it is right to ask a local officer to fill out the intergovernmental relations section because he or she has or ought to have sufficient knowledge on these issues.

Addressing the challenges identified in this section may go beyond the competency of a local government officer. It is important, however, to list them and to be aware of these challenges because the external partners, such as lender banks or potential investors, are keen to know if the intergovernmental framework is stable and supportive of the financial capacity and stability of the local government.

Predictability of transfers: Transfers from higher government tiers play a very substantial role in financing local governments, and local officers are well aware of the situation (table 3.46). In planning time, the issue is whether the amount and installments of transfers are known on time, say because of a set formula or stable common practice. The other

Table 3.46 Predictability of Transfers

Predictability of transfers	A	There is a mature and robust framework for the LG sector with clear definition of transfers. Any changes are made at a deliberate and predictable pace. Transfers are stable and predictable, regulated, timely transmitted; no ad hoc grants.
	B	CG transfers are predictable annually and regulated, but delivery times may vary during the year; no ad hoc grants.
	C	Transfers are not regulated but are, by and large, stable; ad hoc grants appear.
	D	Transfers are unpredictable, and/or not regulated, and/or ad hoc grants are common.

Note: CG = central government; LG = local government.

Table 3.47 Intergovernmental Mandates

Intergovernmental mandate arrangements	A	Revenue and expenditure mandates are clearly stipulated by law, and are respected. Any changes are made at a deliberate and predictable pace.
	B	Revenue and expenditure mandates are stipulated, but not in harmony; rules are respected with some exceptions. Intergovernmental finance changes are mostly discussed with LGs.
	C	Revenue and expenditure mandates are not well regulated, but rarely change.
	D	Revenue and expenditure mandates are unclear, not fully respected, and subject to changes without prior announcement or discussions.

Note: LG = local government.

issue is whether the transfers are conveyed in a timely manner and in accordance with the rules, formulas, or generally accepted practices. This is reflected in the A answer option. Ad hoc grants might play an important role in an extreme situation, such as after natural disasters, but this thematic question addresses the regular, normal situation in which ad hoc grants are considered a deviation from the formula or rules, so use of ad hoc grants downgrades the scoring of transfer predictability. The sample city has marked the C answer, because transfers from higher government tiers are fairly stable, but the country lacks a legislated transfer formula.

Intergovernmental mandates: Intergovernmental mandates include revenue assignments and the expenditure assignments (table 3.47). Law and regulations set the framework and assign specific revenues for local government that typically include transfers from higher government tiers, own-source revenues, and rules for incurring debt (that is, rules on if, when, and how to borrow short-term and long-term loans, issue bonds, and so on). The expenditure assignments stipulate the core responsibilities of the local governments and the corresponding authority to spend money to cover the cost of assigned services and functions. A fundamental principle of the decentralized government systems is that revenue and expenditure assignments should be in harmony, in order to ensure sustainable function of the local governments. However, real life is different, and the mandates may remain unclear or loosely followed, or tend to change without discussions with key stakeholders.

The sample city is in a relatively good situation with a B score, because the mandates are stipulated, but there are shortcomings in harmonies between revenue and expenditure assignments and in implementation of rules.

Debt regulation: Debt regulations show a wide range of approaches across the globe from very liberal market-based financing to total bans of formal debt (although forced credits by unpaid bills are often accepted as informal debt rules in many countries). Prudential debt regulation and harmony with market rules are vital determinants of the quality of local financial systems. For that reason, category A depicts a very robust framework typical in developed countries, although the debt regulations in South Africa also meet the score A requirement.

The sample city faces rules that each borrowing plan should be submitted to the Ministry of Finance for approval, and loan agreements can be signed and valid only with the formal approval of the ministry (table 3.48). This situation earns the sample city a score of C, because the ministry provides for some quality assurance, but it also reduces the responsibility of the local government and, in some cases, may open the gates for politically based approval of loans and moral hazard. In short, the involvement of a ministry is a sort of risk factor, even if it may incentivize some lenders, because it may work as an informal guarantee by the ministry.

Own-source revenue (OSR) confidence: The basic principle of decentralized intergovernmental systems is that local governments not

Table 3.48 Debt Regulations

Debt regulations	A	Debt financing is clearly regulated with market-based rules and insolvency framework.
	B	Debt financing is regulated, but there is no framework for managing insolvencies.
	C	Ministry (of finance) approves loans with or without clear rules for debt financing.
	D	Debt financing is unregulated, OR no borrowing is allowed.

Table 3.49 Own-Source Revenue Confidence

Own-source revenue self-confidence	A	LG has the flexibility to change taxes/fees on a significant share of operating revenues, and increases are politically acceptable at the local level. OSR is about 40% of revenues or above. LG has good collection power and capacities. OSRs are predictable with clear visibility of future revenues.
	B	LG has the flexibility to change base or rate of some taxes/fees, but increases are politically challenging at the local level. Collection power and capacity are reasonable with low incentives to increase revenues. OSRs are substantial (above 20%) and somewhat predictable.
	C	LG has no power to change base or rate of taxes/fees, but may propose changes to the government/ministry. OSRs are somewhat predictable but low (below 20%).
	D	LG has no power to change rates or base of taxes and fees. OSRs are very low (below 10%), not predictable, or both.

Note: LG = local government; OSR = own-source revenue.

Table 3.50 Expenditure Spending Responsibility

Expenditure spending flexibility	A	Spending responsibilities are highly stable and predictable over time. LG has the flexibility to change the level and nature of spending, such as by cutting public services or changing service standards, on a significant share of operating expenditures. These cuts are politically acceptable at the local level.
	B	LG has the legal power to change the level and nature of spending, such as by cutting public services or changing service standards, on a significant share of operating expenditures. These cuts are conceptually acceptable at the local level, but rarely occur and only under extreme situations.
	C	LG has the legal power to change the level and nature of spending, but this occurs on an ad hoc basis against shortages of cash and is not a common practice. Overspending occurs time and again.
	D	LG can change the level and nature of spending, but this happens as quick fixes without long-term plans. Overspending in some line items is very common.

Note: LG = local government.

only have clear revenue-raising mandates but also are empowered to set the base and the rates of the main revenue sources, taxes, fees, and charges (table 3.49). OSR confidence measures the quality of the local financial system from this perspective. Some scholars put high emphasis on whether the local government is empowered to change the revenue bases and rates; however, the effective revenue collection is often far below the capacity that can be calculated using centrally set rates, bases, and rules. Thus, this indicator also should capture the local political support and capacity for raising local revenues as part of the revenue confidence.

The sample city faces multiple challenges in revenue management, because it has no power to change the revenue bases or rates; instead, it may propose and indeed has proposed changes to the finance ministry and, as a result, has reached a high level of OSR (46 percent of total revenues). More than half of this OSR, however, is from nonrecurrent sources (land sale and development fees). Thus, the sample city rightly scored OSR confidence as C.

Expenditure spending responsibility: The expenditure spending responsibility indicator captures the issue of the local ability to manage expenditures in changing situations in order to maintain stable budget balances (table 3.50). The core "A" option reflects the various underlying factors of this ability or capacity, predictable and stable spending responsibility, which is high if (1) OSRs and unconditional transfers represent a high share of total revenues; and (2) the local government has the flexibility to change, rearrange, or specifically cut expenses in case of revenue shortages in order to avoid overspending and forced deficit financing.

The sample city has a strong OSR base and a high share of unconditional grants, and it even has the legal room for changing expenditures. Still, the officer points out the issue that rearranging of expenditures across line items are ad hoc and overspending occurs. Indeed, the city has resulted in budget deficits four times in the last five years, which is an apparent signal of uncontrolled spending (see budget snapshot in historical database, table 3.17). Thus, the city wisely scored this indicator as C.

Planning, Budgeting, and Budget Implementation

This thematic area analyzes the quality of the local financial management system in planning, budgeting, and budget implementation by addressing four specific questions: strategic plan and CIP, budget planning, scope of budget, and budget implementation. There is no

good financial management system without strategic planning and three-to-five-year perspectives, reliable budgeting, and disciplined budget execution where the budget drives the events and the spending during the year rather than just reflects arbitrary changes and results at the end of the year.

Strategic plan and CIP: Developing a strategic plan and multiyear CIP has become a best practice, because it expands the scope of local financial management from the short annual to a strategic three-to-five-year perspective. This is also why the MFSA analysis takes the historical perspective back five years to draw lessons from trends, and then makes financial projections five years ahead. Developing and adopting strategic plans for the medium or long term, often 10–20 years ahead, has a significant value, despite the fact that these plans should be revised against changing circumstances (table 3.51). Likewise, the CIP that is preferably adopted as a rolling five-year plan sets more concrete and specific targets for medium-term development actions and does so in the context of well-identified financing options. Again, this is a very powerful instrument, despite the fact that the CIP can be revised annually, and the plans of the coming year should be carefully analyzed before they are moved from the CIP to the annual budget. Local government practices around the globe show wide variances from well-established and respected systems

Table 3.51 Strategic Plan and CIP

Strategic plan and CIP	A	LG adopts, in line with a strategic plan, 3–5-year CIPs on a rolling basis, where the first year becomes the budget plan and a new year is added to the CIP every year. The CIP is developed in a participatory process and substantially implemented in the annual budgets.
	B	LG adopts CIPs every 3–5 years. The CIPs are substantially included in planning the annual budgets.
	C	LG adopts strategic plan or CIP, some actions are considered in planning the annual budgets, but changing circumstances reduce the scope or use of strategic planning.
	D	LG has no strategic plan or CIP; the planning is limited to annual budgets.

Note: CIP = capital improvement plan; LG = local government.

Table 3.52 Budget Planning

Budget planning	A	LG budgeting is clearly regulated; budget process is mature, iterative, and participatory based on predictable forecast for transfers, clear and robust national guidelines, and local budget circulars. Budget plans are completed on time and approved. Revised budgets are well regulated and timely planned and adopted at the midpoint of the fiscal year.
	B	LG budgeting is clearly regulated, budget process is timely completed based on clear national guidelines and local budget circulars. Revised budgets are adopted at the midpoint of the fiscal year or rarely other times as deemed necessary.
	C	LG budgeting is regulated by national guidelines; budgets are completed mostly on time. Revised budgets are adopted if and when necessary.
	D	There are general rules for local budgets, but multiple changes occur during the fiscal year because of unforeseen circumstances at central or local government level.

Note: LG = local government.

(score A) to nonexistent strategy, lack of CIP, or blurred medium-term vision.

The sample city has a well-established strategic plan and a rolling CIP procedure linked to the annual capital budgeting system. The A score reflects the good framework and the adequate implementation of the CIP and budgeting rules.

Budget planning: Annual budgets play a major role in disciplined planning, expenditure control, citizen participation, and transparent communication with key stakeholders (table 3.52). That's why the quality of budget planning is a self-standing factor in measuring the quality of the local financial management and the quality depends on several factors: (1) budget rules and national and local regulations, (2) a budgeting process that should be iterative and participatory as a best practice, (3) budget approval, and (4) disciplined budget execution that requires respecting specific rules like budget appropriation as a condition of releasing payments and the like. In short, good-quality budget planning empowers the local government to use the budget as a management tool that drives rather than just follows and records service and financial operations.

The sample city has a mature budgeting system with good national and local rules, and

the budget process well respects the rules and regulations. Revised budgets are approved at midpoint of the fiscal year. These factors all support a score of A.

Scope of the budget: Municipal budgets by default cover the revenues and expenditures born and accounted for to reflect and cover the activities of narrow budgetary entities like municipal departments and service units, or functional entities that work as part of the municipality as a singular legal body. Municipalities in developed and developing countries alike, however, often spin off service activities or functions to independent legal entities like public utility companies (PUCs) or independent offices or joint ventures with private service providers. In these cases, the budgets do not inherently reflect the entire scope of services and functions, because they exclude the revenues and expenditures of the independent legal entities.

Responsibility and liabilities with respect to the independent legal entities: There is one significant connection between the municipal budget and the legal entities, namely that entities often require support from the municipal budget in the form of either operation or capital subsidies or both. Some municipalities do not even account these supports as subsidies but rather as "loans" or "regular or other

Table 3.53 Scope of the Budget

Scope of the budget	A	Extra-budgetary entities, PUCs, and/or funds play substantial role in local service delivery, but financial transactions are regulated, are clear, and require low operating subsidies (5%). LG prepares both regular and consolidated budget/financial reports.
	B	Extra-budgetary entities, PUCs, and/or funds play substantial role in local service delivery, but financial transactions are regulated, are clear, and require low operating subsidies (max 10% of current revenues). LG does not prepare consolidated budget/financial reports.
	C	Extra-budgetary entities, PUCs, and/or funds play substantial role in local service delivery, and require substantial operating subsidies (over 10%). Financial transactions between municipality and entities are not regulated and not consolidated in financial reports.
	D	Extra-budgetary entities, PUCs, and/or funds play substantial role in local service delivery, and require substantial operating subsidies (15%). Financial transactions to and from entities are not regulated and not consolidated in financial reports.

Note: LG = local government; PUC = public utility company.

Table 3.54 Budget Implementation

Budget implementation	A	Expenditures are adhered to budget appropriation; variations of actual and planned total expenditures and variation of structures of main lines are within 5% of plans.
	B	Expenditures are adhered to budget appropriation; variations of actual and planned total expenditures and variation of structures of main lines are within 10% of plans.
	C	LG actual expenditures and revenues and revenue and expenditure variations and main line structures are within 15% of plans.
	D	LG actual expenditures and revenues and revenue and expenditure main line structures are over 15% of plans.

Note: LG = local government.

expenditures." Finally, municipalities often commit huge contingent liabilities, because they are financially responsible for services and losses as majority owners of these entities. For these reasons, the scope of the budget is a vital factor of the financial health of the municipalities. Two specific issues deserve close scrutiny: (1) the size and form of accounting of the financial transactions between the municipal budget and the entities, and (2) whether the municipality prepares budget and closing financial reports on consolidated bases, or reports fully and consistently the financial performance of the independent legal entities as part of the budget or financial reports, often as annex or memo items.

The sample city does not prepare a consolidated budget (table 3.53); the financial transactions are well regulated by internal rules with clear accounts of the financial transactions, but the entities require more than 15 percent of the current revenues as operating subsidies that represent a serious risk factor for the budget. This means the budget does not fairly reflect the financial situation of the city, and thus the score D is justified.

Budget implementation: This factor captures the budget implementation/execution practices (table 3.54) that either reinforce or undermine the quality of the budget discussed above. Three issues deserve attention and answers here: (1) whether budget appropriations confine expenditures, in other words if there is a built-in procedure (maybe computerized) that prohibits releasing payments without budget appropriation; (2) quality can be measured by the variation between the planned and actual annual total expenditures and total revenues, a broad signal of implementation quality (within 5 percent, both are best-practice benchmarks); and (3) changes of the composition/share of main line item categories, that is, whether the amounts budgeted for solid waste services, education, administration, or energy/fuel are within close range of the budgeted shares. The proper answer to this question requires revisiting the A/P financial reports and the expenditures by functions. Should this information be left unrecorded, it is a signal of low quality of budget implementation.

The sample city has good budget implementation records, with low variations in total budget within a 10 percent range between plans and actuals; however, it does not have clear records of expenditure composition by function or the respective A/P variations. Furthermore, the persistent budget deficit signals weaknesses in budget execution. Thus, the score of budget implementation quality is rightly C, despite the low budget total variations.

Financial Management Systems and Practices

Financial management systems and practices are the cornerstones of the broad financial management framework of a municipality; specific factors include (1) the financial management framework, and (2) revenue management, expenditure management, cash and debt management, and oversight and internal control systems and practices. Some finance officers may find it difficult to make judgments about the quality of financial management systems, but the specific questions are designed to make the responses and the selection of the relevant score relatively easy. Others may feel, mistakenly, that the existence of an integrated financial management information system (IFMIS) automatically ensures good financial management.

Financial management framework: Financial management is mainly driven by technologies and software; however, the quality and performance of the system largely depend on adapted and enforced procedures, clear segregation of functions, and the skills and experiences of the staff working in the various functions of the FMS. The scoring of this area aims to capture these factors by asking if financial management is well regulated, if the computerized system includes internationally accepted standard templates and generates reports automatically, and finally if there is an adequate squad of qualified staff to run the systems timely and adequately. The score A requires meeting all of these conditions.

The sample city has a reasonable FMS in place (table 3.55); however, the performance

Table 3.55 Financial Management Framework

Financial management framework	A	Financial management framework is well regulated and supported by FMS/IFMIS software system with standard templates and reporting forms; and sufficient number of qualified staff in key positions are assigned to financial management with clear segregation of functions.
	B	Financial management is controlled and supported by FMS/IFMIS system with clear templates and segregation of functions; and qualified staff are assigned to many key positions with some vacant positions.
	C	Financial management is supported by some software and some qualified staff are assigned to financial management.
	D	Financial management is computer enhanced with various software solutions, but staff have various levels of knowledge in financial management area.

Note: FMS = financial management system; IFMIS = integrated financial management information system.

Table 3.56 Revenue Management

Revenue manage-ment	A	LG has effective fiscal cadaster and/or tax and fee payer registration and assessment system with up-to-date and transparent records on bases, rates, and payers' obligations and responsibilities; revenue collection efficiency is high (95%).
	B	LG has effective tax and fee payer registration and assessment system with up-to-date and transparent records on payers' obligations and responsibilities; revenue collection efficiency is good (80%).
	C	LG has several tax and fee payer registration systems with records on payers' obligations and responsibilities in various qualities; revenue collection efficiency is moderate (60–80%).
	D	LG has gaps in several tax and fee payer registration systems with records on payers' obligations and responsibilities in various qualities; revenue collection efficiency is low (60% or below).

Note: LG = local government.

Table 3.57 Expenditure Management

Expenditure management	A	LG has effective commitment control system, clear segregation of duties, internal controls for nonsalary expenditures, and public procurement procedures to ensure value for money. Qualified staff are available.
	B	LG has commitment control system, expenditures are accounted mostly timely, public procurement procedures support investments. Qualified staff are posted in most key positions.
	C	LG has computerized systems for managing and recording expenditures.
	D	Expenditure recording and management is fragmented.

Note: LG = local government.

of the system is not fully regulated and there is shortage of staff is some important positions. These factors justify a B score.

Revenue management: Good revenue management requires several systems and procedures in place together. The most critical components include reliable databases for each important revenue source (taxes and fees), updated records on tax and fee payers' obligations, easy payment systems, and powerful enforcement and remedy systems and procedures. Needless to say, strong political support is vital for good functioning of these systems and procedures; it is not easy to assess, but collection efficiency is a good proxy for the capacity and efficiency of the revenue management system. The lack of reliable databases, however, not only undermines revenue collection; it also weakens the credibility of the revenue collection efficiency figures, which thus deserve a score one notch below the suggested score.

The sample city has no reliable revenue databases, payers' records are in various systems and in diverse quality (table 3.56). Thus, the score D is justified regardless of the fact that the city has managed to collect quite a substantial volume of OSRs. This calls for urgent corrective measures that can and should be included in the very next MFSA Action Plan.

Expenditure management: Expenditure management includes specific subsystems for managing operating and capital investment expenditures, but the quality of the system depends on several specific tools, instruments, rules, and procedures (table 3.57). The commitment control system is vital to ensure that no payment is possible without prior commitment in the system (budget). Controlling operating expenditures requires clear segregation of functions and internal control systems and procedures; managing investment expenditures requires public procurement and good contract management, among others. Most expenditure management functions are supported today by computerized systems; however, the quality and performance of the system depends on the qualified staff and the said procedures.

The sample city does have some computerized systems for expenditure management, but seems to lack adequate commitment control, internal control, and public procurement systems and procedures. Thus, the score C is adequate.

Cash and debt management: Cash management is a system and process aimed at collecting and managing cash, as well as using it for (short-term) investing. It is a key component of ensuring the city's financial stability and solvency by making cash available as needed and investing the surplus cash into short-term instruments to earn as much as possible. These instruments require close interconnection with the revenue and expenditure management systems to ensure early warning and timely corrective measures. Likewise, the debt management system starts with clear consolidated debt records (aging list of debt), competitive selection of financing partners, and a strong liquidity management system to ensure liquidity/solvency in the short, medium and long term. An adequate cash and debt management system includes clear records, not only of loans but also of guarantees or other direct or contingent liabilities, such as the likely payments the city needs to cover on behalf of some independent subordinated entities like the water utility company. The timeliness of debt service and the size and nature of liabilities are indicators of the performance and quality of the cash and debt management system.

The sample city has a reasonable framework for cash and debt management (table 3.58), but it falls short in valuation and management of guarantees and other contingent liabilities. These factors definitely weaken the quality and the reliability of the cash and debt management system, thus a score B, or even C is justified (the officer scored B).

Oversite and control: The internal audit system is the cornerstone of the oversight and control systems; it requires qualified staff to perform the internal audit and analyze the financial performance and risks the city faces. Special attention should be paid to analyzing the performance of subordinated entities and their impacts on municipal budgets and

Table 3.58 Cash Management

Cash and debt management	A	LG has an effective framework for cash and debt management with reliable records on cash balances, debts, guarantees, other liabilities, and payment arrears; LG debt service is stable.
	B	LG has an effective framework for cash and debt management with records on cash balances, debts, and guarantees; but guarantees are not valuated in debt management. LG debt service is mostly timely.
	C	LG has some procedure for cash and debt management with some records on cash balances and some debts; payments delayed time and again.
	D	LG has no debt management framework, but cash balances are reconciled OR neither cash nor debt management procedure is in place and/or ad hoc short-term liquidity borrowing is common.

Note: LG = local government.

Table 3.59   Oversight and Internal Control

Oversight and internal control	A	LG has reliable internal audit system, effective procedures for account reconciliations, and for oversight and analysis of the aggregate fiscal risk born from subordinated legally independent entities (PUCs) based on consolidated financial reports.
	B	LG has reliable internal audit system, some procedures for account reconciliations, and for oversight and analysis of the aggregate fiscal risk born from subordinated legally independent entities (PUCs) without consolidation.
	C	LG has internal audit system, account reconciliations are intermittent, and LG receives the annual reports from the subordinated legally independent entities (PUCs).
	D	LG has no formal internal audit unit or system, and there are no records about the subordinated legally independent entities (PUCs).

Note: LG = local government; PUC = public utility company.

the risks they may induce. For these reasons, municipal budgets should be consolidated with local entities and analyzed on the consolidated basis. This is not the case in most developing countries, which substantially reduces the credibility and power of the oversight and internal control systems.

The sample city has reliable oversite and internal control systems (table 3.59), but it fails to prepare and analyze a consolidated budget. Thus, the score B is justified, especially because the financial reports indicate that the PUCs play very substantial roles in local services and that the city provides a substantial volume of capital and operating subsidies. Institutionalizing development and analysis of a consolidated budget would be among high-priority actions even if the national regulations do not stipulate preparation of consolidated budgets.

Financial Reporting, Disclosure, and Transparency

Financial reporting, disclosure, and transparency are critical elements of good financial management systems and reflect strong commitments, policies, and procedures for transparency, that is, timely sharing relevant information and receiving feedback about the adequacy and results of the financial reports. The four decisive factors are the following: (1)

financial reporting, (2) external audit, (3) financial disclosures, and (4) public procurement.

Financial reporting supports the internal control and the external face of the municipality. The conditions for good financial reporting include four key elements. First, it is important to have a reliable computerized financial reporting system consistent with generally accepted accounting principles and standards. We understand that the computer is only a tool, but it is hardly possible to establish a reliable reporting system today without computers. Second, daily, monthly, quarterly, and annual reports that are generated timely in automated procedures represent another condition that is not a mechanical result of a computer system but is rather an attribute of a good system. Third, ensuring that results are disseminated to respective governing bodies and discussed is good policy, because the mere preparation of reports does not ensure good financial reporting. Finally, good reports indicate and should induce corrective measures. The explained standards represent the A score quality of financial reporting systems and practices. Computerized accounting and reporting systems are available everywhere today, so most local governments do have some system; however, this set of qualifications

Table 3.60 Financial Reporting

Financial reporting	A	The LG has a reliable computerized financial reporting system consistent with generally accepted accounting principles and standards. Daily, monthly, quarterly, and annual reports are generated timely in automated procedures (e.g., by IFMIS); results are disseminated to respective governing bodies and discussed, and corrective measures commenced timely.
	B	The LG has a reliable financial reporting system and procedures in compliance with national legislation; reports are generated and disseminated mostly on time.
	C	The LG has rules and various templates for financial reporting in various LG entities, reports are generated separately, and delays may occur because of missing information.
	D	LG entities generate some reports.

Note: IFMIS = integrated financial management information system; LG = local government.

Table 3.61 External Audit

External audit	A	The LG annual financial reports are audited by external auditor; audit reports are obtained within 8–12 months following a fiscal year. The LG audit committee discusses the audit results and commences corrective measures as it may deem necessary, AND the LG has obtained unqualified audits in the last 3 years.
	B	The LG annual financial reports are audited by external auditor; audit reports are obtained within 2 years following a fiscal year. The LG audit committee discusses the audit results and commences corrective measures. The LG has obtained unqualified audits in the last year.
	C	The LG annual financial reports are audited by external auditor; audit reports are obtained within 2–3 years following a fiscal year. The LG audit committee discusses the audit results. The LG has obtained qualified audits in the last 2 years.
	D	The LG has no external auditor, or the LG has failed to obtain audits or obtained qualified audits or one or more adverse external audits in the last 3 years.

Note: LG = local government.

points to the importance of the quality and implementation of such systems. These are the issues the MFSA user should address.

The sample city seems to have a reliable financial reporting system (table 3.60); however, the filing officer was not sure about the international standards and remained silent about the follow-up corrective measures. These results justify a fair B score or even a C (the officer scored B).

External audit: An external audit performed by a third party provides the local government with a valuable check on the adequacy of financial management and financial reporting, and eventually supports efficiency. This audit supplements internal audits because

external auditors are often better trained for the purpose and thus are able to address key weaknesses that might go unnoticed by the internal auditors, support international standards, and persuade corrective measures. Troubles that cities in developing countries face include (1) long-delayed external audits (2–3 years is not uncommon); (2) central government agencies performing external audits focused on compliance with use of fund rules rather than with international accounting and reporting standards; (3) simple and relaxed audit reports; and (4) lack of follow-up actions. A score of A represents the highest standard on audits, when reports are timely audited, results are discussed and followed with corrective measures, or unqualified (good) audits are obtained persistently.

The sample city faces multiple challenges, including delays in audit reports and qualified audits discussed with an audit committee, but no evidences of corrective measures (table 3.61). These factors justify a C score. It is important for the users of this MFSA to be very precise and disciplined in assessing the quality of external audit framework and practices, and particularly not to assume that merely having external audits (by the auditors general) is satisfactory for a high score, unless the said very specific quality conditions are met.

Financial disclosures: Financial disclosures are essential elements of good financial management systems and policies. A city with a score of A not only has an adequate financial reporting system, with quality financial reports that are generated and audited in a timely manner and with good results (unqualified audits), but also strongly supports transparency and timely and proper disclosure of key financial results. It means the city ensures that external partners—citizens, investors, lenders, and other government entities—understand, recognize, and respect the quality of the city's financial reports and results. The score A qualification includes two specific conditions: (1) the reports are timely and made available in various ways (in tandem); (2) the city engages in dialogues about the results to receive feedback and learn priorities and ideas from respected partners.

Disclosure practices show a wide variety across the globe. In some cases, very regular and tailored reports, even audit reports, are disclosed in a timely manner using the best modern technology. In contrast, local governments in some countries consider financial results to be confidential and not suitable for disclosure, or they simply lack the means and technology to disclose results. MFSA users need to make an honest judgement on the means, ways, and quality of disclosure in their own jurisdiction in order to use this assessment as a guide for future improvements.

The sample city presumably has financial reports, but, as a matter of policy, the reports are made available only on demand (table 3.62). This policy is better than nothing, but key stakeholders, especially citizens, are unlikely to go to local government offices and demand a report they may not even know exists. Thus, the score of C is a fair assessment.

Public procurement and competitive tendering: Public procurement fits into several places in the FMS because it serves several functions, from expenditure management to transparency. *Class A* cities put high emphasis on public procurement for both efficiency and transparency reasons. By default, they use the public procurement system and instruments in various instances and apply open, transparent competitive tendering for infrastructure projects, for

Table 3.62 Financial Disclosure

Financial disclosures	A	The annual financial reports, the audit report, and short briefs on quarterly or monthly reports are made available for public scrutiny (e.g., posted on the LG website, readable at city hall, shared with key stakeholders in print or electronic forms). Town hall meeting is held to discuss results and future plans.
	B	The annual financial reports are made available for public scrutiny (e.g., posted on the LG website, readable at city hall, shared with key stakeholders in print or electronic forms).
	C	The annual financial reports are made available for public scrutiny on demand.
	D	Financial reports are not shared with public.

Note: LG = local government.

Table 3.63 Public Procurement and Competitive Tendering

Public procurement and competitive tendering	A	LG has standard procedures that asset divestitures, all investment construction projects, and bulk purchases are procured by open competitive tendering published in various media and adhere to value for money principles.
	B	LG has standard procedures supporting that large construction projects are procured by open competitive tendering published in various media.
	C	Some projects are published and procured by competitive tenders.
	D	LG has no public procurement procedures.

Note: LG = local government.

Table 3.64 Financial Management Assessment Scoring Results

Financial management assessment themes	Scores
Intergovernmental relations	C, **B**, C, C, C
Planning, budgeting, and budget implementation	A, **D**, B, C
Financial management systems and practices	B, **D**, C, B, B
Financial reporting, disclosure, and transparency	B, C, **C**, B
Summary	C

bulk purchase of materials (fuel, stationary, construction material, and computers), for selecting construction supervisors, for selecting banks for short-term deposits or long-term loans, and for selling or leasing land or buildings via competitive tendering. In contrast, some cities may ignore competitive tendering and public procurement, because the mayor or heads of department feel competent to find good partners using their own knowledge of the city or the specific sector. This kind of knowledge is useful, but may compromise the selection process without transparent public procurement and competitive tendering.

The sample city implements public procurement procedures for selection of large investment projects (table 3.63), but it seems to ignore opportunities to use public procurement and open competitive selection in many other possible areas mentioned above. Thus, the score of B is a fair assessment.

MFSA–FMA Analysis and Scoring: Summary

The FMA needs no detailed summary, because each and every thematic area deserves close attention and needs to be seen individually. Still, a short summary of the results might be useful to signal the overall strength of the financial management system. As noted earlier, it is also important to highlight and address the lowest scores in each thematic area regardless of the general results. We use the scoring results of the sample city to illustrate how to summarize the results of the FMA (table 3.64).

The overall results can be scored as C, because C is the dominant (statistical mode) score in the assessment; the lowest scores are marked in each theme. This overall score is a bit worrisome, because C is a low score just one notch above the lowest that signals a need for careful analysis of some areas and commencement of corrective measures that can be included in the MFSA Action Plan (discussed in the next section of the Handbook).

Intergovernmental relations is an area where possible changes are beyond the competency of local government, except that local governments may join efforts or use the national association of local governments to initiate changes in national legislation or encourage the central government to get rid of bad practices that may ignore or compromise national legislation. For instance, they might use these efforts to improve the practices of biased debt approval by the ministry of finance, or to improve predictability and stability of transfers. There is one particular factor—namely that the sample city has legal power to change the expenditures, but it has not been a practice—which can be changed by local action and may be included in the MFSA Action Plan to achieve a higher score (B instead of C).

Planning, budgeting, and budget implementation: The city has obtained diverse scores in this area because it has good systems in place and follows adequate practices—except in controlling revenues and expenditures, which results in persistent budget deficit. This is a very serious shortcoming that deserves immediate action and should be included in the MFSA Action Plan!

Financial management systems and practices: The scores are very diverse in this thematic area and support the opinion that most financial management systems are in place and of good quality; however, revenue management faces serious gaps and weaknesses. The score of D for revenue management is one of the lowest scores in the entire assessment and requires urgent actions and provisions in the MFSA Action Plan.

Financial reporting, disclosure, and transparency: The city has a good financial reporting system, but it has obtained qualified audits in recent years and follows a restricted disclosure policy. The issue of qualified audits also signals weaknesses in adopting and implementing corrective measures; both of these require close attention and urgent improvements.

Step 6: MFSA Action Plan

The MFSA Action Plan is the final step of the MFSA process and the most important one. This final step enables the city and local government to complete the loop of self-assessment by capturing key solutions and actions on par with the key problems, bottlenecks, and issues identified during the diagnosis phase. The MFSA Action Plan, therefore, brings closure to the diagnostic process and opens the pathway to a solution package along with its implementation details.

Objective: The objective of the Action Plan is to translate the results and lessons learned from the different steps of the MFSA into specific actions to improve the municipality's financial health and financial management in the short and medium term.

Tasks and products: The MFSA Action Plan includes a number of components: (1) a table focusing on short- and medium-term actions that includes specific policy targets, specific actions, timing of actions, budget estimates for execution, expected results in either technical or financial terms or both, and the identified responsible person or entity; and (2) supporting documents annexed to facilitate the implementation of these actions.

MFSA Action Plan: Guiding Principles

MFSA Action Plan Time Frame

The time frame for the MFSA Action Plan is typically one to five years. Experience shows that it is very difficult to set an Action Plan to a longer time frame because many things can happen during that timeframe that may render the Action Plan content either out of date or out of touch with the evolving reality on the ground. The MFSA Action Plan will make a clear distinction between (1) actions of high priority, which need to be implemented in the short term (short list), and (2) actions of lower priority, which can be implemented over the medium term (long list). It will also make a distinction between actions that can be implemented directly and immediately by local governments and actions that require attention or decision by upper levels of government. The latter case will have an influence on the complexity of the implementation of such actions as well as on the realistic time frame allocated to them. Actions that require central government involvement or changes in legislation and regulations or sustained policy dialogue across multiple stakeholders will likely take longer to put in place. Similarly, actions that affect citizens and taxpayers will require some time for "sensitization" and communication. Experience shows that lack of clear communication between cities and their citizens is an important factor in the failure to implement change.

MFSA Action Plan Consultation Process

Just like in the UA/SA, consultation is a big part of the process. Consultation needs to start at the beginning of the MFSA process in order to ensure success of the reform/action agenda. Very early on, the ministry of finance, ministry of local governments, association of local governments, and other stakeholders need to be on board. They need to understand and own the process as well as appreciate what is in it for them. As indicated in chapter 1, the MFSA is a valuable analytic tool, but it is also much more than that. It tells a story about the city and provides the foundational ground for identifying appropriate and realistic solutions to well-defined problems or shortcomings. The quantification of the results or findings facilitates in turn the quantification of targets or goals. These targets will be the expected results of the MFSA Action Plan.

MFSA Action Plan Expected Results

Expected results will focus on a number of policy objectives such as (1) improve revenue sources; (2) control and prioritize expenditures; (3) improve financial management practices including budget realism; (4) increase service sustainability; and (5) increase creditworthiness. This list is indicative and can be expanded or narrowed down according to the MFSA findings. Whatever the focus of action might be (increase tax revenues, increase transfers, improve assets management), an expected quantified target will be attached to it. This quantified target will be realistic because it is calculated on the basis

of the MFSA diagnostic and it will be achievable because all implementation requirements, including costs and responsibilities, will have been vetted and agreed upon.

MFSA Action Plan Roles and Responsibilities

The MFSA Action Plan is drafted by the city department that has carried out the MFSA analysis (typically the finance department) in consultation with respective partner departments. The Action Plan should be discussed and approved by the mayor and the city council and made public. Experience shows that making it public on the city's website, portal, or social network achieves both a higher level of accountability and a higher level of institutional commitment to its successful implementation. In instances when a high level of central government action is required or requested, it may be advisable to enter into partnership agreements. We have previously discussed the "contractual" experience in which some countries engage. Municipal contracts in Africa have been implemented for many years with the explicit objective of holding all parties (local government, central government, and others) accountable for their share of the bargain. This approach has proved to be very successful in reaching quantified targets on local revenue mobilization, intergovernmental transfers, shared taxation, and other reforms requiring politically charged, time sensitive action-taking and moving the MFSA agenda away from politics and short-lived political mandates.

The sections below summarize the results of the MFSA analysis in a formal Action Plan for priority actions derived from the MFSA analysis. They provide a template for the user's own purpose. Appendix D provides detailed guidance for identifying and outlining a long list of possible actions based on systematic reading of the results of the MFSA steps from historical analysis all the way to financial management qualitative assessment.

Table 3.65 MFSA Action Plan: Example

Objective	Specific action	Expected results	Time frame	Cost estimate	Responsible entity
Increase creditworthiness	Reorganize tax administration with computerized databases, easy payment systems, and collection, billing, and enforcement procedures.	Tax revenues start increasing third year and reach 25%, 60%, and 100% increase, respectively, on 2013 results by 2018.	Years 1–5	ShS20,000 million	Council to approve plans; revenue department to implement
	Lobby with municipal associations to increase central government transfers at least to the level of inflation (7.3% in last 5 years).	Increase transfers from 4.4% per year to 7.3%.	Years 1–5 continues	No cost	Mayor to lobby
Increase service sustainability	Increase expenditures for repair and maintenance (R&M) to double gradually by 2018. Additional 10% increase year on year above the trend.	Better services, more reliable assets.	Years 1–5 continues	Increase R&M expenditures from ShS3,900 million to ShS7,800 million	Council to approve; service departments to implement
	Maintain revenues from land development fee by charging developers for off-site infrastructure; improve monitoring and enforcement.	Maintain revenue in the range of ShS5,000 million per year or even above if possible.	Years 1–5 continues	ShS5,000 million	Planning and revenue departments
	Increase investments.	Infrastructure investment on-budget increased to 20,000 (from 10,000 plan) and additional 3,000–5,000 off-budget investments per year.	Years 1–5 continues	ShS10,000 million additional budgeted expenditures with ShS5,000 million loan disbursement	Planning and finance departments to plan; council to approve
Control expenditure	Revise the system and procedures for subsidizing current expenditures of service entities, measure performance, and introduce rules for performance-based subsidization.	Reduce amount spent on subsidizing service and subordinated entities, while improving performance.	Years 1–5	No cost	Finance department and service entities
Improve budget reality	Increase budget reality by good analyses, conservative forecasting, and disciplined planning.	Balanced budget maintained in planning and implementation, actual/plan ratios within (+/–) 5% of plans.	Years 1–5 continues		Planning and finance departments to plan; council to approve

MFSA Action Plan: A Solution Package

Detailed analysis of the MFSA results has helped us define 50 specific possible actions (see appendix D). This list is indicative of what an Action Plan can entail but is not restricted to those actions. Local governments may identify other potential actions that would be specific to the local context and particular circumstances. It would be very difficult, if not impossible, however, for the sample city (or any city) to start implementing all of these actions immediately or even to aim at completing all of them in the medium term. However, it is very valuable to see all of these actions together, consider and discuss the implications, and then select a strategic short list of priority actions manageable in the medium term. There are critical interlinks across some actions that trigger sequencing. The cost of some items may appear to be large, representing a sizable financial commitment. Thus, sequencing will be necessary in order to be in harmony with the technical, human, organizational, and financial absorptive capacity of a municipality and to make such institutional modernization realistic and doable. It is therefore pragmatic to select a short list of specific actions considered as doable in the medium term.

Preliminary Action Plan: Table 3.65 summarizes the preliminary Action Plan of the sample city with a small number of time-bound priority actions. A good action plan includes at least six headings: objectives, specific actions, expected results, time frame, cost estimate, and responsible entity. The table indicates, for instance, that reforming the tax administration includes many sub-actions and may need two or more years to complete. For example, increasing own tax revenues requires establishing a reliable revenue management system, establishing a reliable computerized tax database, revising and expanding the tax base, improving tax collection procedures, collection and management of tax arrears, and eventually property revaluation. *The investment need* (ShS20 million) is comparable to the total local tax revenues collected in year 5 (table 3.19); however, that investment will be recovered by the fifth year from the incremental revenues (table 3.41) and will generate double annual tax revenues in subsequent years. We can also see that several actions need no financial investments; instead they require only improving the internal control or management system or networking and lobbying for national changes.

Some cities may find that the Action Plan stated as an example is too modest and does not do justice to the multitude of possible actions. First, this table is used mostly to illustrate the format and to provide an indicative template. Second, it can be expanded during initial discussions, final prioritization, and approval by the city council. Finally, new actions can be added after the initial implementation in subsequent years.

References

AECOM. 2015. "Public Expenditure and Financial Accountability Assessment for the City of Tshwane, South Africa." AECOM Technology Corporation, Los Angeles, and South African Cities Network.

Bahl, Roy. 2009. "Property Tax Reform in Developing and Transition Countries." Paper for the Fiscal Reform and Economic Governance Project, U.S. Agency for International Development.

Bahl, Roy, Johannes Linn, and Deborah Wetzel. 2013. "Governing and Financing Metropolitan Areas in the Developing World." In *Financing Metropolitan Governments in Developing Countries*, edited by Roy Bahl, Johannes Linn, and Deborah Wetzel. Cambridge, MA: Lincoln Institute of Land Policy.

Berger, Thomas Müller-Marqués, and Jens Heiling. 2013. "European Accounting Standards for the

Public Sectors." European Union Commission Report, Brussels.

Bird, Richard. 2010. "Smart Tax Administration." Economic Premise No. 36, Poverty Reduction and Economic Management Network, World Bank, Washington, DC.

———. 2013. "Foreign Advice and Tax Policy in Developing Countries." International Center for Public Policy Working Paper 13-07, Andrew Young School of Policy Studies, Georgia State University, Atlanta.

Bird, Richard, and Naomi Enid Slack. 2015. *Is Your City Healthy? Measuring Urban Fiscal Health.* University of Toronto Press.

Cabaleiro, Roberto, Enrique Buch, and Antonio Vaamonde. 2013. "Developing a Method to Assessing the Municipal Financial Health." *The American Review of Public Administration* 43 (6): 729–51.

CABRI (Collaborative Africa Budget Reform Initiative). 2017. "Management of Explicit Contingent Liabilities—Credit Guarantees for State-Owned Entities' Debt." CABRI Policy Dialogue Paper, CABRI South Africa.

Colorado General Assembly. 2013. "Fiscal Health Analysis for Colorado Counties and Municipalities." Report No. 2129-13, Colorado General Assembly, Denver.

Farvacque-Vitkovic, Catherine and Lucien Godin. 2006. "Decentralization and Municipal Development: Municipal Contracts." Working Paper, World Bank, Washington, DC.

Farvacque-Vitkovic, Catherine, Lucien Godin, and Anne Sinet. 2014. *Municipal Self-Assessments: A Handbook for Local Governments.* Washington, DC: World Bank.

Farvacque-Vitkovic, Catherine, and Mihaly Kopanyi, eds. 2014. *Municipal Finances: A Handbook for Local Governments.* Washington, DC: World Bank.

Farvacque -Vitkovic, Catherine, and Anne Sinet. 2014. "Achieving Greater Transparency and Accountability: Measuring Municipal Financial Performance and Paving the Path for Reforms." Chapter 8 in *Municipal Finances: A Handbook for Local Governments*, edited by Catherine Farvacque-Vitkovic and Mihaly Kopanyi, 379–445. Washington, DC: World Bank.

Fitch Ratings. 2015. "International Local and Regional Governments Rating Criteria—Outside the United States." Fitch Ratings, www.fitchratings.com.

Fourie, Erika, Tanja Verster, and Gary Wayne van Vuuren. 2016. "A Proposed Quantitative Credit-Rating Methodology for South African Provincial Departments." *South African Journal of Economics and Managements Sciences* 19 (2): 192–214.

Freire, Maria Emilia. 2014. "Managing External Resources." Chapter 7 in *Municipal Finances: A Handbook for Local Governments*, edited by Catherine Farvacque-Vitkovic and Mihaly Kopanyi, 325–78. Washington, DC: World Bank.

Freire, Maria Emilia, and Hernando Garzón. 2014. "Managing Local Revenues." Chapter 3 in *Municipal Finances: A Handbook for Local Governments*, edited by Catherine Farvacque-Vitkovic and Mihaly Kopanyi, 147–214. Washington, DC: World Bank.

Freire, Maria E., and Mihaly Kopanyi. 2018. "Asset and Debt Management for Cities." Cities that Work, International Growth Centre Working Paper, London School of Economics and University of Oxford.

German, Lourdes. 2015. "Creating a Digital Bridge for Municipal Fiscal Health." *Meeting of the Minds* (blog), December 10. https://meetingoftheminds.org/creating-a-digital-bridge-for-municipal-fiscal-health-14597.

Groves, Sanford, and Maureen Godsey Valente. 2003. *Evaluating Financial Condition: A Handbook for Local Governments.* Washington, DC: ICMA.

HM Treasury. 2017. "Contingent Liability Approval Framework: Guidance." Government of the United Kingdom. https://assets.publishing.service.gov.uk/government/uploads/system/uploads/attachment_data/file/635939/contingent_liability_approval_framework_guidance.pdf.

IMF (International Monetary Fund). 2014. *General Finance Statistics Manual.* International Monetary Fund, Washington, DC.

———. 2018. "Public Investment Management Assessment (PIMA)." Fiscal Affairs Department, International Monetary Fund, Washington, DC.

Kaganova, Olga. 2011. "Guidebook on Capital Investment Planning for Local Governments." Urban Development Series Knowledge Papers, World Bank, Washington, DC.

Kaganova, Olga, and Mihaly Kopanyi. 2014. "Managing Local Assets." Chapter 6 in *Municipal Finances: A Handbook for Local Governments*, edited by Catherine Farvacque-Vitkovic and Mihaly Kopanyi, 275–324. Washington, DC: World Bank.

Kelly, Roy. 2013. "Making the Property Tax Work." International Center for Public Policy Working Paper 13-11, Andrew Young School of Policy Studies, Georgia State University, Atlanta.

Kim, Julie. 2018. "CePACs and Their Value Capture Viability in the U.S. for Infrastructure Funding." Working Paper 18Jk1, Lincoln Institute of Land Policy, Cambridge, MA.

Kopanyi, Mihaly. 2015a. "Local Revenue Reform in Rwanda." International Growth Centre Working Paper, London School of Economics and University of Oxford.

———. 2015b. "Local Revenue Reform of Kampala Capital City Authority." International Growth Centre Working Paper, London School of Economics and University of Oxford.

———. 2015c. "Financing Cities in Turkey." Chapter 5 in *The Rise of the Anatolian Tigers: Turkey Urbanization Review*. Report No. 87180-TR. Washington, DC: World Bank.

———. 2016. "Improving Revenue Mobilization in Cities." Conference paper for the East and Central African Cities Development Forum, Kampala, International Growth Centre, London School of Economics and University of Oxford, May 24–26.

———. 2018. "Municipal Finances Self-Assessment (MFSA) Experiences in South-East Europe: Synthesis and Country Reports." Working Paper, World Bank-Austria Urban Partnership Program (UPP), World Bank, Washington, DC.

Kopanyi, Mihaly, and A. Muwonge. Forthcoming. *Managing Municipal Assets in Kenya—Post Devolution Challenges and Responses*. Washington, DC: World Bank.

Liu, Lily, and Kim Song Tan. 2009. "Subnational Credit Ratings." Policy Research Working Paper 5013, World Bank, Washington, DC.

Logan, Sarah. 2016. "Local Revenue Reform with the Kampala Capital City Authority." International Growth Centre (blog). http://www.theigc.org/blog/local-revenue-reform-with-the-kampala-capital-city-authority.

Moody's. 2013. "Rating Scales and Definitions." Moody's Asia Pacific. https://www.moodys.com/sites/products/ProductAttachments/AP075378_1_1408_KI.pdf.

———. 2017. "Rating Methodology: Regional and Local Governments." Report Number 1072625. Moody's Investor Service.

Morell, Lance, and Mihaly Kopanyi. 2014. "Managing Local Expenditures." Chapter 5 in *Municipal Finances: A Handbook for Local Governments*, edited by Catherine Farvacque-Vitkovic and Mihaly Kopanyi, 215–74. Washington, DC: World Bank.

Muwonge, Abdu, and Robert Ebel. 2014. "Intergovernmental Finances in a Decentralized World." Chapter 1 in *Municipal Finances: A Handbook for Local Governments*, edited by Catherine Farvacque-Vitkovic and Mihaly Kopanyi, 1–39. Washington, DC: World Bank.

OECD (Organisation for Economic Co-operation and Development). 2006. "Explicit Contingent Liabilities in Debt Management." Chapter 6 in *Advances in Risk Management of Government Debt*. Paris: OECD Publishing. https://dx.doi.org/10.1787/9789264104433-7-en.

———. 2011. "Classification of the Functions of Government (COFOG)." Annex B in *Government at a Glance 2011*, 194–95. Paris, OECD Publishing.

Ösmen, Türda. 2016. "Principles of Municipal Creditworthiness and Shadow Credit Rating." City Creditworthiness Initiative Workshop, World Bank, Ankara.

PEFA Secretariat. 2016a. *PEFA Handbook Volume I: The PEFA Assessment Process—Planning, Managing and Using PEFA*. PEFA Secretariat, Washington, DC. https://www.pefa.org/sites/default/files/PEFA%20Handbook%20Volume%201%20-%20second%20edition_1.pdf.

——. 2016b. *PEFA Handbook, Volume II: PEFA Assessment Fieldguide.* PEFA Secretariat, Washington, DC. https://www.pefa.org/sites/default/files/PEFA%20Handbook%20Volume%202%20-%20second%20edition%20publication.pdf.

——. 2016c. *PEFA Handbook Volume III: Preparing the PEFA Report.* PEFA Secretariat, Washington, DC. https://www.pefa.org/sites/default/files/PEFA%20Handbook%20Volume%203%20Second%20edition_2.pdf.

——. 2016d. "Supplementary Guidance for Subnational PEFA Assessments." PEFA Secretariat, Washington, DC. https://pefa.org/sites/default/files/SNG%20PEFA%20guide%20revised%2016-03-10%20edited.pdf.

——. 2017. "PEFA Check: Quality endorsement of PEFA assessments from January 1, 2018." PEFA Secretariat, Washington, DC. https://pefa.org/sites/default/files/20180111-PEFA%20Check%20from%20January%201%202018-Final_0.pdf.

PEFINDO. 2016. "Municipal Rating Methodology—Subnational Entity (Province/Regency/City)." PEFINDO Credit Rating Agency. https://www.pefindo.com/index.php/fileman/file?file=91.

Peterson, George. 1998. "Measuring Local Government Credit Risk and Improving Creditworthiness." Working Paper, World Bank, Washington, DC.

——. 2008. *Unlocking Land Values to Finance Urban Infrastructure.* Washington, DC: World Bank.

Shah, Anwar. 2007. *Local Budgeting: Public Sector Governance and Accountability.* Washington, DC: World Bank.

Sirtaine, Sophie. 2014. "Contingent Liability Management." Presentation at the PPPs in Infrastructure Conference, World Bank. http://siteresources.worldbank.org/ECAEXT/Resources/Day2Session8.pdf.

Slack, Enid. 2014. "The Fiscal Health of Ontario Municipalities." Presentation to OMTRA Annual Conference, Kingston, Ontario, December 9. https://munkschool.utoronto.ca/imfg/uploads/291/slack_presentation_to_omtra_september_9_2014.pdf.

Slack, Enid, and Richard Bird. 2015. "How to Reform the Property Tax: Lessons from around the World." IMFG Papers on Municipal Finance and Governance, Institute of Municipal Finance and Governance, University of Toronto.

Standard & Poor's. 2016. "S&P Global Ratings Definitions 2016." Standard & Poor's.

Stiglitz, Joseph E., and Jay K. Rosengard. 2015. "The Five Desirable Characteristics of Any Tax System." In *Economics of the Public Sector,* Fourth Edition, edited by Joseph Stiglitz, J. and J. K. Rosengard. London and New York: W.W. Norton and Company.

Suzuki, Hiraoke, Jin Murakame, Yu-Hung Hong, and Beth Tamayose. 2015. *Financing Transit-Oriented Development with Land Values: Adapting Land Value Capture in Developing Countries.* Urban Development Series. Washington, DC: World Bank.

UN-Habitat. 2009. *Guide to Municipal Finance.* Nairobi: United Nations Human Settlements Programme.

Venkateswaran, Rama Krishnan. 2014. "Municipal Financial Management." Chapter 3 in *Municipal Finances: A Handbook for Local Governments,* edited by Catherine Farvacque-Vitkovic and Mihaly Kopanyi, 93–145. Washington, DC: World Bank.

World Bank. 2014 "Improving Local Government Capacity—The Experience of Municipal Finances Self-Assessment (MFSA) in South-East Europe." World Bank–Austria Urban Partnership Program, World Bank, Washington, DC.

——. 2015. "Debt Management Performance Assessment (DeMPA) Methodology." World Bank, Washington, DC.

——. 2017. *Public–Private Partnerships: Reference Guide Version 3.* Washington, DC: World Bank. https://ppp.worldbank.org/public-private-partnership/library/ppp-reference-guide-3-0.

——. 2018 "Improving Local Government Capacity—The Experience of Municipal Finances Self-Assessment (MFSA) in South-East Europe." World Bank–Austria Urban Partnership Program, World Bank, Washington, DC.

——. (Forthcoming). "Municipal Finances Self-Assessment Online Application."

CHAPTER 4

Way Forward and Perspectives for the Future

Transformative Actions for a New Urban Agenda

Beyond the Nuts and Bolts of Local Governments Self-Assessments: A World of Applications

Local Governments Self-Assessments (LGSAs) have many current and potential applications. Among the multiple applications, the following are worth mentioning again:

- Data collection and curation

- Data sharing and dissemination

- Support to planning documents (both city planning documents and budgeting and financial reporting)

- Support to investment programming

- Support to leveraging financing opportunities for public urban investments

- Support to access to credit

- Support to municipal program/project design

- Support to capacity building of local governments

- Support to professionalization of municipal staff

- Support to city leaders' decision making and policy change

- Support to central government ministries of finance, public works and infrastructure, and local governments.

Box 4.1
Leave No City Behind

"Data gathering capacity is underdeveloped, weak, or dysfunctional in many parts of the world. Africa, Asia, and Latin America are especially data (infrastructure) poor. There is no consensus on who should set the metrics, who might generate and monitor data, or what the architecture of the science–policy interface underpinning global urban governance should be. Implementing a global monitoring mechanism for cities acknowledges that there are transnational drivers of urban change and embraces the idea that the way all cities are run will determine our common future. If the post-2030 agenda logic of 'Leave no one behind' is to incorporate the logic of 'Leave no city behind,' then fundamental attention to fair, accessible, and effective monitoring mechanisms is imperative."

Source: Acuto and Parnell 2016, 873.

Institutionalization of LGSA: Integrating LGSA into Current Practice of Local Governments

As we have seen, national legislation, country regulations, and management rules and requirements typically stipulate the way data collection and reporting are done. On the financial side, there is a list of reporting documents that municipalities are mandated to fill out monthly, quarterly, or yearly; municipalities must also submit financial reports to higher-level government entities, such as the ministry of finance, the ministry of local governments, or sectoral ministries. The central government entities review the reports to verify accuracy and compliance with rules, and may, sometimes, aggregate them into national-level municipal databases. Very rarely, however, do the regulations require municipalities to analyze data with the aim of assessing their financial health, nor do regulations require them to project future trends in order to uncover issues or identify needed corrective measures. On the investment side, we have already discussed the lack of meaningful data, the sporadic nature of data collection and curation, and the disconnect between the various bodies in charge of planning and programming, all of which make the prioritization of municipal investments programs difficult (box 4.1).

The LGSAs outlined in this book represent a radical departure from this culture and promote the use of data and data reporting for a greater good of analysis and policy change. LGSAs indeed have the potential to change the deep-rooted culture of local governments as they move away from simple reporting to storytelling and analysis. Municipalities work more and more like business entities (Bird 2013), and LGSAs support the move toward unified and integrated data reporting and analytical practices, one step closer to more effective and accountable city management. The LGSA methodology and results have been well tested and underscore a great potential toward becoming a new integrated practice of local governments. Supporting arguments include the following:

- Present city analysis and financial results in both format and content that are understood and valued by key partners such as citizens, central governments, banks, capital markets, rating agencies, private partners, and potential donors.

- Institutionalizing benchmarks to enable consistent comparison of city analysis and financial results with national and international benchmarks is very valuable, regardless of how far the city's indicators are from international best practices. The benchmarks serve as signals on where the city stands and where it needs to go.

- Standardizing basic financial reporting and analyses helps make comparison across cities and across countries clear and reliable, regardless of their diverse accounting and financial reporting practices.

- Speak a common language across the various accounting practices ranging from cash-based or modified cash to modified accrual and full accrual accounting practices. The Municipal Finances Self-Assessment (MFSA) helps this unification without requiring or demanding major changes in the various national legislations and rules that govern accounting and financial reporting in various countries.

- Institutionalizing greater collaboration among various departments that typically do not communicate or work together breaks the cycle of poor management practices, disconnected services, and disjointed service delivery.

- Institutionalizing fact-based information and financial forecasting, planning, and budgeting supports policy dialogues and helps city leaders in the decision-making process of reforms or actions.

- Institutionalizing the formulation and adoption of a Priority Investment Plan (PIP) and an MFSA Action Plan with specific measures will help improve the financial health and the quality of investments of the city. This should become part of the new culture and mainstream practice, because substantive corrective measures and reforms require careful planning, calibration, time, and investments that can only be completed over several years. This new culture is a departure from the common practice of ad hoc, shortsighted, and short-lived improvement actions.

With the goal of facilitating access to LGSA templates and scaling up its use, a companion Internet-based, online application has been developed. Details can be found in appendix C.

LGSA Contribution to City-Based Knowledge Products: Data with a Purpose, Data with a Voice, Deep Dive into Storytelling

There are many ways of presenting or curating data. Following are some examples of city-based knowledge products to which LGSAs can contribute.

National and Regional Observatories

National or regional observatories are a common product line. There have been many attempts, and many failures, at creating large-scale observatories. One common shortcoming is trying to get too many data and losing sight of what we want to track. LGSAs can help in many ways with city-based results as well as with national aggregate results combined with international benchmarking indicators.

Municipal associations can benefit from LGSAs results. These associations often engage in policy dialogue with national governments aiming at corrective measures in the intergovernmental finance system. Associations often lack sufficient data to support such a dialogue, however, and they often rely on anecdotal evidence, some of which may be misleading, incorrect, or biased. The systematic set of LGSA data provides a powerful source of unified and reliable information to support fact-based dialogue.

Ministries of finance can also benefit from LGSAs results. These ministries often have good aggregate data on intergovernmental finances but often face difficulties in disaggregating such data. The MFSA provides several supporting options, including (1) templates and an analytic tool for unified data collection; (2) systematic samples for policy analysis to support reform decisions and policy dialogue; (3) unified data and templates for international benchmarking and comparison; and (4) templates and methodology for developing a disaggregated national municipal finance database. For instance, inspired by the MFSA, the Ministry of Finance of Croatia has developed such a national database in cooperation with the Association of Municipalities. This database has greatly improved not only policy dialogue and analysis but also transparency, because the database and the rich set of graphic exhibits on cities, groups of municipalities, or sectors are accessible to local governments, development partners, and financial market entities.

Urban Atlas, Financial Ratios Guide, and City Profiles

Earlier generations of MFSAs have been instrumental in developing Financial Ratios Guides.

These guides, produced on an annual basis, were based on the findings of the early "financial audits" and included city-level as well as aggregated data covering the key financial ratios and providing thereby a quick snapshot of the cities. They were linked to an Urban Atlas, a by-product of Urban Audits, that served the same purpose on urban issues. In Senegal, the Municipal Development Agency has been producing and updating such reports since 1998.

City websites and apps. There are many ways of presenting city data, and cities around the world have proved to be very ingenious when it comes to presenting and branding themselves (see figure 4.1). Our intention is not to confine this creativity but to highlight some fundamentals that will help make city websites more accessible and user friendly. As mentioned previously, map-based data representation supported by a geographic information system as well as interactive apps are incredible assets that cities should tap into. The packaging, however, should not overlook the quality, relevance, or accuracy of data. The overarching principles should be found in the concept of "data with a purpose, data with a voice:"

> "The raw material for this work is data and therefore providing data with a voice is an intrinsic part of this process. Data need to be crafted into a story in order to be heard. If you visualize data as what it is—material, basically—you often end up with confusing results or you fail to communicate the content and the story." (Scherabon 2016).

As we have tried to show throughout this book, data are useful only as long as you make them compelling. The art of storytelling is, generally speaking, not the forte of most government entities. It is becoming clear, however, that a little capacity building around this topic is in order.

Figure 4.1 LGSA Byproducts: Monitoring Dashboard and Informed Decision Making

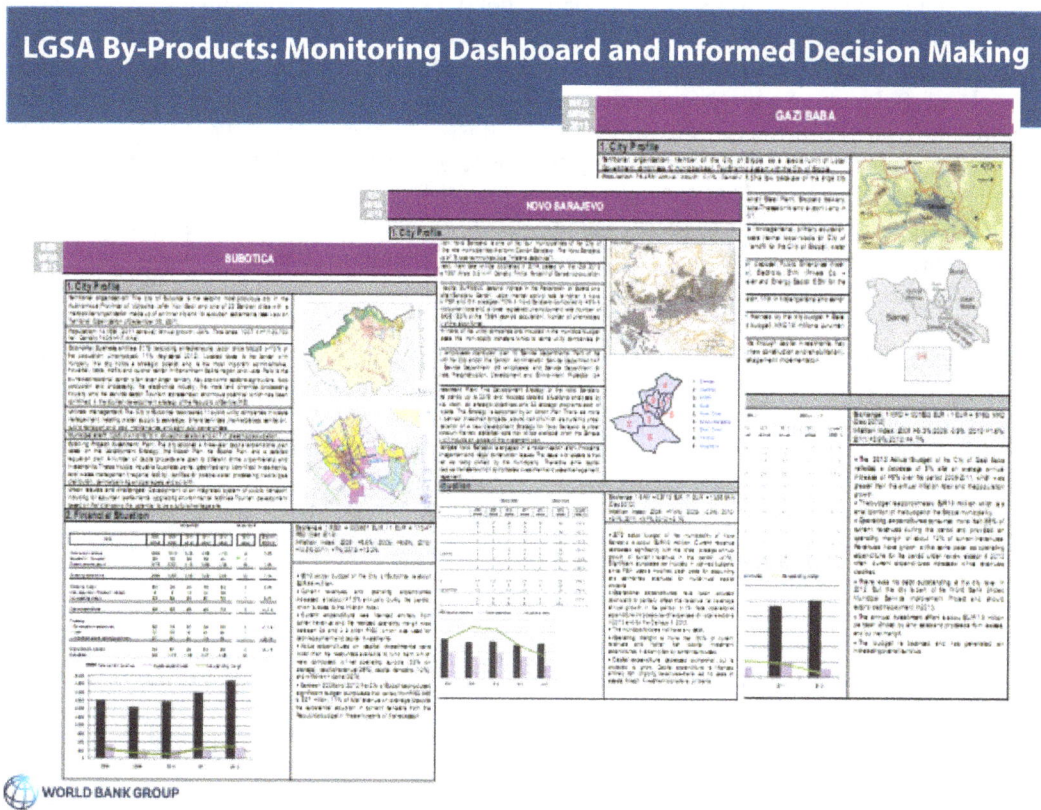

LGSAs: Tapping External Sources of Funding and Accessing Multiple Windows of Financing

The Urban Audit/Self-Assessment (UA/SA) and the MFSA can be instrumental in expanding funding capacity beyond local government budgets and current revenues. There are three ways that local governments can expand their funding capacity: (1) through access to credit from lending institutions and banks; (2) by tapping into innovative instruments through deals with private partners; and (3) through access to grants from central government and multilateral and bilateral development agencies. LGSAs are helping local governments to do so through the following:

- Improved creditworthiness and access to borrowing;

- Tapping into specific instruments (land-value capture and public–private partnerships); and

- Access to donor funding made easier.

Tapping External Sources of Funding: Creditworthiness and Access to Borrowing

The primary objective of the MFSA analysis is to assess the financial health of a municipality and identify issues and corrective measures that can be included in the MFSA Action Plan in order to improve financial health substantially in the medium term (see box 4.2 for the example of Belgrade, Serbia). One inherent component of the MFSA is the assessment of the borrowing capacity of the municipality, its so-called creditworthiness. MFSA users can also complete a simple self-assessed shadow credit rating. Details are explained in various sections of this handbook (see chapter 1 and appendix E).

Creditworthiness is a well-used term, but it is a softer term than some people would expect. The MFSA financial ratios provide a solid basis for creditworthiness assessment because creditworthiness is on a continuum and it is better to assess it in ranges, such as *weak, medium,* or *strong* creditworthiness. Historical data signal creditworthiness in the past; however, investors are more interested in projected future creditworthiness in order to see the capacity for repaying new debts. That is why it is important to measure creditworthiness at both current and future times on the basis of financial projections.

Borrowing capacity refers to how much a city can borrow, that is, what amount of new debt can be procured at a specific point in time. It is a vital indicator for city governments, and it should be estimated in real numbers (as opposed to qualitative creditworthiness measures). Estimating debt capacity requires combining results from ratios, revenues, and debt databases; but borrowing capacity depends also on the debt terms, such as interest rate and maturity. Thus, calculating debt capacity is inevitably more complicated than assessing creditworthiness.

Credit rating is becoming increasingly popular among municipalities in the developed world, because it not only signals the financial and management quality of a municipality but also strongly influences the cost of borrowing or bond issuance. Lenders highly value the rating scores published by internationally renowned rating agencies such as Fitch Ratings, Moody's, and Standard and Poor's. In contrast, cities (mostly in the developing world) lack such published rating results and, thus, borrow with high risk premium.

Is it better for them to obtain *published credit ratings* from the rating agencies and access debt in more favorable terms? The answer is: it depends. The fact that they may pay a substantial amount for a rating does not ensure obtaining a rating favorable enough to obtain good terms for debt. The reason is that not only do they miss published credit ratings, but also, and more importantly, most of them have weak creditworthiness and substandard financial management systems; thus, a rating could show unfavorable scores that cities would not be willing to make public. To address this issue, rating agencies have introduced an interim solution; namely a *shadow credit rating* to help municipalities identify and correct areas of weaknesses and initiate a formal credit rating process later on when likely good results are expected. The challenge is, however, that even a shadow credit rating remains an expensive exercise.

The MFSA offers a solution one notch below this, namely, to complete a *self-assessed shadow credit rating* (SASCR) based on MFSA results at no or very little cost. This SASCR would inform the municipality about its status, weaknesses, and likely rating score, signaling whether or not it would be wise to contract for a formal rating that would provide them with favorable scores. Experiences show that, in most cases, it is better for even the progressive cities in the developing world to first get the results from the SASCR, engage in specific corrective measures, and aim for formal rating at a later stage.

Story from the Field: Belgrade's Credit Rating

The city of Belgrade was among the first municipalities to join the World Bank–Austria Urban Partnership Program (UPP); the city started using the Municipal Finances Self-Assessment (MFSA) among various capacity-building instruments in 2011. It took city officials a year to restructure their original financial reports, fill out MFSA templates using the methodology outlined in this handbook, and then analyze key findings and results. The initial results signaled good creditworthiness, sound financial management, and overall good medium-term outlook. In 2013, the city government decided to embark on a formal credit rating in order to obtain loans with more favorable terms, and finally contracted with Moody's Rating Agency. Rating discussions and analysis went more smoothly and faster than expected, because the city shared with Moody's not only all original financial reports but also the MFSA reports, which Moody's found fully compatible with the rating requirements (see details in chapter 1).

The MFSA has helped the city of Belgrade to obtain and sustain a sound financial position. The most recent rating review was completed with a score of Ba3 and announced by Moody's Investor Services on April 22, 2019. A press statement published in SeeNews, an Internet-based news portal, reported:

BELGRADE (Serbia): Moody's Investors Service has praised Belgrade city government's self-financing capacity and improved liquidity position in a periodic review of the Ba3 credit rating of Serbia's capital, deputy mayor Goran Vesic said. "The rating still takes into account the relatively high level of indebtedness of the city due to the debt of 1.2 billion euros left by the previous mayor, but Moody's states that the level of indebtedness of Belgrade is decreasing and concludes that our city is the centre of the Serbian national economy," Vesic said, according to a press release issued by the city government.

In a periodic review of Belgrade's credit rating Moody's said earlier this month that the credit profile challenges include the city's high investment requirements, associated with pressure stemming from the transport company and limited financial flexibility under the current legislative framework.

"Moody's also considers the City of Belgrade to have a strong likelihood of extraordinary support from the Government of Serbia (Ba3) in the event that the issuer was to face acute liquidity stress," the ratings agency said on April 10, 2019.

In March 2017, Moody's upgraded Belgrade's long-term issuer rating to Ba3 from B1 and changed its rating's outlook to stable from positive following similar actions on Serbia's government bond rating. The creditworthiness of Belgrade is closely linked to that of the sovereign, as Serbian local governments depend on revenues that are linked to the sovereign's macroeconomic and fiscal performance (Ralev 2019).

The SASCR involves a procedure that adopts the principles and key methodology practices of rating agencies in completing credit ratings or shadow credit ratings (Fitch Ratings 2015; Moody's 2017; Standard and Poor's 2016). The scores could be aaa, aa, a, bbb, bb, b, ccc, cc, c, or d. The SASCR, however, applies rating instruments in a self-assessment modality. SASCR analysis and scoring are built on three pillars: (1) the MFSA qualitative municipal finance assessment (MFA), (2) the MFSA ratio analysis, and (3) MFSA financial projections. All of these are assumed to be completed during the MFSA before the SASCR. Therefore, the SASCR does not require new data collection.

SASCR analysis and scoring include the following simple steps: (1) scoring the qualitative results from the MFA; (2) scoring the quantitative results from the ratio analysis; (3) calculating the final score; and (4) establishing a shadow credit rating score based on the final score and a rating table. It is also useful to summarize the results in a short SASCR report. The steps of the SASCR are explained in appendix E by using again the data of the sample city analyzed and explained in the preceding MFSA sections.

Tapping External Sources of Funding: Land Value Capture and Public–Private Partnerships

Land Value Capture

The combination of the UA/SA and MFSA is a powerful instrument for estimating both the projected development funding needs and the existing funding capacity while encouraging users to seek options "outside the box." The UA/SA, through its Land Assessment and its identification of major land development projects in the city, is uniquely positioned to provide a current and accurate picture of the local situation on existing zoning and regulations, population trends, and development pressures. Many cities are very dependent on land-based revenues; therefore, any additional revenues tied to specific land development projects are bound to have a measurable impact on revenue generation. In recent years, cities have explored ways to

capture increases in land values. Cities such as New York; Washington, DC; London; and Paris, and, more recently, Chinese cities, made it a major component of financing their urban infrastructure. Land value capture has also been used to finance large infrastructure in Latin America. The most famous examples are the bus rapid transit (BRT) systems of Bogotá, Colombia, and São Paolo, Brazil. Land value capture (LVC) is a method of funding infrastructure improvements based on the recovery of all or some of the increase in property values generated by public infrastructure investments (Peterson 2008). LVC can help mitigate the challenges cities face in obtaining public funding, while also providing benefits to private sector partners. Below are some of the LVC instruments that local governments can tap into (Freire and Kopanyi 2018; Kim 2018):

- **Tax increment financing (TIF)**: TIF is a funding strategy used by cities to promote economic development within a designated area that is deemed "blighted" or "underdeveloped." TIF is used to divert anticipated property tax increases to a dedicated fund, which is then reinvested into public infrastructure within the TIF district. It is used to promote economic development by earmarking future property tax revenues from increases in assessed values within a zone and issue bonds against these earmarked revenues.

- **Transit development impact fee (TDIF)**: The TDIF is a one-time charge on new development designed to cover costs associated with its impact on public transit systems. TDIF reflects a shift in policy where local governments increasingly look to developers to contribute to the impacts of development.

- *Special assessment district (SAD)/ Betterment levy*: In districts in which land value has increased as a result of public infrastructure improvements, like upgraded transit systems, an additional tax is assessed on parcels to recover the costs of the public improvement project. SADs are most useful to fund localized improvements, such as new transit stations on existing lines or district-specific improvements like bus or light rail. Betterment levies or special assessments are instruments that charge property owners a substantial share of the cost for infrastructure improvements that benefit their properties within a designated area of improvement. One modality of these is known as transit-oriented development (TOD), commonly used to support metro-rail development (Suzuki et al. 2015). Community development facilities (CDFs) represent another modality when cities issue special levies, outside of property tax, based on land (size, not value) without linking them to specific development; cities in California often issue bonds backed by CDFs.

- *Transfer of development rights*: This refers to a set of instruments introduced initially to induce voluntary private transactions to trade development rights (for example, some defined area in square meters) between owners in "selling" and "receiving" zones defined for better urban development by master plans or zoning regulations. Cities have emulated this practice by selling building rights in defined zones directly to developers or to any investors via open auctions (Certificate of Potential Additional Construction, or CePAC in Brazil) in order to collect revenues while promoting higher-density urbanization.

- *Developer exactions/Development fees*: These are charges that a city collects from developers, forcing them to contribute to development of trunk infrastructure. Issuance of building permits will be made upon payment of development fees.

- *Development agreements*: They capture land value via voluntary contracts negotiated between cities and developers where developers promise to make large up-front investments on infrastructure if the city commits not to change land use and zoning regulations during the term of the agreement.

- *Community benefit agreements*: These are voluntary contracts between developers and the community in a defined zone.

LVC's success as a funding tool requires an environment with a smart mix of uses, density, accessibility, and market demand:

- *Regulatory framework*: Local zoning ordinances that allow for a mix of uses— residential, commercial, and recreational— must be in place for LVC to be effective, because mixed-use development near transit stations tends to generate more value than single-use development. If areas near transit are zoned only for a single use, cities may need to rewrite zoning ordinances to include mixed-use zoning, or develop a TOD overlay district.

- *Density*: Development near transit should be sufficiently dense in order to capture the greatest value possible through LVC strategies. Because LVC funds transit projects through a proportional relationship with property values, dense development that creates more value per built square foot is more desirable than comparably less valuable sprawling, suburban style development.

- *Reforming property taxes*: In addition to zoning, reforming general property tax formulas to include a land value tax (LVT) component can be an effective method to promote TOD and raise revenue to finance public transit. LVT as a reform measure results in placing a higher tax rate on land than on buildings, which provides incentives to develop property by making it more costly to hold on to vacant or underused sites. Additionally, placing a lower tax rate on improvement assessments could encourage owners to upgrade or replace obsolete buildings.

Public-Private Partnerships

Municipalities can substantially expand investment capacities by selecting projects to be funded and managed by public–private partnerships (PPPs). Applying PPP arrangements for the right project and with the right conditions can produce a win-win situation for both the private and public partners. PPPs include a wide range of modalities. One modality is a very simple management contract that aims to improve management efficiency by private experiences and procedures. A second modality is joint ventures, when the municipality provides some assets and forms a joint venture company with a private partner who also contributes with substantial funds (for example, working capital or equipment) and when parties share the risk of operation. One of the highest-level modalities is concession, in which the municipality tenders out a license to provide particular services (for example, solid waste collection and disposal, water and wastewater services, or public transport). The private partner signs a concession agreement in exchange for a concession fee; the municipality becomes a regulator of the contracted service, while the private partner provides for all required investments and working capital and builds and operates the facilities until the end of the concession agreement.

From the municipality's perspective, PPPs financed by the private sector allow the spreading of the project cost for the public over a longer period, in line with the expected benefits (such as savings on vehicle operating cost, on travel time, and on accidents). Public funds are, thus, freed up for investments in sectors where private investments are impossible or inappropriate. Experience suggests, however, that PPP is not a panacea, and structuring and managing a PPP is a very demanding task. Typical mistakes cities may make include contracting out services that have failed both in technical and financial terms and expecting private partners to fix all the deficiencies. Another mistake is when the municipality lacks capacity to monitor and control the private service provider, and, as a result, services deteriorate and eventually the contract may be canceled. Finally, the PPP makes the different interests very visible, because the private partner wants fair recovery of costs and return on equity; as a result, PPP partners often demand various guarantees such as off-take warrantees, which means that the municipality must commit to pay a portion of fees to ensure that the private partner generates sufficient revenues in case of low volume of initial customers' demand (for example, due to gradual increase of water use, bus travelers, or volume of waste disposed of in a landfill). In summary, a city needs to get the proper technical and financial advice before engaging in such partnerships in order to make sure that the endeavor is profitable and beneficial for all parties involved.

Tapping External Sources of Funding: Access to Donor Funding Made Easier

There is nothing that donors love better than having a trusted line of communication with key country stakeholders at the central and local levels, knowing that key agreements are based on sound and reliable data, and knowing that due diligence and proper homework have been carried out. Multilateral agencies, bilateral agencies, and foundations are ready to jump in but, more often than not, are concerned about the lack of preparedness of potential investment projects. The European Union in Southeast Europe is a case in point: large funding opportunities have not been fully "captured" by potential beneficiaries. The donor complains about the lack of "bankable" projects or programs, whereas the potential recipient laments the administrative hurdles put in place to access funding. The first group is concerned about not disbursing fast enough whereas the second does not know how to present its agenda and its credentials. Such a situation is hard to fathom in view of the state of urgency and the incredible financing gap outlined in this book. LGSAs can provide a solution to all parties because their use and application will clear the way for the screening and identification of priority actions as well as companion measures.

From LGSAs to Green Financing

Green financing refers to actions aimed at increasing the level of financial flows to sustainable development priorities and project implementation (box 4.3). A key principle of green financing is to better manage environmental and social risks and take opportunities that bring both a decent rate of return and environmental benefit and that deliver greater accountability. Green financing can be promoted through changes in countries' regulatory frameworks, such as harmonization of public financial incentives, increases in green financing from different sectors, alignment of public sector financial decision making with the environmental dimension of the investment projects, increases in investments in clean and green technologies, and increased use of green bonds.

Cities have a major role to play in this agenda, and LGSAs can help push it forward. Today's capital markets do not provide cities with adequate access to affordable financing suited to low-emission, climate-resilient infrastructure. The challenge is not simply to increase the amount of money in the pipeline; it is also to create an enabling environment that encourages existing and new financing to flow from a broad spectrum of sources. Specific recommendations include

Box 4.3
Paris Agreement on Climate Change

This agreement is a global treaty under international law to combat climate change. It was adopted by 195 nations in Paris during the 21st Conference of Parties (COP21) of the United Nations Framework Convention on Climate Change (UNFCCC) on December 12, 2015. The core objective of the Paris Agreement on Climate Change is to limit the global temperature rise to below 2° Celsius as compared to the preindustrial era in the present century. The agreement also emphasizes the need to drive efforts so that the temperature rise can be limited to 1.5 °C.

Funding climate change has always been a contentious issue between rich and poor countries. Under the convention, developed countries are bound to provide support in the amount of US$100 billion per year to developing countries, every year, until 2025 through the **Green Climate Fund**. For the post-2025 period, a new, higher financial goal will be set. With regard to financial support, for the first time in any international agreement, developing countries are also encouraged to come forward voluntarily to contribute financially.

the following: develop a financial policy environment that encourages cities to invest in low-emission, climate-resilient infrastructure; support cities in developing frameworks to price climate externalities; develop and encourage project preparation and maximize support for mitigation and adaptation projects; and collaborate with local financial institutions to develop climate finance infrastructure solutions for cities.

- National government supporting public sectors on creating enabling environments for green investments (Global Green Growth Institute, GGGI)

- Selecting local public investments with green technology modalities and environmental sustainability (for example, public transport with electric vehicles, energy-saving buildings, energy-efficient street lighting (iLEF 2015), solar electricity applications, water conservation, and solid-waste treatment with methane capture)

- Selecting municipal project financing modalities to tap into available international funds set aside to support green development, for example, the Green Climate Fund GCF—the world's largest climate fund—or the Global Environment Facility GEF—managed under the World Bank

- Promoting public-private partnerships on financing mechanisms, such as green bonds.

Carbon emission trade is a well-tested instrument that works well in developing countries. As of September 2015, 39 countries and 23 cities, states, and provinces have employed carbon-pricing instruments, mostly in the form of carbon taxes or emissions-trading systems (Habitat 2016).

Environmental impact bonds (EIBs) are a type of financing that provides different levels of return for investors based on how well the projects funded by the bond perform. If a green infrastructure intervention is more effective than expected, investors get a greater return; if the intervention is less successful, the return is lower. The financing is particularly useful for innovative projects that might be difficult to fund with traditional bonds. Examples of environmental impact bonds include US$12 million, Atlanta, Georgia (2019); US$25 million, Washington, DC, Water Company (2017); and the Massachusetts Bay Transportation Authority's tax-exempt sustainability bonds as part of a US$574 million competitive sale (2017).

Interestingly, India and China have been making progress in green financing. China has issued guidelines for establishing a green financial system. The city of Shanghai has established a special-purpose vehicle, the Shanghai Green Urban Financing and Services Co., Ltd (FSC), and is borrowing from the World Bank in order to finance a very comprehensive green financing program, the Green Urban Financing and Innovation Project, for a total amount of US$520 million (World Bank 2019) (box 4.4).

From LGSAs to Municipal Programs: Partnership Agreements and the Municipal Contract

One possible and powerful outcome of the LGSA process lies in the fact that the UA/SA PIP and the MFSA Action Plan can become the key components of a partnership agreement between the local government and the central government. There is a long legacy of such partnerships. Below is a summary of experience and a reminder of what municipal contracts are and what they can do to support both the decentralization process and greater accountability in municipal affairs and in central–local relationships.

The Green Urban Financing and Innovation Project Development Objective

The Green Urban Financing and Innovation Project development objective is to increase access to sustainable, long-term financing for selected green urban investments benefitting local governments in the Yangtze River Delta (YRD) Region. The YRD Region is very vulnerable to the impact of climate change. Direct economic losses from extreme weather events account for up to 3 percent of China's annual GDP. Of the top 20 cities worldwide affected by rising sea levels, seven are from China; four of the seven are in the YRD Region.

According to a Climate Change Special Assessment Report on the YRD Region, water resources shortages, water environmental degradation, and urban flooding are the top three climate-change-related challenges facing cities in the region. Investments in water supply, wastewater, and solid waste will help cities enhance resilience against climate change threats. Building on experiences with green financing, the proposed financial intermediary (Shanghai Green Urban Financing and Services Co., Ltd, or FSC) is expected to raise medium- to long-term funds in the capital markets and on-lend to specific subprojects based on project appraisal and fiduciary oversight capacity.

The FSC will be the first subnational financing facility of its kind in China. The FSC would be open to public utilities and revenue-earning entities that are service providers for districts and towns in the Shanghai metropolitan area and other cities and towns in adjacent provinces in the YRD Region. They would be responsible for raising the initial financing and would repay loans from operating revenues or government subsidies (World Bank 2019).

Legacy from Europe

In Europe, the rapid development of such contractual arrangements is directly linked to ambitious public policies aimed at addressing social, economic, and environmental problems in urban areas in the 1980s. All these policies feature the same objectives aimed at promoting social cohesion, enhancing public safety, and improving living conditions. In this context, contractualization means a concerted partnership policy that advocates the cofinancing of costly investments and involves several ministries and levels of local governments as well as citizens as partners. In France, municipal contracts were initially introduced on an experimental basis in 1989–94. They were the legacy of a dual history of contractualization—public action contracts of the 1970s and social action contracts (focused on underserviced neighborhoods) of the 1980s. They represented a new form of selectivity in awarding capital grants to urban areas. During the 2000–06 period, 247 municipal contracts involving 2,000 municipalities were signed, providing over 2 billion euros in financing.

Comparable arrangements emerged in Europe to best suit the increasingly integrated nature of urban development programs. The Netherlands adopted the contract formula in its "big city" policy, which was implemented by way of a comprehensive agreement between the central government and 25 cities in 1994 and a city-by-city agreement in 1999–2003.

In Sweden, "local development contracts" were implemented in the 2000s with seven municipalities that provided cofinancing. The contracts targeted 24 poor neighborhoods that were home to a large concentration of immigrants. In Belgium, federal authorities used the law of July 17, 2000, to develop a municipal contracts policy, whereby contracts would specify the conditions under which local authorities may receive financial aid from the state. Beginning in 2000, the first municipal contracts were executed and targeted initially to larger cities, gradually including other municipalities. The United Kingdom adopted an original form of partnership policy that brought together local stakeholders (civil society, private sector, local governments) for the purpose of identifying and outlining local development projects, which gave them access to grants from the central government's Neighborhood Renewal Fund. The United Kingdom is currently expanding the use of city contracts beyond the initial urban renewal objective. Germany also introduced partnership policies between various tiers of governments in which the regions (Landers) played an important role. Its "Social City" program drew 25 percent of its financing from the federal government, and 75 percent came from the Landers and communities.

In Europe, the concept of municipal contracts has been used and scaled up in a very pragmatic and determined way. It has not often been used to seal an all-encompassing agreement or a full-scale municipal program; instead, it has been used to target specific public policy objectives, such as social inclusion, or to help bridge a financing gap for large multi-jurisdiction investment projects. Experiences in Europe, and particularly in France, with regard to central–local government partnerships provided some inspiration for the municipal contracts that emerged in the Maghreb (Morocco and Tunisia) and in Sub-Saharan Africa. There, the model has been very effective: over 200 municipalities have implemented

several generations of municipal contracts, thereby introducing some level of accountability in public spending.

Connecting LGSAs and Municipal Contracts

If financing through own revenues, grants, or donor funding is available, converting the content of the UA/SA PIP and MFSA Action Plan into components of a municipal contract is an effective way to ensure their actual implementation. It provides the following:

- *An accountable binding agreement*: Although this agreement has no legal value, it is a signed public document that stipulates the content of the program both in terms of infrastructure investments and in terms of specific measures pertaining to revenue mobilization, expenditures management, local taxation, asset management, bookkeeping, and financial management with specific annual targets and assignment of responsibilities between the central and local governments.

- *Some measure of stability and visibility on short- and medium-term public spending*: It, in effect, introduces a multiyear planning perspective and "culture" as well as a programmatic approach to city management and investments. To some extent, it takes the politics out of the equation because the duration of the municipal contract (which is typically three to five years) does not necessarily match the duration of the political mandate of the elected leadership, and its content is not likely to be subject to political volatility.

- *Some measure of efficiency in channeling funding for the city*: Because the components of the municipal contract are based on the UA/SA and the MFSA and because the data and key findings are reliable, trustworthy, and packaged in a way that inspires confidence, central governments, private partners, and the donor community are likely to use the municipal contract as a platform for investments, giving the municipality an opportunity to harmonize its many windows of financing and cut down on transaction costs.

- ***Some measure of progress on structural reforms and on the decentralization process***: Because it brings together the key proponents of the decentralization process, typically the ministry of finance and the city, the municipal contract process provides a greater chance to put on the table and work through some fundamental reforms such as local taxation, shared taxes, grant allocation formulas, and intergovernmental transfers.

Again, if funding is available, if the political will is there, and if the partners are committed to change and progress and serious about implementation, then the municipal contract may be the final step of the LGSA process—the icing on the cake.

Keeping an Eye on the Prize: A Bottom-Line Approach to Better City Management

When all is said and done, the LGSA's ultimate goal can be summarized in two words: ***action*** and ***reform***. This is why the UA/SA PIPs and the MFSA Action Plans, which are derived from both the urban and the financial analysis, are so very important. Users of LGSAs should always keep in mind the "solution" side of the equation. For every issue, challenge, and weakness the LGSAs uncover, there should be a solution, a way forward, and, if needed, the outline of a reform. Each solution should come with its *mode d'emploi,* or "how-to," in order to bring realism and accountability to its implementation. Among the questions that should be properly addressed are the following: Who are the gatekeepers, and who has power to unlock a situation? What triggers or key prerequisites need to be unleashed to get the best results? What trade-offs must not be overlooked? What is the proper timing and sequencing of tasks and activities? What mundane or less mundane implementation issues need to be overcome? Ultimately, what matters is not so much how we get there, but what we get in the end. Keeping an eye on the prize comes down to better cities and a better world.

References

Acuto, Michele, and Susan Parnell. 2016. "Leave No City Behind." Science 352 (6288): 873. Urban Planet Special Issue.

ADM (Agence de Développement Municipal). 2008. *Guide de Ratios 2008–2011.* Senegal: ADM.

ADM (Agence de Developpement Municipal). *Atlas Urbain des Villes du Senegal 2008-2011.* Senegal: ADM.

Bird, Richard. 2013. "Foreign Advice and Tax Policy in Developing Countries." International Center for Public Policy Working Paper 13-07, Andrew Young School of Policy Studies, Georgia State University, Atlanta.

Freire, Maria E., and Mihaly Kopanyi. 2018. "Asset and Debt Management for Cities." Cities that Work, International Growth Centre Working Paper, London School of Economics and University of Oxford.

Kim, Julie. 2018. "CePACs and Their Value Capture Viability in the U.S. for Infrastructure Funding." Working Paper 18Jk1, Lincoln Institute of Land Policy, Cambridge, MA.

Peterson, George. 2008. Unlocking Land Values to Finance Urban Infrastructure. Washington, DC: World Bank.

Ralev, Radomir. 2019. "Moody's Praises Belgrade City's Self-Financing Capacity, Liquidity—Deputy Mayor." SeeNews, April 22. https://seenews.com/news/moodys-praises

-belgrade-citys-self-financing-capacity
-liquidity-deputy-mayor-651449.

Scherabon, Herwig. 2016. "The Art of
Gentrification: City Data Made Beautiful."
The Guardian Cities in Numbers gallery.
https://www.theguardian.com/cities/gallery
/2016 /nov/30/art-gentrification-patterns-data
-visualisation-herwig-scherabon-.

Suzuki, Hiraoke, Jin Murakame, Yu-Hung Hong,
and Beth Tamayose. 2015. Financing Transit
Oriented Development with Land Values:
Adapting Land Value Capture in Developing
Countries. Urban Development Series.
Washington, DC: World Bank.

World Bank. 2019. "People's Republic of China:
Green Urban Financing and Innovation
Project." Project Appraisal Document, World
Bank, Washington, DC, April.

Additional Readings

Agence Française de Notation. 2010. Rapport de
l'Observatoire des Finances Locales. Paris:
Agence Française de Notation.

Ammons, D. N. 2001. Municipal Benchmarks:
Assessing Local Performances and Establishing
Community Standards. Thousand Oaks, CA:
Sage Publications Inc.

Cities Alliance. 2006. Guide to City Development
Strategies: Improving Urban Performance.
Brussels: The Cities Alliance, Cities without
Slums.

Farvacque-Vitkovic, Catherine, and Lucien Godin.
2006. "Decentralization and Municipal
Development: Municipal Contracts." Working
Paper, World Bank, Washington, DC.

Farvacque-Vitkovic, Catherine, Lucien Godin, and
Anne Sinet. 2014. "Municipal Self-Assessments:
A Handbook for Local Governments." Working
Paper, World Bank, Washington, DC.

Farvacque-Vitkovic, Catherine, and Anne Sinet.
2014. "Achieving Greater Transparency and
Accountability: Measuring Municipal Finances
Performance and Paving a Path for Reforms."
In Municipal Finances: A Handbook for Local

Governments, edited by Catherine Farvacque-
Vitkovic and Mihaly Kopanyi. Washington, DC:
World Bank.

Goudriaan, Mirco. 2010. "Effective Aid through
Municipal Contracts." Working Paper,
World Bank, Washington, DC.

Habitat. 2016. "Municipal Finance and Local Fiscal
Systems." HABITAT III Policy Paper 5, Quito III.

ILEF (International Lighting Efficiency Financing).
2015. "International Lighting Efficiency
Financing–Facility Financial Model Capital
Estimate and Financial Viability."

NALAS (Network of Associations of Local
Authorities of South-East Europe). 2011.
"Report on Fiscal Decentralization Indicators
in South-East Europe." NALAS, Skopje.

Partenariat pour le Developpement Municipal
(PDM), Banque du Developpement Local au
Maroc, and Institut de la Gestion Deleguee
(IGD). 2007. "Guide pour l'Autoevaluation
financiere des autorites locales."

Paulais, Thierry. 2012. Financing Africa's Cities:
The Imperative of Local Investments. Africa
Development Forum series. Washington, DC:
World Bank.

Poister, H. T., and C. Streib. 1999. "Performance
Measurement in Municipal Government:
Assessing the State of the Practice." Public
Administration Review 59: 325–35.

Smolka, Martin O. 2013. "Implementing Value Capture
in Latin America." Policy Focus Report Series,
Lincoln Institute of Land Policy, Washington, DC.

World Bank. 2013. Planning, Connecting and
Financing Cities—Now: Priorities for City
Leaders. Washington, DC: World Bank.

——. 2014. "Improving Local Governments
Capacity—The Experience of Municipal Finances
Self-Assessment (MFSA) in South-East Europe."
World Bank–Austria Urban Partnership Program,
World Bank, Washington, DC.

——. 2018. "Improving Local Governments
Capacity—The Experience of Municipal Finances
Self-Assessment (MFSA) in South-East Europe."
World Bank–Austria Urban Partnership Program,
World Bank, Washington, DC.

Local Governments Self-Assessments: Simplified Framework or Version "Light"

LGSAs as described in this book require some level of capacity and a high level of commitment from all parties involved. The payoff and results emerging from the process are well worth the effort; however, some cities and towns may not be ready for such an engagement. For those local governments that are on the fence—ready but not quite equipped to carry out a full-fledged Urban Audit/Self-Assessment and a Municipal Finances Self-Assessment/MFSA—this appendix provides a simplified framework for a more modest self-assessment that can provide an entry point into a full-fledged LGSA process later.

The key objective is to carry out a quick assessment or diagnostic focusing on the urban, financial, and organizational situation of the municipality and help it to identify a Priority Investment Program and a MFSA Action Plan. The key goal of this simpler version is to assess the absorptive capacity of the local government and to outline a matching program of investments ready for implementation. The objective is to help the municipality take informed investments decisions while taking steps on improving its urban, organizational, and financial position. This process can easily be carried out by any technical and financial department and would not require, as may be the case with the LGSAs presented in the main core of this book, the initial reliance on local experts. This template/framework has been developed, tested, and implemented on the ground in many cities.

Urban Audit/Self-Assessment: Simplified Framework

Step 1: Regional context

The city in its regional context

- Give a brief description of the region (major geographical features), distances to other major cities, and major access routes.

Regional economy and boundaries of the city's hinterland

- Describe the region's principal activities and products, as well its connectivity with the rest of the country (key transportation nodes and mobility patterns of goods and people). Indicate the principal regional administrative boundaries and population clusters. Define the boundaries of the city's hinterland (area of influence).

Demography

- Provide figures for the regional population according to the most recent censuses and projections for 5, 10, and 15 years from now, as well as the corresponding growth rates.

Map: The city in its regional context

Step 2: Urban setting and organization of the city

Urban setting

- Describe the city's physical context: (a) principal terrain relief, hydrography, undevelopable areas (such as steep slopes, erosion, and flood-prone areas), conservation areas (forests, water tables), open areas, and potential expansion areas; (b) principal connections to other cities; (c) climate (seasonal precipitation table); and (d) assets and constraints that favor or hinder urban expansion.

Organization of the city

- Clarify administrative boundaries of the city and internal organization in districts.

- Identify levels of local government units responsible for infrastructure and service delivery.

Table A.1   Share of Responsibilities: Who Is Responsible for What?

| | | Responsible entities | | | | | | | |
| | | Municipality | | State government | | Utility companies | | Private | |
Sectors	Items	New works	Maintenance	New works	Maintenance	New works	Maintenance	New works	Maintenance
1 Infrastructure	Primary roads			O	O				
	Secondary roads	X	X						
	Drainage	X	X						
	Solid waste	X	X	O	O				
	Street lighting	X	X						
2 Utilities	Electricity					X	X		
	Water supply					X	X		
	Wastewater					X	X		
	Urban transport	X	X			X	X		

continued next page

Sectors	Items	Municipality		State government		Utility companies		Private	
		New works	Maintenance	New works	Maintenance	New works	Maintenance	New works	Maintenance
	Public heating					X	X		
	Others								
3 Services	Education	X	X	O	O				
	Health	X	X	O	O				
	Social	X	X	O	O				
	Culture	X	X	O	O				
	Green spaces	X	X	O	O				
4 Land develop-ment	Housing	X	X	O	O			V	V
	Industrial	X	X	O	O			V	V
	Urban renewal	X	X	O	O			V	V

Note: Responsibility for infrastructure or public utilities denoted by X = municipal level; O = state level; V= private.

Land occupancy

- Review and outline the pros and cons of existing city planning documents and land use regulations and their impact on the city fabric and configuration.

- Map existing land occupancy, highlighting current and future urbanization patterns and trends and locating key pressure points.

Major facilities
Activities
Green space
Roads, open areas
Total - other occupancy

Table A.2 Land Occupancy

Surface area, hectares	Neighborhood					
	1	2	3	...	...	Total
Housing						
Serviced housing						
Underserviced housing						
Irregular housing						
Total housing						
Other occupancy						

Land Markets

- Do a quick review of existing sources (real estate, transaction records) to assess current land prices by neighborhood.

- Map out land value information.

Land Assets

- Do a quick assessment of the city's land assets information.

- Update or jumpstart a quick Land Assets Inventory.

- Map existing locations of public lands.

Main Land Assets

	Property type	Unit	Price	Area	Location/ Address
Plots owned by the municipality					
Plots controlled by the municipality					
Buildings owned by the municipality					
Total					

Step 3: Demography and Densities

Urban population and population by neighborhood

- Provide figures for the city's population according to the most recent censuses and projections for 5, 10, and 15 years from now, as well as the corresponding growth rates.

- Break down the city's population by neighborhood.

- Provide an overview of the city-level population profile and composition, including by age and gender.

- State any salient feature with a long-term impact on the city's infrastructure needs.

- *Map*. Population and density by neighborhood.

Table A.3 Population

Year	Census 1	Census 2	N	N+5	N+10	N+15
Population						

Table A.4 Population by Neighborhood

	Neighborhood			
	1	2	3	Total
Population in serviced housing				
Population in underserviced housing				
Population in irregular housing				
Total population				
Housing				

Step 4: Urban Economy and City Branding

The city is the focal point for shaping the local economy and developing relations with hinterland areas:

- Identify the **"drivers"** of the local economy: principal stakeholders involved (public and private, local and outside the region, "modern" and "informal").

- Describe the **exchanges** of agricultural goods and services and transfers between rural areas and the city, and analyze the interdependencies between these two areas.

- Identify the **decision-making centers** that influence the various components of the local economy, and the major external factors that affect these different components.

- Describe the features and level of urban **employment**: government, commerce, industry, agriculture, "informal" activities. Name the major "employers." List features of large local retailers, the transportation sector, and the public buildings and works sector.

- Identify "modern" businesses and **informal activities**.

- Describe the "brand" and "branding policies" of the city.

Table A.5 Economic Activities and Jobs

Sector of activity	Economic units / services	Type of activity	Number of jobs	Location
Industry				
Crafts				
Commerce				
Public enterprise				
Public administration				
Other				
Informal activities				
Other				

Step 5: Urban Services and Infrastructure

Urban Services and Infrastructure Needs Assessment

- Prepare an inventory of neighborhood access to services, by infrastructure and superstructure facilities. Enter the information in the ISPI table.

- Comment on the results of indicators and scores: (a) brief description of each neighborhood; (b) classification of neighborhoods according to scores received.

- Identify the most underserviced neighborhoods, where access to infrastructure and facilities is the most deficient.

This analysis should help reveal the city's principal needs and serve as a guide for proposals under the Priority Investment Program (PIP). The goal is to determine, for each type of infrastructure or facility, which neighborhood(s) are the most inadequate, and thereby decide on priorities. The data are entered in the "inventory" section (1) of the table. Section 2, "indicators," compares the most significant service data to the populations of each neighborhood (calculated automatically). And finally, the scores determined from these indicators serve as the basis for comparing neighborhood service data to the average for the city. The neighborhood score is defined qualitatively (poor, mediocre, average, fair, or good) by way of a quantitative rating of 0 to 4, with a 4 equal to the city's average. A coefficient is assigned to each score according to its weight.

Maps: (a) Facilities; (b) Roads (by classification, kind, condition); (c) Drainage; (d) Potable water supply (reservoirs, principal network, treatment plant, water towers); (e) Electricity (high voltage lines, medium voltage lines, power plant); (f) Sanitation (sewage, waste disposal, transfer stations).

Table A.6 Infrastructure and Services Programming Inventory (ISPI) (For complete tables, see chapter 2 tables 2.3, 2.4, and 2.5.)

	Neighborhood			
	1	2	3	Total
1. Inventory				
Population				
Land occupancy				
Access to infrastructure				
Roads				
Water and electricity				
Environmental sanitation				
Access to superstructure facilities				
Education				
Health care				
Commercial facilities				
Sports and youth activities				
Culture and recreation				
Public administration				

continued next page

Table A.6 Infrastructure and Services Programming Inventory (ISPI; continued)

	Neighborhood			
	1	2	3	Total

2. Indicators

Population

Land occupancy

Access to infrastructure

  Roads

  Water and electricity

  Environmental sanitation

Access to superstructure facilities

  Education

  Health care

  Commercial facilities

  Sports and youth activities

  Culture and recreation

  Public administration

3. Scores

Population

Land occupancy

Access to infrastructure

  Roads

  Water and electricity

  Environmental sanitation

Access to superstructure facilities

  Education

  Health care

  Commercial facilities

  Sports and youth activities

  Culture and recreation

Public administration

Final score

Municipal assets

- List all municipally owned built assets, indicating their location (a street address), dates of building, and present values.

- Reconcile the list of municipal assets with the municipal assets list of the MFSA.

- Map information.

If street addresses exist, the street addressing database and map will be the first key entry points for this inventory exercise.

Table A.7 Municipal Built Assets

Description	Size	Date purchased /built	Present value
Developed land	m^2		
Undeveloped land	m^2		
Infrastructure	km		
Asphalt roads			
Dirt roads			
Rolling stock			
Total			

Public works maintenance

- Identify the maintenance work performed annually by the municipality: type of work, location, method of execution, resources allocated to maintenance.

- State if a Capital Improvement Plan is available, and indicate its date of approval, content, costs, level of implementation, and key pending issues with either its preparation or its implementation.

Step 6: Deficiencies and needs

Based on the infrastructure and services needs assessment,

- Summarize the main deficiencies and needs identified during the analysis and implementation of the ISPI.

- Indicate feasible intervention types and sectors to help focus the process of identifying projects for the PIP.

Step 7: Urban development projects, recent and future projects

Urban development trends and urban planning projects

- Outline urbanization trends both in the city center and in the peri-urban areas.

- Give an overview of current urban planning documents, assess implementation status.

- Give an overview of the content and implementation status of the Capital Improvement Plan, if it exists.

- Identify key large infrastructure projects/ structuring or restructuring projects in the city, specifically mentioning the location, costs, implementing agency/agencies, involvement of private partners, sources of funding, and timeline for implementation.

- Summarize all projects completed or ongoing during the past three years in the municipality or its immediate surroundings, and work projected for the immediate future.

- *Map:* Urban development trends, recent and future projects, and projects.

Table A.8 Recent, Ongoing, and Scheduled Projects

	Description	Year	Location	Amount	Financing
Recent					
Ongoing					
Projected					
Scheduled					

Step 8: Priority Investments Program: Consultation and Selection

Overview of the consultation process

The consultation process is a key component of the Urban Audit/SA. It includes the following:

- An information/sensibilization session at the beginning of the UA/SA process. This is a crucial time when all stakeholders should be on board with both the process and the expected results.

- A "reinstatement/consultation" phase upon completion of the analysis. This is an equally important stage because it is an opportunity for city officials, funding partners, and civil society to come together to review and discuss the key findings of the UA/SA and to start decanting what it means in terms of (1) needed supporting-capacity-building measures, (2) new investment priorities, and (3) key maintenance/rehabilitation programs. It is also an opportunity to ensure that the selection criteria are agreed upon and that proper attention is placed on green investments, social inclusion, and programs that contribute to the economic and cultural vibrancy of the city.

- A "consultation/cooperative discussion" stage after the costs and feasibility of all the projects have been assessed. This "long list" of projects[1] is examined, discussed, and filtered through the criteria listed. The consultations are followed by discussion as needed to decide which projects are PIP-eligible.

Project eligibility and priority criteria

If the UA/SA is conducted in parallel with the MFSA, one of the first criteria will be the key question of availability of funding. Is funding available, and through what source? What are the cost implications on the existing and projected tax burden? What is the likelihood of partnering with private operators? Does the inclusion of a specific project preclude the financing of other priority projects? Is the project expected to raise revenues for the city and increase land values? What impact will it have on existing residents? Besides the funding issue, there are other equally important criteria which need to be checked. For example, the project should:

- Be executable within the expected time-frame come under municipal authority.

- Not be redundant with other projects planned under other programs.

- Respond to the needs identified in the urban analysis and/or the demands articulated during consultation.

- Meet the requirement for immediate start-up upon completion of the work (for example, availability of staff to run the facility, and connection to utility networks).

- Give priority consideration to underserviced neighborhoods with high population density.

- Be free of land ownership concerns.

- Not cause any major displacement of population or users; but in the event of displacement, a solution should be found within the parameters of the project.

- Correspond to long-term goals for the greening of the city.

- Contribute to the social inclusion vision of the city.

- Do no harm.

- Favor rehabilitation of existing infrastructure and built assets rather than new construction.

- Contribute to the livability of the city.

- Contribute to the branding of the city.

- Contribute to the medium- and long-term urbanization strategy of the city.

9. PIP: Allocation and schedule of investments

- Allocate investments in facilities and infrastructure according to priorities, the nature of the work (for example, rehabilitation or new work), and the amount of the investment.

Table A.9   Priority Investment Program (PIP)

Type of investment	Order of priority	Estimated amount		
		New work	Rehabilitation	Total
1 Infrastructure				
2 Educational and health care facilities				
- Subtotal education				
- Subtotal health care				
3 Community facilities				
4 Government and municipal technical facilities				
- Subtotal government				
- Subtotal municipal technical				
5 Commercial facilities				
6 Environmental facilities				
7 Historical assets				
Total				

Table A.10   PIP Implementation Schedule

Type of investment	Year 1	Year 2	Year 3	Total
1 Infrastructure				
2 Educational and health care facilities				
Subtotal education				
Subtotal health care				
3 Community facilities				

continued next page

Table A.10   PIP Implementation Schedule (continued)

Type of investment	Year 1	Year 2	Year 3	Total
4 Government and municipal technical facilities				
Subtotal government				
Subtotal municipal technical				
5 Commercial facilities				
6 Environmental facilities				
7 Historical assets				
Total				

Table A.11   Project Fact Sheet No. 1

Title of project:

No. Name

I   Project type and eligibility

1.1 Investment category:

1.2 • Location:

1.3 • Beneficiaries:

1.4 Special conditions and eligibility

 • Eligibility:

 • Agreement reached:

 • Assumption of responsibility for maintenance:

II   Justification

2.1 • Priority level:

2.2 • Social impact:

2.3 • Financial/economic analysis:

2.4 • Environmental impact:

III   Description of project

3.1 Number of buildings and/or m^2 to be built:

 • Description:

 • ....

 Construction of fences:

 Development of access roads:

3.2 Project preparation status

 • Availability of technical documents:

 • Cost basis:

 • Dates of meetings with beneficiaries:

3.3 Constraints related to implementation

 • Land ownership status:

 • Deed of land ownership or assignment:

 • Slum clearance:

 • Utilities to be relocated:

 • Easements:

3.4 Practical terms of start-up:

3.5 Execution deadlines

 • Studies:

 • Work:

3.6 Site drawing

 Implementation plan

3.7 Other graphics:

IV   Costs

4.1 Cost of work:

4.2 ....

 Recurring expenses:

Municipal Finances Self-Assessment: Simplified Framework

Step 1: City profile

The city profile is an introductory section with three components: (a) institutional and territorial organization/demography/economy of the city, (b) municipal organization, and (c) main urban issues and challenges that face the city for the next three to five years (for example, presentation of the main content of the Local Economic Development Plan).

1. Institutional organization/city map/demography/economy

Objective: Give a general overview of the situation of the municipality through few indicators. Regarding the complexity of the territorial organization, clarify the consistency of the entity (city, subcity, metropolitan area).

	One city level	City with sub-municipalities	City with inter-communal upper level	
I Territorial organization				
Number/name of subnational/metropolitan entities				
Submunicipalities or metropolitan financed by the city level		**Yes/No**	**Yes/No**	
City level financed by submunicipality level and/or the metropolitan level		**Yes/No**	**Yes/No**	
Area of the municipality and agglomeration in square kilometers				
II Demography	**Year 1**	**Year 2**	**Year 3**	**Year 4**
Country population				
Total resident population				
Annual growth				
Rank in the country (in population)				
III Economy				
GDP per head (country level) in US$ or euros				
City GDP per head (if available) in US$ or euros				
Median disposable annual household income in US$ or euros				
Activity rate				
Unemployment rate (% active population)				

Insert a map of the city (A4)

Insert a short summary on the three items (territorial organization, demography, and economy) with focus on consideration directly linked with financial situation (for example, how territorial organization has direct impact on distribution of the functions and budget; how population increases or specificities impact the budget; how the local taxation takes advantage of the local economy).

2. Local finance and management

***Objective*:** Provide with preliminary summarized information and data on volume of local finance, utilities, management, municipal staff, etc.

Insert a short summary on the different items.

	Year 1	Year 2	Year 3	Year 4
IV Total municipal budget revenue				
Total revenue				
Revenue per capita				
Annual city capital investment				
Debt outstanding				

continued next page

		Year 1	Year 2	Year 3	Year 4
V	**Utilities management**	Denomination	Annex to municipal budget (Yes/No)	Tariff (current)	
	Water supply				
	Wastewater				
	Electricity				
	Urban heating				
	Other				
VI	**Tax policy**	Rate	Last increase	Fixed locally	
	Property tax				
	Local business tax				
	Tax 3				
	Tax 4				
VII	**Municipal staff (regular staff)**	Number	%		
	Total		100%		
	General administration				
	Education				
	Social services				
	Technical service units				
	Environment (including solid waste)				
	Contractual workers total				
VIII	**Financial reporting (Yes/No)**	**Year 1**	**Year 2**	**Year 3**	**Year 4**
	Long-term investment program				
	Annual budget				
	Annual financial statement				
	Audited accounts				

Taxes: Fill property and local business tax lines and name the two most important other local taxes.

3. Urban issues and challenges

Objective and content: Explain and illustrate the development policy of the municipality.

- *Is there a strategic vision for the development of the city?* If yes, provide main content (*city development strategy, long-term development plan*) and mention the level of approval (for example, city assembly or central government).

- *What are the key areas for implementation of the vision?* Present the main *components* of the "Local Economic Development Plan," including capital investment, institutional development, and others.

- *If existing, provide with the Capital Investment Plan.*

Project name	Timeframe	Total costs	Source of financing

Insert a short summary of the multiyear development program approved by the council. List all priority projects; add more lines if needed.

Step 2: Basic accounting and financial database

Objective and content: This step consists of organizing data not in a usual accounting presentation (always different from one country to another or even among municipalities of the same country), but in a financial one (more generic).

This step includes filling out the following five key tables:

- Municipal/city budget + annex public utility company (PUC) budget

- Cash balance and arrears

- Indebtedness

- Capital investment

- Tax potential and performance

These five tables will mention three years of historical (actual data) and one year of planned data.

The sources will be clearly mentioned (document title and source); for example, budget department, taxation department, economic department, other entity than the municipality, Ministry of Finance).

General budget database

- Because the accounting systems and *classifications* are all different (functional classification, classification per category, etc.), the consistency of the budget database will have to be adjusted consequently by the user; *expenditures and revenues will be listed on a strategic basis,* for example (taxation revenue, grants, fees, loans), using a commonly accepted typology as well as the destination they have (for example, payroll, O&M, debts service), rather than a long list of revenues and expenditures without classification.

- *Actual data*, compared to planned budget, will be favored. It can be cash accounting transaction (payment and receipt) or commitment accounting transaction (contract signed and receipt validated through an invoice or equivalent).

- *Current and capital expenditures* will have to be clearly distinguished, even if the accounting format does not make a difference. Usually, expenditures are considered as *capital expenditures* when they contribute to expand the public assets of the municipality.

- The *mandatory expenditures* dedicated or implemented on behalf of the central government level will be separated from the own expenditures of the municipality; the same for the revenues coming from the state and earmarked to specific expenditures. These revenues will have to be outlined.

- The different *types of subsidies or intergovernmental transfers* will be included and will differentiate between transfers for which the municipality does not have any flexibility in the allocation and transfers free of allocation.

- General budget will be analyzed separately from the independent PUC budget. Only consider financial transactions between city budget and budgets accounted in the city budget (for example, subsidy from the general budget to PUC budget will have to be accounted as expenditure in city budget and revenue in PUC budget; the same for dividend or any cash coming from PUC budget to city budget). A consolidated budget will be set up subsequently, if possible.

Step 2: Financial self-evaluation basic database

A	*actual*
P	*projection*

1. GENERAL BUDGET (simplified table)

In millions		Year 1 A	Year 2 A	Year 3 A	Year 4 P
TOTAL REVENUES					
I STATE REVENUES (INTERGOVERNMENTAL)					
1 Shared taxes	City share				
- VAT and sales taxes	... %				
- Personal income tax	... %				
- Corporate income tax (tax on company profit)	... %				
- Tax on the transfer of property rights	... %				
- Motor vehicle tax	... %				
- Others	... %				
2 Unconditional transfers					
- Operating transfer					
- Investment grant					
- Road rehabilitation					
- Education					
...					
3 Conditional transfers					
- For wages	from Ministry ...				
- For social policy (social welfare)	from Ministry ...				
-	from Ministry ...				

continued next page

II LOCAL REVENUES

1 Local taxes and levies
   - Property tax (regardless if centrally collected)
   - Business taxes
2 Local fees
   - Licenses
   - Permits
   - Local development fee
   - Authorizations and issuance
   - Others (fines, etc.)
3 Local asset proceeds
   - Rents
   - Sales
   - Charges
   - Levies on exploitation of natural resources (forest, mineral, water, etc.)
   - Other
4 Dividends, funds, or assets from PUCs
   - Utility 1
   - Utility 2
   - Utility 3
5 Donations
6 Loan proceeds
7 Municipal bond proceeds

In filling up dividends, funds, or assets from PUCs, please add the combined value of all wealth transferred from PUCs to the municipality's property, whether cash, land, or equipment, if any occurred in the given year.

In millions, local currency	Year 1	Year 2	Year 3	Year 4
	A	A	A	P
TOTAL EXPENDITURES				

I EXPENSES ON DELEGATED FUNCTIONS

1 Preschool education
   Wages
   Operating costs
   Maintenance
   Capital investments (new construction)
2 Primary and secondary school
   Wages
   Operating

continued next page

Better Cities, Better World

Continued

In millions, local currency	Year 1 A	Year 2 A	Year 3 A	Year 4 P
TOTAL EXPENDITURES				
Capital investment				
3 Health care				
4 Social assistance and poverty alleviation				
5 Public order and civil protection				
Wages				
Operating costs				
Maintenance				
Capital investment				
6 Environmental protection				
Wastewater				
Solid waste				
7 Other				
II OWN EXPENDITURES				
1 Infrastructure and public services				
- Current expenditures				
Direct expenditures				
Subcontracts				
- Capital expenditures				
Direct expenditures				
Subcontracts				
2 Social, cultural, recreational expenditures				
3 Local economic development				
4 Social housing				
5 Urban development				
6 Civil security				
7 Transfer to local government entities				
8 Support to PUC (subsidies, grants, or in-kind)				
Utility 1				
Utility 2				
Utility 3				
9 Loan repayment				
10 Interest charges				
11 Guarantees called (paid by the municipality)				

Supports to PUC (subsidies, grants, or in-kind): please enter the total combined value of all support provided to PUCs (by sectors/services) regardless if cash (grant, subsidy), equity, or in-kind asset (land, structure, or equipment) was transferred by the municipality.

Cash balance and arrears

- The objective is to complete budgetary and accounting data with information on *cash*; provide a monthly general situation.

- Identify the volume of the arrears (expenses incurred but not paid), with the difference between public and private providers.

2. CASH BALANCE, ARREARS

I Cash Balance

	Cash receipts	Cash payments	Cumulative inflow	Cumulative outflow	Net change in the stock of cash
January					
February					
March					
April					
May					
June					
July					
August					
September					
October					
November					
December					

II Arrears (overdue liabilities by the city or by its entities)

	Year 1	Year 2	Year 3	Year 4
	31.12	31.12	31.12	30.09
Public stakeholders				
- Water supply				
- Electricity				
- Social welfare				
- Transport				
City dues to private contractors				
Labor arrears (wages, salaries)				

Indebtedness database

- List all ongoing loans and bonds (subscribed and not fully reimbursed).

- Differentiate between medium long-term (MLT) debt and short-term (overdraft credit facility) debt.

- Complete the table with *amortization figures* for each loan, for further analysis and financial projections.

3. INDEBTEDNESS DATABASE

	Bank or institution	Year of the loan subscription	Initial amount	Duration	Currency	Maturity	Grace period	Interest Rate (fixed, variable)	Rate (%)
I MLT DEBT									
1 On-lending loan (from central government)									
2 Direct loan									
- Commercial bank									
- State development bank									
3 Municipal bond									
II SHORT-TERM DEBT									
1 Treasury facility from state									
2 Facility from commercial bank									

Note: Give amortization figure for each MLT loan.

Capital investment database

- Provide a figure with capital investment expenditure *per year* (historical and projections) and *per sector* (sectors can be adjusted regarding specific policy).

- Provide simplified tentative financing plan.

4. CAPITAL INVESTMENT DATABASE

	Year 1	Year 2	Year 3	Year 4	Year 5	Year 6	Year 7	Year 8
	A	A	A	P	P	P	P	P
Population								
Inflation rate (annual)								
I TOTAL INVESTMENT 100%								
% growth								

continued next page

Delegated investments (from earmarked grants)	... %
- Education	
- Health care	
- Housing	
- ...	
Municipal investment	... %
- Roads rehabilitation	
- Street lighting	
- Solid waste equipment purchase	
- Urban renewal	
- ...	
Investment into PUC (assets, grants, or equity provided for PUC in cash or in-kind)	... %
- Water supply	
- Wastewater	
- Transport	
- Urban heating	
- Other	
II TOTAL FINANCING	
- Earmarked grants	... %
- Own budgetary revenue	... %
- Loans or municipal bond	... %
- Equity from PUC	... %

Tax potential and tax performance

- The objective is to put together relevant information coming from tax administration about the tax potential of the city.

- The items (property tax, business tax, etc.) have to be adjusted according to the local situation.

- It is important to obtain information on *the number of taxpayers* and to differentiate households from businesses, especially for property tax.

Tax potential and performance	Year 1		Year 2		Year 3		Year 4	
	No. of taxpayers	Amount	No. of taxpayers	Amount	No. of taxpayers	Amount	No. of taxpayers	Amount
I PROPERTY TAX								
Tax base (taxable)								
Households								
Business								
Others								
Tax rate								
Households								
Business								
Others								
Exemption								
Households								
Business								
Others								
Tax collected								
Households								
Business								
Others								
II BUSINESS TAX								
Tax basis								
Rate								
Exemption								
Tax proceed collected								
III Development fees								

Step 3: Generic financial framework

Objective and content: If the database is necessarily different from one municipality to another, the generic financial framework should be the same. The objective is to evaluate at a glance the financial position of the municipality and to assess the following:

- Ability to generate growth savings and operating surplus to finance capital investment budget: *evaluate operating margin or surplus* and see how it contributes to the self-financing of capital investment budget. This will show the financial ability of the municipality, at the end of the year, to self-finance part of its capital investment budget, directly or through additional debt (borrowing).

- Creditworthiness: level of the debt service and adequacy with financial position.

- Level of capital investment effort compared with operating budget.

- Degree of dependency from grants coming from the state government.

- General surplus at the end of the year: to account for the general surplus or deficit coming from year N-1 in the actual budget of the year N.

Figure A.1 **Structure of Current and Capital Budget**

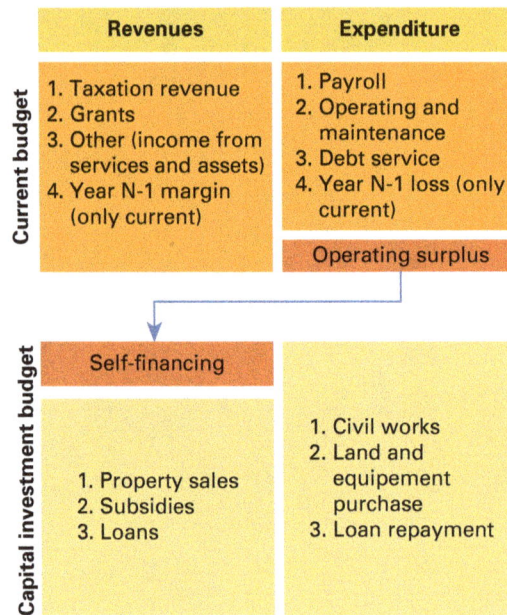

The figure will be completed by a graph showing the operating surplus or margin in comparison with the current revenue and the capital investment expenditures.

Main definitions

Current or operating budget should include the expenses and receipts used to provide for daily operation. They are often considered as mandatory and repeat themselves relatively predictably.

- *Current revenues* include tax receipts, grants from the state or other levels of government, and resources recovered by the local authority in the form of rates, fees, tariffs, etc. generated by the local assets owned by the municipality (for example, land lease, public utilities, and facilities).

- *Current expenditures* mainly include salaries (payroll including social insurance and other charges connected to staff management), operating costs, O&M (often difficult to identify because of subsidies paid by the local authority to assist other structures such as associations or related budgets), and debt service incumbent on the local authority.

Capital revenues and expenditures are operations that increase or reduce the assets of the local authority (acquisitions or sales, civil works). Most of the local public accounting systems are cash-based and thus do not include depreciation or physical amortization of the assets owned by the municipality; they are administrative accounting. Consequently, the capital revenues and expenditures will be yearly operations.

- Usually, capital expenditures are implemented on more than one year (12 months) and have to be split on several fiscal years. Their amount can be variable from one year to another.

- Debt service should be split between the current budget, for loan interest, and the capital budget, for loan repayment. All the debt service (including loan principal repayment) should be covered by the operating surplus as a proof of debt service ability.

- Total budget or annual account can be balanced, positive, or in deficit (negative): net position.

- More precise budget analysis requires taking into account (including in or annexing to the budget report) expenditures that are not paid and that affect apparent surplus at the end of the year; such as revenues billed/levied but not recovered during the year.

Step 4: Historical analysis

Objective and content: To review previous year budget and identify trends and performances in level of services provided to population, taxation efficiency, etc.

The objective is to understand how the budget is structured and to identify the major trends and how they occur. The analysis is mainly based on gross self-financing (or savings) calculated as the positive difference between operating receipts and expenses. Self-financing makes it possible to pay for a portion of investments; it is a crucial indicator of quality management on the part of the local authority, and is a strong component in dialogues with financial partners: no financial partner wants to see its resources used to finance an operating deficit.

After self-financing, the analysis turns to the characteristics of debt already incurred by the local authority, for example:

- Is the level of debt acceptable?

- Who are the lenders?

- What is the cost of the debt?

- How much time will be needed to pay it back?

The capacity of the local authority to develop a summary table, such as the one recommended here, based on a transparent and easy-to-control methodology, reinforces the credibility of the municipal financial management.

Main outputs: Ten tables have to be produced:

- Table 1: Financial position

- Table 2: Main revenue sources

- Table 3: Tax potential and tax performance

- Table 4: Grants and transfers

- Table 5: Main operating expenses line items by category

- Table 6: Municipal assets and maintenance

- Table 7: Indebtedness situation

- Table 8: Capital investment budget financing

- Table 9: Cash balance

- Table 10: Arrears

These tables and figures have to be set up from the database (five tables) prepared in step 2.

Table 1 **Financial position**

	Items	Calculation	Year 1 actual	Year 2 actual	Year 3 actual	Year 4 plan	Average annual growth	% structure
1	Total current revenues							
2	Balance N-1 (if surplus)							
3	Current revenues year N	(1 − 2)						
4	Operating expenditures							
5	Operating margin	(1 − 4)						
6	Debt repayment							
7	Net margin	(5 − 6)						
8	Capital expenditures							
9	Financing requirements	(8 − 7)						
10	- Own capital revenues							
11	- Investment grants							
12	- Loan	(9 − (10 + 11))						
13	Investment balance	(8 − (7 + 10 + 11 + 12))						
14	Overall closing balance	(1 + 10 + 11 + 12) − (4 + 8)						

Insert a short summary and comment on the main lessons learned from the financial position data on the basis of ratio structure.

Table 2   Main revenue sources

Items	Calculation	Year 1 actual	Year 2 actual	Year 3 actual	Year 4 plan	Average annual growth	% structure (total)
TOTAL CURRENT REVENUES							
1 State transfers							
- Shared taxes							
- Unconditional transfers/grants							
- Conditional operating transfers	Refer to database						
2 Own revenues							
- Local taxes and levies							
- Local fees							
- Local asset proceeds							
3 Other revenues							
- Surplus Y-1							
- Revenues received from PUC							
TOTAL NONRECURRENT REVENUES							
1 State transfers and grants							
- Unconditional development transfers							
- Conditional development grants	Refer to database						
2 Own revenues							
- Property sales							
- Long-term leases							
3 External revenues							
- Loans proceeds							
- Municipal bonds							
- Donations							
TOTAL REVENUES							
1 State transfers							
2 Own revenues	Refer to database						
3 External revenues							

Insert a short summary and comment on the main lessons drawn from the main revenue source data: analyze the principal sources of municipal financing (taxation, grants, local taxes, etc.); evaluate revenues and potentials from the local taxation system; and estimate revenues from commercial facilities.

Table 3 Tax potential and performance analysis

Items	Source	Year 1 actual	Year 2 actual	Year 3 actual	Year 4 plan	2009–08 growth	2010–09 growth
1 Property tax (residential)							
- Number of items							
- Number of taxpayers							
- Amount taxable							
- Amount collected							
- Collection rate							
2 Property tax (commercial and business)							
- Number of items							
- Number of taxpayers							
- Amount taxable							
- Amount collected							
- Collection rate							
3 Business tax							
- Number of items							
- Number of taxpayers							
- Amount taxable							
- Amount collected							
- Collection rate							
Main taxpayers							
List of the 10 to 50 major taxpayers							

Insert a short summary and comment on the main lessons learned from the above data: analyze the tax potential and pressure for land, property, and business taxes: (a) economic fabric and tax potential of the modern and informal sectors; (b) assessment rate; (c) collection rate overall and by category of tax paid (concentration).

Table 4 Transfer predictability and city dependence

Items	Allocation criteria	Year 1 actual	Year 2 actual	Year 3 actual	Year 4 plan	Average annual growth	% structure (total revenue)
1 Unconditional transfers							
- Transfer 1							
- Transfer 2							
- ...							

continued next page

Table 4 Transfer predictability and city dependence (continued)

Items	Allocation criteria	Year 1 actual	Year 2 actual	Year 3 actual	Year 4 plan	Average annual growth	% structure (total revenue)
2 Conditional transfers							
- Transfer 1							
- Transfer 2							
- …							

Insert a short summary and comments on the main lessons learned from the above data on predictability of transfers and level of city dependence: % of transfers compared to total revenues.

Provide information on allocation criteria for grants and assess the degree to which local governments can affect the volume allocated to them (performance criteria, if any).

Table 5 Main operating expenditures line items by category

Items	Year 1 actual	Year 2 actual	Year 3 actual	Year 4 plan	Average annual growth	% structure (total rev.)
CURRENT EXPENDITURES						
1 Payroll (including employees benefits & misc.)						
- Administrative staff						
- Technical department staff						
- Other staff (contractual workers)						
2 Operating costs						
- Office supplies						
- Electricity						
- Communication (telephone, etc.)						
- Fuel and gas						
- …						
3 Maintenance costs						
…						
4 Costs to maintain state assets						
Total						

Insert a short summary of the main operating expenditures line items. Evaluate specific expenditures (for example, maintenance of infrastructure and facilities).

Table 6   Municipal assets and maintenance expenditures

Items	Tentative assets inventory	Year 1 actual	Year 2 actual	Year 3 actual	Year 4 plan	Average annual growth	Dominant implementation arrangement (1)
Roads, streets (m²)							
o.w. Artery roads km							
Residential streets km							
Paved roads total km							
Public lighting (number of lighting posts)							
Water, networks km							
Water treatment plants (number)							
Sewer network (km)							
Wastewater treatment plants (number)							
Solid waste management facilities trucks							
Solid waste (transfer stations, landfill total capacity ton per day)							
Other public infrastructure and equipment (parks, cemeteries, parking and garage, etc.) (m²)							
Educational facilities (number of class or m²)							
Health care facilities (m²)							
Administrative facilities (m²)							
Cultural facilities (m²)							
Sport facilities (m²)							
Commercial facilities (m²)							
Environmental facilities							
Public housing (number of apartments and other units, m²)							
Cultural heritage							
Vacant municipal land (hectare)							

(1) directed by the city, by contractors and private partners, by residents ...

Insert a short summary on the asset composition and management, more specifically if there is public housing and land property. Provide a short description of the maintenance implementation: directed by municipal staff, by municipal enterprise, by private contractors, or by residents themselves.

No information is requested on valuation of the assets because of the complexity of the calculation. If the municipality has already conducted an evaluation of its assets, provide the main results and analysis. If an Urban Audit/SA is being conducted, it is important to include consolidated data on location and mapping of municipal assets. Similarly, if a street addressing program is in place, it would be very useful to connect with the existing data from the street addressing database and map.

Table 7 Indebtedness situation

Items	Donor/bank terms and Conditions	Year 1 actual	Year 2 actual	Year 3 actual	Year 4 plan
Loan 1					
- Outstanding					
- K repayment					
- Interest charge					
Loan 2					
- Outstanding					
- K repayment					
- Interest charge					
Loan 3					
- Outstanding					
- K repayment					
- Interest charge					
Municipal bond					
- Outstanding					
- K repayment					
- Interest charge					
Cash facility (short term)					
Loan					
Overdraft					
Suppliers' credit					

Insert a short summary on existing debt of the municipality: (a) number of loans or other existing external financing, (b) terms and conditions of these loans, (c) contribution to annual debt service. The amortization tables will be useful to make projections on the next 5 to 10 years.

Table 8 Capital investment financing

Items	Year 1 actual	Year 2 actual	Year 3 actual	Year 4 plan	Average annual growth	% structure (total rev.)
Total capital investment costs						
- Civil works						
- Equipment purchase						
- Others						
Financing						
- Grants from state						
- Investment revenues (sales of assets, etc.)						
- Self-financing (Y1 or -1)						
- Loan						

Insert a short summary about the structure of the municipality's capital budget and its financing.

Insert a short summary on the cash balance at the end of the year but also about the monthly cash flow: possible difficulties faced during the year with fluctuation between inflows (for example, grants payment rate or tax collection rate) and outflows rate every month. Mention any specific arrangements with the Treasury or the banks (cash facility).

Table 9 **Cash balance**

	Inflows	Cumulative	Outflows	Cumulative	Balance
January					
February					
March					
April					
May					
June					
July					
August					
September					
October					
November					
December					

Table 10 **Arrears**

	Items	Calculation	Year 1 actual	Year 2 actual	Year 3 actual	Year 4 plan	Average annual growth	% outflows current and capital inv.
CURRENT BUDGET								
Energy	-							
Material	-							
Salaries or other labor costs	-							
Social security dues								
CAPITAL BUDGET								
Public institutions	-							
Private entities	-							
TOTAL								

Insert a short summary about evaluation of unpaid invoices and commitments amount by the municipality, differentiating between current and capital expenditures. Analysis can also distinguish between institutional debt or arrears and private contractors arrears.

Step 5: Ratio analysis

The objective of the ratio analysis is to get familiar with and to adopt municipal finances benchmarks, for internal purpose (financial management dashboard) and regional comparative purpose. The following ratios and benchmarks are based on international standards used in Western European countries and in the United States.

Through the MFSA, each municipality will get a better understanding of its position compared to others in the region and in the world and will also be able to highlight its potentials and key gaps. The ratio analysis tables can be filled out by linking the respective cells of the historical analysis tables.

It is important to work closely with the Ministry of Finance in order to publish annually these ratios at the national level for all the municipalities as a tool for self-comparison and self-improvement.

Reference to ratios already used by the Ministry of Finance or the Ministry of Interior, or even to ratios calculated by regional associations of local governments, is recommended.

Finally, ratios comparing local finance performance and GDP are not suggested at this stage but could be usefully added if local GDP data are available. This comparison is common at the national level: weight of local expenditures and local taxation/GDP.

Step 5. Ratio analysis (municipal finance dashboard)

Criteria	Indicator (definition)	Objective	Comparative index (benchmark)	City index — Year 1	Year 2	Year 3	Graph with mention of the benchmark if possible
STOCK RATIO							
Creditworthiness							
	Operating savings before interests/current actual revenues	The local government has the capacity to borrow and to invest	> 0.3				Graph with mention of the benchmark if possible
	Net operating surplus (after debt service including capital repayment)/ current actual revenues	The local government has the capacity to borrow more	> 0.2				Graph with mention of the benchmark if possible

continued next page

Continued

Criteria	Indicator (definition)	Objective	Comparative index (benchmark)	City index			Graph with mention of the benchmark if possible
				Year 1	Year 2	Year 3	
	Cash (end of the year)/current liabilities (divided by 365 days)	The local government has the ability to meet its short-term obligations	90 days				Graph with mention of the benchmark if possible
Indebtedness							
	Debt outstanding/operating surplus (capacity to clear its debt)	The local government has the capacity to clear its debt with operating surplus	< 10 years				Graph with mention of the benchmark if possible
	Debt service/ total current revenues	The annual debt burden is correct regarding current revenue	< 10%				Graph with mention of the benchmark if possible
Fiscal autonomy							
	Own tax receipts + unconditional grants/current actual revenues	The local government has the ability to increase its revenue	> 80%				Graph with mention of the benchmark if possible
	Tax pressure (tax receipts/ tax potential)		< 70%				
Capital investment effort							
	Capital investment expenditures/current actual revenues	The local government favors development expenditures	> 40%				Graph with mention of the benchmark if possible

continued next page

Better Cities, Better World

Continued

Criteria	Indicator (definition)	Objective	Comparative index (benchmark)	City index			Graph with mention of the benchmark if possible
				Year 1	Year 2	Year 3	
	Capital investment expenditures delegated by state/total investment expenditures	The local government functions are still weak	> 50%				Graph with mention of the benchmark if possible

Level of service

	Maintenance works expenditures/operating expenditures	The local government has important noncurrent assets to maintain and make it a priority	> 30%				Graph with mention of the benchmark if possible

Others

	Total number of municipal employees/population	The local government has limited room for financing maintenance and capital investment	> 25 employees for 1,000 inhabitants				Graph with mention of the benchmark if possible
	Salaries and wages/operating actual expenses		> 40%				
	Actual revenues/estimated revenues	The local government has a good visibility and Budget is reliable	> 95%				Graph with mention of the benchmark if possible
	Arrears amount/net cash (end of the year)	The local government accumulates short-term debt and reduces its credibility toward contractors	> 1				Graph with mention of the benchmark if possible

Criteria	Indicator (definition)	Objective	Comparative index (benchmark)	City index Year 1	Year 2	Year 3	Graph with mention of the benchmark if possible
FLOW RATIO							
1	Margin ratio: Total financial resources (cash)/total financial obligations (payment + arrears)	The city is living (or not) within its financial means	1.02				Graph with mention of the benchmark if possible
COMPARISON RATIO							
	Total revenues per capita	Comparison with local governments of the same size in the country or abroad					Graph with mention of the benchmark if possible
	Total expenditures per capita						
	Current actual revenues per capita						
	Debt outstanding per capita						
	Capital investment expenditures per capita						

Insert a short summary about the key findings and lessons learned from the ratio analysis.

Step 6: Financial projections

The five-year financial projections are performed with the objective to confirm and complete ratio analysis main results. It provides a review of the financial position of the municipality with focus on creditworthiness. The main objective is to formalize through assumptions the impact of policy decisions (expenses, borrowing, tax pressure) on the financial position of the municipality. Usually, several assumptions and scenarios are tested: past trends projections and projections on the basis of significant changes. The method will be adjusted depending on the size of the municipality and the issues it currently faces (for example, specific investment program for the future years, specific indebtedness situation to solve).

The following figures provide a preliminary and simplified framework for projections. Insert a short summary about the lessons learned from the preliminary results obtained.

Step 6. Five-year financial projections

In current currency

Items	Last 3 actual years trends	Main assumptions	Index	Specific calculation	Year 1 Actual	Year 2 Estimated	Year 3 Projection	Year 4 Projection	Year 5 Projection	Year 6 Projection	Year 7 Projection
A TOTAL CURRENT REVENUES											
Own tax revenues											
- Property tax											
- Business tax											
- Others (development fee)											
State transfers											
- Shared tax											
- Unconditional grants											
- Conditional grants											
Other revenues											
- Asset rent, interest											
B TOTAL OPERATING EXPENDITURES											
Payroll (including employees' benefits and misc.)											
- Administrative staff											
- Technical department staff											
- Other staff (specific …)											
Operating costs											
- Office supplies											
- Electricity											
- Communication (telephone, etc.)											
- Fuel and gas											
- Maintenance costs											
- …											

continued next page

					Year 1		Year 2	Year 3	Year 4	Year 5	Year 6	Year 7
Items	**Last 3 actual years trends**	**Main as- sump- tions**	**Index**	**Specific calcula- tion**	**Actual**	**Esti- mated**	**Pro- jec- tion**	**Pro- jec- tion**	**Pro- jec- tion**	**Pro- jec- tion**	**Pro- jec- tion**	**Pro- jec- tion**

Continued

C   GROSS OPERATING SAVINGS (A – B)

D   DEBT SERVICE
   Existing debt
   - Interest charge
   - Loan repayment
   New debt
   - Interest charge
   - Loan repayment
   Total debt service
   - Interest charge
   - Loan repayment

E   NET SAVINGS (C – D)

F   CAPITAL EXPENDI- TURES

G   INVESTMENT FINANCING (F – E)
   Investment grants
   Own capital revenues excl. operation surplus
   Loans

H   OVERALL CLOSING BALANCE (CASH- FLOW) (A + G) – (B + D + F)

Step 7: Financial management assessment

Objective and content: The objective is to assess the financial management of the municipality.

A municipality may have a good financial situation but weak financial management; likewise, a municipality may have poor financial capacity but a fair financial management system.

This section capitalizes on the PEFA methodology, also developed by the World Bank and its partners, and provides a checklist of six key indicators of financial management.

Insert comments on the different items and propose specific actions for improvement.

	Aggregate fiscal discipline	Strategic allocation of resources	Efficient service delivery
1. Credibility of the budget	Overoptimistic revenue forecasts/underbudgeting of nondiscretionary spending/noncompliance in budget.	Revenues shortfalls/underestimation of the costs of the policy priorities/noncompliance in the use of resources.	Efficiency of resources used at the service delivery level; a shift across expenditure categories, reflecting personal preferences rather than efficiency of service delivery.
2. Comprehensiveness and transparency	Activities not managed and reported through adequate budget processes are unlikely to be subject to the same kind of scrutiny and controls (included from financial markets) as are operations included in the budget.	Extrabudgetary funds/earmarking of some revenues to certain programs/limits the capacity of the legislature, civil society, and media to assess the extent to which the government is implementing its policy priorities.	Lack of comprehensiveness/increase waste of resources/decrease the provision of services/limit competition in the review of the efficiency and effectiveness of the different programs and their inputs/may facilitate the development of patronage or corrupt practices.
3. Policy-based budgeting	Weak planning process/no respect for the fiscal and macroeconomic framework/lead to unsustainable policies.	Process of allocation of the global resource envelope in line with LG priorities/annual budget too short to introduce significant changes in expenditure/ costs of new policy systematically underestimated.	The lack of multiyear perspective may contribute to inadequate planning of the recurrent costs of investment decisions and of the funding for multiyear procurement.
4. Predictability and control in budget execution	Impact on fiscal management/inadequate debt policy/excess of expenditures.	Planned reallocations/authorized expenditures/fraudulent payments.	Plan and use resources in a timely and efficient manner/competitive tendering process practices/control of payrolls.
5. Accounting, recording and reporting	To allow management for long-term fiscal sustainability and affordability of policies: timely and adequate information on revenue forecasting and collection/existing liquidity levels and expenditures flows/debt levels, guarantees/contingent liability and forward costs of investment programs.	Regular information on budget execution allows monitoring on the use of resources, but also facilitates identification of bottlenecks and problems that may lead to significant changes in the executed budget.	Inadequate information and records would reduce the availability of evidence that is required for effective audit and oversight of the use of funds and could provide the opportunity for leakages, corrupt procurement practices, or use of resources in a unintended manner.

continued next page

	Aggregate fiscal discipline	**Strategic allocation of resources**	**Efficient Service Delivery**
6. External scrutiny and audit	Consider long-term fiscal sustainability issues and respect its targets.	Pressure on LG to allocate and execute the budget in line with its stated policies.	LG is held accountable for efficient and rule-based management of resources, without which the value of services is likely to be diminished. The accounting and use of funds is subject to detailed review and verification.

Step 7. Financial management assessment

Criteria	Indicator

A. Credibility of the budget

Aggregate expenditure compared to original approved budget

Composition of expenditure compared to original approved budget

Aggregate revenue compared to original approved budget

Stock and monitoring of expenditure payment arrears

B. Comprehensiveness and transparency

Classification of the budget

Comprehensiveness of information included in budget documentation

Extent of unreported government operations

Transparency of intergovernmental fiscal relations

Oversight of aggregate fiscal risk from other public sector entities

Public access to key fiscal information

C. Budget cycle

Policy-based budgeting

Orderliness and participation in the annual budget process

Multiyear perspective in fiscal planning, expenditure policy, and budgeting

Predictability and control in budget execution

Transparency of taxpayer obligations and liabilities

Effectiveness of measures for taxpayer registration and tax assessment

Effectiveness in collection of tax payments

Predictability in the availability of funds for commitment of expenditures

continued next page

Step 7. Financial management assessment (continued)	
Criteria	**Indicator**
	Recording and management of cash balances, debt, and guarantees
	Effectiveness of payroll controls
	Competition, value for money, and controls in procurement
	Effectiveness of internal controls for nonsalary expenditures
	Effectiveness of internal audit
	Accounting, recording, and reporting
	Timeliness and regularity of accounts reconciliation
	Availability of information on resources received by service delivery units
	Quality and timeliness of in-year budget reports
	Quality and timeliness of annual financial statements
	External scrutiny and audit
	Scope, nature, and follow-up of external audit
	Scrutiny of the annual budget law by the city council
	Scrutiny of external audit reports by the city council
D. Donor practices	
	Predictability of direct budget support
	Financial information provided by donors for budgeting and reporting on project and program aid
	Proportion of aid that is managed by use of national procedures
	Predictability of transfers from higher level of government

Step 8: MFSA Action Plan

Objective and content: The goal is to translate lessons learned from the different steps of the MFSA into a few actions to be implemented by the municipality to improve its financial situation and its financial management. The template below is indicative and should be further developed based on the findings of the MFSA. The municipality is free to list any action it considers as a priority. The actions that are not under the full control of the municipality can be mentioned if they are part of state reforms currently under discussion or if they are included in the current agenda of National Associations of Local Governments (that is, they need to have some traction for actual implementation and should include precisely what is expected from central government).

The MFSA Action Plan can be divided into:

- Short-term actions: 1 year

- Medium-term actions: (1 to 3 years)

All of them need to include a specific description of what needs to be done and why, with quantified targets in some cases, and explain when (timeline), how, and by whom these actions will be implemented. It should also indicate if there is a cost attached to them.

MFSA Action Plan (nonexhaustive sample)

Specific objective	Items	Priority action	Expected result	Schedule: Short term/ long term	Cost estimate, if any	Responsible entity/ person
Objective 1: Improve financial situation of the municipality						
Leverage under the control of state						
Increase fiscal autonomy	Replace conditional grants with unconditional grants or shared taxes					
	Give more flexibility on the local tax policy					
…						
Action to plan and to implement at the LG level						
Increase fiscal autonomy	Increase local tax collection					
	Reconsider the rate of property tax for households					
…						
Objective 2: Improve financial management of the municipality						
Specific objective	Items	Priority action	Expected result	Schedule short-term/ long-term	Cost estimate, if any	Responsible entity/person
Credibility of the budget	Improve forecast reliability					
Policy-based budgeting	Improve cost analysis of main expenditure					
Improve budget execution	Improve expenditure control	E.g., competitive bidding, performance contacts				

Detailed Methodology and Procedures to Help Calculate Specific Results in MFSA

This appendix provides specific and detailed methodology and procedures for completing some MFSA analytical steps. The technical notes might be useful for those who lack experience with technical proficiency on various statistical, econometric, or other data-processing procedures, such as means, mode, and median, or the use of respective software, such as various Microsoft Excel applications on trends or forecasting steps. Users who are familiar with these methodologies and software applications will omit this section and will focus instead on the analysis of the results explained in chapter 3. The technical notes (also called *technical details* or *TD*) are numbered for reference purposes in the text from TD1 to TD5 and discussed in numeric order in this section.

TD1: Analyzing Historical Trends

Historical trends can be approached in various ways, but we limit our discussion to the following three options: (1) estimating the annual growth indexes; (2) estimating the average changes over the given time period; and (3) developing trend equations and graph trend lines. There is no one single best method for historical analysis, because each procedure includes benefits and shortcomings. We will explain these three analysis options by using the data from table 3.18 of chapter 3. We also recommend that, in parallel with reading the technical notes, users open an Excel table and enter the data from table 3.18 in order to test the procedures and increase their own knowledge with real data processed.

TD1.1: Estimating Annual Growth Rate and Growth Indexes with Geometric Averages

Total changes. We can calculate annual growth rate for each financial line in table 3.18. The first step is to calculate the total changes in five years (meaning four years added on top of the beginning year). The total changes can be calculated by the following formula: $[x = Y_2/Y_1 * Y_3/Y_2 * Y_4/Y_3 * Y_5/Y_4 = Y_5/Y_1$ after simplification]. Please note that there are four steps between Year 1 (Y_1) and Year 5 (Y_5), but also that the total change can be simply calculated by dividing the last year data with the first year.

Average growth (the growth index) is a geometric average of the growth ratios, which means that the first year actual revenue could grow steadily with this rate four times to reach the actual revenues of the fifth year. Let's take current revenue data (the first line of table 3.18):

Total change: x = 41,214/41,999 *
48,636/41,214 *
52,743/48,636 *
65,821/52,743 =
65,821/41,999 = 1.567

The x shows the total change over the five years. The geometric average is the *fourth root of the total change*. The fourth root of x is a number g = 1.11887 with which we can multiply the first year revenue (41,999) four times to reach the last year results with negligible error: 41,999 * g * g * g * g = 65,820. For calculation of the root, we use the following formula:

Geometric average = Root formula:
growth ratio = g = $\sqrt[4]{x}$ = $x^{1/4}$ or more generally;

Root formula: g = $\sqrt[(N-1)]{x}$ = $x^{1/(N-1)}$

where N is the number of years, x is the total change ratio over the given time period, g is the growth ratio, and $1/(N–1)$ is the root factor.

Growth index: In communicating financial results, we often talk about "growth index" (g_i), which refers to the percentages by which the revenues grow annually over the period of analysis [Growth index: $g_i = (g–1) * 100$]. This means that we use $g–1$ instead of g in communicating results; for example, [$g_i = (1.11887–1) * 100 = 0.11887 * 100 = 11.887\%$] or 11.9 percent after rounding. Thus, the key finding is that *the municipal revenues have grown on average by 11.9 percent annually between Year 1 and Year 5* (first line in table 3.18). That is one easy, clear, and common way to analyze and communicate the growth indexes in the historical position tables.

Using root formulas: Root formulas can be downloaded via Google or other search engines, but MFSA users can also use Microsoft Excel more conveniently.

Methods to calculate roots in Excel: We show two possible methods:

1. Click on a cell for which you need to compute the result (for example, the index) => enter the equal sign "=" => type POWER **(Y_N/Y_1,1/(N–1)) or => in our case** =POWER **(Y_5/Y_1,1/4)**

2. Click on a cell for which you need to compute the result (the index) => enter the equal sign "=" => enter the total growth (x in above formula) between brackets "( )" in the following way (Y_5/Y_1) by clicking on the respective cells in the table => enter the sign "^" (upper case the number 6 on the keyboard) => enter the root factor "(1/(N–1)" in brackets => click "Enter"

The Excel formula to calculate g will appear like the following in the cell window:

- In our case: = **(I9/E9)^(1/4)** = POWER **(Y_5/Y_1,1/4)**

- In general form: $= (Y_N/Y_1)\char`^(1/(N-1))$

This formula should appear in your cell and gives the g growth ratio after your click "Enter," where Y_1 and Y_5 are the revenue in Year 1 and Year 5, ˆ is a sign above the number 6 on the keyboard, and N is the number of total years in your data series ($N = 5$ and $N-1 = 4$ and $1/(N-1)$ is ¼ in our case).

The Excel formula to calculate g_i growth index in table 3.18 is

$$g_i = ((I9/E9)\char`^(1/4))-1$$

This may seem complicated but is, in fact, simple because you need to enter this formula only once in a top cell of a respective column of an analyzed table and roll it down to the bottom of the table/column to generate dozens of growth indexes.

Benefits: One major benefit to using this formula is its simplicity to calculate: you enter the formula in one cell once to create dozens of growth indexes very quickly. The other benefit is that this is the way economists or finance officers commonly talk about the results, the growth, or achievements. Finally, these indexes are easily comparable across lines or tables: 11.9 percent is far greater than 1.2 percent regardless of the nature of the subject. In contrast, most other indicators that reflect trends may be more precise, but either they provide for absolute numbers that are hard to compare across lines or their results are buried in complex formulas that are difficult to translate into simple and well-known percentages. For instance, it is difficult to compare a current revenue change of 24,000 with an operating margin change of 400, but it is easier to understand that current revenues grew by 11.9 percent while operating margin grew by only 1.2 percent in the same time period.

Caveats and shortcomings: Calculating growth index this way provides a rough estimate, not a very precise one; it measures growth in smooth data series, but the results are less reliable if the data are volatile over the years. This is the case with interest, debt repayment, or overall balance in table 3.18. The index is still good in these lines to shed light on alarming movements (without being precise in measuring growth). There is, however, no one good method to represent a data series in a much better way; if the data are volatile or a year sticks out, that also means that the data series is less predictable.

TD1.2: Measuring Growth by Arithmetic Averages

Estimating the arithmetic average of annual changes is another simple method for computing growth indexes, and some users may find it easier to handle. Using again the usual signs such as Y_1, Y_2, Y_3, Y_4, and Y_5 representing the annual figures of the time series (for example, revenues), g = growth ratio (Y_2/Y_1), and growth index = $g_i = (g-1)$.

Procedure: The calculation procedure is to compute g_i for each pair of years, and take the arithmetic average as the g_i for the time period (for example, for a line of revenues). Notice that there are four pairs in a five-year time series of financial data.

Growth average formula: $g_i = \{[(Y_2/Y_1)-1] + [(Y_3/Y_2)-1] + [(Y_4/Y_3)-1] + [(Y_5/Y_1)-1]\} / 4$

or, more generally,

$$g_i = \{[(Y_2/Y_1)-1] + [(Y_3/Y_2)-1] + ... + [(Y_N/Y_{N-1})-1]\} / (N-1)$$

Benefits: The first benefit of this formula is simplicity. This formula provides users with the same kinds of benefits that the geometric average formula provides.

Caveats and shortcomings: This growth average formula (unlike the g_i growth index above) captures the volatility of the time series in every year and adds them into the average ratio, which means that it can distort the average with any extreme movement (drop or raise in revenues) during years that might not be representative of the time period. The index is useful for signaling issues, but less effective for computing or projecting growth in volatile time series. For projecting future growth, this index can be used only with great caution. Let's compare the results of the indexes computed by the two formulas in table B.1, which is a copy of table 3.18.

The results of the two growth indexes are often similar, but table B.1 shows great variations between arithmetic and geometric averages in a few critical areas that are highlighted. First, the arithmetic average formula indicates a 19.1 percent growth of the operating margin annually (line 3), which is apparently wrong because the margin is greater than the first year only once (that is, in the last year); and, except for a drop in Year 2, the movement is moderate. Thus, the geometric average index (1.2 percent) is far more realistic.

Table B.1   Historical Trends in Financial Snapshot with Two Indexes

	Items	Year 1 actual	Year 2 actual	Year 3 actual	Year 4 actual	Year 5 actual	Growth indexes Geometric average	Arithmetic average
1	Current revenue	41,999	41,214	48,636	52,743	65,821	11.9%	12.3%
2	Operating expenditure	33,498	37,785	41,187	44,610	56,893	14.2%	14.4%
3	Gross operating margin/balance	8,501	3,430	7,449	8,132	8,927	1.2%	19.1%
4	Interests and borrowing costs	321	502	695	1,450	2,212	62.1%	64.0%
5	Current margin/ balance	8,181	2,928	6,753	6,682	6,715	−4.8%	16.5%
6	Debt principal repayment	425	490	768	687	2,982	62.7%	98.8%
7	Net margin - net current balance	7,756	2,438	5,985	5,995	3,733	−16.7%	9.8%
8	Capital revenues	17,734	12,564	9,303	8,220	7,407	−19.6%	−19.2%
9	Own capital revenues	12,724	9,607	8,938	7,904	7,078	−13.6%	−13.4%
10	Investment grants and donations	32	90	365	316	329	79.0%	119.4%
11	Cash reserve from previous years	4,978	2,867	0	0	0	−100.0%	
12	Capital expenditures	25,845	23,770	28,222	29,100	22,614	−3.3%	−2.1%
13	Investment balance before loan	−355	−8,768	−12,933	−14,886	−11,474	138.4%	601.8%
14	Loan proceeds (disbursed)	3,222	4,956	10,192	12,548	7,022	21.5%	34.6%
15	Overall closing balance with loans	2,866	−3,812	−2,741	−2,337	−4,452		−46.3%

Second, the net margin data show an apparent decreasing trend, a sharp contrast to the arithmetic average index that measures a 16.5 percent annual increase. Again, the geometric index (−4.8 percent) is more realistic. Finally, the trend in investment balance (601.8 percent increase by year) is exaggerated by the arithmetic average formula. Thus, the geometric average formula is preferable and recommended for MFSA users.

TD 1.3: Trend Analysis

Trend analysis requires more effort, but it provides some benefits and is, for example, better for projecting financial figures in the future. Users can generate charts with trend lines, trend equations, and future projections, or even test the predicting quality (R^2) of the trend equation. There are easy applications in Excel.

Benefits: The major benefit of the trend analysis is that it conceptually positions a trend line somewhere between the dots of actual financial figures, and so somewhat counterbalances the volatility of the annual figures. Trend lines and equations are less sensitive to the first and last year figures regardless of whether those are in harmony with the other years or stand out either as extremely low or extremely high compared to the other years. For this reason, the trend equations are the best instruments for conservatively projecting future financial figures.

Shortcomings: Trend analyses have one major shortcoming, namely that most of the coefficients and constants that appear in trend equations are hard to interpret in economic terms, unlike the simple percentage from growth indexes used in the other two methods above. Another, less substantial shortcoming is that very precise trends are not necessarily better for projecting future financial results because

they may project unrealistically high figures, as will be shown later.

Procedures: MFSA users who are unfamiliar with Excel chart applications may read and use the following guidance; others may skip it. Excel offers easy procedures for drawing charts/figures with trends and including trend equations, which are important for projecting revenues/expenditures years ahead. We intentionally ignore the statistical details needed to establish a trend equation from raw data because Excel does everything "behind the screen" for users.

Excel procedure: Choose and select a data series like current revenues (line 1 in table B.1) => click on "Insert" => select "scatter" graph and a graph will appear in a box beside the table => click on the graph line depicting the actual data, and => select "Add trend line," and a box appears with options on trend forms => select a trend form (Linear trend is a default and also advisable as a first choice), but also mark "Display equation on chart," which you will see in the box of trend options. You are done, and your graph shows a line chart of actual data, a crossing trend line, and an equation. Let's look at three charts side by side in Figure B.1.

Results: Reading the results that appear in figure B.1 depends on the trend line you have selected. Look at the first box in figure B.1; the linear trend line is the simplest: the equation $y = 5917.1x + 32,331$ appears. The coefficient before the x is the most important result and measures the amount of money by which current revenues grow annually according to this trend. The x is the serial number of the years (1, 2, 3, 4, 5). By putting the serial number of the year into the formula, you can compute the trend estimate of the revenue for any year within this five-year period or beyond (for year

5 it is: 5,917.1 * 5 + 32,331 = 61,916.5), somewhat lower than the actual figure in the table as the trend line also suggests. But you can also put 10 into the equation to see the estimated revenue five years ahead, such as y = 5,917.1 * 10 + 32,331 = 91,502.

Benefits and shortcomings: The major benefits of linear trend include (1) its simplicity and ease for projecting future revenues; (2) that it provides for a conservative estimate in projections ahead, because it counterbalances data volatility; and (3) that some results are easy to explain when comparing trend results of various revenue or expenditure lines. By establishing trend equations for current revenues, current expenditures, and capital expenditures in table B.1, we find that current revenues grew by ShS5,917 per year, current expenditures grew by ShS5,361 per year, and capital expenditures grew by only ShS418 per year. One shortcoming of the trend analysis is that it indicates the growth factor only in absolute number (for example, volume in shillings), which is hard to translate into general percentage growth typically used in various comparisons and benchmarks.

Two other trends in Figure B.1: The other two trends (panels b and c in figure B.1) produce apparently more complex equations and provide for factors or coefficients that are difficult to interpret in the course of financial analyses. Please notice also that the polynomial trend seems to fit best with the actual data in this financial line; however, its coefficients cannot be transformed into financial categories, and by nature this equation would provide for extremely high (overly optimistic) revenue projection for year 10 (ShS173,450 as opposed to ShS91,502 projected by the linear tend). We can make an interesting test, namely, to estimate the average annual growth indexes over 10 years by using the geometric average index formula with the year 10 revenues of the three trend projections. The Y_{10}/Y_1 growth indexes computed back from these projected revenues with ninth roots suggest that the linear trend projects about 9.1 percent annual growth whereas the polynomial projects 15.3 percent annual growth, which is an overly optimistic projection compared to the conservative 9 percent.

TD 1.4: Lessons from the Three Different Growth Analyses

We can draw the following lessons by comparing results of the three methods:

- The geometric average seems to provide for an easy procedure to estimate annual

Figure B.1   Current Revenues: Three Different Trends

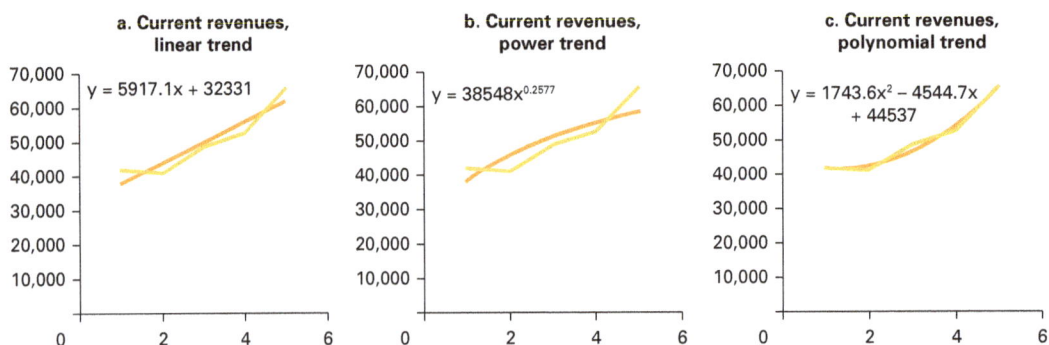

a. Current revenues, linear trend — y = 5917.1x + 32331

b. Current revenues, power trend — y = 38548x$^{0.2577}$

c. Current revenues, polynomial trend — y = 1743.6x^2 − 4544.7x + 44537

growth and seems more reliable than the arithmetic average formula to compute growth indexes.

- Growth indexes are useful for highlighting warning trends, but it is better to use them with caution for projections of future revenues or expenditures. It is better to use trends instead for projections.

- The linear trend is often the best instrument for projecting future financial numbers years ahead, particularly when we have short time series (five years or fewer).

- There are more trend formulas and other estimating procedures that the MFSA users may try testing. Experience shows, however, that these formulas and procedures are more complex and more difficult to use or interpret without providing visibly better results.

- Short time series (fewer than five years) provide very preliminary estimates in growth indexes and are not suitable for trend analyses. Thus, users are strongly advised to collect historical data for at least five years or longer, or to use the results from short time series with extreme caution.

TD2: Average Absolute Deviation from 100 Percent

Deviation issues: Deviation from 100 percent is an important measure of efficiency of planning and execution of budgets, because an ideal plan is fulfilled to 100 percent. The problem with negative deviation is obvious; for instance, if property tax collection is, say, 78 percent of the planned collection, the city faces both a revenue shortage and a case of ill-predicted revenue that needs attention and corrective measures. Interestingly, however, a case where actual revenues greatly exceed the plans in a year (collection of business tax appears to be 34 percent above the plan) is good for revenue collection but still signals poor revenue planning.

A good plan and disciplined execution of budget result in small deviations, meaning that the actual figures are close to the planned figures (ideally within the ±5 percent range). Deviations can be either positive or negative; thus, a simple sum of deviations may underestimate the actual/plan (A/P) variations because pluses and minuses eliminate each other even if they are big. For example, a positive 20 percent deviation (A/P = 120 percent) and a negative 20 percent deviation (A/P = 80 percent) next year would show a zero deviation on average. Therefore, estimating the budget reality and true variations should sum the absolute value of deviations—that is, SUM of $|+20\%| + |-20\%| = 20\% + 20\% = 40\%$, and the *average absolute deviation* is 20 percent as opposed to zero (average deviation).

Methodology: Measuring planning efficiency requires calculating the *average absolute deviation* from 100 percent rather than using simply the *average deviation*. For example, in table 3.6 in main text, the line *Participation of firms and individuals* shows the following A/P budget performances between Year 1 and Year 5: 169.1 percent, 69.4 percent, 59.2 percent 48.2 percent, and 120.5 percent; these numbers signal very unpredictable and volatile budget execution. The deviations from 100 percent are: +69 percent, –31 percent, –41 percent, –52 percent, and +20 percent. The average deviation would be 6.7 percent, because pluses and minuses eliminate each other. In contrast, the *absolute deviations* show the real and very substantial variations: $|+69\%|$, $|-31\%|$, $|-41\%|$, $|-52\%|$, $|+20\%|$ = +69%, +31%, +41%, +52%, +20%; and the average absolute deviation is 213%/5 = 42.5%.

TD3: Projecting Local Tax Revenues by Using Trend Functions in Excel

For illustrating the technical details in using trend functions of Excel, we copy into table B.2 and follow table 3.39 from chapter 3 and provide explanations step by step from 1 to 4.

1. Let's take line 6, *Local tax revenues*, in table B.2. Generate linear trend line equation with Excel by following the next steps: highlight/mark the respective cells in line 6 (4,235, 4,818, 6,212, 7,584, and 8,037) => click on "Insert" icon => select "Scatter" charts => click on a graph icon => click on the graph that appears in a chart => click on "Linear trend" option with "Display Equation on Chart" .. =>.. click on "Close," and you will see the trend equation beside the trend line => type the equation to the respective cell (Taxes $y = 1,033.4x + 3,069.6$) of the *Assumption* column of the financial projection table B.2.

2. *Create a technical line* above line A that includes the serial numbers of the years, which should be used as the values of the x variable in the equations (see the cells highlighted in table B.2).

3. *Compute the projected local tax revenues* by using the equations for the taxes in Year 6: => click in the cell => insert [=1,033.4 * 6 + 3,069.6], and you see the projected tax revenues as 9,270. (Please note that we assume the cell is y in the equation, but do not write the "y" or the "x" letters: we use them only to show clearly the inserted equation.) =>.. Scroll the cell to Year 10, and now you have computed the first line of financial projections. We will apply this procedure to all the lines of financial projections unless we note reasons for not doing so, but we will not explain them again. Below we focus on only the lines that require special attention or procedures; we also highlight them in memo

items and indicate the respective memo references with (*) star marks like (*1) for tax revenues.

4. *Projection challenge—unusual data flow* (*2): Line 7, *Local fees and charges*, shows an unusual flow, namely that the Year 5 revenues stand out from the previous trend (flow) because they more than doubled compared to Year 4. Let's address the projection challenges. First, the high revenue of Year 5 would steepen the slope of the trend and may result in unrealistic revenue projections (figure B.2). In contrast, using the trend of the four years and excluding the outstanding year would result in unrealistic low projections. One way to mitigate the above challenges is to estimate the trend on the basis of the first four years and then elevate the trend line to the last year by changing the *base* in the trend formula with the *same slope* (see the trend line in figure B.3). This is what we recommend for MFSA users.

Figures B.2 and B.3 show the impact of an outstanding fee volume (12,347) in Year 5: (1) a combined linear trend would project over 20,000 in revenues in Year 10; (2) a trend that ignores the outstanding volume in Year 5 would project only about 12,000 in fee revenues, the amount that has been reached already in Year 5; and (3) the adjusted trend would start from the level of Year 5 (12,347 in revenues) but follow the slope of the previous years. This is realistic in a sense that the expansion of the fee base and increase of fee rates increased the revenues one time substantially and created a new basis for the future, but it is unrealistic to assume that it has also changed the slope of the fee trend. This means it is not realistic to expect an additional ShS2,000 in fee revenues year on year (see x coefficient) after this large increase; rather the revenues are likely to increase the same way as before, by about ShS1,000 annually from the elevated level of Year 5, and thus would reach about ShS16,000 in Year 10. Note that this projection would still

Table B.2 Projection of Current Revenues, Operating Expenditures, and Gross Operating Margin—Conservative Estimates Scenario (Copy of Table 3.39)

Items	Year 1 Actual	Year 2 Actual	Year 3 Actual	Year 4 Actual	Year 5 Actual	Assumptions, formulas	Year 6 Projection	Year 7 Projection	Year 8 Projection	Year 9 Projection	Year 10 Projection
	1	2	3	4	5	serial number of years (x)	6	7	8	9	10
A Total current revenue	**41,999**	**41,214**	**48,636**	**52,743**	**65,821**	sum lines 1+6	**69,588**	**75,633**	**83,209**	**93,118**	**97,398**
1 Transfers from higher government	30,300	25,162	26,120	29,933	35,984	sum lines (7,10)	35,032	37,859	40,686	43,513	46,340
2 – Shared taxes	24,053	22,255	22,747	26,915	35,631	y=2781.6x+17975	34,665	37,446	40,228	43,009	45,791
3 – Unconditional transfers *4	6,192	2,613	3,076	2,865		y=-6588.6-1213.2 USE zero!	0	0	0	0	0
4 – Conditional transfers	55	294	297	153	353	y=-45.565x+93.67	367	413	458	504	549
5 Own revenue	11,700	16,053	22,516	22,810	29,837	sum lines (2,5)	34,556	37,774	42,523	49,605	51,058
6 – Local tax revenues *1	4,235	4,818	6,212	7,548	8,037	y=1033.4x+3069.6	9,270	10,303	11,337	12,370	13,404
7 – Local fees and charges *2	2,496	4,389	5,571	5,397	12,347	y=988.63x+1991.6+5412	13,335	14,324	16,844	21,697	20,921
8 – Local asset revenues	4,969	6,847	9,778	8,723	8,989	y=991.61x+4886.3	10,836	11,828	12,819	13,811	14,802
9 – Local mixed revenues *3			955	1,142	464	y=204x-108.84	1,115	1,319	1,523	1,727	1,931
B Total operating expenditure	**33,498**	**37,784**	**41,187**	**44,610**	**56,893**		**59,274**	**65,115**	**71,054**	**77,102**	**83,273**
10 Labor (wages, salaries, taxes, charges)	6,592	7,635	8,141	9,075	10,034	y=832.38x+5798.2	10,792	11,625	12,457	13,290	14,122
11 – Administrative staff											
12 – Technical, service, and other staff											
13 Goods and services	10,052	10,917	11,386	12,737	15,044	y=1180.3x+8486	15,568	16,748	17,928	19,109	20,289
14 – Office supply											
15 – Electricity											
16 – Fuel and gas											
17 – Repair and maintenance *5	2,956	3,234	2,813	3,472	3,940	y=(220.62x+2621.1)*1.1	4,339	5,040	5,838	6,745	7,774
18 – Other goods and services											
19 Current subsidies to service entities *6	7,606	6,023	9,134	8,612	11,242	y=986.19x+5564.9	11,482	12,468	13,454	14,441	15,427
20 Current grants and transfers *7	3,128	5,466	4,582	5,549	11,577	y=1698x+966.46	11,154	12,852	14,550	16,248	17,946
21 Social care/welfare support	1,946	3,274	3,827	3,774	3,492	y=359.18x+2185	4,340	4,699	5,058	5,418	5,777
22 Other current expenditures	1,217	1,236	1,305	1,392	1,563	y=84.93x+10878	1,597	1,682	1,767	1,852	1,937
C Gross operating saving (A – B)	8,502	3,430	7,449	8,133	8,928		10,315	10,517	12,155	16,016	14,126

Note: Empty cells in lines 11, 12, 14, 15, 16, and 18 reflect missing data (only aggregate figures were available); ShS (shillings) is a notional name of the currency of the sample city.

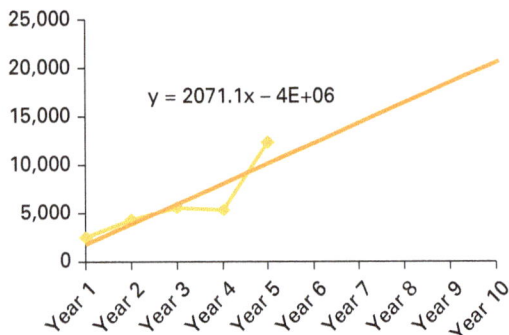

Figure B.2   Linear Trend for Fee Revenues

$y = 2071.1x - 4E+06$

Figure B.3   Modified Linear Trend for Fee Revenues

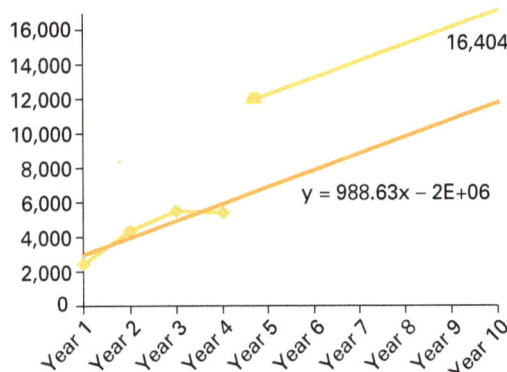

16,404

$y = 988.63x - 2E+06$

show a sixfold increase over 10 years, a quite remarkable increase. In sum, we recommend that MFSA users follow this logic and careful procedure to mitigate the outstanding end-year figures by changing either the *slope* or the *base* of the historical trend for projecting future revenues or expenditures.

TD4: Calculating Debt Capacity by Using the Annuity Function in Excel

Calculating the capacity for procuring new debts in the projected Year 10 requires the following procedure.

1. The sample city will have a projected current revenue of ShS97.4billion (bn) in the planned Year 10 (table B.2) that allows ShS9.74bn debt service according to the ratio *Debt service ≤ 10% of Current revenues*.

2. The debt capacity, however, also depends on the debt terms, such as interest rate and maturity (that is, the number of years to repay). The existing debt stock of the sample city indicates various interest rates (table 3.8 in chapter 3), so for the matter of simplicity let's assume that a 5 percent rate for debts will be available with a 15-year maturity investment loan to be procured in Year 10.

3. The city will have high debt service of ShS8.6bn in Year 10 (table 3.38), so it will have room for additional debt service only up to ShS1.14.bn (9.74bn – 8.6bn).

4. The present value calculation below suggests that the sample city will have capacity to procure ShS11.83bn in new debt in the planned Year 10, much less than the other ratios would allow.

The calculation of debt capacity follows the logic of a standard annuity calculation, that is to find the present value of a loan that can be repaid in 15 years and 15 equal Shs1.14bn installments, with a 5 percent interest rate. According to this ratio and the data above, the city has a capacity to pay an additional ShS1.14bn installment (debt service) above and beyond the already committed and due debt service of ShS8.6bn and comply with the rule that debt service is not more than 10 percent of the current revenues (projected to be ShS97.4bn in Year 10.

Excel has a function to calculate the present value of a loan with a 5 percent interest rate, 15 installments, and amount of ShS1.14bn per installment. Formula in Excel: [*=PV(interest rate in decimals, maturity years or number of installments, installment amount)*] =>

[=PV(0.05,15,1.14)] = 11.83. With these numbers the estimated present value of a loan, that is, the amount of new debt capacity, appears as ShS11.83bn.

TD5: Financial Management Scoring Templates

1. Intergovernmental Relations

Predictability of transfers	A	There is a mature and robust framework for the LG sector with clear definition of transfers. Any changes are made at a deliberate and predictable pace. Transfers are stable and predictable, regulated, timely transmitted; no ad hoc grants.
	B	CG transfers are predictable annually, regulated, but delivery times may vary during the year; no ad hoc grants.
	C	Transfers are not regulated but are by and large stable; ad hoc grants appear.
	D	Transfers are unpredictable, and/or not regulated, and/or ad hoc grants are common.
Intergovern-mental mandate arrangements	A	Revenue and expenditure mandates are clearly stipulated by law, and are respected. Any changes are made at a deliberate and predictable pace.
	B	Revenue and expenditure mandates are stipulated, but not in harmony, rules are respected with some exceptions. Intergovernmental finance changes are mostly discussed with LGs.
	C	Revenue and expenditure mandates are not well regulated, but rarely change.
	D	Revenue and expenditure mandates are unclear, not fully respected, and subject to changes without prior announcement or discussions.
Debt regula-tions	A	Debt financing is clearly regulated with market-based rules and insolvency framework; LG debt service is stable.
	B	Debt financing is regulated; LG debt service is mostly timely.
	C	Ministry (of finance) approves loans with no clear rules for debt financing. Payments may be delayed.
	D	Debt financing is unregulated, loans may rolled over, ad hoc short-term liquidity borrowing is common OR no borrowing is allowed.
Own revenue self-confidence	A	LG has the flexibility to change taxes/fees on a significant share of operating revenues, and increases are politically acceptable at the local level. LG has good collection power and capacities. Own revenues are predictable with clear visibility of future revenues.
	B	LG has the flexibility to change base or rate of some taxes/fees, but increases are politically challenging at the local level. Collection power and capacity are reason-able with low incentives to increase revenues. Own revenues are substantial and somewhat predictable.
	C	LG has no power to change base or rate of taxes/fees, may propose changes to the government/ministry. Own revenues are somewhat predictable.
	D	LG has no power to change rates or base of taxes and fees. Own revenues are not predictable or are very low.

Expenditure spending flexibility	A	Spending responsibilities are highly stable and predictable over time. LG has the flexibility to change the level and nature of spending, such as by cutting public services or changing service standards, on a significant share of operating expenditures. These cuts are politically acceptable at the local level.
	B	LG has the legal power to change the level and nature of spending, such as by cutting public services or changing service standards, on a significant share of operating expenditures. These cuts are conceptually acceptable at the local level, but rarely occur and only under extreme situations.
	C	LG has the legal power to change the level and nature of spending, but this occurs on an ad hoc basis against shortages of cash, and it is not a common practice. Overspending occurs time and again.
	D	LG can change the level and nature of spending, but this happens as quick fixes without long-term plans. Overspending is very common.

2. Planning, Budgeting, and Budget Implementation

Strategic plan and CIP	A	LG adopts, in line with a strategic plan, 3–5-year capital improvement plans (CIPs) on a rolling basis, whereas the first year becomes the budget plan and a new year is added to the CIP every year. The CIP is developed in participatory process and substantially implemented in the annual budgets.
	B	LG adopts CIPs every 3–5 years. The CIPs are substantially included in planning the annual budgets.
	C	LG adopts strategic plan or CIP, some actions are considered in planning the annual budgets, but changing circumstances reduce the scope or use of strategic planning.
	D	LG has no strategic plan or CIP; the planning is limited to annual budgets.
Budget planning	A	LG budgeting is clearly regulated, budget process is mature, iterative, and participatory based on predictable forecast for transfers, clear and robust national guidelines, and local budget circulars. Budget plans are completed on time and approved. Revised budgets are well regulated and timely planned and adopted at the midpoint of the fiscal year.
	B	LG budgeting is clearly regulated; budget process is timely completed based on clear national guidelines and local budget circulars. Revised budgets are adopted as deemed necessary.
	C	LG budgeting is regulated by national guidelines; budgets are completed mostly on time. Revised budgets are adopted several times a year if and when necessary.
	D	There are general rules for local budgets; multiple changes occur because of unforeseen circumstances at central or local government level.
Scope of budget	A	Extrabudgetary entities, PUCs, and/or funds play substantial role in local service delivery; but financial transactions are regulated, clear, and require low operating subsidies (5%). LG prepares both regular and consolidated budget/financial reports.
	B	Extrabudgetary entities, PUCs, and/or funds play substantial role in local service delivery; but financial transactions are regulated, clear, and require low operating subsidies (max 10% of current revenues). LG does not prepare consolidated budget/financial reports.

	C	Extrabudgetary entities, PUCs, and/or funds play substantial role in local service delivery, and require substantial operating subsidies (over 10%). Financial transactions are accounted but not regulated and not consolidated in financial reports.
	D	Extrabudgetary entities, PUCs, and/or funds play substantial role in local service delivery, and require substantial operating subsidies (15%). Financial transactions to and from entities are not regulated, accounted in various forms, but not consolidated in financial reports.
Budget implementa-tion	A	Expenditures adhere to budget appropriations; variations of actual and planned total expenditures and variation of structures of main lines are within 5% of plans.
	B	Expenditures adhere to budget appropriation; variations of actual and planned total expenditures and variation of structures of main lines are within 10% of plans.
	C	LG actual expenditures and revenues and revenue and expenditure variations and main line structures are within 15% of plans.
	D	LG actual expenditures and revenues and revenue and expenditure main line structures are over 15% of plans.

3. Financial Management

Financial management framework	A	Financial management framework is well regulated and supported by IFMS/FMS software system with standard templates and reporting forms, and sufficient number of qualified staff in key positions are assigned to financial management with clear segregation of functions.
	B	Financial management is controlled and supported by IFMS/FMS system with clear templates and segregation of functions, and qualified staff are assigned to many key positions with some vacant positions.
	C	Financial management is supported by some software, and some qualified staff are assigned to financial management.
	D	Financial management is computer enhanced with various software solutions, but staff have varying levels of knowledge in financial management area.
Revenue management	A	LG has effective fiscal cadaster and/or tax and fee payer registration and assessment system with up-to-date and transparent records on bases, rates, and payers' obligations and responsibilities; revenue collection efficiency is high (95%).
	B	LG has effective tax and fee payer registration and assessment system with up-to-date and transparent records on payers' obligations and responsibilities; revenue collection efficiency is good (80%).
	C	LG has several tax and fee payer registration systems with records on payers' obligations and responsibilities in various qualities; revenue collection efficiency is moderate (60–80%).
	D	LG has no or has several tax and fee payer registration systems with records on payers' obligations and responsibilities in varying qualities; revenue collection efficiency is low (60% or below).

Expenditure management	A	LG has effective commitment control system, clear segregation of duties, internal controls for nonsalary expenditures, and public procurement procedures to ensure value for money.
	B	LG has commitment control system, expenditures are accounted mostly on time, public procurement procedures support investments.
	C	LG has computerized systems for managing and recording expenditures.
	D	Expenditure recording and management are fragmented.
Cash and debt management	A	LG has an effective framework for cash and debt management with reliable records on cash balances, debts, guarantees, other liabilities, and payment arrears.
	B	LG has an effective framework for cash and debt management with records on cash balances, debts, and guarantees; but guarantees are not valued in debt management.
	C	LG has some procedure for cash and debt management with some records on cash balances and some debts.
	D	LG has no debt management framework but cash balances are reconciled or neither cash nor debt management procedure is in place.
Oversight and internal control	A	LG has reliable internal audit system, effective procedures for account reconciliations, and for oversight and analysis of the aggregate fiscal risk born from subordinated legally independent entities (PUCs) based on consolidated financial reports.
	B	LG has reliable internal audit system, some procedures for accounts' reconciliations, and for oversight and analysis of the aggregate fiscal risk born from subordinated legally independent entities (PUCs) without consolidation.
	C	LG has internal audit system, accounts reconciliations are intermittent, and LG receives the annual reports from the subordinated legally independent entities (PUCs).
	D	LG has no formal internal audit unit or system, and there are no records about the subordinated legally independent entities (PUCs).

4. Financial Reporting, Disclosure, and Transparency

Financial reporting	A	The LG has a reliable computerized financial reporting system consistent with generally accepted accounting principles and standards. Daily, monthly, quarterly, and annual reports are generated timely in automated procedures (e.g., by IFMS); results are disseminated to respective governing bodies, discussed, and corrective measures commenced timely.
	B	The LG has a reliable financial reporting system and procedures in compliance with national legislation; reports are generated and disseminated mostly on due courses.
	C	The LG has rules and various templates for financial reporting in various LG entities, reports are generated separately and delays may occur because of missing information.
	D	LG entities do generate some reports.

External audit	A	The LG annual financial reports are audited by external auditor; audit reports are obtained within 8-12 month following a fiscal year. The LG audit committee discusses the audit results and commences corrective measures as may deem necessary AND the LG has obtained unqualified audits in the last 3 years.
	B	The LG annual financial reports are audited by external auditor; audit reports are obtained within 2 years following a fiscal year. The LG audit committee discusses the audit results and commences corrective measures AND the LG has obtained unqualified audits in the last year.
	C	The LG annual financial reports are audited by external auditor; audit reports are obtained within 2–3 years following a fiscal year. The LG audit committee discusses the audit results. The LG has obtained qualified audits in the last 2 years.
	D	The LG has no external auditor or the LG has failed to obtain audits or has obtained qualified audits or one or more adverse external audits in the last 3 years.
Financial disclosures	A	The annual financial reports, the audit report, and short briefs on quarterly or monthly reports are made available for public scrutiny (e.g., posted on the LG website, readable at city hall, shared with key stakeholders in print or electronic forms). Town hall meeting is held to discuss results and future plans.
	B	The annual financial reports are made available for public scrutiny (e.g., posted on the LG website, readable at city hall, shared with key stakeholders in print or electronic forms).
	C	The annual financial reports are made available for public scrutiny on demand.
	D	Financial reports are not shared with the public.
Public procure-ment	A	LG has standard procedures that asset divestitures, all investment construction projects, and bulk purchases are procured by open competitive tendering published in various media and adhere to value-for-money principles.
	B	LG has standard procedures supporting that large construction projects are procured by open competitive tendering published in various media.
	C	Some projects are published and procured by competitive tenders.
	D	LG has no public procurement procedures.

Note: CG = central government; FMS = financial management system; IFMS = integrated financial management system; LG = local government; PUC = public utility company.

Municipal Finances Self-Assessment Online Application: An Interactive Platform for Mainstreaming of Use

The authors of *Better Cities, Better World: A Handbook on Local Governments Self-Assessments* have also developed a Municipal Finances Self-Assessment Online Application (World Bank 2019). The platform will be accessible by application via the World Bank website: www.worldbank.org. It is a follow-up companion document to *Municipal Finances: A Handbook for Local Governments* (Farvacque-Vitkovic and Kopanyi 2014), which also included a weblink to the MFSA Version "Light" and, more specifically, to this current publication. The MFSA online application is identical to the MFSA described in chapter 3 of this book in substance, content,

process, and methodology. The online application enables quick results because calculations are done automatically on the basis of the city data entered by the user; however, it does not contain the detailed step-by-step guidance and data interpretation that the book provides. The readers of *Better Cities, Better World* are encouraged to sign up and use the online application to save time on data entry and focus instead on analyzing results, drawing lessons, and seeking options for future improvements. A combined use of the LGSA Handbook and the MFSA online application is the most effective way to proceed.

Salient Features

The MFSA Online Application includes the following:

- A built-in, easy-to-access *Users Guide* to aid users in learning and operating the platform.

- A detailed built-in *Glossary* that explains the meanings and relations of over 300 terms, in order to ensure consistency of the financial terminology and analyses across cities and countries.

- Minimized data entry requirements with a single-entry method, whereby specific data are entered only once, and then the system populates all the relevant tables and cells automatically. Users can focus more on analyses and on forming and testing assumptions to project future scenarios.

- Performance of all routine calculations in the tables and automatic population of derivative and output tables, such as subtotals and totals, growth indexes, trends, and financial ratios. All the tables are interlinked following standard finance and accounting principles. There are still numerous actions users need to perform besides entering data, such as selecting options, defining assumptions and entering variations accordingly, and analyzing and summarizing results in short reports. The system includes icons to help users to either export to local databases or print tables from the system.

How to Use the Online Application

The users of this MFSA online application will need to populate only the Financial Database and the supplementary tables, and the system will automatically populate the standard derivative or output tables. Users will need to analyze the results of both the standard and the supplementary tables and perform the prescribed actions.

Tables that users are advised to fill out include the following:

- Financial Database, which is the most fundamental database in the MFSA

- Expenditures by sector

- Capital investments

- Debt database

- Tax performance database

- Liabilities and arrears

- Cash balance

- Asset maintenance database

- Actual/Plan variations financial database

Should a user be missing some of the information needed to fill out supplementary tables, the system will still perform most of the MFSA analysis. Should tables or lines be left unfilled, the system will still work; but it will show gaps in some output tables, such as financial projections or ratio analysis. It also may provide a low score on the shadow credit rating, which assumes that missing information signals financial weaknesses and risks of low creditworthiness. Such gaps actually do point to weaknesses, and they signal areas that need special attention and corrective measures. In short, systematically pointing out gaps is already one valuable result of an MFSA analysis, because users who are not aware of such gaps have little chance to address them or to improve the respective areas of financial management.

The *standard tables* can be generated from the regular budgets or financial reports of a municipality. The template tables that appear on the screen in each step are self-explanatory, but users may visit the *Glossary* and *Users Guide* for help, clarification, and ensuring quality of entries for the respective cells.

The *supplementary tables* include items that are not recorded within regular budgets. Most of these supplementary tables, though, can be developed with a moderate workload, and many may already exist in various municipal departments, with various levels of sophistication. It is important to bring these tables into the spotlight with MFSA analysis, because most national regulations exclude or do not make these tables mandatory; hence, many local governments ignore or fail to record these additional data in a timely or consistent fashion. Developing these tables under the MFSA requires close cooperation across various municipal departments and entities, and this cross-fertilization is an added bonus of the MFSA process.

Populating the initial *Financial Database* from the *raw municipal data* is the most critical task that users should complete first. Challenges include, first, reducing the details of the original local reports from hundreds of lines to a short 60-line report called the *Financial Database* and, second, identifying and streamlining the categories to the international standard structure of the Financial Database. Entering new lines and categories is not possible, yet leaving out financial data because of an unspecified category is not advisable. A third challenge is making adjustments to fit the cash accounting principles from the various local practices (for example, accrual reports, performance-based budgeting, or other local peculiarities). A final challenge is to screen and compare the entries to ensure that all the main entries, subtotals, and totals are identical with the numbers found in the original local reports, such as operating revenues; operating expenditures; capital revenue; capital expenditures; and loans, borrowing, and savings.

Local own-source revenues may need careful adjustment and may even require changing the built-in categories (lines are editable in the platform); for example, property tax might be the most significant revenue source in one city, but negligible in another one where business tax and communal tax are the most important. Thus, users are enabled and encouraged to change the name of the own taxes or fees to reflect the local reality. However, the subtotal lines such as *Local taxes* or *Local fees* should remain unchanged, and the sum figures should be identical to the original local financial reports.

References

Farvacque-Vitkovic, Catherine, and Mihaly Kopanyi, eds. 2014. *Municipal Finances: A Handbook for Local Governments.* Washington, DC: World Bank.

Farvacque-Vitkovic, Catherine, and Anne Sinet. 2014. "Achieving Greater Transparency and Accountability: Measuring Municipal Finances Performance." In *Municipal Finances: A Handbook for Local Governments,* edited by Catherine Farvacque-Vitkovic and Mihaly Kopanyi. Washington, DC: World Bank.

World Bank. 2019. "Municipal Finances Self-Assessment Online Application." World Bank, Washington, DC.

MFSA Action Plan: Long List of Possible Key Actions

The MFSA Action Plan is the most important final product of the MFSA process. It is also the step that proves to be the most difficult for MFSA users. MFSA users find it sometimes difficult to translate key issues into key actions, and they also need support for the implementation phase of the Action Plan. This section provides guidance for identifying specific actions based on the MFSA analysis and results. It follows the sequence of MFSA steps and identifies potential actions for each step. It is based on the key findings of our Sample City (chapter 3). It is advisable in a real-life situation to revisit such a long list and to select a shorter list for the city council's consideration against the available funding after simple estimates of timing and costs. We have included a short list with a few specific actions with cost and timing in order to exemplify the process of costing and based on our limited knowledge of the sample city. Users may further structure the action plan into specific clusters of actions and they may follow a different logic than the MFSA steps (see table 3.4 in chapter 3).

MFSA Action Plans should include a summary table of key actions. This summary table will include the following information, which is essential for implementation and monitoring costs, timelines, and responsibilities. In addition, the summary table will make a distinction between (1) short-term actions that can be carried out by local government with little involvement from other stakeholders and (2) medium-term actions that may require intervention from higher levels of government. The latter case will make any implementation schedule more difficult to predict, but mapping the path and highlighting the requirements on the way (regulatory or legislative changes) will make implementation easier and more feasible.

Historical Analysis (Sample City)

The financial snapshot signals three major weaknesses (table 3.18 in chapter 3), all of which can be corrected by internal actions. Main findings include that the overall closing balance became steadily negative in the last years, the debt service skyrocketed, and the gross margin grew a mere 1.2 percent per year, well below the 7.3 percent national inflation. Corrective actions may include the following:

1. Improve budgeting practices to ensure balance in both planned and actual budgets. This action requires no cost, but revising and improving both budgeting and budget execution control procedure by the budget and finance departments, as well as tightening the council's budget approval.

2. High debt service requires establishment of a debt management system with procedures and an appointed debt management team in the finance department. The action needs moderate costs to improve respective information technology if any, because there is already a simple debt database in place, suitable for managing a small number of debt items.

3. The decreasing gross margin should be addressed in the course of revenue and expenditure actions aiming to boost own-source revenue and expand gross margin.

The revenue trends signal three major challenges (table 3.19): shrinking government transfers, insufficient local tax revenues, and shrinking own capital revenues.

a) The transfers from central government grew by a mere 4.4 percent per year, which is slightly higher than half of annual national inflation. This is because the government phased out unconditional transfers, which the growing shared taxes failed to counterbalance, thus apparently reducing transfers to the local government sector. Specific action could include:

4. The mayor and finance officer initiate or join policy dialogue together with municipal association and other cities on the issue of government's hidden modification of the transfer system and silent reduction of share of transfers, and then request that it reestablish the unconditional grants and ensure increasing transfers at least in proportion to inflation or increase the local shares of designated taxes to counterbalance the lost grants.

b) Local own tax revenues are stable and growing but seem to be far below the tax potential; they are hard to measure because of nonexistent tax databases. Specific actions may include the following, but technical issues and cost estimates require further analyses:

5. Establish a reliable revenue management system with standard procedures and solid professional capacities that may require insourcing trained specialists.

6. Establish a reliable computerized tax database for all or the five largest own tax revenue sources.

7. Revise and expand the tax bases and tax nets and aim to reach over 95 percent coverage rate.

8. Improve tax collection procedures to ensure over 95 percent collection rate and aim to double annual collection in the next five years.

9. Initiate a program for collection and workout of tax arrears; measure and then adopt program to reduce the stock of historical arrears to 5 percent of total tax revenues.

10. Address issue of property valuation and plan a revaluation or updating program by the end of this medium-term period and after completion of the first five actions above (actions 5 through 9)—doable by the end of this medium term.

c) Fee revenues have just increased substantially, but a specific plan should be adopted:

11. Adopt a program to collect historical fee arrears; measure and reduce the volume of stock of fee arrears to 5 percent of total fee revenues.

d) Improve cash management:

12. Introduce a cash and liquidity management system with a dedicated team to ensure strong liquidity; in the meantime, invest free cash into short-term instruments that gain revenues with low risk.

e) Introduce new revenue sources:

13. Analyze revenue options and performances and adopt program to boost some revenues or introduce new revenue sources within the current legal limits. Seek specifically options for using various land-value-capture instruments.

14. Initiate or join policy dialogue to change the local revenue assignments for the entire municipal sector with new revenue sources based on international practices.

f) Own capital revenues include two major items: (1) asset proceeds that are basically from lease or sale of land or buildings, and (2) land development fee; both items shrank in the last period. Corrective actions may include the following:

15. Establish an asset management system with reliable registers, strategy, and policy; there is currently no formal asset register.

16. Revise land-lease contracts to explore hidden losses and initiate corrective measures.

17. Institutionalize competitive tendering procedures for sale or lease of land, buildings, or other assets.

18. Commence analysis of underlying reasons behind decreasing land development fee revenues and initiate corrective measures. Institutionalize regular annual analysis of the private land and real estate market to explore tendencies and make solid projections for land development fee revenues five years ahead on a rolling basis.

19. Establish or revise procedures for systematic and rule-based collection of participation fee (hook-up charge) from new users of service networks to ensure collecting a fair but substantial participation from beneficiaries for expanding the service infrastructure.

20. Revise methodology for analyzing options for investment financing to expand private financing in public infrastructure based on careful risk analyses.

Expenditures: The current expenditures seem to be under good control exemplified by the low share of labor costs and cost of goods and services (tables 3.20 and 3.21 in chapter 3). Nevertheless, operating expenses have grown much faster than current revenues (14.4 percent and 12.3 percent, respectively). Weaknesses explored include missing reliable expenditure data; low control on current subsidies to service entities and current grants and transfers to subordinated entities, both of which represent substantial shares of expenditures; and expenditures signaling low asset sustainability, because the share of repair and maintenance expenses are low and the money spent for repair of assets grew 7 percent annually, a pace about equal to annual inflation. Corrective actions may include the following:

a) Expenditure databases should be established or enhanced on several fronts:

21. Establish databases on functional classification of expenditures in compliance with the classification of the functions of government (COFOG) classification, which would not only improve planning but also enhance communication of plans and results with citizens and other stakeholders.

22. Improve databases and enhance control cost of labor (administrative and technical staff), cost of goods and services such as office supply, fuel and gas, and electricity.

23. Develop database on repair and maintenance prior to and later as part of asset management system (action 15).

b) Control subsidies and grants, because they represent a substantial share of current expenditures (nearly 40 percent in Year 5). Actions may include the following:

24. Revise the system and procedures for subsidizing current expenditures of service entities, measure performance, and introduce rules for performance-based subsidization.

25. Introduce control procedure for rule-based provision of current grants and transfers to subordinated entities (districts, wards, communities).

c) Improve service sustainability by enhanced procedures for asset development planning and maintenance. Actions may include the following:

26. Increase expenditures for asset repair and maintenance, at least double real volume in the medium term.

27. Increase expansion of assets by revision of current capital improvement plans in line with the forecasted revenue increases against the expected reform actions and enhanced financing strategies, but in parallel maintain budget balances and comply with indebtedness regulations.

Ratio Analysis (Sample City)

The ratio analysis results underscore several findings and actions listed before and point to some further weaknesses and actions for improvement (table 3.29 in chapter 3). It is unnecessary to repeat here the 27 actions already mentioned, so we focus discussions on new aspects or actions to be considered. One general observation is clear, namely that the initial financial projections do not indicate substantial changes in the systems or results measured by financial ratios in the medium term. Thus, the ratio analysis also supports the idea that the city may seek more ambitious improvements and more visible enhancements and gradual reduction of gaps between a few selected city ratios and the international benchmarks in the medium term. In the interim, the city should also maintain or improve compliance with regulations.

Creditworthiness: Creditworthiness ratios signal two warning lessons: namely that the operating savings are low in both the gross and the net term.

a) The ratio of [Operating savings before interests/Current revenue] is not bad in comparison to similar developing countries, but it is far below the benchmark. This ratio largely depends on the current revenues, which further depend on transfers and own revenues because the explored actions do not signal substantial savings on operating expenditures. Thus, increasing revenues is the only way to improve this ratio and creditworthiness. We have identified specific corresponding actions for both local and national level (see actions 4 through 14).

b) The ratio of [Net Operating Surplus/Current revenue ratio] depends on the revenues just like the gross ratio, but it further depends on the volume and share of debt service expenditures. Because the debt service has been largely predetermined by loans contracted and disbursed before, the improvement of the net ratio practically depends on the revenue actions mentioned above.

Indebtedness: There are two warning signals of indebtedness, both of which come from regulations; they got close to the regulatory limits by the end of the analyzed period and may even breach the limits in the planned period.

a) The ratio of [Debt service/Total current revenue] has grown fast and has nearly reached the set regulatory limit (8 percent against the 10 percent limit in Year 5); it is likely to grow further in the planned period. Increasing own revenues or receiving substantially larger transfers would solve this issue.

b) The ratio of [Debt outstanding/Budget total] has nearly reached the regulatory limit, it was 56 percent in Year 5; however, it will go far above 60 percent in the beginning of the projected period. The trouble is that it is hard if not impossible and really not advisable to reduce the stock of outstanding debt on short notice, on the one hand. However, increasing revenues by adopting and implementing revenue enhancement actions takes time and is unlikely to generate substantial additional own revenues in the first one to two years of the planned period. Thus, increased government transfers seem to be the only simple solution. This underlines the importance of national actions mentioned before, namely to improve transfer revenues (action 4); meanwhile the city should establish effective cash and debt management system, procedures, and capacities (action 12).

Service sustainability includes two direct service and two financial ratios, namely capital investment expenditures and repair and maintenance work expenditures. These two could move against each other, so offer no solution when both are lower than the benchmarks. The collection efficiency of taxes and fees provides the vital underlying ratios that could support or rather further undermine the two direct service sustainability ratios.

a) The ratio of [Capital investment expenditure/Current revenue] was far above the benchmarks in the beginning and for much of the analyzed period, but it dropped down to a reasonable level by the end of the period. However, financial projections and investment plans signal a radical drop of this ratio to the range below or about half of the benchmark in the optimistic scenario. This is good, on the one hand, from the financial control point of view and signals city leaders' intention to comply with various rules and especially to avoid unmanageable debt burden. On the other hand, such a radical reduction for an entire medium-term period may undermine the scope, coverage, or quality of local services. Actions identified before include substantial increase of revenues and are promising options that can improve capital investments in the medium term. Introduce new revenue sources (actions 13 and 14).

28. Enhance and diversify investment financing. This is a bold option that offers room for expansion of investments outside the budget, thus without violating the regulatory or solvency rules. The city may establish a team or hire an expert to explore technically and legally possible options for enhanced financing of investments.

b) The ratio of [Maintenance works expenditure/Operating expenditures] is far below the benchmark, but more important it signals inadequate maintenance and raises risk of deteriorating local assets and services in the medium term. Even in the optimistic scenario where the amount of money for maintenance is planned to double, it would only help to marginally increase the maintenance ratio. A possible specific action beyond those already stated:

29. Carry out *a specific risk-based analysis* of assets to measure the current quality of assets and *to calculate more precise technical and financial requirements for systematic preventive repair and maintenance of the most critical assets*. Without such analysis, nobody knows what would be the adequate expenditure plan for repair and maintenance, or what would be a realistic repair and maintenance over operating expenditures ratios in the medium term.

c) Tax efficiency measured by the ratio of [Taxes collected/Taxes levied] is vital for service sustainability because tax revenues provide an important part of own-source revenues and operating savings. The fact that the sample city (like many users of MFSA) does not have reliable tax databases can be seen as a red flag from the perspective of lenders, investors, or other possible partners. (See actions 6 through 10.)

d) The fee efficiency ratio measured by [Fees collected/Fees billed] is vital for service sustainability; they may not generate revenue surplus, but fee revenues are vital for cost recovery of key urban services. Lack of reliable fee databases and/or low collection efficiency gravely undermine services, but it also induces using up other revenues like general taxes or transfers, which would otherwise be usable for development financing. Furthermore, reliable fee databases are vital to help measure and improve cost recovery of services. The actions mentioned before—namely to establish reliable databases—are good signals toward customers (who pay better if they know a good database exists) and partners, but they also help stringent expenditure control, cost recovery and tariff management, and performance measurement of respective staff and entities (actions 11 and 14). A possible additional specific action not mentioned before:

30. Carry out a detailed *revenue* analysis covering all main tax revenues, each of which generates a substantial volume of money.

Quality of operations includes several ratios. The sample city is doing well in controlling employment and labor costs (unlike many cities in the developing world that follow a tradition of reckless employment and escalated labor costs to the detriment of services). Weaknesses appear in the area of budget predictability, managing liabilities, and cash management.

a) *Budget reality*: The ratio of [Actual revenue/ Planned revenue] indicates the reality of the budget plan (ideally by comparing the very first/initial rather than the revised plan) against the actual final account/ budget at the end of the fiscal year. The sample city shows a relatively stable and well-controlled overall management of current revenues and expenditures (despite said shortcomings). However, the budget fluctuates far beyond the 5 percent range of 100 percent, and it does so largely because of movements in development expenditures. One possible action to improve budget reality:

31. Initiate a detailed analysis of actual/plan variation by checking each line of the main revenue and expenditure figures in the course of the last five years and identify areas where large variations are persistent. Then, commence dialogue with respective departments or units to find out the underlying reasons and to explore options for corrective measures.

b) The ratio of [Financial resources (cash + cash-like)/Financial obligations (due liabilities + arrears)] reflects a broader scope of resources and dues, a sort of gross account of the ratio on arrears discussed above. The sample city was unable to manage a balance between liabilities and cash-like financial resources, which remain far below liabilities, but this ratio also shows worsening tendency. This is a very bad signal that undermines creditworthiness and encourages lenders and investors to calculate a higher entity risk when working with such city.

32. Establish an asset-liability management unit within the finance department to systematically monitor and control regular and overdue liabilities in connection with current assets.

Financial Projections (Sample City)

Financial projections were made initially on the basis of the historical trends and by factoring in a few imminent specific actions to enhance revenues and funding (tables 3.39 and 3.41 in chapter 3). The plans indicate moderate changes, however, even in the optimistic scenario. Possible specific actions include the following:

33. Initiate an iterative forecasting and projection process that includes preliminary selection and analysis of a longer list from the revenue-improvement and expenditure-enhancement actions listed. Beware of the fact that some actions are interlinked, reinforce, or supplement each other, whereas many other actions can be postponed without major short-term impacts.

34. Recalculate a third scenario that factors in the projected results of the said new preliminary actions.

35. Perform a reality check against the selected actions, and then analyze the effects on general revenue and expenditure trends, balances, and impacts on asset development and maintenance.

36. Perform revised projections based on lessons learned from the third forecasting model and analyze a fourth forecasting scenario.

Financial Management Assessment (Sample City)

The financial management assessment covers four thematic areas, each with four or five sets of questions: (1) intergovernmental relations; (2) planning, budgeting, and budget implementation; (3) financial management; and (4) financial reporting, disclosure, and transparency. These areas constitute the main underlying causes of the good or weak financial performance of a local government; many of the respective issues have already been mentioned and actions defined. We focus on the specific public financial management aspects of the financial management system in this section and identify specific actions to improve areas of low performance exemplified by low C or D scores in each of the said four thematic areas discussed in chapter 3 (Step 5 and summarized in table 3.64).

Intergovernmental relations include five specific questions: predictability of transfers, intergovernmental mandate, debt regulations, own revenue self-confidence, and expenditure spending flexibility.

a) *Predictability of transfers* got a C score because transfers are not regulated although are by and large stable and ad hoc grants appear. Indeed, as we have seen, the government gradually decreased the unconditional grants/block grants and limited the growth of transfers far below the inflation rate (table 3.19). *Corrective action* could be the following:

37. Initiate or join a national policy dialogue on setting clear rules for transfers, make them more predictable, and avoid or make ad hoc grants exceptional.

b) *Debt regulation* got a C score because the ministry of finance approves municipal loans with or without clear rules for debt financing. This distorts lenders' risk management, allows subjectivity for borrowing approvals, and opens room for political interference. *Corrective action* could be the following:

38. Initiate or join a national policy dialogue to set national regulations for *municipal* borrowing, debt management, and insolvency resolution; and then reduce or terminate the ministry's loan approval mandate.

c) *Own revenue self-confidence* got a C score because municipalities have no power to change the base or rate of taxes and most fees; instead, they may propose changes to the government/ministry. Own revenues are somewhat predictable but low. Corrective actions include increasing own revenues (actions 4 through 14) and the following:

39. Initiate or join a national policy dialogue to empower municipalities to change the base or rate of local taxes and fees, possibly within a set minimum and maximum range—a common international practice.

d) *Expenditure spending flexibility* got a C score because municipalities have legal power to control and change spending; however, this is not a common practice, and overspending occurs. Corrective actions could be the following:

40. Review internal control systems and initiate adequate operating procedures to improve budget appropriation control, local expenditure policy, and expenditure management practices.

41. Initiate procedure to tighten budget control and rules for identifying and enforcing budget cuts as deemed necessary, especially during preparation of revised budgets.

Planning, budgeting, and budget implementation includes four specific questions: strategic plan and CIP, budget planning, scope of budget, and budget implementation. The first three of these areas are under good control and performing well. The issues appear in the fourth area.

a) *Budget implementation* got a C score because the city experiences high plan/actual variations (over 15 percent) in both revenue and expenditures. This score signals weaknesses in both planning and implementation practices. These issues are interrelated with several challenges mentioned before, such as low predictability of some transfers, or reliance on revenues that reflect market volatility such as land development fees. Corrective actions have already been mentioned, for example, detailed analysis of actual/plan variations to identify the most persistent and critical areas. One more can be added:

42. Improve revenue and expenditure analysis and forecasting practices (for example, use MFSA), set realistic targets, and

plan contingencies in some specific critical areas (such as fuel).

The financial management systems and practices area includes five specific factors: financial management framework, revenue management, expenditure management, cash and debt management, and oversight and internal control systems and practices. Of these factors, revenue management and expenditure management appear to be the problematic areas. Revenue management got a lowest D score, but all critical actions have been mentioned earlier (actions 4 through 14).

Financial reporting, disclosure, and transparency includes four decisive factors: financial reporting, external audit, financial disclosures, and public procurement. Of these factors, external audit and financial disclosures appear to be problematic and need corrective measures.

a) *External audit* got a C score because the annual financial reports are audited by an external auditor; however, audit reports are obtained within two to three years following a fiscal year. The city has obtained qualified audits in the last two years. The local audit committee discussed the audit results, but there is no evidence of adopting corrective measures. Specific actions could include the following:

43. Initiate or join a national policy dialogue to legalize private external audits and aim to provide municipalities with audit reports within six months after submission of financial reports for audits.

44. Carry out investigation and consultancy analysis to unfold the reasons behind qualified audits obtained in the last two years and define specific, time-bound corrective measures.

45. Adopt a rule that the local audit committee should commence detailed discussion with auditor for clarifications, define specific time-bound corrective measures, and then discuss them with respective stakeholders.

46. Mandate and encourage the mayor and/or town clerk to oversee and enforce implementation of the corrective measures about audit reports in a timely fashion.

b) *Financial disclosures* got a C score because the annual financial reports are made available for public scrutiny on demand, but this is a passive form of communication and results in low levels of citizen outreach. Specific actions could include the following:

47. Establish a cell/team responsible for policy analysis, customer education, communication, and collection and analysis of feedback information.

48. Adopt a communication and citizen outreach strategy based on analyses and national or international best practices, and include a list of standard short budget and other reports designed for easy understanding by citizens.

49. Develop specific communication tools such as leaflets, media news, and web-based communication, public hearings, and town hall meetings to timely communicate the city's plans and financial results.

50. Publish financial results on a recurrent basis; in parallel make them permanently accessible via various media tools, and enable citizens' easy feedback.

Self-Assessed Shadow Credit Rating

Self-assessed shadow credit rating (SASCR) is a procedure that adopts the principles and key methodology practices of rating agencies in completing credit ratings or shadow credit ratings (Fitch Ratings 2015; Moody's 2017; Standard and Poor's 2016). The SASCR, however, applies rating instruments in a self-assessment modality. We use the SASCR acronym in order to clearly distinguish this procedure and its results from other shadow credit ratings and in particular from published credit ratings set by rating committees and professional rating agencies, including the Fitch, Moody's, Standard and Poor's Global Ratings, or their national or regional affiliates (PEFINDO 2016). Thus, it is important to clarify the nature and position of the SASCR in relation to the published formal credit ratings or the shadow credit ratings or credit assessment conducted by third-party expert teams or rating agencies (see box E.1 for a discussion of Standard and Poor's credit assessment).

The SASCR resembles more an entity's *idiosyncratic risk assessment* than a credit rating of a debt instrument, that is, it aims to indicate the general financial health or creditworthiness of a municipality similar to such general assessments by rating agencies (Ösmen 2016). Compared to professional and published third-party credit ratings, the SASCR leans more toward a self-assessment with messages geared to the finance department, finance subcommittee of the city council, city council, and city mayor instead of investors; therefore, by no means can it serve or can it be understood as a publishable rating result (box E.2).

The SASCR is structured in a way to encourage honest scoring and factors applied are in harmony with the regular rating principles, but the SASCR inevitably includes some level of subjectivity that emerges from the self-assessment modality. Therefore, comparison of the SASCR rating scores, if any, may be adequate for a domestic shadow credit rating;

it is presumably fair even to downgrade some SASCR results. For example, a "ccc" score in SASCR may be comparable to a "c" score in a domestic shadow credit rating, but it is better not to compare it to external ratings at all.

The SASCR also differs from the third-party shadow or internationally recognized professional credit ratings in terms of the scope of rating drivers considered and assessed. The main reason is that the SASCR aims to use the results of the MFSA quantitative and qualitative assessments without requiring substantial additional data gathering and analysis. In short, simplicity is a major objective of the SASCR. A more sophisticated SASCR would require significantly greater efforts while providing marginally improved precision; however, it would still not be considered a formal credit rating.

The SASCR relies more on scorecards, but we do encourage the users to identify and write a short summary report, pointing out strengths and weaknesses of their financial system as well as specific factors that play a major role in credit scores (qualitative and quantitative modifiers). The SASCR final summary scores and rating are set by the user of the scoring templates. These templates also incorporate experiences from various creditworthiness assessments and analysis completed under international donors such as the World Bank, academia, and subnational assessments (Bird and Slack 2015; Cabaleiro, Buch, and Vaamonde 2013; Colorado General Assembly 2013; Fourie, Verster, and van Vuuren 2016; German 2015; Groves and Valente 2003; Liu and Tan 2009: Peterson 1998). In contrast, rating agencies assign rating committees to establish the final rating on the basis of "baseline credit assessments" by scorecard tables, but also taking additional national, market, policy, or political information into account (box E.3). This is one important reason why the SASCR should only be considered as a limited shadow rating.

The SASCR is based on historical results with an opportunity to score the results of financial projections five years ahead, but it is still not comparable to a formal rating that is strongly focused on predicting the future creditworthiness and likelihood of risks that hamper debt service during the repayment period of a loan or bond.

Finally, formal credit ratings are geared to investors and lenders, so they value positively the likelihood of extra government support in case of financial distress or disability of a municipality to service a debt. They do so regardless of whether there is a formal commitment of the government in the form of either a sovereign guarantee behind a debt (loan or bond) or a general legislation that suggests such intervention, or even whether there is just a general practice for providing ad hoc grants if a municipality needs them. This is understandable from the investor or lender perspective, because the assurance or likelihood of government support is a credit enhancement for them; however, many question those assurances because they are often the source of moral hazard on both the lender's and borrower's side. They could induce perverse incentives for lenders who may compromise due diligence and ignore business risks, because they assume protection from a higher government tier regardless of the borrower's performance.

In contrast, the MFSA and the SASCR score a government's extra financial support or evidence of ad hoc grants outside the formula-based transfers as negative characteristics of the intergovernmental framework. In short, SASCR intends to assess the financial health of a city without the extra support and protection by the central government.

Box E.3
Moody's Guidelines on Scorecards

The scorecards are not meant to be a substitute for rating committee judgments on individual baseline credit assessment. Scorecard results have limitations in that they generally use historical data, while credit assessments are forward-looking opinions of credit strength. The limited number of variables included in the scorecard cannot fully capture all idiosyncratic risks nor the breadth and depth of the analysis considered by rating committees.

Source: Moody's 2017 (page 2).

SASCR Analysis and Scoring

SASCR analysis and scoring are built on three pillars: (1) the MFSA qualitative municipal finance assessment (MFA), which is a derivative of the Public Expenditure and Financial Accountability (PEFA) Assessments, (2) the MFSA ratio analysis, and (3) MFSA financial projections. All of these are assumed to be completed during the MFSA before the SASCR. Therefore, the SASCR does not require new data collection.

SASCR analysis and scoring include the following simple steps: (1) scoring the qualitative results from the MFA; (2) scoring the quantitative results from the ratio analysis; (3) calculating the final score; (4) establishing a shadow credit rating based on the final score and a rating table. It is also useful to summarize the results in a short SASCR report. The steps of the SASCR are explained in this section by using again the data of the sample city analyzed and explained in chapter 3.

Scoring Qualitative Results

The SASCR analysis and scoring include the following simple steps users are advised to follow:

1. Read and score the municipal finance (qualitative) assessment (MFA) line by line and score each factor. Users who have filled out the MFA assessment can borrow the results, and then attach SASCR scores to the factors in each of the four qualitative areas:
   a. Intergovernmental relations (IR)
   b. Planning, budgeting, and budget implementation (PB)
   c. Financial management (FM)
   d. Financial reporting, disclosure, and transparency (RDT).

2. Calculate the average score in each qualitative area as a simple arithmetic average of the factor scores; compared to the MFA score, A = 5, B = 4, C = 3, and D = 2. Table E.1 summarizes the scoring of the sample city on the basis of the MFA tables in "Step 5 Financial Management Assessment FMA" and the MFSA–MFA Analysis and Scoring (see table 3.64). In this case, however, the lowest score, not the average, should be attached to the *financial reporting, disclosure, and transparency* qualitative area to capture the weakest link in the chain of creditworthiness factors. Users may use table E.1 as a template for their own scoring.

3. Calculate the final score of the qualitative assessment as a weighted average of the scores of the qualitative areas by applying the following formula (using the acronyms identified in the first step for the four qualitative areas):

$$\text{MFA score} = (0.4*\text{IR} + 0.2\text{PB} + 0.2\text{FM} + 0.2\text{RDT})/4$$

The formula applies higher weight for intergovernmental relations (IR), because that factor plays a particularly important role in financial stability and eventually creditworthiness of a city.

Scoring Quantitative Results

Scoring the quantitative results uses the results of the ratio analysis (Step 3 of the MFSA Analysis). The scoring scales are summarized in table E.2. Users just need to look into the ratio analysis results and set the scores accordingly. One specific rule is to use the score 2 (the lowest score) if there are no data, and no ratio established in a specific line. The reason is that missing data represent

SASCR Scoring of Qualitative Areas and Factors from Sample City, 2013

	Factor Scores		Factor Scores
Intergovernmental relations scoring summary (IR)		**Financial management (FM)**	
Predictability of transfers	C=3	Financial management framework	B=4
Intergovernmental mandate arrangements	B=4	Revenue management	C=3
Debt regulations	C=3	Expenditure management	C=3
Own revenue self-confidence	C=3	Cash and debt management	B=4
Expenditure spending flexibility	D=2	Oversite and internal control	B=4
Average score	3.00	Average score	3.60
Planning, budgeting, and budget implementation (PB)		**Financial reporting, disclosure, and transparency (RDT)**	
Strategic plan and CIP	A=5	Financial reporting	B=4
Budget planning	A=5	External audit	C=3
Scope of budget	B=4	Financial disclosures	C=3
Budget implementation	B=4	Public procurement	B=4
Average score	4.50	Lowest score!	3.00
Qualitative assessment final scores = 0.4*IR+0.2*PB+0.2*FM+0.2*RDT =			3.42

Note: CIP = capital investment plan; SASCR = self-assessed shadow credit rating.

Table E.2 **Scoring Financial Ratios**

Creditworthiness (CW)	3.75
Indebtedness (ID)	4.67
Fiscal autonomy (FA)	5.00
Capital investment effort (CE)	4.50
Service sustainability (SS)	2.33
Quality of operations(QO)	3.80
Financial ratios final score	4.06

risks, downscale financial health measurement, and may reduce creditworthiness. The fact that a city has no data for an area that is supposed to be measured and for which a financial ratio should be established is an apparent risk factor and a shortcoming that may hide financial health issues. For instance, the sample city does not have reliable fee databases and does not measure collection efficiency, which are financial health issues

regardless of the fact that the city indeed collects substantial own-source revenue. Without measurement, it remains unclear if the collection could have substantial growth potential or has exhausted capacities under the current revenue management system.

The ratio analysis measures six clusters of ratios: creditworthiness, indebtedness, fiscal autonomy, capital investment efforts, service sustainability, and quality of operations. Each of these measurements includes several specific ratios that signal factors that influence financial health and creditworthiness. The scoring of the financial ratios includes the following steps:

1. Calculate the average score for each factor by using a qualified weighted average of scores for five years (Y1 through Y5) = (1*Y5+0.9*Y4+0.8*Y3+0.7*Y2+0.6*Y1)/4 to put higher emphasis on more recent scores.

2. Score each ratio/factor from table 3.29 using the set scales presented in table E.3.

3. Establish average scores for each measurement area by calculating the arithmetic average of the factor scores. Table E.3 shows the results of the sample city and can be used as a template for summary of the scoring of ratio analyses.

4. Calculate the final score for the financial ratios by applying the following formula:

Final Score for Ratios = 0.25*CW+0.25*ID+ 0.125*FA+0.125 CE + 0.125*SS+0.125*QO =

Ratios for Sample City: 0.25*3.75+0.25* 4.67+0.125*5+0. 125*4.50+0.125* 2.33+0.125*3.25=4.06

The creditworthiness and the indebtedness measurement ratios are given double the weight of the other four measurements, because they strongly influence the financial health and the creditworthiness of the city. It is also important, however, to account the other measurements because financial sustainability depends not only on the direct creditworthiness ratios but also on the sustainability of services, capital investments, and quality of operations. For instance, many municipalities cut expenditures on repair and maintenance, which may improve operating savings and creditworthiness ratios in the short term but will induce higher costs of operation and future repair and may undermine creditworthiness in the medium to long term. Likewise, a high level of spending on administration and labor indicates a substantial imbalance between the city's main functions (that is, services and the bureaucracy). Therefore, the low scores on the quality of operations have negative impacts on financial health and eventually on creditworthiness. The results of the sample city show low scores in service sustainability and quality of operation, moderate results in creditworthiness and indebtedness, and higher scores in capital investments and fiscal autonomy. The overall result of the financial scores is 4.06 (tables E.2 and E.3).

Table E.3 Scoring of Financial Ratios with Projections

	Scoring 5, 4, 3, 2	Scores	5-year average
Creditworthiness		3.75	
Operating savings before interests/ Current revenue	≥30%, ≥15%, ≥0%, <0%	3	14%
Net operating surplus/Current revenue	≥ 20%, ≥10%, ≥0%, <0%	4	12%
Investment balance before loan/Total revenue	≥ –15%, ≥ –20%, ≥ –25 %, ≥ –30%	4	–17%
Financing gap after loan proceeds/Total revenue	≥0%, ≥ –3%, ≥ –6%, < –6%	4	–4%
Indebtedness		4.7	
Debt outstanding/operating surplus (years)	≤ 10y, ≤15y, ≤20y, ≤25y	5	4

continued next page

	Scoring 5, 4, 3, 2	Scores	5-year average
Debt outstanding/Budget total	≤60%, ≤80%, ≤100%, ≤120%	5	39%
Debt service/Total current revenue	≤10%, ≤15%, ≤20%, ≤25%	5	4%
Operating margin/Interest payment (x)	≥15x, ≥10x, ≥5x, ≤5x	4	10
Borrowing/Current revenues	≤15%, ≤20%, ≤25%, ≤30%	4	17%
Debt outstanding/Total current revenue	<100%, <120%, <140%, 160%	5	52%
Fiscal autonomy		5	
Own (taxes + fees + unconditional grants)/Total Current revenue	>80%, >65%, >50%, <50%	5	0.94
Capital investment effort		4.5	
Capital investment expenditure/Total Current revenue	≥40%, ≥30%, ≥20%, ≤20%	5	50%
Capital investment expenditure/Total Expenditure	≥30%, ≥2 5%, ≥20%, ≤20%	5	36%
Current margin/Capital investment expenditure	≥30%, ≥25%, ≥20%, ≤20%	3	26%
Capital investments from earmarked grants/Total investment expenditures	≤50%, ≤70%, ≤90%, ≥90%	5	1%
Service sustainability		2.3	
Maintenance works expenditure/Operating expenditures	≥15 %, ≥10%, ≥5%, <5%	3	8%
Taxes collected/Taxes levied*	≥95 %, ≥80%, ≥70%, <70%	2	
Fees Collected/Fees billed*	≥95 %, ≥80%, ≥70%, <70%	2	
Quality of operations		3.8	
Salaries & wages/Operating expenditures	≤40%, ≤50%, ≤60%, ≥60%	5	19%
Number of municipal employees/1000 citizens	<25, <40,<60, <80, <100	5	22
Actual revenue/Planned revenue	± 5%, ±10%, ±15%, ±20% or more	5	98%
Arrears due/net cash (end of the year).	≤100%, ≤1 20%, ≤140%, >140%	2	0%
Financial resources (cash + cash-like)/Financial obligations (due liabilities + arrears)*	≥100%, ≥90%, ≥80%, <80%	2	
Average of total financial ratio scores		4.06	n.a.
Average of total qualitative scores		3.42	
Shadow credit rating score		3.23	

Note: *The city has no data on these two ratios; thus, a score of "2" should be added. n.a. = not applicable.

Calculating the Total Score and the SASCR

Calculating the final results of the SASCR requires two steps: (1) calculating the total score of qualitative and quantitative assessments and (2) applying a rating scale. The total score of the SASCR is a simple (arithmetic average) of the qualitative and quantitative summary scores. The rating scale presented in table E.4 has been established on the basis of international experiences and taking into account all the caveats of self-assessment mentioned before. We repeat that this is just one possible rating approach and there might be many similar or different, but still adequate, rating options.

The possible range of scores is between 5 and 2. The 5 has been retained as a single score for the "aaa" rate, which is extremely difficult if not impossible for a city to reach. The SASCR discourages scoring too liberally and presenting ratings to please city management and politicians. An "aaa" rating in the SASCR would not be a fair or accurate reflection of the financial health of a city in the developing world and would presumably be above the national sovereign rating, which rating agencies consider as an upper limit for subnational entities. A rating of "b" or better would signal good financial health and that the city could consider commencing a pro forma external credit rating.

The other rating brackets have been established in adjusting the total range. It is clear, however, that any SASCR rating score below "b" should be considered low and should encourage plans for improvements. It also means that a city with an SASCR rate in the "ccc" to "c" range should focus on medium-term improvement plans to increase scores and strengthen financial health and creditworthiness; it should not plan to spend money immediately for obtaining a pro forma external credit rating. A good credit rating is beneficial, but a bad formal credit rating would be counterproductive, a waste of money, or even harmful if published or leaked.

Should your SASCR scores conclude with a "d" rating, it is recommended that you consider that the SASCR is incomplete because of a severe shortage of data and information entered. Rather than naming the results as an SASCR at all, it is better to repeat the entire SASCR exercise right away or in the next fiscal year. Even in such a situation, however, the MFSA results, the SASCR results of the qualitative assessments, and especially the weaknesses explored may convey useful messages and valuable issues to be discussed, first in the finance department and then shared with the higher-level administration of your city.

On the basis of the financial projections, the financial ratios can be calculated for five years ahead to show the medium-term outlook of a city (table E.5).

The sample city's financial projections show remarkable but still moderate improvements in financial ratios (table 3.42) The financial ratios, however, are projected to remain in the range of the historical results, and do not support increase of the financial scores of the SASCR. The medium-term forecasts summarized in table E.5 show that the sample city is likely to remain in the "b" rating level during the projected five-year time period (See summary in table E.6). It may improve, however, provided

Table E.4 Shadow Credit Rating Scores

aaa	5
a	≥4.5
bbb	≥4.0
b	≥3.5
ccc	≥3.0
c	≥2.5
d	≥2.0

Table E.5 Scoring Financial Ratios with Medium-Term Projections

	Ratio scoring	Scoring 5, 4, 3, 2	Scores based on 5-year weighted averages		Past average	Future average
	Creditworthiness		3.75	4.25	5 year	5 year
89	Operating savings before interests/ Current revenue	≥30%, ≥15%, ≥0%, <0%	3	4	14%	15%
90	Net operating surplus/ Current revenue	≥20%, ≥10%, ≥0%, <0%	4	3	12%	6%
91	Investment balance before loan/Total revenue	≥ −15%, ≥ −20%, ≥ −25%, ≥ −30%	4	5	−17%	−8%
92	Financing gap after loan proceeds/Total revenue	≥0%, ≥ −3%, ≥ −6%, ≤ −6%	4	5	−4%	18%
	Indebtedness		4.7	4.7		
93	Debt outstanding/ operating surplus (years).	≤10y, ≤15y, ≤20y, ≤25y	5	5	4	4
94	Debt outstanding/ Budget total	≤60%, ≤80%, ≤100%, ≤120%	5	5	39%	59%
95	Debt service/Total current revenue	≤10%, ≤15%, ≤20%, ≤25%	5	5	4%	9%
96	Operating margin/ Interest payment (x)	≥15x, ≥10x, ≥5x, ≤5x	4	3	10	6
97	Borrowing/Current revenues	≤15%, ≤20%, ≤25%, ≤30%	4	5	17%	7%
98	Debt outstanding/ Total current revenue	<100%, <120%, <140%, 160%	5	5	52%	62%
	Fiscal autonomy		5	5		
99	Own (taxes + fees + unconditional grants)/ Total Current revenue	≥80%, ≥65%, ≥50%, ≤50%	5	5	0.94	0.99
	Capital investment effort		4.5	3.5		
100	Capital investment expenditure/ Total Current revenue	≥40%, ≥30%, ≥20%, ≤20%	5	2	50%	16%
101	Capital investment expenditure/ Total Expenditure	≥30%, ≥25%, ≥20%, ≤20%	5	2	36%	14%
102	Current margin/Capital investment expenditure	≥30%, ≥25%, ≥20%, ≤20%	3	5	26%	92%

continued next page

Ratio scoring	Scoring 5, 4, 3, 2	Scores based on 5-year weighted averages		Past average	Future average
103 Capital investments from earmarked grants/ Total investment expenditures	≤50%, ≤70%, ≤90%, >90%	5	5	1%	5%
Service sustainability		2.3	2.3		
104 Maintenance works expenditure/Operating expenditures	≥15%, ≥10%, ≥5%, <5%	3	3	8%	8%
105 Taxes collected/Taxes levied	≥95%, ≥80%, ≥70%, <70%	2	2		69%
106 Fees collected/Fees billed	≥95%, ≥80%, ≥70%, <70%	2	2		69%
Quality of operations		3.8	3.6		
107 Salaries & wages/ Operating expenditures	≤40%, ≤50%, ≤ 60%, >60%	5	5	19%	18%
108 Number of municipal employees/1,000 citizens	≥25, ≥40, ≥60, ≥80, ≥100	5	5	22	24
109 Actual revenue/Planned revenue	±5%, ±10%, ±15%, ±20% or more	5	4	98%	109%
110 Arrears due/Net cash (end of the year).	≤100%, ≤120%, ≤140%, >140%	2	2	0%	0%
111 Financial resources (cash + cash-like)/ Financial obligations (due liabilities + arrears)	≥100%, ≥90%, ≥80%, <80%	2	2		
Average of total financial ratio scores		4.06	4.03	n.a.	n.a.

Note: n.a. = not applicable.

that it successfully completes the actions listed in the action plan and accounted in the financial projections. A revision of the action plan and inclusion of measures particularly important for improving the results of the quantitative ratios are well justified and would further improve the SASCR results in the medium term.

The optimistic scenario of the financial projections plan indicates additional measures that could improve revenues, creditworthiness, and several SASCR factors. For instance, the planned establishment of reliable tax and fee databases would improve service sustainability, increase revenues, and elevate the scores on service sustainability factors. Some of these results are accounted for in the medium-term future scores.

In sum, the medium-term outlook of the sample city is stable and shows improvements in both the qualitative and quantitative scores. Data in the city profile further

Table E.6 Financial Management Scoring Summary

Scoring items	Scores past 5 years average	Scores 5 years ahead average
Intergovernmental relations	3.00	3.20
Planning, budgeting, and budget implementation	4.50	4.50
Financial management	3.60	4.00
Financial reporting and disclosure	3.00	4.00
Qualitative scores total	**3.42**	**3.78**
Creditworthiness	3.75	4.25
Indebtedness	4.67	4.67
Fiscal autonomy	5.00	5.00
Capital investment effort	4.50	3.50
Service sustainability	2.33	2.33
Quality of operations	3.80	3.60
Financial ratios total	**4.06**	**4.03**
Shadow credit rating total scores	**3.74**	**3.91**
Shadow credit rating sample city	b	b

reconfirm a good medium-term outlook, because growth of key industries in the city has been higher than national gross domestic product growth. Overall the projections suggest (table E.6) that the city may improve credit scores from 3.74 to 3.91, reaching a rating score of "bb" and moving closer to the "bbb" score that is ≥4.0. It is worth mentioning that this credit score is not an overarching objective of the SASCR. Instead the credit score just provides a sort of metric to improve understanding of the underlying factors and the signals toward potential improvements, which are the most significant results of this SASCR shadow credit rating.

Finally, it is worth mentioning that the sample city, in this case, is a well-managed city in Eastern Europe, and its results may not represent most cities in the developing world. Thus, users in less-developed countries should not be surprised if the SASCR results of their own city fall below the "b" range. As said, identifying the factors and inducing corrective measures are the most important results of a self-assessed shadow credit rating.

Glossary

This glossary summarizes the terms used in the MFSA modules. Many of these terms are used in various contexts such as banking, financial or capital markets, corporate finance, or general economics. This glossary, however, defines the terms only in the context of the municipalities and MFSA modules without explaining the broader context or broader meaning of the terms.

Accrual accounting: Accounting method that records revenues and expenses when they are incurred (that is, bill received), regardless of when the corresponding cash is exchanged (that is, bill paid). Under this method, the municipality accounts for expenses as bills are received and records revenues when taxes or services are billed (see also cash-based accounting, modified cash-based accounting, modified accrual accounting).

Action plan: A list of specific time-bound actions aimed at improving the performance of a municipality.

Adverse audit opinion: An auditor issues a disclaimer with adverse opinion if he or she has no confidence that a municipality's financial statements accurately reflect its true financial status because of misstatements found to be material and pervasive.

Aging list of debt: A detailed list of various debt instruments that reflects the date of debt procured, terms, and the amount of projected payments of interest and principal based on the loan agreement or bond contracts till maturity (final repayment). The payments of principal and interest for actual years may be somewhat different from projections because of subsequent changes or delayed or early repayments. The list indicates the *stock of outstanding debt* principals at a particular date, and the total *debt service*, as a sum of due or repaid principal and/or interest at a given period (year). See debt stock, debt service, debt maturity.

Amortization: Accounting for the depreciation in value of fixed assets (due to usage or obsolescence) as operational costs; also used to refer to gradual repayment of debt (for example, amortization of loan principal).

Annuity: Repayment of debt in equal installments, that is, when the sum of principal and interest is equal in each payment period (year).

Appropriation: Assignment of money for spending on specific purposes or budget lines with authorization of respective entities (for example, municipal departments) to spend the assigned money in a fiscal year. Appropriation is the term for the expenditure section of the annual budget (see budget).

Area-based property tax: Tax based on measured area (for example, square meter or square feet) of properties such as land or buildings (see also property tax, value-based property tax, market value–based property tax).

Arrears: Overdue debts, liabilities, or collectibles. The municipality's overdue debts, fees, charges, or bills to suppliers, creditors, taxes, or employees are arrears of the municipality. Arrears may refer to overdue collectibles, that is, arrears by citizens or legal entities with respect to the municipality such as overdue uncollected taxes, fees, charges, or debts (see also liabilities, overdue liabilities, tax arrears).

Assets: All tangible and intangible properties of a municipality including real property such as land, buildings, structures, equipment, cash, or receivables; also includes intangibles such as intellectual properties, rights of way, and so on.

Asset-based financing: Borrowing in the form of loans or selling debt by securing it with dedicated assets of a municipality (for example, fixed assets and revenue flows). It offers a debt financing option when a municipality is not otherwise creditworthy (see also land-based financing, credit enhancements).

Asset proceeds: Revenues or gains obtained from municipal assets, which include operating revenues like rents, charges, and levies on natural resource exploitation. Also includes capital revenues from divestiture of assets;

capital revenues ought to be used for funding capital investments or debt service in order to maintain the net wealth of the municipality. Asset sale revenues may be used to cover cost of operations only in emergency situations.

Asset transfers: Assets (whether fixed/physical or financial) transferred from the municipality to municipal entities or from the entities to the municipality (see subsidies and in-kind donations).

Audit: An independent examination of the financial statements, project studies, or financial projections from the perspective of completeness, correctness, and/or compliance.

Audited financial reports: A status given to a municipality's financial reports once they are audited, and accompanied by an audit letter with an audit statement issued by the auditor. The audit letter may include an audit statement with an unqualified, qualified, or adverse opinion.

Average rate of return (ARR): The ratio of average net earnings to average investment.

Balanced budget: A municipal budget or final account where all revenues are equal to all expenditures; more generally this refers to a budget that has no deficit but may show a positive balance. Good planning principles require a budget plan (planned budget) to be balanced; in contrast an actual (closing) budget ought to be balanced, too, but may show a positive or negative balance because of unforeseen movements in revenues and expenditures during the fiscal year (see also overall balance, closing balance, and budget reality ratio).

Balance sheet: A financial statement that summarizes the municipality's assets and liabilities at a point in time (typically end of fiscal year).

Municipalities that follow accrual accounting prepare balance sheets (some of which are limited to financial assets and liabilities), income statements, and cash-flow statements.

Bailout: Action by an owner or higher-level government entity to pay the obligations of a municipality or municipal entity in order to avoid formal bankruptcy or disruption of services.

Base year: A selected specific year for comparison of results in a series of years, for example, the first year of a five-year period.

Benchmark: A figure or ratio that serves as a reference point against which to measure financial or service performance on the basis of internationally accepted practices or ratios.

Betterment levies: Forms of taxes levied on land or property that has gained value because of public infrastructure investments. Betterment levies are calculated on the basis of investment cost of a specific public infrastructure (for example, Tokyo metro-rail) and allocated across beneficiaries according to estimated impacts, albeit sometimes collected somewhat arbitrarily (see development fee).

Betterment tax: See betterment levies.

Billing efficiency: The ratio of number of taxpayers billed to the number of taxpayers in the tax net.

Block grants: Grants from higher government tiers with some general provisions, for example, for development or for human services, but without specific rules and limits attached to ways and amounts of spending.

Bond: A security that represents the debt of the issuing municipality and a commitment to repay at a defined date (with interest paid annually or at maturity). The issuer receives the principal amount from the buyers who invest in the bonds. Bond financing is an alternative to loans (that is, borrowing from banks or other creditors). See also securities, general obligation bonds, revenue bonds.

Bond proceeds: The total amount of money collected by selling the bonds issued by a municipality. As opposed to loan proceeds, which may disburse over a period of years, bond proceeds are transferred to the municipal budget by selling the bonds over a short time period, and they may be deposited into a special account from which the investment will be financed gradually in subsequent months or years.

Bridge financing or bridge loan: Short-term loan that provides interim financing before long-term financing is put in place.

Budget plan, or opening budget: A financial plan that serves as an estimate of future expenditures and revenues adopted for one fiscal year (see also revised budget, closing budget, and final accounts).

Business license fee: A fee collected from business owners when a business license is granted or renewed; it can be a small administrative fee or a substantial charge collected annually. It is a form of tax if it is substantial (see business tax).

Business tax: A tax levied on business ownership according to the size or value of the business (as measured by net turnover or balance sheet), often levied under the designation of "business license fee."

CAPEX: See capital expenditure.

Capital appreciation: The increase in value of an asset over time (land, building, financial).

Capital budget: List and sum total of revenues generated and available for financing capital expenditures, including net savings, asset sales, capital grants, and debts. The expenditure side of the capital budget includes costs of capital investments (acquisition of land or buildings, construction of buildings, structures, infrastructure networks, and so on), capital grants to municipal entities, and repayment of debt principal (see also current budget, development budget, operating budget).

Capital cost: The cost of financing construction or equipment; the total one-off expenses of a project that may include cost of equipment, land, labor, material, energy and transactions.

Capital expenditure: Long-term expenditures spent for acquiring or developing fixed assets such as land, buildings, plants, and equipment that have substantial value and whose benefits will last over a period of more than one year (antonym: current or operating expenditures).

Capital gains tax: Tax levied on the basis of the value gained on capital or properties between acquisition and divestiture, assumed to be a result of improvements to nearby public infrastructure during this period.

Capital Improvement Plan: A medium-term (three-to-five-year) plan or program that incorporates capital investment priority projects and implementation timing; it identifies funding sources, including the municipal budget, specific grants or donations from public or private donors, and equity transfers from third parties (public utility companies, private investor partners).

Capital investment: The amount invested to develop or acquire fixed assets.

Capital investment costs: All costs required to make a project, asset, or service fully operational. These may include acquisition costs for land, building, or equipment; construction costs; and the costs of designing, managing, and/or monitoring the construction (see capital cost).

Capital investment plan: Capital improvement plan.

Capital market: Segment of the financial system; a market of tradeable debts, securities, and equities distinct from other segments such as banking or private exchange of debts.

Capitalized interest: Accrued interest that is not paid but is instead added to the principal amount of debt at the end of each interest payment period or by a specific action (see debt rollover).

Capital subsidies: Financial support to preferred entities often earmarked to specific investment projects without repayment obligation. Capital subsidies reduce the cost of services because the beneficiaries need only cover the cost of operation to remain financially sustainable and are therefore able to keep the service charges low; thus the end users/customers are the final beneficiaries of the capital subsidies. Municipalities often provide capital subsidies by fully financing and managing the construction of (expansion of) local service infrastructure and handing it over to public utility companies as an in-kind asset transfer.

Carryovers: Appropriations, encumbrances, or unspent grants and capital funds carried over from the current to the next fiscal year in final accounts and budget plans at the end of one fiscal year.

Cash balance: The stock of cash the municipality owns that is accessible in various bank accounts at a point of time; or the difference between the total cash inflows and outflows during a certain time period (such as a month or a year).

Cash-based accounting: A method of recording accounting transactions for revenues and expenses only when the corresponding cash is received or payments are made. A bill a municipality has received but not yet paid is not accounted for in the budget or financial statements; likewise, taxes or fees levied but not yet collected are not recorded. The vast majority of municipalities follow some version of cash-based accounting (see also accrual accounting, modified cash-based accounting, or modified accrual accounting).

Cash flow: Incoming and outgoing cash during a fiscal year or project cycle that eventually shows the difference between cash available at the beginning of a period and cash available at the end (see revenue flow).

Cash flow analysis: A procedure to segregate from various financial statements of a municipality the items that induce and represent cash in- or outflows and to include these in a dedicated cash flow statement. For instance, collection of taxes or payments for energy, machinery, or salaries are cash flow items; but amortization costs of assets do not represent cash outflow and therefore would not be part of the cash flow statements (see cash flow statement, cash-based accounting, balance sheet, income statement).

Cash flow statement: A financial statement that summarizes financial transactions that involved cash movement and thus shows how changes in the balance sheet and income accounts affect cash and cash-equivalents in the fields of operating, investing, and financing activities.

Cash-like securities: Bank accounts, marketable securities, commercial papers, treasury bills, and short-term government bonds with maturities of three months or less that can be easily transformed into cash by selling them.

Cash transfers received from municipal enterprises: Although municipal enterprises (MEs) or public utility companies (PUCs) are legally independent entities, the municipality as sole owner of MEs or PUCs may request and receive cash transfers from MEs or PUCs to fill a liquidity gap temporarily. Such cases may occur as formal loans or transfers from enterprise fund to general fund of the municipality, or may be obscured when the MEs/PUCs simply pay invoices for an event or services on behalf of the municipality.

CIP: Capital improvement plan or capital investment plan.

City unemployed population: People who are registered citizens of a city's jurisdiction and registered as unemployed on the basis of national employment registration systems and statistics, measured and published by the bureau of statistics or similar national entity.

City unemployment rate: The ratio of registered unemployed citizens to the city's active population based on the national population and employment registration system and statistics, measured and published by the bureau of statistics or similar national entity.

Closing budget: A municipal budget that reflects the actual volume of revenues and expenditures as of the end of the fiscal year;

this is why it is also known as an "actual budget: (see also actual budget, final accounts).

Co-financing: Joint financing by different entities such as municipalities, other government entities, and/or the private sector.

COFOG (classification of functions of governments): A widely accepted and used list with definitions of expenditures by function; adopted by the Organisation for Economic Co-operation and Development (OECD) and also published by the United Nations.

Collateral: An asset pledged as security to support a loan and secure creditors' recovery.

Commercial bank: A common bank that collects deposits and lends money that pays interest to a wide range of customers such as private persons or entities (antonyms: specialized banks, investment banks).

Commercial risk, or business risk: Risk born from uncertain and unpredictable market events during financing, construction, or operation of assets or while performing services.

Commission: A fee paid to an agent that performs some management functions; the commission is based on a percentage of the collected revenues (for example, taxes, fees) or the sales price.

Communal tax: Tax levied to cover the cost of communal services, often based on or attached to some characteristic (for example, size, value) of the properties, or electricity bills.

Community benefit agreements are voluntary contracts between developers and the community in a defined zone.

Community development facility (CDF): A modality of betterment levies when cities issue special levies based on land (size not value), not linked to specific development, and levied outside the property tax; cities in California often issue bonds backed by CDFs (see betterment levies).

Comparison ratios: Ratios that compare municipal performance to the national average, to international averages, or to other municipalities, comparing measures such as per capita revenues, per capita expenditures, per capita debts, or per capita investments.

Compound interest: Interest calculated on the initial principal plus on the accumulated interest of previous periods of a deposit or loan.

Concession: Right (of service or development) granted by a central or local government to a private entity for a period of time in exchange for a one-time or annual payment of concession fee.

Conditional grants: Grants provided to local governments with specific conditions on obtaining or spending attached.

Contingent liability: A liability that is uncertain either in amount or in timing until it occurs or crystallizes (for example, the guarantee the municipality issued to support its public utility company in repaying a loan). It becomes a direct financial liability if the company defaults and the municipality must step in and pay the interest or the unpaid principal. Thus, the value of this contingent liability decreases over time as the company repays the installments of the loan principal and interests.

Corporatized utility: A utility company owned by a municipality but structured and operating like a private or public corporate entity with independent legal status.

Cost-benefit analysis, benefit-cost analysis, or cost-effectiveness analysis: An analytical technique to support policy/business decisions by comparing the total financial and nonfinancial costs and total financial and nonfinancial benefits of proposed programs or policy actions based on the estimated net present value of alternatives (see also net present value, NPV, and internal rate of return).

Cost of capital: The rate of return that could have been earned by putting the same money into a different investment with equal risk. The yields of long-term bonds are often used as a reference rate to reflect the cost of capital, but a company or a municipality may use a higher rate if it is relevant on the basis of the assumed risks (see hurdle rate).

Cost of debt: The total cost of interest until maturity/repayment plus the cost of financial structuring required to obtain the debt.

Cost of financing: The cost of debt.

Coupon: The interest amount or annual rate of a bond attached physically or electronically to a bond certificate.

CPI (consumer price index): An index that measures changes in the level of prices of goods; it is calculated and published by the bureau of statistics using a selected list of products (consumer basket).

Creditor: Person or entity providing debt for a project or another entity (municipality) on purpose or in form of issuers of unpaid bills/claims (see lenders, forced creditor).

Credit rating agency: A company that analyzes creditworthiness and assigns credit ratings, which rate a debtor's ability to pay back debt by making timely interest payments and the estimated likelihood of default. The most notable rating agencies include Moody's, Standard & Poor's, and Fitch Ratings (see rating agency).

Credit risk: A risk that a counterpart in a financial transaction (debtor) fails to perform according to the terms and agreed conditions (also known as default risk).

Creditworthiness: An entity's current and future ability and inclination to honor debt obligations as agreed upon. It is usually measured according to the credit history, credit rating, and character of the entity.

Creditworthiness ratio: A municipality's creditworthiness is measured as a ratio of operating savings to current actual revenues, but also using the debt service coverage ratio; it reflects the municipality's capacity to borrow or service debts.

Current assets: Cash, cash-like securities, and other financial assets (for example, receivables, uncollected fees, taxes, and so on) that are expected to be converted to cash within a year.

Current budget: Budget that includes recurrent revenues (operating revenues and financial gains) and recurrent expenditures (labor, goods and services, administrative costs, and interest and financial costs paid) in a fiscal year. The term current budget is also used to refer to the budget of the current year that includes both operating and capital budgets (see budget plan).

Current expenditures, or recurrent expenditures: Expenditures on goods and services consumed within the current year, which need to be made recurrently to sustain administrative functions and deliver services; in contrast, spending money for investments is a nonrecurrent expenditure that can be postponed, reduced, or canceled if the finances appear to be insufficient (see also capital expenditures).

Current liabilities: Amounts due within 12 months to creditors, suppliers, contractors, workers, or other government entities.

Current margin/balance: The difference between the *total current (or recurrent) revenues* and *total current expenditures*. Current balance is also equal to the *operating balance/ margin* minus *nonoperating current expenditures,* such as interest payments, financing costs, or insurance premiums, because these are due and paid regardless of operation (see current revenues, current expenditures, operating margin/balance).

Current revenues, or recurrent revenues: Revenues a municipality receives on a recurring basis from higher government tiers and from collection of own taxes, fees, and charges (see also operating revenues, nonrecurrent revenues).

Debt: An obligation to pay cash to another entity under agreed terms and on an agreed schedule (see also liability).

Debt capacity: The total volume of debt a municipality can prudently acquire at a point in time given the net current revenues or assets available for debt service.

Debt maturity: The time period in which the debt is expected to be fully repaid (5 years, 10 years, and so on) based on the initial or actual (amended) debt agreements, terms, and conditions.

Debt rescheduling: Modifying the tenor/ maturity, interest rate, or other conditions of an existing debt agreement (see also loan rollover, debt restructuring).

Debt restructuring: An arrangement to replace an existing debt with a new one, typically one with longer maturity and/or that is of a different type (see also refinancing, debt rescheduling).

Debt service: The total amount of interest and principal payment, often measured and accounted as one year or one installment (see also debt amortization).

Debt service coverage ratio (DSCR): The ratio of cash available for debt servicing to interest, principal, and lease payments (the ratio of net operating income to debt service).

Debt service reserve fund (DSRF): An amount set aside or accumulated to ensure uninterrupted service of a debt in the future. Lenders may require municipalities or municipal entities to enhance loan security by establishing a debt service reserve fund (for example, set aside three installments of debt service in a special account accessible by the lender).

Debt stock (outstanding debt total): The total value of the principal of various debt instruments a municipality owes at a point in time (for example, end or beginning of a fiscal year); the stock includes the principal of short- and long-term loans a municipality borrowed and the face value of bonds a municipality issued/sold. The debt stock changes monthly/ yearly because of repayment of principal in installments, maturity (final payment) of some debts, or procurement of new debts (see aging list of debts).

Debt-to-equity ratio, or D/E ratio: The proportion of debt to equities in a balance sheet.

Default: Inability of a debtor municipality to service a debt's interest or principal or both, or failure to fulfill other agreed-upon legal and contractual obligations (for example paying contractors). In some countries a default triggers formal declaration of default or bankruptcy (Hungary, South Africa, and the United States). In most of the developing world, municipal defaults remain hidden, undeclared, and settled without formal rules; and overdue payment obligations keep accumulating (see also overdue liabilities, arrears, insolvency).

Default risk: The risk that reflects the likelihood that a borrower may default, that is, be unable or unwilling to serve the debt (see credit risk).

Deficit credit: An amount of money by which the total sum of expenditures and/or liabilities is greater than the available income and/or revenues in a fiscal year (see balanced budget). Municipalities should not adopt a budget plan with deficit (except in extreme circumstances such as financial restructuring), but the final account or closing budget may end with deficit because of unforeseen changes during the fiscal year or poor management of expenditures or revenues.

Delegated functions: Local service functions that the law assigns to higher government tiers, but that are provided by local government as agent and financed by conditional funding received from the higher government tier (see earmarked grants).

Depreciation: Reduction of an asset's value over time; the corresponding amortization for accounting, tax, or income calculation.

Developer exaction (or development fee): A charge cities collect from developers forcing them to contribute development of trunk infrastructure, because the city issues building permits only against these payments.

Development agreements: A tool to capture land value via voluntary contracts negotiated between cities and developers where developers promise to make large up-front investments on infrastructure if the city commits not to change land use and zoning regulations during the term of the agreement.

Development bank: A lending agency that is focused on financing development projects and assisting development by mobilizing financing for development.

Development fee (or land development fee): A tax collected from developers often during the permitting procedure to enforce contribution by the developer to the expansion of respective infrastructure (for example, water and sanitation, roads, and so on). It can be charged as a percent of investment costs or be somewhat arbitrarily negotiated. Revenues from development fees should be accounted for as development revenues and used for development and not for covering costs of operation.

Development fund/municipal fund: Specialized financial intermediary that exclusively supports municipalities or other local governments and entities and that, besides investment financing, often provides technical assistance in structuring financing and development projects.

Direct liability: An obligation to pay an amount of money under agreed/contracted conditions, for example, repayment of debt principal and interest or payment of a bill against delivered products or services such as electricity bill or contractors' bills (see also contingent liability).

Disclaimer: A formal statement that the issuer is not (legally) responsible for something; for example, an auditor is not responsible legally for the reliability of the municipality's financial reports because of limited obtainable information (see also auditor, qualified audit, unqualified audit).

Disbursement: Payout (by a bank) of funds/cash from the principal of an approved loan; for example, a municipality may withdraw 4 million from a 10 million loan in the first year of a project and 6 million in the second year. Or disbursement of funds from one to another government entity within the intergovernmental financial system.

Dividends: Distribution of cash to holders of stock or equity ownership stake based on the financial results of a financial year. Municipalities may receive dividends from public companies or joint ventures as cash transfers to the municipal budget.

Donations: Gifts provided to municipalities by natural or legal persons in the form of cash, services, or assets. Financial donations should be accounted for as external revenues, because they are obtained from entities outside the intergovernmental finance system.

DSCR: Debt service coverage ratio.

DSRF: Debt service reserve fund.

Due date: Date on which a payment of interest or principal, or a supplier bill, becomes payable.

Due diligence: A detailed and reasonable review of a borrower's overall position, management, and financial abilities.

Earmarked grants: Grants provided to local governments with conditions that they can be used only for a set specific purpose (for example, paying teachers' salaries, building a hospital ward, and so on) and with the exact amount set aside (unused amounts should be returned to the grantor). Earmarked grants are often provided to fund delegated functions (see delegated functions, conditional grants).

Earnings: Excess of revenue over all respective expenses for a given time (typically a year) in a project or venture.

Economic rate of return (ERR) (or economic internal rate of return [EIRR]): A project's rate of return after combining the direct financial returns and the monetized nonfinancial economic, environmental, and social costs and benefits; the maximum rate at which the project's net present value equals to zero (see also financial rate of return, FIR).

EIRR: Economic internal rate of return.

Encumbrance: An accounting commitment that reserves appropriated funds for a future expenditure related to unperformed contracts for goods or services. The total of all expenditures and encumbrances for a department or agency in a fiscal year, or for a capital project, may not exceed its total appropriation.

Equity: The total value of municipal properties minus the current liabilities. In accounting terms equity is the difference between the assets and liabilities on a municipality's balance sheet (if one is prepared).

Equity-based financing: Sale of an ownership interest to raise funds (see asset-based financing).

Escrow account: A special financial account for the temporary deposit of funds (inflow of money) before they are paid out according to agreed conditions (deed). Lenders to municipalities may demand an escrow account and that the fee revenues of a project or tax revenues are directly deposited to this account from which the debt service is performed monthly, after which only the excess amount is transferred to the regular accounts of the municipality.

Expenditures on delegated functions: Expenditures spent on functions that are assigned to higher government tiers, but provision is delegated to the municipality (such as primary education, primary health, or social protection). Delegated expenditures are typically financed from earmarked grants provided by the higher government with specific amounts and rules governing spending. Municipalities are allowed (or sometimes forced) to co-finance the delegated functions from their general revenues (like add a new classroom to a school or top up labor, electricity, or water expenditures, and so on if the earmarked grants received appear to be insufficient).

Explicit contingent liabilities: Liabilities that are contingent upon the occurrence of some events, stipulated by law, or committed explicitly in contracts with clear measurable timing and volume (which may also depend on the timing) that may become directly payable; also known as direct liability when some agreed foreseen event occurs. A municipality's guarantee issued/committed to support a debt of a municipal entity (water company) is a common example that becomes directly payable if the company fails to service a debt guaranteed by the municipality (see implicit contingent liability).

External revenues: Revenues or funds a municipality may incur from resources outside the fiscal intergovernmental finance stream (transfers or own revenues). These can be loans, bond proceeds, or private external donations and inflow of foreign investments.

Fiscal autonomy ratio: A ratio that reflects the sovereignty of a municipality in financial decisions on increasing revenues or saving costs, measured as a ratio of own revenues plus unconditional grants to current revenues.

Fiscal year (FY): A 12-month period designated as the operating year for accounting and budgeting purposes in a country. A fiscal year can start on different dates, such as January 1, March 20, or July 1, depending upon the country.

Final account: Financial statement (budget report) prepared to summarize the actual revenues and actual expenditures at the end of a fiscal year (see also closing budget or actual budget).

Financial internal rate of return (FIRR): See internal rate of return.

Financial management assessment (FMA): Assessment of the factors and quality of the financial management system and performance of a municipality using specific qualitative indicators and scores. It is a module of the Municipal Finances Self-Assessment that includes assessment of intergovernmental relations; planning, budgeting, and budget implementation; the financial management framework and practices; and the financial reporting, disclosure, and transparency assessment (see also MFSA, MFA, PEFA).

Financial projection: Medium-term projection of revenues, expenditures, or balances, projected with statistical tools using historical figures and trends, while also taking into account specific assumptions or expected future events that divert results from the historical trends.

Financial ratios: Ratios calculated from the financial reports of the municipality such as creditworthiness ratios (ratio of operating savings / current revenues, net savings / current revenues, cash in hand / liabilities); indebtedness ratios (ratio of outstanding debt / operating balance, debt service / current revenues); and fiscal autonomy (own revenues plus unconditional grants / current revenues).

Financial statements: Statements a municipality prepares to reflect and declare its financial position periodically and at the end of the fiscal year; they depend on the accounting system applied, but may include a balance sheet, income statement, and cash flow statement, or just a final account or closing budget (see also balance sheet, income statement, cash flow statement, final account).

Financing gap before loan proceeds: The amount of money required to cover the planned development expenditures from loan proceeds or other forms of external financing; this gap is the difference between the amount of planned development expenditures and the available financing from net savings, own capital revenues, and cash reserves from previous years, and investment grants received.

Financing requirement: The amount of money required to cover the cost of planned capital expenditures after covering all current expenditures; financing sources include net margin, own capital revenues, investment grants received, and loan proceeds.

FIRR: Financial internal rate of return.

Fixed rate: An interest rate fixed for a defined time period of a loan typically till maturity.

Fixed rate loan: A loan with a fixed interest rate for the life of the loan till repayment.

Floating interest rate: An interest rate that fluctuates during the loan term in accordance with an agreed-upon benchmark index and/or formula (for example, central bank rate or Treasury bill rates).

FMA (financial management assessment): A module in the Municipal Finances Self-Assessment.

FMIS: Financial management information system is a methodology and tools a municipality uses to fulfill financial management functions. The FMIS term may be used to reflect that the various tools or functions (payroll, revenues, expenditures and so on) are not organized into one integrated system. In short, all kinds of information systems municipalities use can be named as FMIS (see IFMIS, IFMS).

Forced creditors: Entities or persons who issued bills or other forms of claims and forced by the municipality or its entity to become unwilling creditor by postponing due and undisputed payments. (see creditors)

Foreign exchange rate (FX rate): A price at which the currency of a country can be bought with or exchanged for the currency of another country.

Foreign exchange risk: A risk that the movement of the FX rate substantially affects a project's costs, revenues, or debt service.

Forex (FX): Foreign exchange.

Full-fledged guarantee: A guarantee whereby a guarantor commits to pay the full amount of principal and interest if the supported debtor defaults and the guarantee is called (see guarantee called, partial risk guarantee, partial credit guarantee).

Fund: A sum of money set aside for a specific purpose with specific rules regulated by law or by the donor entity. For example, an education fund, road fund, social welfare fund in a municipality, or private trust fund to support disabled students (see trust fund).

Fund accounting: An accounting system in which the revenues and expenditures are structured by specific activities or functions into funds with special regulations and limitations (health fund, education fund, road fund, and general fund in a municipality). Fund accounting is a common practice by U.S. local governments that supports accountability.

Future value: The value of a specific investment after a specified period at a certain interest rate.

FX rate: See foreign exchange rate.

FX risk: See foreign exchange risk.

General contractor: A contractor who takes full responsibility for completion of a project with full management competency; he/she remains the key contact of the municipality even if subcontracts are part of the construction or procurement activities.

General fund: In fund accounting, municipalities use the general fund to cover expenditures of general administration or general functions, as opposed to special-purpose funds that are dedicated to special functions (for example, health or education fund). See fund accounting.

Geographic information system (GIS): A computer system for capturing, storing, checking, and displaying data related to positions on the Earth's surface. GIS is also used to display and identify properties in a municipal jurisdiction, municipal service networks, and structures for planning, development, or taxation purposes.

General obligation bonds: Bonds issued with the obligation to repay from the general budget of the municipality; thus, they are backed by the taxing and other revenue-collecting power of the municipality without pledging any specific project or revenue source for repayment (see also GO bonds and revenue bonds).

GIS: Geographic information system.

GO bonds: See general obligation bonds.

Grants: Grants are transfers for which no repayment is required; often used interchangeably with the term "transfers," and in this broad sense all transfers from higher to local governments are grants. In the narrower sense grants are parts of the transfers from higher to local governments that are provided in addition to shared taxes, which are considered joint revenues or some as own revenues of the local governments (see also transfers, conditional grants, earmarked grants, unconditional grants).

Gross (operating) margin: The difference between recurrent revenues from operation and direct cost of operation (see also operating margin).

Guarantee: Commitment to fulfill the obligations of a third party in the event of default (a municipality may issue a guarantee to support a debt of a municipal company); it could be a full-fledged financial guarantee or a partial one with limited provisions either in time, amount, or instrument (for example, to support interest payment only).

Guarantees called: Guarantees that become a payment obligation of a municipality because of the default of the supported project or entity. Guarantees remain contingent liabilities until or unless they are called and crystallized, because contracts assume that the debtor will serve the debt in a timely manner, but there is a risk of default in terms of timing and/or payment amount (see also full-fledged guarantee, partial risk guarantee, partial credit guarantee, contingent liabilities).

Guarantor: A party that guarantees repayment or performance of covenants.

Hurdle rate: Minimum acceptable rate of return on an investment defined by an entity or an evaluator; often used to calculate net present value of a project.

Idiosyncratic credit risk assessment: Assessment of credit risks for an entity or cluster of entities (such as municipalities) to explore specific risks and risk profiles uniquely and particularly relevant to such entities (see credit risk, risk assessment, credit rating).

IFMIS: Integrated financial management information system is a methodology and integrated software a municipality uses for fulfilling the financial management functions. (see FMS, IFMS).

IFMS: Financial management information system; synonym of IFMIS.

Implicit contingent liabilities: Liabilities that are contingent upon the occurrence of some events but are measurable neither by volume/size nor in terms of timing. Implicit contingent liabilities are born from political, moral, or social obligations or from environmental events. Examples include the municipality's obligation to support citizens after environmental disasters, flood, and fire; to support the poorest of the poor; or to build a bridge a winning politician had promised. Unlike explicit contingent liabilities, implicit contingent liabilities cannot be estimated in advance, and thus they are not accounted in a balance sheet (see explicit contingent liabilities).

Income statement: A report of a municipality's revenues and expenditures and the resulting net income for a period such as a fiscal year (see profit and loss account for municipal companies).

Indebtedness ratios: Ratios that reflect the ability of a municipality to clear its debts from operating surplus, such as outstanding debt/operating balance, outstanding debt/total budget, and debt service/current revenues.

Inflows: All kinds of revenues, incomes, or financial proceeds that are accounted for in the budget of a municipality, such as taxes, fees, charges, transfers from other government entities, interests received, proceeds from sale or lease of assets, legal gains, loan proceeds, security deposits, and so on. In contrast, inflows do not include the value of fixed assets received as in-kind contributions from other government entities or donors (land, buildings, networks, structures, equipment) if those do not imply financial transactions. In-kind transfers affect the balance sheet, but not the budget, cash flow, or income statements of municipalities (see financial transfers, in-kind donations).

Inheritance tax: A tax levied on the property of a person who has died and that is due to be paid by the persons who inherit the property or assets.

Initial budget plan: A budget plan adopted before or at the beginning of a fiscal year as a first official and approved budget of the respective year; it is binding and can only be changed by formal approval of a revised budget (see also revised budget, closing budget, final accounts).

In-kind donations: Donations of assets (land, structures, or buildings) to municipal entities, including cases when a municipality finances from the budget expansion of service infrastructure (for example, water, road, or school building) and transfers the constructed assets to the entities (for example, public utility companies, schools, and health centers) in the form of an asset transfer without repayment obligations (see also asset transfer, capital subsidies). A municipality may receive in-kind donations from private or legal persons who may donate a building, land, park, sculpture, or vehicle.

Insolvency: A situation when a municipality (or other municipal entity) is unable to service its debts or other liabilities (for example, it is unable to pay contractors' or suppliers' bills on time). Solutions of insolvencies may include legal procedures or grants from higher government (see also municipal bankruptcy, debt restructuring, bailout, ad hoc grants).

Insolvency status: A legal status of an entity (for example, municipality or municipal company) that is declared or recognized as insolvent. Insolvency status aims to help the debtor in restructuring operations and debts in order to stabilize finances and maintain operations or services under controlled and agreed terms.

Intangible assets: Assets that have no tangible forms, such as good will, patents, rights of way, permissions, and ownership share/bond premiums.

Interest: Cash amount paid by borrowers to lenders for the use of money, expressed in percentage terms.

Interest rate: A percentage of the principal amount expressed as an annual rate.

Intergovernmental revenues: Funds/money/transfers municipalities receive from federal, state, or other government entities in the form of grants, shared taxes, reimbursements, or payments instead of taxes.

Intergovernmental system: A network and hierarchic system of governing entities (tiers) at the national, provincial, regional, and local level.

Intergovernmental finance system: A system of financial arrangements across various tiers of government entities that enables and supports ability at each level to finance the mandated responsibilities and services.

Internal rate of return (IRR): The interest rate at which the net present value of all the cash flows (both positive and negative) from a project or investment equals to zero. Internal rate of return is used to evaluate the attractiveness of a project or investment or to compare various alternatives.

Investment balance: The difference between the capital expenditures and the available financing sources (net balance plus own capital revenues, plus investment grants and donations) without loan proceeds taken into account.

Investment bank: Specialized bank that mobilizes funding and financial services for projects and investments (see also development bank).

Investment grants: Grants to local government provided for capital investments with or without specific conditions for use (see unconditional grants, conditional grants).

IRR: Internal rate of return.

Joint venture: Jointly owned corporation and arrangement between two or more parties for joint operation of a company or other entity, which shares the net income according to an agreed-upon formula which is often the ownership shares.

Jurisdiction: A geographic area defined by law within which the appointed administration or elected local government is the ruling local authority with administrative and legislative power (see intergovernmental systems, local administration).

Labor cost: Wages or salaries paid to employees and contractual workers, plus the cost of other employee benefits and payroll taxes paid by the municipality.

Land development fee: A fee local governments charge developers in order to finance a portion of the services required for proper functioning of the planned development; the fee is often regulated, published, and calculated as a percentage of development cost, or set ad hoc by negotiations in some developing countries.

Land value capture (LVC): also known as land-based financing, refers to a group of instruments that are used to tap into the private gains of land owners, developers, or the general community that resulted in public infrastructure development or in smart strategic planning or zoning of a city (see betterment levies, development fees, contributions).

Lenders: Persons or entities providing debt for a project or another entity (municipality). See creditors.

Lending arrangement: A legal document that includes the terms and conditions for lending and financing.

Lessee: User who obtains rights to use specific assets for a set time and under agreed conditions and pays rentals or lease fees to the owner (lessor).

Lessor: An owner of assets who hands over their use to a lessee for an agreed time period and under an agreed use and price arrangement.

Liability: An obligation to pay an amount of money or perform a service under agreed or assumed conditions set by law or defined and agreed in contracts.

Liabilities with respect to national government entities: Liabilities a municipality/city is obliged to pay by law (for example, to national social or health insurance authorities) also known as statutory deductions, taxes due to national government, or fees and charges against services received from national government entities or state corporations (for example, electricity bills to the national electricity supplier).

Lien: A legal security interest registered on an asset in national cadasters.

Life cycle: Time period and stages of an asset from procurement/construction through repair, maintenance, refurbishment during useful life, and then final disposal.

Life cycle asset management: A core process of asset management whereby all management decisions are evaluated and alternatives compared in the context of the entire life cycle; these include systematic scheduled maintenance as well as timely repair and refurbishment, which are performed in order to reduce the total life cycle costs and maintain the economic value of the asset.

Life cycle costing: Accounting for the present value of the costs of an asset—actual and projected—for the entire life cycle.

Line-item budget: A budget or financial statement where the individual financial lines are grouped by departments or cost centers (see also program budgeting, performance budgeting).

Line of credit: A bank's commitment to a borrower to extend a series of credits up to a specific maximum amount under agreed terms and conditions; thus, the borrower can withdraw portions of the credit as a unilateral action, without seeking permits or approval of the lender.

Liquidity: The ability to serve a debt or pay any financial obligation due; beyond cash on hand, it may include the ability to exchange assets for cash or reschedule liabilities (see also current assets, solvency).

Loan proceeds: The amount disbursed to a municipality from a loan (under a loan agreement) in a particular time period such as a fiscal year. Development loans are often disbursed gradually as the construction of assets progresses; for example, a municipality may withdraw 7 million from a 20 million loan in the first year. In cash accounting the line item "Loans" should indicate the disbursed volume (proceeds) in a year rather than the contracted total principal of a loan (see bond proceeds).

Loan repayment: The amount of principal and interest due or repaid in a certain period of time like a fiscal year; repayment of principal is often accounted for as a capital expenditure, whereas interest costs are accounted for as current expenditures (see also debt service).

Local administration: Single administrative entity granted with ruling administrative powers of self-government by appointment or by popular votes.

Local currency: The official currency of a country.

Local fees and charges: Fees and charges assigned to be levied, managed, and collected by local governments, including licenses, permits, user charges for urban services, stamp duties, and local development fees.

Local service tax: A tax levied on some self-employed professionals or persons who hold jobs.

Local taxes: Taxes assigned to be levied, managed, and collected by local governments, which may delegate or contract out some of these functions (like collection). The most common local taxes include property tax, business tax, hotel tax, local service tax, communal tax, or betterment levies.

Long-term debt: Debt (bank loan) with maturity of five years or more.

Maintenance: Routine or periodic repair and maintenance of assets in order to ensure sustainable use until the end of its regular operating time period without changing the capacity or quality of the asset; that is, without major refurbishment or replacement of main parts that would increase value or extend useful life (see O&M, R&M).

Maintenance cost: Operating costs spent for routine maintenance of assets (as opposed to major refurbishment or expansion, which would constitute investment or development expenditures).

Maintenance expenditures: See maintenance cost.

Management contract: When a municipality hands over assets and services to a private company or other entity for full management of operations following agreed performance benchmarks and for a fee paid by the municipality.

Market risks: Risks emerging from market factors and movements beyond the control of the municipality or contractual parties that may impact costs, sales, or revenues.

Market value: The price an asset or property could be sold for on the market by a willing seller to a willing buyer under free market conditions.

Maturity: The date or time period upon or by which full repayment of a debt becomes due.

Medium term: Generally denotes two to five years.

MFSA: Municipal Finances Self-Assessment.

Modified accrual accounting: An accounting method that is midway between and mixes cash and accrual principles. In modified accrual accounting revenues are accounted for in the period when they are collected, but expenditures are accounted for in the period the corresponding liability is incurred (bill received).

In fact, most municipalities follow modified accrual accounting rather than full accrual accounting (see also accrual accounting, cash-based accounting, modified cash-based accounting).

Modified cash-based accounting: See modified accrual accounting, although there might be minor differences in the detailed rules like accounting for large cash outflows for invested assets.

Mortgage: A pledge or assignment of security of a particular property for payment of debt or for performance of other obligations.

Municipal bankruptcy: A legal status of a municipality, recognized in only a few countries, including Hungary, South Africa, and the United States (chapter 9 procedure); it aims to help the debtor in restructuring operations and debts in order to stabilize finances while maintaining operation or services under controlled and agreed-upon terms (see insolvency, municipal insolvency, debt restructuring).

Municipal enterprises (MEs), or public utility companies (PUCs): Legally independent often incorporated entities owned fully or in majority by the local governments.

Municipal financial improvement plan: A list of specific time-bound actions aimed at improving the financial performance of a municipality (see action plan).

Municipal Finances Self-Assessment (MFSA): A methodology and procedure to assess the financial health of municipalities using a self-paced approach that includes six modules: historical analysis, financial projections, ratio analysis, financial management qualitative assessment, action plan, and self-assessed shadow credit rating (SASCR) with qualitative and quantitative assessments.

Municipal insolvency: A situation and/or status when a municipality is unable to service its debts or other financial liabilities such as paying suppliers or contractors (see municipal bankruptcy, insolvency).

Negative pledge: The borrower's commitment not to pledge any of its assets as security and/or not to incur further debts until the end of an agreed-upon time period (usually maturity of a debt supported by this negative pledge).

Net income: Operating cash flow minus (overhead + depreciation).

Net margin: Gross margin minus debt payment expenditures, that is, current revenues minus operating expenditures minus debt payment.

Net operating surplus, or net margin: The amount of revenue net of operating expenditures, debt service, and other recurrent nonoperating expenses (legal fees, insurance premiums paid, cost of financial structuring).

Net present value (NPV): The difference between the discounted cash inflows and outflows of a project at a set discount rate in a set time period; a profitable project should show positive NPV (see also hurdle rate, cost of capital).

Net saving: See net operating surplus.

Net wealth, or net worth: A municipality's net wealth is estimated as the value of total assets minus total liabilities.

Nonrecourse debt: A loan secured exclusively by a project's cash flow as pledged collateral; thus, the lender has no recourse to other sources of revenue or other municipal assets in the case of a default.

NPV: Net present value.

O&M: Operation and maintenance.

Off-balance sheet liabilities: Obligations that do not need to be accounted for in municipal budgets or balance sheets such as costs and revenues of a ring-fenced project financing.

Off-budget entities: Legally independent entities with management, operations, balance sheet, and finances fully separated from the municipal budget, although often owned fully or dominantly by the municipality; these may include public utility companies as well as sport, culture, or commercial entities under municipal ownership. Municipalities often support their entities by means of cash transfers or in-kind subsidies (see transfers to municipal entities, in-kind asset transfers).

Operation and maintenance (O&M) cost: The cost of operating an asset such as a plant or service system and covering ongoing expenses such as labor, energy, repairs, and routine maintenance.

O&M expenditures: Incurred costs for operating an asset such as a plant or service system. This is also a name of an accounting line used to account such expenditures from all kinds of assets.

Operating budget: List and total sum of revenues gained from operations and expenditures (planned or spent) on operating and maintenance in a year (see also current budget, capital budget).

Operating cash flow: A financial statement that summarizes a project's net cash revenues generated by a project's operation (see also cash inflow).

Operating margin: The difference between the current revenues and the operating expenditures (see also gross margin, net margin).

Operating risks: Risks related to market factors and management components of the project that have an impact on project's output, revenues, or profitability.

Operating surplus: Operating revenues minus operating expenditures (see also gross margin).

Operating transfers: Transfers from higher government tiers provided for general operating expenditures, which may come with or without conditions for spending (see also unconditional grants or transfers, conditional transfers, earmarked grants).

Operator: A person or entity that undertakes the operation and maintenance of a plant, system, or equipment for a fee or salary.

OPEX: Operating expenditures costs and expenses incurred to cover municipal administration, ensure services, and maintain assets (antonym: CAPEX).

Outflow: The amount of money spent/flowing out of the municipal budget for all kinds of forms and all kinds of reasons—for example, costs of goods or services, purchase of assets, fees, charges, penalties, taxes, grants, and donations or transfers to public utility companies or other government tiers like city districts or wards (see expenditures, inflow, transfers).

Outsourcing: Assigning services or operations to an external person or entity (usually private), such as simple janitorial services, solid waste collection, public transport, construction, or repair of assets.

Outstanding loan: Unpaid portion of a debt at a point in time that may include accrued interest (see also stock of debt).

Overall closing balance, or budget balance: Difference between the total revenues (current and capital revenues, grants, savings from previous years, and loan proceeds disbursed in a year) and the total current and capital expenditures. In budget plans the balance should be zero or positive; in real life deficit may occur because of unexpected changes in revenues and/or expenditures (for example, increased energy prices, disasters, or mismanagement of revenues and/or expenditures).

Overdraft: Deficit on an account caused by drawing more money than the account holds; it is often based on an agreement between a bank and a municipality.

Overdraft agreement: Arrangement that allows account holders (a municipality) to withdraw money up to a certain agreed amount that is beyond and above the zero balance of its account, and thus to temporarily maintain a negative balance and obtain a short-term loan.

Overdue: A term that means "behind schedule"; a bill, charge, tax, or other liability that remains unpaid beyond the legally defined or regulated due date (for example, 45, 60, or 90 days after receiving a bill).

Own expenditures: Expenditures spent to cover administrative and service functions or activities assigned to a municipality by law; these expenditures include operational and recurrent as well as development and capital investment expenditures (see also expenditure assignment, delegated expenditures, earmarked expenditures).

Own tax revenues: Tax revenues levied and collected by local governments or third parties under collection agreements (signed with national entities or even private collectors); the shared taxes can be considered as own revenues if the shared amount is returned to the source jurisdiction according to the collection; in contrast, the shared tax is a grant if any allocation formula is used.

Partnership: An arrangement when two or more parties agree to jointly undertake production or services through joint investment financing and sharing of both risks and net revenues.

Payback period: A period (in years) during which a loan or initial investment recovers.

Payroll expenditures: Salaries and wages, employment benefits, and taxes (see labor expenditures).

PEFA: Public Expenditure and Financial Accountability Assessment.

PEFA guidelines: Guidelines for commencing and completing PEFA, issued by the PEFA Secretariat.

PEFA Secretariat: A multidonor agency supported by the European Commission, International Monetary Fund, World Bank, and several bilateral agencies; it issues guidelines for commencing and implementing PEFA.

Performance-based budgeting: A budgeting practice that links the inputs and outputs of municipal entities or services to set performance indicators in order to help measure budget execution performance (see also program budgeting).

Performance ratios: Financial or other ratios that reflect the performance of a municipality such as the service sustainability ratio (ratio of capital investments to current expenditures; ratio of maintenance expenditures to operating expenditures), labor efficiency (ratio of salaries to total operating expenditures; ratio of number of municipal employees to population), budget reliability (ratio of the actual to planned revenues or expenditures), collection efficiency (ratio of billed to collected taxes/fees; ratio of arrears [uncollected taxes, fees] to total budget).

Political risk: Risk emerging from political disturbances such as war, terrorism, currency inconvertibility, expropriation, nongovernmental activities, and so on (see also country risk).

Present value: The present value of a future payment or income calculated by discounting the projected amount with a set discount rate (cost of capital or hurdle rate).

Principal, or loan principal: The original total amount loaned, upon which interest payments are based and on which interest accrues. A principal may refer to the total amount remaining on a loan.

Principal repayment: The amount of money the borrower repays to amortize the principal amount.

Priority Investment Program (PIP): Detailed explanation of priority investment plans or projects with supporting arguments, data, and figures published in the form of a small book or brochure. Some municipalities may adopt such a PIP formally and publish it after public scrutiny; others draft and name the program as a PIP without formal approval or publication. Latter PIPs could be as simple as a very short list of projects drafted without a detailed selection process and approval (see CIP).

Priority maintenance program: A list of major maintenance actions planned in the medium term, with or without detailed analysis and explanation.

Proceeds from domestic loans and bonds: Inflow of cash or cash equivalents to the city budget as a form of earning or income from disbursing portions of a domestic loan or selling bonds.

Proceeds from foreign borrowing: Inflow of cash or cash equivalents to the city budget as a form of earning or income from disbursing portions of foreign loan or selling bonds abroad. Proceeds from foreign loans borrowed by national government and on-lent to local governments are domestic loans if the national government/treasury takes up the foreign exchange risk.

Proceeds from sale of assets: Revenues, income, or all kinds of money inflow to the budget in exchange for sale or lease of assets (for example, selling land; leasing out office spaces; selling vehicles, plants, or equipment).

Procurement: A process by which a municipality procures assets, debt, or inventories; it could be an adopted principle and procedure aiming to obtain the best available quality at the least cost.

Program budgeting: Budgeting practices where the financial items are grouped first by program and then by subject with or without performance measurements (see also performance budgeting, line-item budgeting).

PPP: Public–private partnership.

Project: A package of actions required to expand municipal assets or services or refurbish assets, including planning, designing, financing, constructing, or procuring assets.

Project financing: A financing arrangement where the repayment of the debt/loan is secured primarily by the project's cash flow and the project's assets, rights, and interests (see also recourse financing, nonrecourse financing).

Property tax: A tax levied on the basis of immovable properties (houses, land) to cover general expenditures of the local government; the base on which the tax is calculated can be the market value, rental value, or area of the property, or an estimated flat rate.

Property transfer tax: See TTIP.

Public Expenditure and Financial Accountability Assessment (PEFA): Methodology to assess the quality of the public financial management framework and practices of a country or a municipality (see also PEFA, financial management assessment, FMA, PEFA guidelines).

Public–private partnership (PPP): An arrangement whereby public entities (municipalities) engage in partnership with private entities to develop and/or operate assets, aiming to pass through the corresponding commercial and management risks to the private partner in exchange for a fee or shared income. In contrast, outsourcing such as hiring a firm to supply material, to refurbish an office building, or to repair a truck is not a PPP (see also outsourcing).

Public utility companies (PUCs), or municipal enterprises (MEs): Legally independent, often incorporated entities owned fully or in majority by local governments.

Qualified audit opinion: The auditor issues a disclaimer with qualified opinion if the municipality provided a limited scope of information and/or deviated from generally accepted accounting principles.

Qualitative scores: The scoring of the qualitative assessment of the financial and accountability framework and practices of a municipality in the self-assessed shadow credit rating (SASCR), based on the current situation and projected improvements five years out (see also SASCR, PEFA, quantitative scores).

Quantitative scores: The scoring of the financial and performance abilities of a municipality based on weighted averages of the relevant ratios, using aggregated data from the past five years as well as five-year financial projections of future ratios, calculated in line with rating agencies' practices; quantitative scores are established from ratios on creditworthiness, indebtedness, fiscal autonomy, capital investment efforts, service sustainability, and quality of operations (see also SASCR, qualitative scores).

Rating agency: See credit rating agency.

Ratio analysis: A procedure to calculate ratios from the municipal financial or other reports and analyze the status or financial health of a municipality by comparing the ratios to generally accepted benchmark ratios. Ratio analysis is a powerful tool to interpret and analyze the status of a municipality in a quick and simple format (see also ratios, financial ratios, performance ratios, comparison ratios, credit rating).

Ratios: The generally accepted ratios are used by rating agencies, financial institutions, and

insurance companies or municipalities themselves to measure municipal performance. They can be clustered into stock, flow, or comparison ratios, or financial, performance, or comparison ratios.

Real estate tax: See property tax.

Reallocation of appropriation: Transfer of unencumbered appropriations from one municipal entity, budget line, or fund to another entity, budget line, or fund.

Recourse: Financing arrangement when the lender has power to access cash or securities from other sponsors in case the project in question does not generate sufficient revenues to service the debt.

Refinancing: Repaying existing debt with a new loan to obtain better terms, lengthen maturity, or capitalize overdue accrued interests (see also debt rollover and debt rescheduling).

Rental value: One possible value base upon which to levy property taxes; calculated using market evidence that indicates the amount of money a willing renter/lessee would pay for renting/leasing the property to a willing lessor/owner under free market conditions.

Reserve account: A special account to hold cash or letters of credit to secure uninterrupted debt service in support of a loan/debt.

Repair and maintenance (R&M): The costs or expenditures planned or spent for repairing or maintaining an asset (such as plant, service system, school building). R&M is part of operation and maintenance, but excludes expenditures spent for operation such as labor, energy, water and sanitation and so on.

Revenues: Municipal revenues include transfers from higher levels of government (federal, state, or provincial); own-source revenues from taxes, service fees, and charges, and asset proceeds; and external funds like loans (see also current revenues, capital revenues, external revenues).

Revenue bonds: Municipal bonds issued with repayment commitment from revenues of a specific (revenue generating) project or service and without backing repayment from the general budget of the municipality—that is, without general obligation (see also ring-fenced project financing, GO bonds).

Revenue expenditures, or operating and maintenance expenditures: Expenditures incurred on fixed assets that are aimed at maintaining (rather than enhancing) the useful life or earning capacity; but also, this is an amount that is spent for an expense that will be matched immediately with the revenues reported on the current period's income statement of the assets such as costs of repair, maintenance, repainting, or renewal expenses. This term is used to make distinction between capital and revenue expenses incurred on assets, and to classify and account repair and maintenance expenses as *revenue expenses* (see also repair and maintenance, R&M, operation and maintenance, O&M expenditures).

Revenue-generating projects: Investment projects whereby municipalities may invest in commercial activities that are beyond municipal mandated services or functions; they do these projects purely in order to generate revenue for the budget (albeit they may incur losses instead of revenues).

Revised budget, or amended budget: A budget plan that has been revised and approved by the council, typically at mid-fiscal year, but it can be done at any time of the fiscal year in response to substantial unforeseen changes in planned revenues or expenditures (see also budget plan, initial budget plan).

Ring-fenced project financing: Financing arrangement whereby a municipal project is separated from the general assets of the municipality and financed as a closed independent entity, regardless of whether it is a legally independent company or just a selected regular asset of the municipality. Ring-fenced project financing carves out both the respective assets, revenues, and the finances from the municipal budget for risk management purposes and provides higher security for the creditors, which in turn lowers the interest rate for the municipality.

Risk premium: An additional (higher) amount of interest rate that lenders or investors require from municipalities because of identified or assumed risks above and beyond the generally assumed market risks; the main incremental risks assumed could include political, regulatory, or financial.

Royalty: A share of revenue or fee paid to the central and/or local government by a concessionaire under a concession or license agreement on mining, service provision, land use, and so on (see concession).

SASCR: Self-assessed shadow credit rating.

Secondary market: A market of bonds or other securities traded among investors after the initial sale of the security by the issuer.

Secured creditor: A creditor who has a secured debt, meaning a debt backed by a pledge of assets or cash that is secured by the debtor or a third party.

Secured debt: Debt secured by assets or specific rights that are unconditionally accessible to the lender in the event of debtor's default.

Securities: Tradable financial papers (bonds, stocks, bank notes, debentures) that represent asset ownership without possession and are freely tradeable (see bonds, stocks, shares).

Self-assessed shadow credit rating (SASCR): A methodology and procedure for municipalities to complete a shadow credit rating in a self-paced manner; it combines scoring of a qualitative assessment based on PEFA indicators and quantitative scoring based on historical and projected financial and performance ratios following the rating agencies' practices.

Self-financing: The portion of financing an investment funded from the municipality's own resources, or in a narrow sense from the net balance. In project finance terms, a project is self-financing if it has the capacity to finance itself without subsidies, grants, and loans.

Shared taxes: Taxes levied and collected by national government, but a part of them are shared with local government entities with no restrictions on the use of the funds (for example, personal income tax, value added tax, or concessions). The sharing can be general and formula based, or can return to source the exact share of the amount collected in a jurisdiction.

Short-term debt: Debt with less than one-year maturity.

Sinking fund: A fund reserve set aside to secure paying out a liability that is expected to become due at a later date (see also DSRF, reserve funds).

Social assistance expenditures: Money spent on providing financial or in-kind assistance to defined disadvantaged groups of citizens in the municipal jurisdiction. Social assistance is often a delegated service where the municipality acts as an agent of the higher government and finances these expenditures from earmarked grants.

Solvency, or liquidity: Debtor's ability to pay the debt or installment on time; also measured as liquidity of assets that can be sold for paying due debts or liabilities.

Stamp duty: A tax paid to validate a legal document (historically in the form of buying and sticking to the document a duty stamp), such as a land transaction contract or land registry form. The amount of stamp duty aims to cover the cost of administration; however, in many countries the stamp duty has elevated to a substantial tax; it is easier to enforce than many other taxes because the seller and buyer of land properties are motivated to be registered (see also TTIP).

Standby credit: Lending arrangement that enables a borrower to withdraw money if needed; banks provide these against a commitment fee; it becomes a debt upon withdrawal (see also line of credit, overdraft).

Subsovereign entities: Public entities that are below the highest national entities (federal or state governments), such as provinces, counties, municipalities, or municipal entities.

Sunk cost: Costs or capital already spent that thus cannot be recovered.

Surtax: An additional tax on something already taxed (see tax surcharge).

Tax: A mandatory levy or financial charge imposed upon a taxpayer by a governmental organization without directly enumerating any specific services in exchange. Taxes levied in order to finance general administration or various general public expenditures that are provided without charge, such as street lights, roads, and so on (see direct taxes, indirect taxes, own taxes, shared taxes, tax surcharge).

Tax arrears: Overdue uncollected taxes and penalties.

Tax capacity: See tax potential.

Tax efficiency: The ratio between the collected actual amount of taxes and the billed amounts.

Tax effort: A ratio between the actual collected taxes and the tax potential or tax capacity.

Tax enforcement: Legal and/or regulatory measures to collect the billed tax from nonpayers (see also tax arrears).

Tax increment financing (TIF): A financing instrument cities use to promote economic development by earmarking future property tax revenues from increases in assessed values within a zone and issue bonds against these earmarked incremental revenues (not the total property tax).

Tax on transfer of immovable properties (TTIP): A tax levied at the transfer of ownership of immovable properties (houses, land); this could be a small amount to cover administrative costs, or rather a substantial revenue, for example, 3 percent of property value.

Tax potential: The amount of revenue a municipality could reasonably raise from a tax source if all tax payers were well identified and all tax levies were billed and fully collected.

Tax surcharge: An additional tax that is levied together with the national tax but collected by or for the local authorities—for example, a 2.3 percent tax local surcharge attached to a 16 percent national personal income tax.

Taxes on properties: Various taxes levied on properties, including the property tax, property transfer tax, inheritance tax, capital gain tax, stamp duties, and communal tax.

Tenor, or tenure: A period of time for holding a particular status, like the number of years a loan is outstanding (see also maturity, term).

Term: Conditions in the lending or other legal agreements, including the interest rate and time period in number of years for a debt or loan (see maturity, tenor).

Transfer of development rights: A set of instruments introduced initially to induce voluntary private transactions to trade development rights between owners in "selling" and in "receiving" zones defined for better urban development by master plans and/or zoning regulations. Cities have emulated this by selling building rights in defined zones direct to developers or even to any investor via open auctions (Certificate of Potential Additional Construction, or CePAC, in Brazil) in order to collect revenues while promoting higher-density urbanization.

Transfers: A general term that refers to all types of money channeled from higher government tiers to local governments; these may include shared taxes, formula-based transfers, ad hoc transfers, and conditional or unconditional or block grants; some countries use the term grant interchangeably with transfer (see grants).

Transfers to local government entities: Financial support a municipality provides without repayment obligations to its legally independent (off-budget) entities in order to subsidize capital investments and operations, or to cover deficits of the entity (see also CAPEX, OPEX subsidies, bailout, off-budget entities).

Trust fund: A portfolio of assets established by a grantor in the form of a fund to support specific activities or specific beneficiaries (for example, food for children) often managed by a dedicated trustee.

TTIP, or property transfer tax: Tax on transfer of immovable property (see also stamp duty).

Unconditional grants: Central government grants provided to beneficiaries without any conditions attached concerning either obtaining or spending the money.

Unconditional transfers: Transfers provided to local governments without any repayment or use conditions attached; these include shared taxes, operational grants, equalization grants, and development or ad hoc grants (see unconditional grants).

Underwriting: A bank's commitment to buy a certain amount of a newly issued debt (municipal bond) if it is not sold in the market within an agreed time period.

Unsecured loan: A loan granted on the general credit of a borrower without pledging assets or other securities; the lender assumes it will recover debt from the budget or balance sheet of the debtor (for example, a short-term liquidity loan for a municipality). (See also overdraft, liquidity loan.)

Useful life: Time period within which an asset has positive economic value and remains usable with routine maintenance (see life cycle costing).

Yield: Rate of return on an investment.

www.ingramcontent.com/pod-product-compliance
Lightning Source LLC
Chambersburg PA
CBHW081428270326
41932CB00019B/3126